Praise for *Happy Alchemy*

"A refreshing medley . . . Davies is the ideal theater buddy, a generous audience member with a classicist's appreciation of form. . . . The book in thoroughly entertaining fashion acquaints us with Davies's expansive erudition and gift for rendering literary and historical complexities in simple, human terms."
—*The New York Times*

"[Davies] is nothing if not a literary entertainer, a Chautauqua-style crowd-pleaser. . . . This second posthumous collection allow[s] us to hear his voice on the page: opinionated, melodramatic, occasionally faux-naif, slyly humorous." —*The Washington Post Book World*

"Even the slightest of these highly diverse essays, speeches, parodies and playlets display such wit, charm and insight that readers will come away with renewed appreciation of the ease with which Davies routinely transformed his sometimes erudite passions into delightful entertainments. Throughout, Davies's voice is characteristically wry."
—*The New York Times Book Review*

"Delightful reading. Davies has quirky opinions about everything and expresses himself with an almost Shavian verve. He is not afraid to tweak a few noses here and there, either—but everything is said and done with abundant good nature."
—*The Cleveland Plain Dealer*

"In this posthumously published collection of highly literate essays, lectures and reviews by Davies, one discovers what a great fan he truly was of the stage." —*The Seattle Times*

PENGUIN BOOKS

HAPPY ALCHEMY

Robertson Davies's death in December 1995 was marked in obituaries around the world. Not only was he one of Canada's most distinguished men of letters, but he was also a novelist whose unique voice spoke to a vast international audience.

His twelve novels, all available in Penguin editions, include such memorable works as *Fifth Business, The Manticore, The Rebel Angels, What's Bred in the Bone, Murther and Walking Spirits*, and his last, much acclaimed novel, *The Cunning Man*.

Robertson Davies was born and raised in Ontario and was educated at a variety of schools, including Balliol College, Oxford. He had three successive careers: first as an actor with the Old Vic Company in England; then as publisher of the *Peterborough Examiner*; and later as a university professor and first Master of Massey College at the University of Toronto, from which he retired in 1981 with the title of Master Emeritus.

His career was marked by many honors: He was, for example, the first Canadian to become an Honorary Member of the American Academy of Arts and Letters, and he received honorary degrees from Oxford; Trinity College, Dublin; and the University of Wales, as well as from twenty-three American and Canadian universities.

Two posthumous collections, *The Merry Heart* and *Happy Alchemy*, have been published in collaboration with Davies's Canadian publisher, his widow, Brenda Davies, and his daughter, Jennifer Surridge.

BOOKS BY ROBERTSON DAVIES

HAPPY ALCHEMY

On the Pleasures of Music and the Theatre

Robertson Davies

Edited by Jennifer Surridge and Brenda Davies

PENGUIN BOOKS

PENGUIN BOOKS
Published by the Penguin Group
Penguin Putnam Inc., 375 Hudson Street, New York, New York 10014, U.S.A.
Penguin Books Ltd, 27 Wrights Lane, London W8 5TZ, England
Penguin Books Australia Ltd, Ringwood, Victoria, Australia
Penguin Books Canada Ltd, 10 Alcorn Avenue, Toronto, Ontario, Canada M4V 3B2
Penguin Books (N.Z.) Ltd, 182–190 Wairau Road, Auckland 10, New Zealand

Penguin Books Ltd, Registered Offices: Harmondsworth, Middlesex, England

First published in Canada by McClelland & Stewart Inc. 1997
First published in the United States of America by Viking Penguin,
a member of Penguin Putnam Inc. 1998
Published in Penguin Books 1999

1 3 5 7 9 10 8 6 4 2

Grateful acknowledgement is made for permission to use the following selections:
"Alchemy in the Theatre," *The New Theater Review*, Fall 1994,
Lincoln Center Theater, New York.
Excerpt from *Journey's End* by R. C. Sherriff, Penguin Books Ltd.
"Tanya Moiseiwitsch" from Tanya Moiseiwitsch exhibition catalog, David and Alfred Smart
Museum of Art, The University of Chicago; The Stratford Shakespearean
Festival Foundation of Canada; and the Parnassus Foundation, Ridgewood, New Jersey.
Introduction ("Introduction to an Anthology of Canadian Plays") to
Major Plays of the Canadian Theatre, 1934–1984, edited by Richard Perkyns,
Stoddart Publishing Co. Ltd., North York, Ontario.
Introductions to *"At My Heart's Core"* and *"Overlaid"*; *"Fortune, My Foe"* and
"Eros at Breakfast"; and *"Hunting Stuart"* and *"The Voice of the People"*
by Robertson Davies, Simon & Pierre Publishing Co. Ltd, Toronto.
"Dickens and Music" from *A Christmas Carol Re-Harmonized*
by Robertson Davies, Penguin Books Ltd.
Excerpt from *The Myth of the Eternal Return* by Mircea Eliade.
Copyright 1954 by Princeton University Press.
"The Value of a Coherent Notion of Culture," Massey College, Toronto.

THE LIBRARY OF CONGRESS HAS CATALOGUED THE VIKING EDITION AS FOLLOWS:
Davies, Robertson, 1913–1995
Happy alchemy: on the pleasures of music and the theatre / Robertson Davies;
Edited by Jennifer Surridge and Brenda Davies.
p.   cm.
ISBN 0-670-88019-1 (hc.)
ISBN 0 14 02.7562 2 (pbk.)
I. Davies, Robertson, 1913–1995 —Aesthetics.   2. Music—History and criticism.
3. Drama—History and criticism.   I. Surridge, Jennifer.   II. Davies, Brenda.   III. Title.
PR9199.3.D3H37   1998
814'.54—dc21   98–5622

Printed in the United States of America
Set in Bembo OS

By happy alchemy of mind
They turn to pleasure all they find.

MATTHEW GREEN (1696–1737)

CONTENTS

———— ·❧· ————

INTRODUCTION

WHEN DOUGLAS GIBSON WROTE the Introduction to *The Merry Heart*, he mentioned the large number of unpublished speeches, commissioned book reviews, and other short pieces that Robertson Davies had accumulated in his files before his death in December of 1995. Given the impressive variety and scope of this material, it was decided to have two books: one about reading, writing, and books, which is *The Merry Heart*, published in 1996; and one mostly about theatre, opera, and music, which is *Happy Alchemy*, the book you hold in your hands.

The title, *Happy Alchemy*, comes directly from the English poet Matthew Green, still remembered by some for the couplet:

By happy alchemy of mind
They turn to pleasure all they find.

The metaphorical alchemy here is very distant from the "prim- itive chemistry and mystification" discussed in the first essay in the book. There Robertson Davies explains the magic that can attend a live performance. "What alchemy really means is something which has attained to such excellence, such nearness to perfection, that it offers a glory, an expansion of life and understanding, to those who have been brought into contact with it." He continues, "What the critics mean, then, when they talk of alchemy in the theatre, is something so good that it seems to have gone beyond what may be explained in terms of talent."

We have included in *Happy Alchemy* selections that show the diversity of Robertson Davies, whether writing for himself to read or for others to perform. There are speeches, prologues to plays, articles about the theatre and opera, a lengthy discussion of folk-song, a libretto for a children's opera, a ghost story set to music, even a suggestion for a film scenario. There are also some thoughts about his own plays when they were published again in the early 1990s that shed light on his own play-writing ambitions and on the theatre in general. And towards the end of the book the focus widens as he discusses Jung or savages contemporary politicians. This is, in short, a lively book about more than "the lively arts."

We have left the speeches in their full text including the introductory paragraphs: they cover thanks to the host, how the lecture came about, apologetics for the title, and how the topic was decided upon. As Robertson Davies explained in the introduction to *One Half of Robertson Davies*, this is where the speaker clears his throat and gets over his nerves. There is some repetition or overlapping between pieces in the course of the book; but we thought, for example, that his account of the differences between the novel *The Bride of Lammermoor* by Sir Walter Scott and the opera *Lucia di Lammermoor* by Donizetti was so interesting that it could be read in different contexts.

At the beginning of each of the thirty-three items in the book you will find a brief introduction that sets the scene, followed usually by a diary entry or two. Robertson Davies had a life-long fascination with the diary form, starting with diaries he kept as a schoolboy. He went on to make use of the form in his books *The Diary of Samuel Marchbanks* and *The Table Talk of Samuel*

Marchbanks, which were published in the late 1940s, and again in 1985, this time in one volume as *The Papers of Samuel Marchbanks*.

He kept many diaries over the years but in 1957 he decided to start Theatre Notes which would include his opinions of all the theatrical productions he saw. At the beginning of 1962 he changed these notes into a Theatre Diary to resemble similar records that had become an important resource in the study of drama, his own specific academic field, which he taught at the University of Toronto for twenty years. As Canada had no such records, he decided to create some for use in his own teaching of the history of drama and as an aide memoire. He kept this diary for the rest of his life, with the final entry describing a production by the Canadian Opera Company on October 17, 1995.

On the opening page of these Theatre Notes he wrote:

In this book I want to make a record, as complete as memory will allow, of my experiences, chiefly as a *playgoer*, but with some references also to what I have done at one time and another, as an *actor* and *playwright*. For as long as I can remember, playgoing has stood first among all pleasures with me, and although to most people it is simply a pastime, I think that I have brought qualities to it which raised it above that. I have never really been a good actor (though I have had my moments), and it may prove that I was not a good playwright, but I sincerely believe that I have been a good *playgoer*, and that is something better, perhaps, than having been a well-known critic. Critics often do not like the theatre; I have never liked anything better.

To give Robertson Davies' perspective on the events surrounding some of the plays and operas that are the topics of speeches, we have selected from these Theatre Diaries the entries that give his opinion of the actual performance, or of a related production. We know, of course, from the warm reception accorded to *The Merry Heart* that readers enjoyed the entries from Davies' daily diaries or his travel diaries that described the circumstances in which he wrote or read these selections. We have followed the same practice here, in the belief that they (with the additional bonus of the Theatre Diary entries) take us behind the scenes with him in a revealing, interesting, and sometimes controversial way. It was Robertson Davies' wish that his diaries be sealed for a period of time following his death, so that now we are able only to have small glimpses of his thoughts on plays he saw and on his eventful life, but can look forward to more of this fascinating material in the future. His publisher has even suggested that in time, to the list of Robertson Davies, teacher, critic, playwright, and novelist, the world may add the category "Robertson Davies, diarist."

Happy Alchemy has been organized so that pieces flow from theatre to opera to music to wider topics that lead to the final selection on collecting, which sums up all the topics in the book. The reader should, of course, keep in mind that many of these pieces were written to be spoken. To get the full impact of them, try reading them aloud, and those who have heard Robertson Davies read may hear him again in the "mind's ear."

We would like to thank Douglas Gibson for all his help in making both *The Merry Heart* and *Happy Alchemy* a reality; Judith Grant for her biography, *Robertson Davies, Man of Myth*, on which we have drawn; Moira Whalon for her aid, suggestions, and incredible proofreader's eye; and Thomas Surridge for his encouragement, patience, and advice on computer matters.

Now let Robertson Davies take over and tell you about the many things he discovered as a lifelong theatregoer, and convey the pleasure he found in a good performance, production, or piece of business in the theatre or opera house when the mixture became *Happy Alchemy*.

Jennifer Surridge
Brenda Davies
Pendragon Ink, April 1997

HAPPY ALCHEMY

1

— ⧫ —

Alchemy in the Theatre

IN 1994, ROBERTSON DAVIES was asked to write an article for *The New Theater Review*, which is published by Lincoln Center Theater in New York. As always he wrote pieces like this well ahead of their due date, and on July 1 (defiantly avoiding the modern usage *Canada Day*) he noted in his diary: *Dominion Day: did not like what I wrote yesterday so buckle down and rewrite and finish the Lincoln Center piece. Am pleased with myself; the old journalistic skill has not deserted me. . . . p.m. help Brenda transplant some lily-of-the-valley to the upper garden, then dig part of a bed, and enjoy it.*

Davies refers here to a production of *Pericles* as an occasion for alchemy in the theatre. This is what he wrote in his Theatre Diary about the production in question, which he saw at The Stratford Festival, Stratford, Ontario in 1973.

July 24, Tuesday: . . . *At 7:30 the opening performance of* Pericles. *Very fine and we quickly abandoned any doubts which the preliminary stuff by* [the critic Herbert] *Whittaker, about bad play, necessity to hack, patch, rewrite and smooth over, might have provoked. Jean* [Gasçon] *had treated it as fairy-tale on a high level, with respectful care for the mythological and ceremonial elements in it; Leslie Hurry had designed it in accord, with all the splendour of barbaric colour which is his – except for the women's costumes, and Hurry does not understand women, for he had put them in tight peek-a-boo skirts and bosom-huggers, so that they lacked flow and mystery. Still, it was otherwise splendid. Notable performance by* [Nicholas] *Pennell as Pericles, noble, suffering under the gods, trusting – a true hero, indeed. We see the controversial Nachum Buchman as Antiochus, and he has as fine a voice as I have ever heard, and great command. Christine Forester, as his daughter, was a lump of bare Eve's flesh which seemed small incitement to incest; they needed some beautiful Jewess, tawny and mysterious. Martha Henry a fine, grave Thaisa but she was outshone by Pamela Brook as a first-rate Marina, playing in noble strain as Pennell did, and carrying full conviction in her virtue. Milly Hall strained rather as the Bawd and her girls were comic, as stage whores commonly are – healthy, pink kids with gleaming teeth, who had painted them-selves hollow-eyed, and put fancy mormals on their hams, without achieving any effect save that of rude health and rather dull virtue. Powys Thomas a fine magician as Cerimon. Barry MacGregor played Boult: consulted his doctor about pox and wore a pox-rotted nose and a left contact lens which gave him an eerie bleared, greyish eye. Also held his pizzle much of the time to simulate priapism. But despite all this elaborate decay he con-tinued to look like a hero trying to be a wreck. Nice chap. A notable evening.*

———— ∾ ————

Alchemy is one of those useful words often employed by critics when they want to suggest that some good work has been done in the theatre with unlikely material. Why unlikely? Because, in general usage, alchemy means the transmutation of base metal into gold. But the word, like "glamour," has been too freely and loosely employed; both words have magical implications, but their magic is not cheap. What was alchemy, and how has it come to its present condition as a drudge-word for critics – who are, it must be said, often careless writers?

Alchemy was the chemistry of the Middle Ages, and it persisted into the sixteenth century. Indeed, it had few practitioners until comparatively modern times. Goethe was perhaps the most celebrated of these, and I am sure that there are a few alchemists in New York at this moment, if we knew where to look for them. It once had a secret significance which I shall touch on shortly, but to most people it meant elaborate processes by means of which it was hoped to turn base metals into gold. Of course it attracted crooks, and they gouged money out of gullible or greedy people, as we see in Ben Jonson's wonderful play *The Alchemist*. But beneath the primitive chemistry and mystification lay something deeper, the true alchemy, which had to be closely guarded because it was founded on a heresy – nothing less than that there was a way to salvation outside the Church. The alchemists pursued a path which was supposed to lead to spiritual perfection, or at least to point out the road to it. (If you are curious to know more, the subject has been thoroughly and fascinatingly explored in volumes 12 and 13 in *The Collected Works of C. G. Jung*.) They are deeply interesting once you accustom yourself to the oddity of the subject. Of course this sort of rivalry could not be countenanced by the Church, and alchemists stood in peril of persecution as heretics – very dangerous heretics – because most of them were, in terms of their time, learned men and women and advanced thinkers. (Learned women? Oh yes, for each alchemist had his *soror mystica* who shared in his work, and some of these, like the famed Maria Prophetissa – still remembered in the kitchen as the originator of the *bain-marie* – were among the most famous of the initiates.)

What alchemy really means is something which has attained to such excellence, such nearness to perfection, that it offers a glory, an expansion of life and understanding, to those who have been brought into contact with it.

What the critics mean, then, when they talk of alchemy in the theatre, is something so good that it seems to have gone beyond what may be explained in terms of talent.

Is such a usage justifiable? Judging from my own theatre experience I would say so, for I have encountered theatre alchemy several times in a life in which theatre-going has been the principal and most cherished experience of art.

I think of the Habima Players in *The Dybbuk*; of a performance on successive nights of both parts of Goethe's *Faust* at Salzburg. (The Second Part of that play, which has puzzled so many students, reveals itself in terms of alchemy, among other concepts.) I recall a performance by the Old Vic Company when it visited New York after the end of the Second World War, of *Uncle Vanya*, which seemed to explain so much about what that war was fought to defend. Heavy stuff, do you say? Theatre which has been touched by alchemy is never heavy. I have seen comedy which was in the alchemical vein too, and I could go on about it if I had limitless space. But I have never seen a theatre performance in which alchemy was at work in any play that lacked literary substance – the hand of the writer who is himself a true theatre artist. You cannot make gold out of garbage though, distressingly, there are theatre directors intent on some inner revelation of their own, who can make gold into garbage.

Sometimes unlikely substances may be transmuted, and I am thinking now of a production at the Shakespeare Festival in Stratford, Ontario, of Shakespeare's *Pericles, Prince of Tyre*. It has never been counted as one of Shakespeare's greatest, but as it appeared in that production it was a truly great and deeply moving drama of loss and reconciliation, and as we saw it we knew that under the dust of its chronicle form glowed the true theatre gold, which alchemy had revealed.

The alchemy begins with the playwright, just as great music begins with the composer but has no life until it is played by great musicians. Shakespeare is the mighty magician here. By means of a dropped handkerchief, as Coleridge says, he sets in motion the tragedy of *Othello*; out of lovers' quarrels and amateur actors and the often mauled and degraded notion of a fairy world he contrives the truly alchemical wonder of *A Midsummer Night's Dream*. But Shakespeare is *hors concours*. Must a playwright be a poet to bring about alchemy?

No, but he must be aware of what Thomas Mann, tongue in cheek, spoke of as the much more complex rhythms of prose, and he must have weeded and cultivated his vocabulary – not to produce exotics, but to root out faded blooms. As Synge says in his Preface to *The Playboy*, "In a good play every speech should be as fully flavoured as a nut or an apple and such speeches cannot be written by anyone who works among people who have shut their lips on poetry."

We think of playwrights who know nothing of poetry but who are deft hands with the wisecrack. The real delight of the theatre is not to rock from guffaw to guffaw until – as critics love to say and producers love to put in their advertisements – the audience is "rolling in the aisles." This is not comedy. Comedy may certainly deploy as splendid wit, but the greatest comedies are those which reveal character. Nor is simple gloom the stuff of tragedy and it is here that playwrights and theatre artists fall into the booby-trap of "realism." Unrelieved realism – the photographic reconstruction of raw life – is impossible in the theatre, which is illusion.

I recall the hosannas that greeted Elmer Rice's *Street Scene* in 1929, because of its supposed unrelenting realism, but even as a very young playgoer I knew that the realism was another form of illusion; nobody who had ever lived on a street could believe that so much incident, however commonplace, could happen in the space of a day in so ordered a fashion. Realism is a form of Puritanism, a rejection of illusion as a cheat, unworthy of serious artists. In the great days of alchemy there were hopeful people who thought that heaps of old iron, fences and fire-tongs, could be transmuted into gold. It is for this rubbish that the realists have sought alchemical transformation in the theatre. A few great playwrights, notably Henrik Ibsen, have pretended to realism, but nowadays the plays of Ibsen are given brilliant and revealing productions in which the clumsy trappings of realism have been set aside.

Perhaps the biggest booby-trap of all those that lie in wait for the theatre artists of our day is the yearning for "relevance," for the treatment that will reveal some supposed "message" for our time in an acknowledged classic. Of course the play would not be a classic if its relevance did not extend to our time and its message was not plain. A recent production of *Othello* that I saw put the action in an American tropical army base, trashed the poetry and reduced the pride, pomp, and circumstance of glorious war to a political wrangle and brought the tragedy of the great leader to something resembling the journalistic story of O. J. Simpson. It is true that the history of a commonplace soldier may be tragic; Wozzeck proves it, but Wozzeck's realism is entirely deceptive, a distillation of the misery of unhappy millions. It is a tragedy of mankind, not of an individual. It is a dangerous example for the unwary. "Tragedy concerneth a high fellow," said Sir Philip Sidney, and you reduce the high fellow to the ranks at your peril. You cannot reduce the Doge of Venice to, for instance, Richard Nixon, without losing something of dimension.

Great drama, drama that may reach the alchemical level, must have dimension and its relevance will take care of itself. Writing about AIDS rather than the cocktail set, or possibly the fairy kingdom, will not guarantee importance. The problems and predicaments of mankind are unchanging; that is what Ibsen meant when he replied to a query about where he found his plots that he found them in the Bible and the newspapers. Classics are not given added relevance by putting them in modern dress, where the men are in bare feet and the ladies make devastating play with their revealed navels. The old comment that all periods of time are at an equal distance from eternity says much, and pondering on it will lead to alchemical theatre while relevance becomes old hat.

2

—— ❧ ——

THE NOBLE GREEKS

THIS IS THE FIRST of three lectures in this collection which were part of the Celebrated Writers Series at the Stratford Festival. An original member of the Board from 1953 to 1971, Robertson Davies was always a great supporter of the Festival and lectured there whenever he could. This lecture took place at the Avon Theatre on August 22, 1993. His diaries record:

July 8, 1993: struggle with the Stratford speech; it gives me great trouble . . . Read it to B in p.m. and she does not like it; says talk about the play too long deferred. So – back at it, wretched thing . . .

August 22: my lecture at the Avon; house sold out. A triumph, Brenda says I spoke it well, not too fast and with lots of variety. Good jokes, enough but not too much (one must not be a stand-up comedian). Received with great applause and a standing ovation which seems absurd for a lecture but I shall not find fault with it. Everybody much pleased and was glad that David William, the director of The Bacchae, *spoke well of it.*

August 22: Matinée: Tom Patterson Theatre, The Bacchae, by Euripides, translated by Kenneth Cavender. Splendidly and grippingly directed by David William. Finely cast and spoken. Fine to look at, truly archaic in feeling, masks effective. Erotic note struck when the Chorus – women – doffed their heavy robes and appeared in body-stockings, stained and decorated in archaic designs. Intense, stirring and alarming. Appearance of Penthens' remains – a tray of bloody remnants – electrifying. (How audience tolerance alters: Martin-Harvey was slated for giving the blinded Oedipus bloody eyes and Prof. Gordon assured me that Oedipus wearing a black blindfold was all an audience could endure.) Lasted an hour and a half, and more of such intensity would have been too much. Mind you, I think The Bacchae *is a fine play, and speaks strongly to our dreadful, bloody, repressive age.*

———— ∾ ————

The Festival program tells you that I am going to speak on "The Noble Greeks," and I suppose that at some time long past I must have agreed to that title. But I am sure you know that any single lecture that tries to come to terms with so great a civilization as that of Greece at its best must do it with a hop, skip, and jump. But I want to do more than simply talk about the play we are going to see this afternoon – though I shall certainly do that. I want to attempt to give you some notion of the atmosphere in which that play first appeared, and to do a little to suggest the kind of people who saw it. How did they look at life? We can only form an opinion about that if we know something about their religion, which affected every aspect of their lives, just as ours does. For, although formal religion seems to be in decline in our world, the structure of our legal system, and the whole complex of social security and of the government which supports and regulates social security, is rooted in our Judaeo–Christian outlook on the world. The Greek religion was very different from ours, and unless we take it into account much of what we discover of their culture must seem strange to us. Therefore I shall talk for a while about Greek religion.

The world in which the Greeks lived – I speak chiefly about the Athenians, who were the intellectual leaders of Greek civilization – was governed by a system of democracy from which we rather presumptuously suppose our own democratic system is derived. But the Greeks would have found the trust we place in elected persons utterly naive; they assumed, not quite that all men are crooks, but that all men are the better for watching. They knew how quickly power corrupts. Therefore, they invited the gods to have a say in all important elections. How did they do that? After the votes had been cast by throwing balls of different colours into a vase, the presiding priest threw in a handful of balls chosen at random, so that the gods – or blind chance – might be represented. It was also a way of preventing a packed election. The Greeks were very subtle, and hard-headed in ways that we are not.

Why do we refer to them, so often, as the Noble Greeks? It is because they have for so long been presented to us as a greatly superior people, of whose splendid vision of life we are the unworthy inheritors. This notion comes from the extraordinary enthusiasm for Greek culture during the nineteenth century, which has somewhat skewed our vision of it. Noble the Greeks undoubtedly were at their best, but their common humanity was in many ways much like ours. In our day nobility is not popular. Can you imagine what would happen to a politician who declared that he intended to behave nobly? He would be laughed at and he would be hated. We mistrust anything that too strongly challenges our ideal of mediocrity. But we can admire nobility when it is safely in the past, in literature and in art. But Greek democracy had a place for nobility. It did not insist, as ours does, on a rather squalid levelling, which is really superficial, and repressive. Why do the Greeks appear to be noble in comparison with ourselves? It was because of the mythic understructure of their lives, which gave them a coherent, common intellectual background of a kind we lack, and it encouraged a sense of the possibility of nobility in life.

We are like the Greeks, but not in obvious ways, and before I have finished I hope I shall have persuaded you that the horrors and psychological extravagances of the play we are going to see this afternoon do not belong to a savage past, but are plainly to be seen in our savage present. Though I shall spend quite a lot of our time talking about Greek government and Greek religion, I assure you that it all has a bearing on *The Bacchae*. The power of Greek drama lies in the fact that, although its form and its theatre were so much unlike what we know, the themes it put on its stage were, and are still, deeply rooted in the human spirit. Under the skin, we are very like the Greeks.

One of the most deeply rooted notions of civilized man is that there existed, at some time in the remote past, an era when humanity reached a glory from which it has been in decline ever since. This is the belief in the Golden Age.

The Greeks dreamed of a Golden Age –

When Saturn did reign, there lived no poor
The King and the beggar on roots did dine –

but when we think of a Golden Age we think most often of that classical period in ancient Greece, roughly defined as from 480 B.C. to 323 B.C., distinguished for great philosophy, great drama, and an art of a serene and restrained majesty, an ideal beauty of proportion, form, and expression, to which we have never again attained.

It was not always so. Greek art was little understood in the Western world until the middle of the eighteenth century, although examples of it were to be seen in great collections. It was the art historian Johann Joachim Winckelmann (1717–1768) who spent a life discussing, cataloguing, and praising what was known and what was newly discovered of Greek sculpture, for its serenity and noble simplicity. He may be said to have brought about Neo-Classicism in European art history, and his influence persists. It was he who brought into focus the Golden Age of Greece.

Not that the Greek heritage was unknown until its art came into vogue. During the Dark Ages manuscripts of Greek literature lingered in the libraries of monasteries, often neglected and little studied, but not wholly forgotten. In an era committed to the learning and culture of the Christian Church, however, such stuff had always a dubious reputation, for it was rooted in paganism. It was not until the Renaissance of the fourteenth and fifteenth centuries that such manuscripts were dusted off and eagerly acclaimed as wondrous revelations of an intellectual splendour that had existed before Christianity and the Church were dreamed of.

This knowledge of the literary and philosophical riches of ancient Greece spread and dominated European culture, especially after the Reformation had put an end to the overwhelming psychological domination of the Church of Rome. Schoolboys and ripe scholars who had never beheld a Greek sculpture or even a Greek vase were nevertheless deep in Greek literature which, in company with that of Rome, dominated European education for at least four centuries. Scholars of renown, and scholars who were merely competent, and schoolboys who were never likely to become competent, all knew the heroes of Homer, but they could not have formed any idea of what those heroes may have looked like. The more they knew the more adroit they became in managing Greek metre; lads of eighteen could, and did, write correct Greek verse, which derived from and imitated Greek thought. But of the actual manner of performance of a Greek play they knew nothing whatever. Greece was, for them, a literary rather than a living concept.

We find evidence of this in their translations from the Greek and their imitations of Greek drama. Chapman's version of Homer is remembered now chiefly because Keats asserted in a famous sonnet that he owed his classical enthusiasm to it. But when we read it not all of us persist to the end, because to the irreverent it seems often like riding over cobblestones in an unsprung cart; the flavour that rises to us from the pages is clumsy Elizabethan rather than soaring Hellenic. The best plays of the Golden Age of English Drama that deal with Greek themes, such as Shakespeare's *Troilus and Cressida*, are wholly Jacobean; the arguments in that play of the wise Ulysses on order and degree, excellent in themselves, would have been unlikely to occur to a Greek dramatist. The thought is English; the characters are Elizabethans. Greece provides only the plot.

Nor have any of the tragedies written in Europe during the three centuries following the Renaissance much about them that speaks to us of Greece. The works of Corneille and Racine owe much of structure but little of spirit to the Greek drama from which they have drawn inspiration. But these are the works of poets great in themselves, and unmistakably French. To understand the icy grip that Greek drama had on the imagination of the learned and the merely educated world of the seventeenth and eighteenth centuries one must read a few of the countless tragedies written by earnest clergymen, armed only with ambition and a grounding in Greek, which were offered to the theatre, and appear now as precisely what they were – talentless and imperceptive imitations, in which the Greeks became Englishmen in white wigs.

When they showed some dramatic flair they were even less Greek in feeling. Consider a play which held the stage for fifty years and provided a role splendidly acted by the great Mrs. Siddons; it is *The Grecian Daughter* (1772) by Arthur Murphy. In it Euphrasia saves the life of her father, Evander, who is in prison, but he has a delicate digestion and starves on the prison diet; Euphrasia visits him and suckles him at her flowing breasts. In classical style this is not shown on the stage but is described by a guard, something of a Peeping Tom, who spies on it and relates what he sees to the audience, with moral gloating. To put the scene on the stage might have drawn irreverent laughter. It is not easy for Euphrasia to surpass this purely feminine exploit, but she does so by employing "a daughter's arm" to stab the tyrant, whereat her father cries

My child! my daughter! sav'd again by thee!

This is the voice, not of the Golden Age of Athens, but of the Age of Sentiment in England. *The Grecian Daughter* is a very feminist play, and I wonder why some feminist group does not revive it.

After the Renaissance, every age invented its own Greece. In seventeenth-century Florence a form of monodic music drama was thought to imitate the high declamatory style of the Greek actors, and from it modern opera evolved. Alexander Pope produced

(1715–1726) a splendid translation of Homer, but as the critic Richard Bentley said, "It is a pretty poem, Mr. Pope, but you must not call it Homer." And indeed it reads like Homer in a white wig. There were many translations, and it is instructive to compare some of them, and to wonder that one original could inspire so many disparate versions. But if we talk of the marvels of translation, let us turn, not to Homer, who was not of the fifth century, but to Sophocles, who was. Here is what a superb modern scholar, Professor R. C. Jebb, offers at the conclusion of the final Chorus of *Oedipus the King*:

> Therefore, while our eyes wait to see the destined final
> day, we must call no one happy who is of mortal race
> until he hath crossed life's border, free from pain.

Now hear what a great poet, W. B. Yeats, makes of the same passage:

> Call no man fortunate that is not dead,
> The dead are free from pain.

And here is the romantic, Swinburnian version of a notable classicist, Gilbert Murray:

> Therefore, O Man, beware, and look toward the end of things
>   that be,
> The last of sights, the last of days; and no man's life account as
>   gain
> Ere the full tale be finished and the darkness find him without
>   pain.

All three obviously stem from the same source, but they are sufficiently different to make us wonder what we, if we had been Greeks, would have heard and understood had we been among the 17,000 Athenians who first heard the words spoken in the great theatre of Dionysus. What would the tone have been? What shade of emotion would have been aroused? Even if we are fully proficient in Greek today (as few are) how much can we recapture of the savour of Greece?

For us it has become a Golden Age, and perhaps it is best if we do not understand it too well. Consider, for instance, the matter of democracy. It is a commonplace today to speak of Greece as the cradle of democracy. But consider; at its peak, the population of Athens was about 180,000; a conservative estimate puts the slave population at 20,000 and these had no voice in government; women had no voice in affairs and they probably numbered 70,000 at a guess; therefore there were about 90,000 – or half the population – to *decide* who should rule a comparatively small community. The Athenians were not trustful of elected persons, and many offices were assigned by lot, rather than by simple vote, to control peculation. Nor was truth and the sanctity of the given word highly regarded (it was assumed in the courts that slaves never spoke truth except under torture) and public officials were kept in check by a number of controls. Our Canadian senators vote themselves a six-thousand-dollar rise in pay in a time of recession; the Greeks would not have put up with that. Our democracy means that once you have won a popularity contest called an election, you can do pretty much as you please. The senators have been made to retract, but their foolish greed will not be forgotten.

The freedoms of Athenian democracy were by no means limitless and when we refer to it as a model for our own democratic governments we do well to preserve a certain vagueness. "Democracy" meant something to the Greeks, by no means what it means to us.

We are on firmer ground when we consider our artistic and literary legacy from Greece, but even here we must take heed of our posture as observers twenty-four hundred years after the fact, and of the presuppositions we bring to our appreciation of the Greek heritage. In particular we must beware of mingling our Christian–Judaic ideas about mankind and society with what we can discern of Greek attitudes. When Elizabeth Barrett Browning wrote of

Our Euripides, the human,
   With his droppings of warm tears,

she created a Euripides in her own image, as well as perpetrating an unintentional, ludicrous portrait. The Greeks knew pity, not sentimentality. The Greeks were not ourselves in fancy dress, and to discover who and what they were with greater precision requires careful, undeluded study of their underlying beliefs. Let us begin with Greek religion.

The rediscovery of Greek belief at the time of the Renaissance let a wonderful breath of fresh air into the European imagination. That imagination had been for a thousand years or more dominated by the Christian Church, which made available to the people what portions of the Christian faith were thought to be good for them, and made it amply clear that there was no salvation for their souls outside its walls. Though Christianity was a sophisticated belief with a coherent philosophy, it never wholly shook off its Oriental origins and its powerful Hebrew foundations. It was not a religion that encouraged free speculation and it regarded art as a handmaid rather than a creature of priestly authority. Art was decoration, not inspiration. The Christian attitude toward women bespoke its Oriental associations and, although the Blessed Virgin was accorded high honours, it was as a mother, and never as a lover, that she was adored. There was no female figure in the Trinity and the women of the New Testament were virtually all servitors or penitents. Love, in so far as it was considered at all, was an adjunct of faith. Such teaching flew in the face of reality, as the more intelligent part of the populace during the Middle Ages perceived, and the revival of Greek learning brought a splendid release. Until Winckelmann's time – that is, the latter part of the eighteenth century – it was chiefly literary in its influence.

It was a rediscovery of the Greek Pantheon, a consideration of gods long forgotten, which, to spirits in chains, gave a psychological freedom which blew through orthodox Christianity like a frolic wind, and the rigours of Puritanism never wholly overcame it. Here was a religion which had a god who was in charge, so to speak, of every aspect of human life, a religion which considered nothing human alien to it and encouraged and venerated freely speculative thought. It embraced womanhood (though not, of course, as voters) and thought love not merely important but in the centre of human concern. Here was a religion which exalted, instead of deriding, the human form, which adored beauty and thought that, upon the whole, men were as beautiful or even more beautiful than women. With the Renaissance, and even more plainly when appreciation of Greek art became general, the beauty and the presence of the Greek Pantheon became a part of our Western culture and imagination. The old gods had returned, and they are still with us.

Some of their spirit, that is to say, is still with us, but the man on the street is not likely to be able to name more than two or three. *Zeus*, the father of the gods, the cloud-bearer and the hurler of thunderbolts, is still well remembered. Zeus, with his horde of divine and mortal children, and his appetite for pretty girls, is in sharp contrast to the God of Christianity, the monolith Creator of a monotheistic faith.

Zeus had a wife, as well as all his occasional loves, and she was a consort and a powerful one. She was *Hera*, and her sphere of influence was in marriage and affairs of family and childbirth. She knew jealousy, rage, and revenge, and she was certainly no benign Mother Goddess.

We might be inclined to think that *Athena* was a more pacific figure, for her concern was with arts and crafts and wisdom and she is well known in the modern world; the owl of Athena (she was herself sometimes called *glauskopi*, which may mean owl-faced or perhaps bright-eyed) is to be seen in the insignia of scores of educational institutions. But we would be wrong; Athena was first of all a war goddess; but hers were the nobler aspects of conflict. It was *Ares* who was the god of the terrors and horrors of war, and like *Poseidon*, who ruled over earthquakes and the sea, he was a god more feared than loved.

If Athena ruled wisdom and literature, it was *Apollo* who ruled music and prophecy. He was the god of male beauty, which he combined, somewhat astonishingly to the Christian mind, with moral excellence. Apollo was beneficent; he had virtually no shadow, nor had his twin sister, *Artemis*, who was goddess of fertility and shared the cares of childbirth with Hera, showing herself more beneficent as she did so. But she was no Blessed Virgin; motherhood and all the sentimentality that goes with Mother's Day was not congenial to the Greek mind. They were a remarkably unsentimental people; they had no particular reverence for children, nor did they regard them as a special and privileged portion of society. It would not have occurred to them to erect a vast temple to Mickey Mouse. They left that for us.

Aphrodite was the goddess of love, both intellectual and sensual, and to the Renaissance she brought a great expansion of spirit. *Demeter* was goddess of generation and rebirth; her grief-laden pursuit of her daughter *Persephone*, who was carried away to the underworld, might make us see her as a sentimental mother-goddess, if it were not for her trick of holding a child over a blazing fire, to purge it of its mortality and thus make it immortal. The Greek gods were incalculable, and to our eyes sometimes barbarous.

A somewhat sinister figure was *Hephaestus*, god of fire, of metalwork and of crafts; lame from birth and of a cankered nature, his temper was not improved by the love affair between his wife, Aphrodite, and the disagreeable Ares; he trapped them in a net and exhibited them in their confusion to the other gods, who laughed heartily. Neither the Greeks nor their gods were notably tender toward human folly. They thought deformity and old age great jokes. To catch someone with his, or her, pants down – so to speak – was their idea of a really good joke. They laughed; they laughed a great deal. There is no suggestion that the Christian God ever laughed, and to the post-Renaissance world the idea of deities with a sense of humour was an immense and freeing revelation.

Two dark gods remain, whose influence was great but whose nature remains incalculable. The first of these, *Hermes*, was the herald of the gods and as such a great tattler and tale-teller, which may be why he invades Athena's realm of literature, or at least as far as journalism. He was god of thieves, of finance, and of merchants, for he was the god of luck and whatever is shadowy and chancy. He was the god of sleep and dreams, and thus associated with the modern art of psychoanalysis. Anthropologists will recognize him at once as the trickster of the gods. The other dark god was *Dionysus*, whose realm was all that is irrational, drunken, and possessed; much crime of the passionate sort is ruled by Dionysus for he is the god of the drug-taker, the serial murderer, and the child-abuser. He was the god of ecstasy, which has two faces, one inspired and the other demonic. I shall talk more of Dionysus later.

These are the mighty twelve of Olympus. There are more than twenty lesser gods, of whom Asclepius, the god of healing, Hecate, associated with ghosts and demons and black magic, and of course the Nine Muses, who had special care of artists of all kinds, are immediately familiar. Thus it may be seen that every Greek had several deities who could be appealed to at necessity.

We must not forget that, although these gods have come down to us as fantastic figures shorn of their divinity, they were cloaked for the Greeks in their *thambos*, the reverential awe that surrounds the supernatural. We have their statues, but we do not know the prayers and rituals by which the gods were invoked, and we are left with only the iconic, the representational portion of their godhead. Splendid as it is, we must never mistake it for the whole.

Unless we give some understanding to Greek religion, we shall not come close to understanding Greek drama. It is, however, a religion unlike any we know. It was rooted in no revelation; it possessed no prophet and no holy book; it was not codified or dogmatic, and it was defined in no creed. But it arose from a great body of myth.

Dispute about the nature of myth is unending, and ranges from Robert Graves's determination that myths embody versions of historical and political realities, to the equally strongly asserted opinion of the psychoanalytical thinkers who declare that myths shadow forth in narrative the condition of the human soul. It is not impossible, of course, that myth is both these things, for history and politics must surely arise from the depths of human consciousness. But we must not suppose that the Greeks of the Golden Age bothered their heads about such matters; myth was, for them, part of the atmosphere in which they lived, and when they went to the theatre they went for a religious rather than a secular edification, and the stories of the great tragedies were fully familiar to the educated and the humble alike; their pleasure was found in the poetic splendour in which their poets enfolded what was already known.

Here we meet with a fact that is puzzling to the modern mind: the Greek theatre was religious in intent, and the tragedies were based upon religiously accepted myths; but with these profound, solemn, and numinous dramas appeared also comedies of such astonishing bawdry that we have trouble in comprehending them. Who has not grubbed among the footnotes of a comedy by Aristophanes to try to find what he is being dirty about? For dirty these comedies are, not simply free-spoken and uninhibited. As Professor Eugene O'Neill writes: "There is no escaping the fact that Aristophanes wrote just as obscenely as he could on every possible occasion," and speaks of such writing as "the very part of his work which the poet clearly took the greatest delight in composing." At this moment one of the chief delights of the London theatre is a production of Aristophanes' *Lysistrata*, which by all reports is so bawdy in language and action that many proper people leave the theatre during every performance, grossly affronted. Yet the choruses in *Lysistrata* are poetry of enchanting beauty. We marvel at the comprehensive and flexible taste that enjoyed both.

Compare this with the concern for public morality that makes our television producers warn their audience for even quite mild programs that there may be language and actions that will offend some viewers. Our painfully solemn scenes in which a couple of actors gloomily pretend to be engaged in sexual intercourse would have meant nothing in the Greek theatre, in full sunshine, with an audience of 17,000 Athenians looking on. The later, degenerate Roman theatre went so far as it is possible to go in sexual action, and to liven up scenes of carnage they really killed a few slaves or criminals in full view of the audience. For us, that is still to come. At its height the Greek theatre did not descend to actual murder, but it supped full with psychological horrors, and its comedy was frankly dirty, and as the theatre was first and foremost a temple of Apollo, nobody felt that they had to walk out in order to assert their respectability.

Many people today may gain a more immediate and fuller sense of the Greek world from the contemplation of Greek art than from any amount of studying translations of Greek literature. Some knowledge of Greek, once the hallmark of a gentleman's education, is now a rarity.

Let us not forget that Greek sculpture, familiar to us since the Renaissance in monochrome marble, washed white by weather and often by the sea, was originally brightly painted to imitate and improve on nature; eyes and lips glowed, nipples were rosy, hair might be bound with circlets of precious metal, even eyelashes of fine wire might be affixed. The effect, to the austere eye of modernity, might seem vulgar, but it glowed with life and it was authentically Greek as the grey stone images that remain to us are not. When we think of the Greeks we must banish solemnity; serious they were – solemn never.

Something which we must never allow ourselves to forget is that the Greeks lived in an outdoor world. They discussed public affairs, they held elections, they gave parties, they held all their ceremonies except the most secret ones, and they taught mathematics and philosophy out-of-doors. Their climate was not an ideal one, but it was more endurable outside than in a dwelling that might have no heating except what was needed for cooking. Our indoor world is very much involved with the coming of reading and writing as common pursuits. It is difficult to read or write seriously in the open air. But the Greeks were not great readers – indeed probably more than half the population was wholly illiterate and the remainder read and wrote as necessities, rather than as common pursuits. Only scholars, poets, and playwrights, and of course the court secretaries, were ready writers. Reading and writing now hold the place that speaking and listening held in the Greek world. We shall see *The Bacchae* under a roof. Unthinkable in Greek terms.

Now let us talk about the play we are going to see this afternoon, and about the playwright. For many scholars, Euripides is the supreme Greek dramatist; of the three whose works have come down to us – Aeschylus, Sophocles, and Euripides – he seems to them to have the widest scope. He wrote ninety-two plays, of which nineteen survive, and we know that on two occasions he won the dramatic competition at Athens, which was the supreme honour for a theatre poet.

We should talk about that for a moment. The production of plays in Greece during the classical period was part of regular religious celebrations, and the most important of these took place in March; many playwrights offered their work for performance, but only three were chosen, and one of these was accorded the crown of ivy, and the money that went with it, and was acclaimed as a great man. Each playwright offered three tragedies, and a satyr play (which was a "take-off" or "skit" related to the tragedies, or one of them, that had gone before); only one of these burlesque pieces survives, and it happens to be by Euripides; it is pretty rough stuff, reminiscent of the *Mutt and Jeff* shows that used to tour this continent – dirty and obvious but filling a need in the human spirit. We should not be surprised that Euripides, who has been called "the most tragic of the poets" by Aristotle, could have written such a thing; we must remember that a great poet is not wholly a tragic author; to have depth, he must also have height and breadth; he must be able to play on the black keys as well as on the white. Think of the dirty jokes in Shakespeare, mixed with unrivalled tragic feeling, and splendid lyric verse. Euripides could not have raised the emotional storm of *The Bacchae* if he had not known the rowdy side of human nature.

Though he was successful twice, that is not much in a long life, and poets are not without self-esteem. We do not know for sure, but it appears that Euripides became disillusioned with Athens, and the judges at the dramatic contests, and accepted the invitation of King Archelaos to live in Macedonia, which was, in Greek terms, the boondocks. He seems not to have had much luck there, because the story is that he was torn to death by the King's dogs. It is ironic that his plays, entered by his son, won the Athenian contest posthumously in 406 B.C.

To us it may seem strange that a man would devote his life to writing for dramatic contests where his four plays might not be chosen at all, or if chosen, presented once, on a single day, and then little heard of except by that small part of the population that could, and did, read. We may wonder, also, who the judges were, who held such power? We do know that the religious aspect of the drama contest was assured by the fact that the best seat in the theatre – which seated 17,000 people, and at which attendance, if not compulsory, was strongly advised – was reserved for the priest of Dionysus.

We know also that the audience behaved as audiences always have done: people chattered so that their neighbours could not hear the actors, stingy people brought all their children on a free day, shameless people brought foreign guests and thus sneaked in without paying, people fell asleep and sometimes were left in the theatre at the end of the long day. Think of it: three tragedies and a funny play all in one session, sitting often in full sunlight! Of course there were the people who brought wine and got drunk as the day progressed. The audience, by the way, sat from dawn till late afternoon on stone seats, unless they hired a leather cushion at the door. One wonders what the sanitary conveniences were like, or if there were any in that predominantly outdoor civilization. And what was the performance like?

It was probably more like modern opera than modern theatre. There were only three actors, who played all the parts among them; they wore large masks, the fixed expression of which could be seen in the huge theatre where a naked face would be no more than a spot of light; they had magnificent voices, and their declamation was of a variety and emphasis more like singing than speech; because they wore masks and heavy robes, and were mounted on built-up shoes, they moved deliberately, and their movement may have been like stately dancing. There was a Chorus, usually of fifteen singers, who declaimed their part to the accompaniment of a flute; the Chorus offered comment on the action, and appealed to the gods, and the words they spoke are usually the noblest verse in the play. All the actors were men, even when they played women's roles. The Athenian audience, apart from the nuisances I have mentioned, must have been splendidly appreciative to have seized and responded to verse of this kind. Perhaps we might say that the Greek theatre was more for the ear than for the eye – again, like modern opera.

The director, in modern terms, was the poet himself, and the expenses were defrayed by a rich citizen who considered it a mark of status to be allowed to pay the bills. He was called the Choregus.

Now, about the play we are to see, *The Bacchae*. The title means simply *The Women of Bacchus* and Bacchus is another name of

Dionysus. It is about a new freedom granted to women – which is probably why the Stratford Festival considers the play especially relevant now. The story is simple.

The god Dionysus is travelling the world, to make himself known, and he has arrived at Thebes. The city has special meaning for him, because here is the tomb of his mother, Semele. The tale is that Semele was loved by Zeus, the greatest of the gods, and begged that he would appear to her in his full glory; he did so and she was reduced to ashes by the lightning-like splendour of her lover. But the child in her womb was saved, and embedded by Zeus in his thigh, until it was ready for birth. Dionysus has a deep filial feeling for his mother and is offended because his mother's sister Agave, who is Queen of Thebes and mother of the King, Pentheus, has tried to diminish this family relationship by denying that Dionysus, son of Zeus and Semele, is a god.

To make known his godhead, Dionysus drives all the women of Thebes mad, and sends them to the nearby Mount Cithaeron to perform rites in his honour. The report is that these rites are wild, erotic, and frenzied, and thus alarming to conventional minds.

This is bitterly displeasing to the King, Pentheus, and he seizes and imprisons Dionysus, who is in human form and is thus not identifiable as a god; but that proved unwise, for Dionysus made Pentheus imprison and bind a bull in his place, and destroyed the royal palace with an earthquake. He made Pentheus put on women's dress and go to the mountain to see for himself what the women were doing. Pentheus agrees to this mad scheme because he seems to be under a spell, as well he might be, in the presence of the god. When he arrived at the orgy Dionysus betrayed Pentheus to the enraged women, who tore him to pieces.

It is his mother, Agave, who is his chief destroyer; in her religious ecstasy she mistakes her son for a lion, and it is with a supposed lion's head that she returns to Thebes, where she drunkenly confronts her son's grandfather, Cadmus, the founder of the city of Thebes, and all is revealed. Dionysus implacably exiles the family of Cadmus from Thebes, and thus the tragedy ends.

Are we to dismiss this as an old tale of horror, redeemed for us by great poetry? We would be as mad as the women of Thebes if we did so. You will recall that when we were talking about the gods of Greece I said that Dionysus was god of all that was irrational, the god of ecstasy, the god of all that probes the darkest and sometimes the most important places in the human spirit. King Pentheus will allow nothing of that; he seeks to repress it, he cannot comprehend it or find a place for it in a well-ordered society. He is the right-minded, clear-thinking, narrow-souled man. Thus, in the end, the irrational overwhelms the purely rational; Pentheus, and the idea of society he represents, is utterly destroyed; and a great city lies in ruins. Dionysus, without regard for the consequences to mere humanity, has asserted his godhead.

The gods of ancient Greece are not dead, and Dionysus is busily at work in our world, where we seem – at least in North America and rather less strenuously in Europe and in the other lands that we think of as civilized – to be anxious to stamp out every inequality, every injustice, everything that some aggrieved minority might con- sider "politically incorrect," and to establish a great, grey world in which everybody gets what he thinks is his due and nobody gets his lumps. Nothing in history or in the nature of man suggests that such a world lies anywhere near possibility, but the zealously right-minded, the blindfolded righters-of-wrongs continue like the dutiful sons and daughters of King Pentheus that they are, to behave as though we could bring it about by endless legislation, and a frantic tut-tutting at anything which is not universally acceptable.

So – where do we see Dionysus at work? Sometimes in horrors that ring around the world, as in 1978 Guyana, when at the direc- tion of a religious leader named Jim Jones some hundreds of his fol- lowers committed mass suicide by drinking – this is burlesque that might have come from a satyr-play – cyanide concealed in draughts of Kool-Aid. They were determined that the end of the world was at hand, so they fled from the United States, and obediently killed themselves to support the position taken by their prophet. Was not Dionysus there?

And this year, between February 28 and April 19 in Waco, Texas, a group called the Branch Davidians held out in a stronghold against armed police, rather than submit to the laws of their country, and at last perished in a great fire – 780 men, women, and children – rather than disobey David Koresh, their religious leader. Dionysian frenzy, surely?

When we look at film records of the great assemblies of the Nazi Party, do we not see thousands in the grip of Dionysus? When we look at the television news of any large riot, do we not see Dionysus at work? What inspires football riots? And when we read the daily papers do we not, if we are attentive, sense a Dionysian note in the stories of crime, of bloody warfare, of drug trafficking and mass murder? Was not the man who shot seventeen college girls in Montreal under the spell of the great, irrational god whose commands run contrary to everything that civilization thinks it stands for?

So, what are we to do about it? Surely the answer is obvious: we must let Dionysus have his due, and not insist that the world is, all the time, obliged to serve Athena and Apollo, or to grub and grumble in the workshops with Hephaestus, earning more money so that we may pay more taxes. These gods of sunlight and daily duty must have their proper service, but Dionysus is neglected at our peril. So, let us not grumble about the rock concerts where thousands of devotees shriek and clamour while some latter-day priest of Dionysus strums his guitar and howls his hymn to the irrational. Let us not run about declaring that the sky is falling if people who crave that sort of release are found smoking marijuana. Let us look a little more leniently at the question of tobacco smoking, which mankind survived for two centuries before we were born. We do not have to join any Dionysian worship that does not appeal to us, but let us be sure that somebody else's worship is harmful to anyone but himself before we roar "Thou shalt not," and begin to make laws and, of course, heap on taxes. The perfectibility of the human race will be achieved, if it ever is achieved, by intelligent indirection, rather than by ill-understood legislation. Remember what happened to Pentheus, whose mother mistook him for a lion but who was, it must be feared, simply an ass.

I spoke earlier about the difficulties of translating these Greek plays in order to make them understandable by us. One of the great problems is that the Greeks wrote in language which was not the ordinary language of their daily life, but in an exalted strain, capable of great poetry, but devilishly hard to find equivalents for in modern verse. That kind of language, in English, soon wears out our patience. Any of you who have seen a performance of Milton's tragedy *Samson Agonistes* will know what I am talking about. That solemn thunder has a numbing effect on the hearer; our greatest dramatic poetry is not like that; it has a wider variety of mood, of vocabulary, of speed. So what is the translator to do? He is expected to be scholarly; he is expected to be poetic, and he is expected to speak to us, but not to roar at us.

I can ask the question: I am not obliged to give the answer. But let me conclude by giving you three renderings of a vital passage from *The Bacchae*. Here is how Kenneth Cavender, whose translation we shall hear, translates the conclusion of one of the most important speeches in the play, in which a Messenger tells of what happened to the unhappy Pentheus when he fell into the hands of the god-possessed women:

The best and safest way to live
Is to keep a balance, acknowledge
The great powers around us and in us.
I think that is what is meant by wisdom.
If you can live that way, if you have
That balance, you are a wise man indeed.

Now listen to the rendering of the same passage by an eminent scholar, F. L. Lucas, who is not usually honoured as a poet, but who sticks with scholarly reverence to his original:

Surely restraint and reverence for Heaven
Are the better way – indeed the truest wisdom,
For all that follows them.

And here is the rendering of a very great Greek scholar who was also a poet of no mean stature, Gilbert Murray:

Oh, to fulfil
God's laws, and have no thought beyond His will
Is man's best treasure. Aye, and wisdom true,
Methinks, for things of dust to cleave unto!

Which is the truest rendering? I cannot tell you. All the Greek I know could easily be written on a postage stamp. But I think I can tell you what this afternoon's play, *The Bacchae*, means: it means that all excess, including and perhaps especially excess in rationality, in law-making, in regimenting humanity, is extremely dangerous, for its opposite, the Dionysian fury, will burst up from underneath all the restraints, and bring about horrors unimaginable. On the great temple of Apollo at Delphi, one of the supreme shrines of the Greek world, was written these words: NOTHING IN EXCESS. No, not even excess in reason, in doing "good," in insisting on some program for the supposed betterment of others.

That wisdom is older than Euripides. It has its great prophet in another Greek, Heracleitus, who lived a century earlier. All Creation, all Nature, he proclaimed, was in a state of flux, and wisdom lay in seeking a balance between opposites. The way to do that was to observe the wisdom NOTHING IN EXCESS, which is as true, and as often forgotten, in our time as it was long ago when *The Bacchae* was a new play.

3

———— ∽ ————

LOOK AT THE CLOCK!
(A Suggestion for a Film Scenario)

WHEN BRIAN MCGING, a Classics Professor at Trinity College in the University of Dublin, and a former Junior Fellow of Massey College, became the editor of *Hermathena*, he turned to the Founding Master of his old College for a contribution. Robertson Davies never had difficulty with such a request as he had many ideas he wished to express, and when he had a chance to have some fun with an idea, he did not hesitate.

On December 7, 1991 Davies wrote: *Complete revision of* Look at the Clock! *for Hermathena; an odd piece but I like it and have always wanted to have some sport with the overblown Oedipus business.*

———— ∽ ————

The room is empty when first we see it, but we need a moment to take it in. At first glance it looks like any room reserved for the private use of some great person in any one of a hundred European palaces; the carpet is richly coloured, the furniture in French eighteenth-century style, of gilt wood and silk upholstery; a handsome bookcase has not been able to contain all the books the owner of the room needs, and some large folios are heaped on the floor; an imposing clock stands near the door. But as we look more closely, we see that this furnishing is in a room with old stone walls, not fully concealed by tapestries; the ceiling is supported on heavy old beams. An archaic room, in fact, immeasurably old, that has been brought to modernity, as royalty encounters modernity. Through the window we see a landscape, harsh but beautiful, that tells us that this must be Greece. It is morning.

The door bursts open and a woman dashes into the room in high agitation; she is splendidly but simply dressed; her clothing is less significant than her beauty and palpable vitality. She unwinds the heavy sash that is her girdle, throws it over a hook which is fastened in a central roof-beam, and rapidly and expertly makes a noose. She draws up a chair, climbs on it, puts the noose around her neck, then pauses for a moment, seems to reflect, takes her neck out of the noose, steps from the chair, seats herself at ease on a sofa, takes a cigarette from a box on the table, and lights it, drawing in the smoke with obvious satisfaction. She is smiling, now.

Cries are heard outside, and they come nearer until the door bursts open and a magnificent young man dashes into the room, his sword drawn. He has the air of a king and wears a uniform which might be that of a field marshal. But it is not in the best of military taste; there is a flashiness about it, and a multiplicity of Orders and Medals that suggests vanity rather than glory in the field. He is shouting.

THE KING: A sword, a sword, and show me here
              That wife, no wife, that field of bloodstained earth
              Where husband, father, sin on sin, had birth,
              Polluted generations!

THE QUEEN: Ah, we're having Gilbert Murray today, are we?

THE KING: We are having The Great Myth, and we are having it in English. You know I prefer Murray to any of the others.

THE QUEEN: Certainly he offers great opportunities to a man of your rhetorical gifts. Sophocles in English. Personally I prefer Seneca's version of our little trouble —

THE KING: Seneca gives you a suicide scene all to yourself. Obviously you like it. But Sophocles was immeasurably the superior playwright.

THE QUEEN: I don't grudge you your Sophocles. I don't even grudge you Gilbert Murray. But now and again I wish I didn't have to play such a docile second fiddle to you, my dear boy.

THE KING: Don't call me your dear boy!

THE QUEEN: I've called you that for years. It's a simple endearment.

THE KING: In the light of what we know — what we discover every time we play out my personal tragedy, such a term is indecent in the highest extreme.

THE QUEEN: And we play out your personal tragedy, as you insist it is (though I carry a lot of the weight of it), on the last day of every lunar month, and have done for the last twenty-eight hundred years, give or take a little. "When 'Omer smote 'is bloomin' lyre," as a contemporary of Gilbert Murray wrote. Don't you ever tire of it?

THE KING: It is not for me to tire of it. I have my place in the great world of myth, and it is my duty to body it forth for the enlargement and guidance of mankind. Tire of it! You are frivolous.

THE QUEEN: O, my dear — you can't imagine how I long for a little frivolity.

THE KING: Well, you can't have it now. Don't you hear the Citizens of Thebes crying for me?

(The Screen shows us the Citizens of Thebes, and they are indeed crying for this unhappy King. Anyone who has had experience with films knows how hard it is to assemble a good Mob, and this one is composed of theatrical extras of all sorts and degrees of education. The English ones cry EEdipus, the Americans cry EDDYpus, and those who have been to Drama School and are waiting for their big chance OIDYPOOS. Now we cut back to the Queen's Chamber.)

THE QUEEN: Well, go to them and say that there has been a change in the script.

THE KING: After – after – A change in the script? You are out of your mind! After – (*He is trying to do a sum in his head.*)

THE QUEEN: You needn't cudgel your brains. You were never any good at reckoning –

THE KING: It is an unkingly accomplishment.

THE QUEEN: Very well. But you have only to look at the clock over there to see that it comes to about twenty-eight hundred years or – or quite a few thousand lunar months. Are we never to have anything new? I am bored to death with this old script and my part in it.

THE KING: How often must I explain that we have the ineffable honour to be creatures of myth, fixed forever in the deepest consciousness of mankind, eternal and unchangeable. You are talking like a woman –

THE QUEEN: Indeed I am. And please don't shout at me. Not for nothing have you been called Oedipus Tyrannus.

THE KING: I glory in the title. I rule single-solus. I brook no contradiction or opposition. What else should I be called?

THE QUEEN: Well, I know you don't like hearing about him, but my first husband was called Laius Basileus. He wasn't a tyrant; he was a king, and wasn't afraid to take advice.

THE KING: Oh, that old ass –

THE QUEEN: Please! He *was* your father, and my first husband. Not so old and not in the least an ass. A very capable ruler, until you murdered him – and with your usual unfailing tact, managed to do it before the altar of two major gods. Your way of meeting a difficulty is to kill somebody. I have been killed thirty-six thousand, four hundred times, if you want accuracy, and I'm fed up with it!

THE KING: I see. One of your tantrums. I'll get Creon to talk to you.

THE QUEEN: You mean you'll get Creon to advise you. You – a tyrant! My lad, without Creon you'd have been assassinated years ago!

THE KING: We are wasting time. (*He rings a bell and the Messenger, who has been listening at the door, almost falls into the room.*) Ask the Lord Creon to join us.

THE MESSENGER: O King –

THE QUEEN: And ask the Prophet Teiresias to join us also.

THE MESSENGER: But what shall I say to the people?

THE KING: The people must wait. Go at once.

(*The Messenger goes.*)

THE KING: Why do you want that old fool?

THE QUEEN: I don't know, but I hope to find out.

THE KING: Ye gods! (*And he must be careful to say it as an invocation, like a Greek, and not "Yee gahds" like an exasperated American schoolgirl.*) The vagarious irrationality of women! – Listen to that Crowd.

(The Camera cuts again to the Mob, whose outcry is increasing. The drama students, remembering that "The city breathes/Heavy with incense, heavy with dim prayer/And shrieks to affright the Slayer" are breathing with difficulty, and a few of the more creative souls utter the most frightening shrieks they can manage. Then we see the Lord Creon, a thoroughly capable bureaucrat, making his masterful way up the palace steps. Not far after him is the aged Teiresias, who is supposed to be blind, but manages astonishingly well with the aid of a staff. Creon wears Court dress, with plenty of gold braid. The Prophet looks as if he had just come from a university lecture room, wears odd socks and a rusty, somewhat tattered academic gown. We now see them enter the Queen's room. Creon gives Oedipus the most perfunctory of bows, and kisses his sister. Teiresias whacks about him with his stick until he finds a chair, and sits immediately.)

THE KING: (*Ironically*) Be seated gentlemen.

TEIRESIAS: Oh, dreadfully sorry. Quite forgot.

(*He bobs up and sits again at once. Creon sits in the middle of the stage, like a man accustomed to chairing meetings.*)

CREON: I needn't tell you that the people of Thebes are waiting for the reappearance of their King. What has caused this delay?

THE KING: She won't go ahead with it.

CREON: Won't hang yourself? Why, may I ask.

THE QUEEN: Look at the clock, brother. Look at the clock! We are very near the end of the Aeon of Pisces. Are we to go into Aquarius acting out this same rowdy puppet-show of cruelty, and vengeance, and incest and remorse? Is there never to be any change?

CREON: Let me see, isn't this the day you do the Gilbert Murray version? In Gilbert Murray's day they believed in the Myth of Progress. Don't tell me you've fallen for that, sister?

THE QUEEN: I have not "fallen for" anything. I have been thinking, which is quite another matter.

THE KING: And usually the beginning of trouble.

CREON: What have you been thinking about, sister?

THE QUEEN: Time.

THE KING: (*amazed*) ⎫
CREON: (*enquiring*) ⎬ Time!
TEIRESIAS: (*delighted*) ⎭

THE QUEEN: Yes, time. It is rather the fashion these days to be derisive about it. People scold about Time as if it were a prison. Yet without it, how should we see men and things in more than one light? Without Time, life would stand still.

THE KING: But you surely understand that with people like ourselves, life does stand still. We are myth. We are Eternal.

THE QUEEN: I have been eternal for quite long enough. Without Time, mind stands still. And don't sneer at the notion of Progress, Creon. If you think of it as a sort of plant-food to secure quick, lavish growth, of course, it's silly. But things *do* change, you know. Slowly, slowly, very, very slowly. But surely, all the same.

CREON: Do I understand that you are proposing that we should change our great Myth?

THE QUEEN: We could talk about it.

THE KING: Blasphemy!

THE QUEEN: Blasphemy against what?

THE KING: Can you ask? Against one of the supreme myths of mankind. Against one of the forces that has shaped man's mind and man's destiny. Against one of the most profoundly rooted of the archetypes that govern the life of man, the highest achievement of Creation.

THE QUEEN: Oh balls!

THE KING: What did you say?

THE QUEEN: You heard me. This great myth of yours was just another old story – a very fine story I freely admit – until that cigar-smoking wizard at Berggasse 19, Vienna District IX blew it up into something which he insisted was universal – meaning that every man was supposed to share it. Women didn't matter.

THE KING: Madam, you are belittling my Complex. The Oedipus Complex, the discovery of which revolutionized the world's attitude toward – toward – toward a great many very significant things. And don't say women didn't matter. They mattered as fiercely desired mothers.

TEIRESIAS: Yes, and without a mother, where's your Complex? She's the bone father and son are fighting over. Thus far, she's central. Passive, but central. She's the prize that goes to the stronger. Daddy hangs on to Mummy, and Baby sulks for life. Baby wrests Mummy

from Daddy, and Daddy shrivels up and blows away. But Mummy
is always pig-in-the-middle, as in the children's game.

THE KING: You are quite wrong. I detest your reductive names for
the characters in the struggle, but if that's the way you understand
it, you must know that Baby kills Daddy and has Mummy all to
himself.

THE QUEEN: Always killing somebody!

THE KING: Well, what about it?

TEIRESIAS: I'll tell you what about it –

THE KING: Have you entirely forgotten your palace manners? Don't
speak to royal persons until you're spoken to.

TEIRESIAS: But then I should never get a chance. I like to talk, but
we prophets are never asked to talk unless everybody else is utterly
exhausted. I want to talk about fathers. This father business is
greatly misunderstood.

THE KING: Not at all. The man who does not kill his father and thus
deliver himself from servitude must be content to live as his father's
shadow. Simple.

TEIRESIAS: Not simple at all, O King. The Queen is right; things do
change, but not quickly. I grant you that every man must kill his
father, not in the flesh but in the spirit, if he is to be his own man.
And as things are now – you see, O Queen, that I share your
respect for Time – every man has many fathers – one of the flesh
but more than one of the spirit. The teacher, the benefactor, the
father in craft or art – every one a father and the free man must,
as humanely as he can, kill them all. That is to say, he must take
what they have to give and make it his own, and then be quit of

them. And the wise father – teacher, benefactor, craftsman, or artist – will take the blow as handsomely as he can, for it is his last blessing on his son.

THE KING: I detest these amplifications and explanations. I am for the simplicity and splendour of life, and the nobility of tragedy. Man is never so truly man as when he is implicated in a tragic situation. You people have no understanding of that. None whatever. Look at you. All sitting down. In tragedy one *never* sits. Sit down and you immediately reduce a situation to comedy.

THE QUEEN: Always the actor.

THE KING: The principal actor in the greatest tragedy the world has known. I am proud of my role.

TEIRESIAS: You are young, O King, and the young are great ones for standing. And for tragedy. They love a great uproar and tempest of feeling. The old know tragedy too well to enjoy it.

THE KING: Spare us the tedious wisdom of age, prophet.

TEIRESIAS: Willingly. I know better than anyone how unavailing it is. Have I not, in my long life, been both a man and a woman? Yes, many long years I spent in a woman's body, and it was because I had loved women's bodies too much. Athena caught me spying on her beauty while she bathed, and turned me into a woman so that I should learn what a woman's body really was. I was soon sick of it, I can tell you.

(The Camera shows us a dark alley in Athens. Teiresias, now a woman, stands at a corner and as a soldier passes, she beckons to him. After a brief colloquy, he possesses her fiercely against the wall, and when she puts out her hand for her fee he strikes her brutally across the face, and walks away, laughing.)

TEIRESIAS: I was glad when Zeus mercifully turned me back into a man, and I was able to get on with my real vocation, which is prophecy. Female prophets are too easily discredited.

CREON: But when you were a woman you were able to answer the great question: which enjoys sexual congress the more – the man, or the woman?

TEIRESIAS: Yes, I was able to settle that. The women are the fortunate ones. They get nine times more pleasure from that exercise than do men.

THE QUEEN: Yes, and they pay for it with nine months' tedious work. Whatever way you look at it, it's a swindle.

CREON: May I remind you that the people of Thebes are waiting for the resolution – the ancient, time-honoured resolution – of this situation. If we begin talking about sex we shall go on quarrelling and boasting for hours. What are we to tell the people? The Messenger is hanging about outside waiting for his summons. Surely I do not have to remind you drama-conscious people that nothing destroys a tragedy so much as superfluous talk. What's it to be? Make haste!

THE KING: It's as plain as day. I burst into the room, crying for the blood of the woman who has betrayed me into incest and thus brought a horrible plague upon Thebes. I find her hanging from the roof, her own girdle tight about her neck. She has discharged her role, and her duty. – But there she sits, smoking and laughing at me.

CREON: Well – order her to discharge her role, and her duty.

THE KING: I don't know that I altogether want to do that. Of course I'm furious with her, but I am fond of her. It goes against the grain. I'd rather she did it out of a sense of – well, a sense of fitness.

CREON: And you call yourself a tyrant!

THE KING: You tell her to hang herself. You're her brother.

CREON: When a brother tells his sister to hang herself, it is mere family pleasantry. You're the offended party. You do it.

THE KING: I am a doer, not a talker. When I came into this room, I was whirled in a tempest of tragic fury. At that moment, I could have chopped her into messes. But I was taken off guard. What I was prepared to do, by tragic necessity and long custom, was to seize the gold pin from her breast and blind myself with it. I was not prepared to meet an arguing, laughing, obstinate woman.

CREON: That is an explanation, but not a proposal. I repeat — what are we to tell the people?

THE QUEEN: Why not tell them the truth?

THE KING: ⎫
CREON: ⎭ The truth?

THE QUEEN: Yes. Tell them that the plague in Thebes is not because of the incest of their King, but is the predictable consequence of their own stupidity. If they persist in dumping their household refuse and their close-stools in the streets, and throwing dead donkeys and corpses into the waterways, they must expect plague, and dirt is far more dangerous than a trivial sexual transgression.

THE KING: Trivial? You call our tragic mating trivial?

THE QUEEN: The fuss about incest is absurd. If it doesn't hurt anybody, or debauch anybody, what's so bad about it?

THE KING: It's all these damned books you read! I knew you were perverse, but not depraved!

TEIRESIAS: Incest is not really likely to catch on in a big way, even if you decide to recognize it, as people now recognize homosexuality. Kindly Nature has so ordained things that most siblings are deeply repugnant to one another. O Queen, would you consent to wed your brother Creon?

THE QUEEN: What a perfectly revolting idea!

CREON: Thank you. And I return the compliment.

TEIRESIAS: You see? Even though King Creon and Queen Jocasta would make an infinitely better royal couple than the present arrangement.

CREON: The Messenger is waiting. We have no time to spare for these compliments. What are we to tell the people? You hear them.

(The Camera once again shows us the Mob, which has increased its clamour, but at considerable personal discomfort. Vendors of throat lozenges, who pass among them, are doing a brisk trade.)

TEIRESIAS: The Queen has suggested the truth.

CREON: When has any Mob ever been ready for the truth?

THE QUEEN: You are right, brother. And we must have some regard for the King. He demands tragedy. It is his milieu. If we tell the people that their agony is caused by a dirty water supply, we reduce this tragedy to a drama of social betterment, like something by Henrik Ibsen.

CREON: And what do you suggest?

THE QUEEN: Couldn't the King and I go out, hand in hand, and explain to the people that the whole thing was an unfortunate mistake, and neither of us knew what we were doing then, but we know now, and intend to go right on doing it?

THE KING: I should look like a fool. Marrying a woman old enough to be my mother!

THE QUEEN: I wasn't so old. And I am your mother.

TEIRESIAS: When Helen ran off with Paris, and brought about the Trojan War, she was only twelve – though a well-developed twelve. We folk of the mythic world are allowed quite a bit of latitude with Time. If you were to ask me, I should say, give it a try.

THE KING: We haven't asked you. – Very well, if that is how it is to be, I shall speak to the people – but alone.

CREON: No, brother-in-law, you'll make a mess of it: I shall speak to the people.

THE QUEEN: And what exactly are you going to say?

CREON: I shall want a few minutes to collect my thoughts.

THE QUEEN: The Messenger is waiting. You'd better listen to me. Tell them that the World Clock is moving toward the new Aeon. The Aeon of Pisces is nearly done, and extraordinary new things are to be expected. The Aeon of Aquarius is very near, and we must prepare for the new beliefs, attitudes, feelings, and all that it brings. Tell them that the King and I will appear, more deeply united than before, but that our example must be followed, if at all, with the uttermost circumspection.

CREON: No, no: very crude. I shall find my own way.

THE QUEEN: Spoken like a ruler. Now – think up your speech.

THE KING: This leaves me in a pretty predicament, I must say.

TEIRESIAS: Not so bad, really; if the old drama had been played out, and you were now blinded, you would have to retire to Colonus, and become a sage. You would have time for reflection. But now, of course, you must continue your reign, and your much-admired association with the Queen. Wouldn't you rather be a King than a sage?

THE KING: I shall miss the long nights of reflection at Colonus.

THE QUEEN: What did you reflect about?

THE KING: Ah – I've never told anybody. But when the Sphinx asked me her famous riddle, and I gave the right answer and she destroyed herself, she actually asked me two riddles. The first, of course, was –

TEIRESIAS: What walks on four legs at dawn, on two legs at noonday, and on three legs at sundown?

THE QUEEN: It seems easy now, when everybody knows the answer. But I don't suppose it was easy when the Sphinx asked you.

THE KING: No indeed. I think I acquitted myself not badly that time, stupid though Creon supposes me to be. But that isn't the whole story. The Sphinx was furious. She raged, because she knew she had to destroy herself. But she shrieked, before she leapt into the chasm, "O clever one, answer this: 'What shall be yours that no one else would have? What shall be yours that King Creon will pay for? What shall be yours that you cannot see?'"

TEIRESIAS: And you have never guessed it?

THE KING: Never. Though I have puzzled for countless hours.

TEIRESIAS: Shall I tell you?

THE QUEEN: No. The Sphinx will be answered in plenty of time.

TEIRESIAS: It will be something for you to work on at Colonus.

THE KING: If we are changing the script I don't think I shall go to Colonus.

CREON: I am ready now.

THE QUEEN: You have it?

CREON: Oh yes. I shall tell the people that the gods have spoken. They have forgiven the King and Queen their transgression, and what has been regarded as their sin is a sin no longer, but a royal prerogative. For which reason, if it is uncovered among lesser folk, it will be subject to an extremely heavy fine.

THE KING: But the Complex? My Complex – the Oedipus Complex: what is to become of that?

CREON: Well, I don't want to be immodest but I think this rather a fine stroke. Homosexuality was botched. An opportunity for a tax thrown away. But henceforth anyone who lays claim to, or is discovered to possess, an Oedipus Complex must pay a substantial yearly tax so long as it persists. A tax on neurosis!

TEIRESIAS: What a mind! What an introduction to a new age!

CREON: Not bad, if I may say so. Of course the Complex will continue to be popular among the neurotic well-to-do, so the tax should bring in a substantial yearly sum.

(Creon claps his hands and The Messenger dashes through the Doorway.)

CREON: Tell the people that I shall address them immediately. Tell them that I bring great news from the gods. And you, sister and brother-in-law, you lurk inside the doorway, until I give you your cue, then come forward hand in hand, and be gracious. Assume a noble port –

THE QUEEN: A what?

CREON: Look your best. Don't snigger. No – wait. You, O King, come first, and when the shouts are over their peak make a splendid gesture, and you, sister, come forward in your role as mother, consort, and goddess. Better put on your Moon tiara.

TEIRESIAS (*to the Messenger*): Is there a side door? I don't want to miss any of this.

(The Messenger beckons, and Teiresias goes.)

CREON: Come, O King. Think of this as a new role.

THE KING: You know, I feel I may be glad of a change.

(THE KING and CREON go, and as we hear a great roar of acclaim from the Mob – some cry, "Hail O King" and others whisper, "Look, he hasn't blinded himself" – we see the front of the Palace, with Oedipus more kindly than ever before in his career, at the top of the steps. Then we cut back to the Queen's chamber. She goes to a large cupboard which, when opened, reveals a store of treasure and jewels of every kind. She selects with great care a silver tiara on the top of which, cut from a single moonstone, is a crescent. As she is adjusting it to her liking before a mirror, there is a tap on the door, and when she cries, "Come," a very old man – a cobwebby old man who might almost have been carved out of the root of a yew tree – enters softly. He bows.)

OLD MAN: If you please, O Queen –

THE QUEEN: Yes, what is it?

OLD MAN: The clock. It's time for me to wind the clock.

THE QUEEN: Very well. – I don't think I have ever known that clock to be wound before.

OLD MAN: Well, you see – I only wind it once in two thousand years. Every Aeon, that's to say. And when I wind it, there are quite a few changes. Because the gods change their minds, every Aeon. Not much, you know, but it's surprising what that little brings about.

THE QUEEN: And a new Aeon is coming.

OLD MAN: O yes, my lady. Indeed, it's a little bit on its way already. But when I wind up the clock, the big changes will begin. The gods must change their minds from time to time. They'd shrivel away with boredom else.

THE QUEEN: You don't sound like a servant. Certainly not a slave.

OLD MAN: Oh no indeed, my lady. I've had my day, and I'm not really finished yet.

THE QUEEN: I wish I had more time to talk, but I have a most important appearance to make.

OLD MAN: Yes. One of the big changes. Or perhaps not such a big one. I don't know. I just wind the clock.

THE QUEEN: We must talk again, clock-winder. – What is your name?

OLD MAN: Cronus, my lady. Or Saturn, if you prefer.

(But the Queen has gone before she hears his name. The Old Man opens the great clock, takes a key from his pouch, and sets to work to wind it. Superimposed on the image of the Old Man at his work we see that of Oedipus and Queen Jocasta acknowledging the welcome of the Mob, as they set out on their new myth. But the noise of winding the Clock grows louder and louder until it drowns out the Mob, and the trumpets, as the film ends.)

4

— ❧ —

ON SEEING PLAYS

ONCE AGAIN TO THE Celebrated Writers Series at the Stratford Festival, this time in June 1990. We are very pleased to be able to include the Theatre Diary entries for three of the four plays that are the subject of this lecture. They are *As You Like It*, *Love for Love*, and *Macbeth*. There is no entry for the production of *The Merry Wives of Windsor*. The mention of *World of Wonders* is of the play that Elliott Hayes adapted from Robertson Davies' novel of the same name, staged at Stratford in June 1992.

On June 10, 1990 Davies wrote: *Very nervous. Lecture in Third Stage at 10:30 a.m. Sold out! Lectures goes very well. Lunch with Elliott Hayes in Green Room: re-greet Desmond Heeley. To Matinée:* As You Like It *very finely done in Canadian setting. Champagne with John and Joanne Hayes: their 41st anniversary. To dinner at the Old Prune with Elliott Hayes, David William, and David Rose. Talk about the Alexander Technique, the occult, and* World of Wonders, *about which they have very interesting ideas.*

June 8: *Friday, Avon Theatre:* Love for Love *produced by David William. Lacked style. Colm Feore an under-par Valentine: his mad scene went for nothing. Goldie Semple good as Angelica but in Congreve one player cannot lift a bad partner. Atienza a good Foresight, but the prevailing style was against him. Ben and Prue (Roger Honeywell and Vickie Papava) coarse and out of key: he hauled her about the stage by her legs and she brayed in a low Canadian voice – not Foresight's daughter. A weary production and dully spoken.*

June 9: *Saturday, Festival Theatre:* Macbeth – *the best I have ever seen of this tragedy. Ensemble did it, for Brian Bedford has not the voice for it, though his depiction of tragic decline was superb. A truly Jungian production: the Hero is dominated by his demonic Anima until he is out of her grasp and wholly in the grip of his Unconscious (very fine that Macbeth showed no regret, only self-concern); at the end, in a terrible flash of light, Macbeth sees all his victims as he falls. Pennell a splendid Banquo, noble and a living rebuke to Macbeth: Scott Wentworth a saturnine, implacable Macduff: Atienza – for once a real King as Duncan: Goldie Semple a brilliant, truly fiend-like Lady. The only bad performance was William Dunlop as the Porter – an impossible part, anyhow. Supernatural scenes splendid; truly archetypal figures in the Masque of Kings. And a true regality about the throne of Scotland – lots of splendid accoutrements. Thrilling and chilling as I have never known Macbeth to be. Fine music by Lou Applebaum.*

June 10: *Sunday: Festival Theatre:* As You Like It. *Brilliant, witty production by Richard Monette. Action in New France, about 1760: coureurs de bois, Indians, canoes, maple leaves, habitants, and score by the usually villainous Carrière which used French-Canadian folk-song simply and movingly. Lucy Peacock a splendid Rosalind, witty, boyish and delightful. And Marie Baron made a witty charmer of that lump Celia. William Dunlop a very funny, restrained Touchstone, played as a Scot in Highland dress. David William a fine Jacques, stressing the bitterness and*

*misanthropy of the role: Seven Ages transformed, the ugliness
and futility stressed. The whole production a brilliant joke and
warming because the Canadian approach has been made to fit so
charmingly. The best* As You Like It *I have seen, I think, and I
have seen some fine productions.*

———— ∽ ————

W hen I was asked to talk to you
this morning I was given no specific direction about the kind of talk
it should be; that was left to my discretion. This sounds complimentary and as if things had been made easy for me, but, in fact, the contrary was the case; to be asked to talk, but not told what to talk about,
throws the speaker into confusion, particularly if, like myself, he has
spent part of his life as a professor. Professors, you see, have a sneaking feeling that they ought to say the last word about anything that
presents itself. They know they won't succeed, but they think they
ought to try. If I had obeyed the promptings of the professor side of
my nature I should now set to work to tell you everything that is
known, or might be guessed, about the plays you have seen here at
Stratford, and wrap it all up so that you would never feel doubt or
be obliged to think about those plays, or see them, again.

But there is another side to my nature. Where the professor is earnest
and weighted down with knowledge, this other fellow is simply a
delighted playgoer, who goes to the theatre as often as he can, because
playgoing is the greatest pleasure he knows. Lord Byron wrote, in a
letter to his friend Thomas Moore: "I am acquainted with no immaterial sensuality so delightful as good acting," and I applaud his lordship, loud and long. And I would add that I consider good plays to
be among the highest achievements of literature and to see them performed – not always greatly but often pretty well – to be among the
highest pleasures possible. So I am going to talk to you this morning
about *seeing* plays, rather than about the plays themselves. I have seen
all the plays we are attending this weekend many times, and I am

going to tell you about what I saw. If any of you came expecting a scholarly lecture, now is the time for you to leave, because this is just going to be a friendly talk.

I may even be boring, and you have been warned. We have all been bored almost to the point of paralysis by old playgoers who want to tell us about the actors far greater than any now living, in productions of plays that have never been equalled in any memory but their own. I promise you that I won't do that. But I shall tell you about some productions that I have greatly enjoyed, and which are now, I am sorry to say, quite a long time in the past. Because I am – it gives me no pleasure to say so – rather an Old Playgoer.

When I was thinking about what I am going to say I stood for quite a while in front of my bookshelves, which is something I often do when I am trying to think. And as I did so my eye lit on a book I have not read for years – and I am not going to read it again – called *The Old Playgoer*. It is rather a rare book – that is why I bought it – and it was written in 1846 by a man called William Robson. You will not have heard of him, and you need not regret it. It is said of him that his criticisms are always scholarly and his comments always interesting. That is true enough. But for all of that, he is rather a bore, because in his book he insists that nobody will ever see anything to equal what he has seen. All the great actors are dead, and nobody understands Shakespeare. I don't want to take the cheap revenge of making fun of a dead man, so I shall simply say that I disagree. I have seen plenty of fine actors who are now dead, but I have also seen many who are still living, and some of them I have seen here at Stratford. Robson says: "Although the pleasure I have received from this retrospective review of by-gone excellence has been one of the reasons for my thus stringing together my dramatic recollections, my principal motive has been to prove the vast superiority of the stage of my day over the present, and to endeavour to show the cause of the deterioration." He wrote that when he was only sixty-one – a mere boy. I am older than he was then, and so I have the senior's right to contradict him. And I do. I think the stage now is better – so far as Shakespeare goes, at least – than it used to be. But it was very fine a long time ago. And I shall begin a long time ago.

I shall begin, in fact, in the spring of 1928, when I first saw a play by Shakespeare professionally performed. I had seen dreadful student assaults on Shakespeare: I recall one of my older brothers playing the role of Julius Caesar's Ghost in the scene at the Battle of Philippi; in order that there should be no mistake about whose Ghost he was, he carried a white plaster bust of Caesar on top of his head, and veiled the rest of himself in a white sheet, so that when he appeared on the battlefield it looked as if Caesar had been seven feet tall. It was athletically, rather than dramatically, impressive and my brother had a headache for two days afterward.

I had studied Shakespeare at school, in the horrible Copp Clarke editions, which were bound in a smelly green oil-cloth. They had been edited to remove any passages unsuitable for the young, and you can imagine my surprise when, in later life, I discovered that Shakespeare was full of dirty jokes. Those school editions had copious notes – more notes than play, sometimes – and they made Shakespeare seem a very great bore.

I was astonished, therefore, when my parents took me from Kingston to Toronto to see *The Merry Wives of Windsor*, performed by an all-star cast. And indeed they were all stars. Falstaff was played by Otis Skinner, Mistress Page by Mrs. Minnie Maddern Fiske, and Mistress Ford by Miss Henrietta Crosman. These names may not be immediately familiar to you, but they were great names for three or four decades on the American stage, which in those days was able to present the plays of Shakespeare splendidly – an ability which it does not seem to have at the present time. I think that even in those days it was a somewhat old-fashioned production, because scenery was going out of fashion then, and this production had carloads of wonderful scenery. I shall never forget the astonishment I felt when the curtain rose on a street in Windsor, marvellously painted, with real doors on the houses for people to come out of, a distant church tower which seemed to give out a sound of bells, and most astounding of all, a slight incline in the cobblestone pavement, so that everybody seemed to come downhill to the front of the stage. There were splendid costumes; it was not one of those starved productions where everybody has just one suit of clothes. There were even dogs, who came on with Master Slender, and got caught up in his legs.

But because I was agog at the scenery you must not think I missed a word of the play. Indeed, the words were best of all, because those actors spoke so beautifully, and I had never heard Shakespeare spoken like that before. I do not mean that they mouthed and sucked their words, like elocutionists (has anybody here under fifty ever heard an elocutionist?) but because long training in a theatre where microphones and amplification were unheard of had made these actors master the art of speech, and the clarity and beauty of their words was like clear water in the desert.

I can remember now the cadence and tone of Otis Skinner's voice when he said: "I had been drowned, but that the shore was shelvy and shallow . . . a death that I abhor; for water swells a man; and what a thing should I have been, when I had been swelled! I should have been a mountain of mummy."

Otis Skinner played Falstaff as a gentleman down on his luck, and not as a fat clown, and all the best Falstaffs I have seen since, including the greatest of them all, Ralph Richardson, have played him from that point of view. Falstaff is great, even when he is most foolish.

He is foolish because he is meddling with love, and he is insincere in his meddling. So love revenges itself on him, because love is a serious matter. Great as Falstaff is, he is not great in everything. Like many witty people, he thinks wit and invention will pull him through any trouble, but it didn't pull him through the mess he got into in *The Merry Wives* until he had been soaked and beaten. Wit did not enable him to see deeply into the nature of young Prince Hal, in *Henry IV*, or he would not have been so astonished and brokenhearted when, at the end of the second part of that play, Hal rejects him. Sentimentalists say that it hurt Hal to have to turn his back on an old friend, but it is clear in the three plays in which he appears that Hal, or King Henry V as he later becomes, was a tough opportunist, and a great leader. If you don't think such men can turn on old friends who have become embarrassing, read a few biographies of great men of our own time, and see what you find. Being a great man may be costly in personal relationships.

I am speaking enthusiastically about the voices of those star players, because they were a revelation to me. I had not thought that human utterance could be so splendid, so clear, so immediately understandable. Otis Skinner, and Mrs. Fiske, and Miss Crosman were not young; I have reckoned that in 1928 their total ages came to 196 years; but they did not seem old, or sound old. They had very good people in the subordinate roles, and I remember one, who played the Host of the Garter, who thrilled me with his inventive, imaginative brilliance: "Is he dead, my Ethiopian? is he dead, my Francisco? What says my Aesculapius, my Galen, my heart of elder? Is he dead, bully-stale? is he dead?" I wished that I could talk like that. I still do. I had fallen totally under the spell of Shakespeare's language. Of Shakespeare's prose; thralldom to his poetry came later, with *Hamlet*.

Scholars are apt to sneer at *The Merry Wives*, as beneath Shakespeare's genius, but I think they are wrong. It contains little poetry, it is true. But it contains much splendid prose, and that is no trifling matter. It is Shakespeare's only play in which he devotes himself to the ordinary, middle-class life of his time, and there is no such comedy by any of his contemporaries that shows us ordinary people more convincingly. The glimpses it gives of common life are delightful in their simplicity. Take that little scene where Mistress Page and her son William meet Sir Hugh Evans, the schoolmaster, and Sir Hugh puts William through a brief test in Latin. William, it is plain to see, is no scholar. But the scene has a sweetness, a charm which is indefinable, and whether it brings the Elizabethan age into our own, or takes our age back to the first Elizabeth I cannot say, but it is an enduring scrap of real life, and we are charmed when, at the end, William having shown himself to be a reasonable scholar, his mother says he is a better scholar than she had thought, and the kindly schoolmaster sends the boy away to play. Shakespeare was very good in the scenes in which he shows us children. Always tender but never sentimental.

I have seen *The Merry Wives* many times, and even directed a production of it myself. One of the very best Falstaffs I ever saw was named Roy Byford, and he was fat enough to play the part without padding. Some Falstaffs are too heavily cushioned and they don't look so much fat as stuffed; they struggle and puff, which real fat men never do. But Byford was properly fat, and he had beautifully formed legs, upon which he could dance with delightful agility. Falstaff surely should not look as if he were dangerously, malignantly, obscenely fat and in perpetual danger of a heart attack. He is, quite simply, a fat man, and that was what Byford was. He was also extremely short-sighted, and on the stage his eyes had a gleaming, moist, vigilant look which gave him a special air of mental alertness. He was attractive; it was not out of the question that the merry wives might have been drawn to him, if they had not thought physical appearance more important than intellect. Byford was a genial, charming Falstaff, but he never let you forget that Falstaff is rather dangerous. He is exploitive and he is on the make. It was in this aspect of the character that Ralph Richardson was supreme; he was so plainly the ablest man on the stage, except for Prince Hal; but he was also an impenitent old crook. A Falstaff who is nothing but charm is not the whole man. Falstaff is a gentleman, a courtier mixing with middle-class folk, and nobody ever forgets it.

My passion for Shakespeare was whetted to a keener edge not long after, when I saw *Hamlet* for the first time. The player was Walter Hampden, who was fifty-two then, and a princely Hamlet he was, and he spoke splendidly. Since then I have seen many Hamlets, and some of them were admired chiefly because they were young. Some of them didn't look old enough to vote. Because they were young, it was said that they were "contemporary," and had banished the older, more intellectual Hamlets forever. But not for me. The young Hamlets never have looked as though, if they had been luckier, they could have ruled a kingdom. Hamlet was the son of a great warrior king, and though he is intellectual, he is not therefore ineffectual. What was Hamlet studying at Wittenberg? It must have been Protestant theology. A prince and a scholar. Give me a princely, scholarly Hamlet every time.

I got another one very shortly after Hampden had settled my taste in that direction, and he was George Hayes, the grandfather of Elliott Hayes, whom you may have met in this theatre. He was one of the leading actors in a company that visited Canada from the Shakespeare

Memorial Theatre in Stratford-on-Avon about 1930. They brought several plays with them, and one of them was *Macbeth*, which is in the repertoire here this year, and which you have seen. It was my first *Macbeth*, and the actor was Wilfrid Walter, who had the enormous advantage of a warrior's physique – a tall, handsome man, with compelling eyes and an admirable bass voice. I mention that because I have heard Macbeths whose voices were too light for the role – voices that suggested romance rather than ruin. Not that a high voice is unsuitable for tragedy. Years ago I saw Maurice Evans play *Richard II* and a friend was with me who was a musician with perfect pitch. When Richard cried

> God, for his Richard, hath in heaven'ly pay
> A glorious angel . . .

my friend nudged me, and said, "A." Afterward I asked him what he had meant. "That was a tenor A," he said, "and it's astonishing to hear anybody speak, and speak magnificently, on such a high note." Evans had one of the great voices of the stage in our time. But a tenor Macbeth would hardly do, and Walter's velvety bass was perfect for it.

An actor in Shakespeare needs a big vocal range. Sir Johnston Forbes-Robertson, who was one of the very great actors of the early part of this century, and famous for his splendid voice, said that a range of at least two octaves was needed, and he himself did exercises every day at the piano, to keep his voice in tune. Yes, I said *in tune*, for those great actors of the past, and the really good ones of today, knew the art of speaking in intervals which are as musical and as carefully calculated as anything in Wagner, and what is more, they could speak in minor as well as major modulations – and that is the secret of many greatly poetic efforts.

But to get back to *Macbeth*, a first-rate voice is essential because without it the actor will become tired – his voice will show strain, and in the last act of *Macbeth* you have no time to indulge fatigue. Some years ago I heard that fine actor Frederick Valk play Othello, and his voice was tired by the end of act three. He was then an old man. He barely made it to the curtain. Members of an audience rarely

understand what a variety and strength of vocal technique goes into
the acting of a great Shakespearean role. Perhaps some of you saw
Richard Burton as Hamlet. A fine voice, but he was not in physical
condition for a great role and the last two acts were very dull. No
amount of pretending that it is all colloquial, and that Shakespeare is
our contemporary, is of any use whatever. You might as well try to
be colloquial singing Mozart. The comparison is apt. A great actor
and a great singer are not far apart in physical equipment.

You have all heard that *Macbeth* has the reputation of being an
unlucky play, and actors love to tell stories of the mishaps that have
taken place when it is put on the stage. My wife was stage manager
at the Old Vic in 1937 during a first-rate example of the *Macbeth* ill-
fortune. To begin, the scenery which had been made for the play
proved, when it was put on the stage, not to fit, although such a mis-
calculation is almost unheard of. Next, the dearly loved dog of the
great manager, Lilian Baylis, was killed in the street outside the stage
door. Third, a heavy iron bar fell, inexplicably, from the area above
the stage and very nearly killed some of the flower of the English
theatre, which would have been a great misfortune indeed. What followed was that the production was not ready – not sufficiently
rehearsed – to be seen on the opening night, and for the first time
in the history of that great theatre an opening had to be postponed.
That was too much for Lilian Baylis, who was in delicate health, and
she took to her bed and died. A succession of misfortunes, which the
theatre folk, who are inclined toward superstition, laid at the door
of what was often called "the Scottish play" – to avoid speaking its
name. I recall once, when I was a young actor, quoting *Macbeth* in
the dressing-room at the Old Vic, and being asked to leave the room
and re-enter it, to ward off ill luck.

That Old Vic production was ill luck indeed. I can tell you another
Macbeth tale in which I was myself involved, and it is not so much
tragic as farcical. It happened at Oxford, where the Oxford University
Dramatic Society, which is a very good amateur group, I may tell
you, was presenting the tragedy in what is called The New Theatre,
although it is really the old theatre. It was the custom of the Society
to retain the services of professional directors, and the man who was

directing us in *Macbeth* (1937) was, and still is, one of the foremost directors in Great Britain. I shall not mention his name because he is still alive, and still famous, and I do not want to recall a sad period in his younger days, and in mine. Because I, you see, was the stage manager, and that was no light responsibility.

The director was a charming man, but an Irishman, and not the best organized man I have ever met. He kept putting off arrangements for the supernatural scenes in the play – you know, the disappearance of the witches, the magic cauldron, the procession of Kings that Macbeth sees in the witches' cavern – all that sort of thing. At last, two days before the play was to open for a week's run, I went to him and said we must have magic, and we must have it right away. To which he said, in tones of a man too fine to be bothered with trivialities, "You arrange something."

And so I did. I had a friend, an American Rhodes Scholar, who loved the theatre, and who was a scientist. In fact, he was a biologist, and all scientists look alike to me, and I thought he must be pretty handy with test-tubes, and smoke, and bad smells, and all those scientific things. I threw myself upon his mercy. "Leave everything to me," said he, with wonderful confidence, and I did so.

Now – do you think he made a mess of it? Not at all. He devised wonderful illusions and at the final rehearsals they worked like a charm. But the director did not work like a charm. He seemed to be a man under an evil spell, and probably it was the spell of that unlucky play.

What he did was this: we were to have our dress rehearsal on Sunday night, to appear before the public on Monday; but it had been arranged by some evil spirit that the London critics were to come to the dress rehearsal on Sunday night so that they could write about our *Macbeth* for the Monday papers. The hour for the curtain came, and the theatre contained about twenty critics, all of whom had been given an excellent dinner beforehand.

The New Theatre was a well-equipped theatre. It had electric equipment of every sort. You could have put on *Les Misérables* there without any difficulty. And that meant that I, as stage manager, was standing beside a large console of switches, and warning lights, and electric bells which kept me in touch with all the men, far up in the flies of the theatre, who would respond to whatever number I pressed, and change the scenery accordingly.

O, unhappy day! Or rather, O unhappy night. Just as we were about to begin – indeed, the orchestra was playing the introductory witch music – the director appeared at my side, and said: "I want you to put in a new cue. Number Four becomes Number Five, and the new Number Four will signal the dimming of the lights at the exit of King Malcolm." I was aghast. "But the cues are all arranged," I said; "we can't put in a new one now." "Oh of course you can," said the Great Director; "just phone through to the fly gallery and tell them."

So I did that. Or rather, I tried to do it, but the chief flyman didn't answer the phone, and one of his assistants did – not a man of capacious intellect, and when I tried to tell him what was wanted, he seemed confused. His intellect appeared to be under a cloud. Meanwhile the orchestra was completing the introductory music, and if I didn't take up the curtain on the right music cue, there would be chaos.

I prayed, but surely some evil spirit, attendant on productions of *Macbeth*, intercepted my prayer. And when the time came, I shut my eyes and pressed the button for Cue Number Four. And as swiftly as you could wish, the backdrop of the battle scene swept up into the air, and to the astonishment of everybody the Three Witches were revealed, totally unprepared for this sudden appearance, transfixed with unwitchlike horror on a papier-maché crag. King Malcolm, thinking he must have done something wrong, hot-footed it off the stage, and the great tragedy lurched forward.

Someone had blundered. My message about the changed cues had never reached the head flyman. And henceforth, every time I pressed a button, the thing that happened was just one jump ahead of what ought to have happened.

The critics loved it. They shrieked and fell about in mirth. But we who were concerned with the play were in agony. We were young men, horribly accustomed to misfortune as only the young can be. But at last a moment came when the Great Director – I told you he was an Irishman – lost all control, and threw himself on the carpet in the main aisle of the theatre, and wept, and shouted to the critics that he took no responsibility – none whatever – for this fearful mess.

There was a conference backstage and I went on the stage and announced that there had been a technical hitch, and that we would begin again. And so we did, but we were a pitifully demoralized group of players.

Oh – and about the magic. It was splendid. Terrific. But my scientific friend had somewhat overdone the fumes in which the Witches usually appeared, and the Witches had a rough week of it, but they all lived to tell the tale, as I am telling it now.

Macbeth is Shakespeare's most wholly evil play; it is about the growth and consequences of evil, and violent disruption of the natural order. It is also about the uncanny nobility and attraction of great evil, from which we prefer to avert our eyes. Sometimes people who are putting it on the stage become so caught up in thoughts of eleventh-century Scotland that they forget about seventeenth-century England, and King James the First, who certainly saw this play, and for whom we may guess that it was written. James knew a great deal about witchcraft; he wrote an interesting book about it. He also knew a great deal about the dangers of kingship and he was a firm believer in the Divine Right of Kings. That doctrine is not so absurd as you might think. In our day, we are so convinced that nobody is meant to rule who has not won a popularity contest called an election, that we forget that a man might very reasonably think that if God had put him on the throne, he was there to do God's will. And if anybody kills God's chosen ruler, he has contradicted God's manifest will, and will certainly suffer the fate of a blasphemer. What King James saw in *Macbeth* was a tyrant who had killed his King and seized his throne, and who was fittingly destroyed by his own evil. The evil was seen at work, palpably, in the form of the Witches. They embody the spirit of Contrary Destiny which destroys the tragic hero, and his wife as well, not as helpless creatures trapped by Fate, but as conscious evil-doers who got their just reward.

This is tough doctrine, and quite against the permissive thinking of our time, which might well argue that Macbeth came from a broken home, and that his wife was protesting against the manifold wrongs of her sex. But that is not what Shakespeare thought, or what King James thought. They thought Macbeth was a tyrant, and that his wife was an embodiment of the evil in his soul, and that that evil had constellated all the horrors of the tragedy – not only the murders, but the psychological sufferings of Macbeth and his Lady.

Can we argue successfully against such thinking? Many of us here today have lived in the greatest age of tyranny in human history, when we have seen Stalin, Hitler, Mao, Idi Amin, and the Ayatollah Khomeini stride the world's stage, creating untold misery and wretchedness. Tyrants are a terrible reality; they are seen on the stage because the stage is what Shakespeare called it – the Mirror of Nature.

I have seen productions of *Macbeth* that were obviously the work of directors who did not really believe in Evil except as a human aberration, and who thought that the supernatural was not part of the reality of nature itself. The supernatural is only what our limited perceptions do not understand, but which we see in life and sometimes suffer appallingly because of it. For myself, I believe that Evil is a reality – a mighty force – not created by Man, but a force of Nature which may manifest itself horribly in the life of Man, and though I do not attempt to read Shakespeare's mind, a lifelong study of his work makes me think that he believed so, as well. A director who does not at least admit the possibility of such a thing must work to make this play convincing on purely human grounds, and sometimes such directors struggle with the Witches, and the Apparitions and prophecies, in an attempt to explain them away, or present them as the superstitions of an earlier age.

Did Shakespeare believe in witches and ghosts? Certainly he believed in them as convenient agencies by means of which he could make the spirit of Evil convincing on the stage. In the production of the play we see here in this Festival, we have the good fortune to be in the hands of a director with a good Celtic conviction of the reality of Evil, and that is what gives the tragedy its force.

If we believe in Evil as a reality, we must believe also in Good, not only as the power which slowly and sometimes incomprehensibly asserts itself in human destiny, but as the sweetener of life and the power that offers the beauty and splendour of life, and this is what we find in the comedy of *As You Like It*. It is one of Shakespeare's loveliest comedies, and when we see it well done – I have been lucky enough to see it well done several times – it is as if the play conferred a blessing on us, and we leave the theatre uplifted and enlarged. There is some Evil in it; Orlando's brother Frederick is first seen as an evil man, and we could not do without him, because it is his wrongdoing that sets the action in motion. A depiction of a world that is all good, all sunshine, quickly sinks into insipidity, and has no drama. In the end the wicked brother Frederick is redeemed, and his redemption is vital to the total effect of the play. Do we care if his redemption is somewhat arbitrary? I don't think so. It is not necessary for a comedy on the great scale to be always convincing in terms of ordinary life. The play persuades us that we want Good to be victorious, and so it is. It is not a picture of ordinary life. Shakespeare gives us that in *The Merry Wives*, and even there it is ordinary life transfigured by comedy. *As You Like It* does something that is possible in the theatre and which is rooted deep in our own hearts: it shows us life as we wish it to be. In the theatre we are able to see what we wish were true, and we are able to see that which we fear because we have met it head on, or have at least heard about it, and that is the terrible spirit of Evil. A play like *As You Like It* is an assertion of the spirit of Good. If you want realism – that is to say, a photographic representation of the life of ordinary people doing ordinary things in ordinary ways – don't look for it in Shakespeare. He had little patience with that sort of thing. He shows us not the externals of life, but the essence of life in its extraordinary variety, and he was able to do that because he was a poet of superlative genius.

The word "poet" has been much abused. Too many people think that a poet is somebody who deals in fantasies and unrealities, whereas true poets are people who see beyond the commonplaces of life to its deepest realities. Poets write poetry because it sets them free from the obligations that weigh so heavily on novelists, who are often expected to explain everything and make everything seem possible in life at a commonplace level. I am well acquainted with that, because I often receive letters from people who complain that my novels contain what the writers regard as improbabilities. To which I can only reply that the things complained of do not seem improbable to me. The poet goes right to the heart of things, and deals with deeper truths than everyday life allows to be clear.

This play, *As You Like It*, as much as any in the Shakespeare canon, brings up a question of Shakespeare criticism, and production, which is of great interest. You all know that until 1660 women did not appear on the stage in Britain, and all the women's parts in Shakespeare's plays were written to be acted by boys. Were the boys any good? Surely they must have been, because Shakespeare would hardly have written great roles for actors whom he knew would be incompetent. But were they as good as modern actresses? It is a pretty problem, and I would like to talk about it for a while.

In the first place, what do we mean when we say that the actors of Lady Macbeth and Rosalind and all the others were boys? This is a matter to which I have given a great deal of attention, and I know for a certainty that they were not "boys" in the modern sense of the word. First of all, they were not children. They were apprenticed to adult actors when they were children, in many cases, and they learned their art as an apprentice does. But they seem to have played leading roles when they were sixteen or seventeen, when they had learned their art. Just as in the Chinese theatre men play women's parts and play them brilliantly, and assume feminine dress and appearance convincingly, may we not assume that in the Elizabethan and Jacobean theatre these young men were entirely acceptable as Rosalind, or Lady Macbeth or whoever it might be? We have no record of their performances, but we have records of plays of Shakespeare and his contemporaries by people who saw them, and nobody says that the boys were not up to their work.

What do we mean by "boy"? If we mean a young man who has been encouraged to believe that his destiny is to go on the football field and knock people down, and be knocked down himself, and to growl in a deep voice and destroy the furniture and eat like a wolf, certainly that is one idea of a boy. But if we look at another sort of modern boy, who has been trained in the ballet school, and who is just as strong as the footballer, and has learned every skill of presenting his body gracefully to evoke beauty, we are getting close to the young Elizabethan actors.

When we say "boy" today we really mean a male creature who has been kept artificially young because our economy has to keep him out of the workforce as long as possible. But a boy of fourteen has plenty of brains, if he is encouraged to use them and if his livelihood and personal success depend on his using them. The musical world is full of young instrumentalists who are technically brilliant and often interpretatively brilliant as well. We all know about boys in their teens who are wizards at chess, or with computers. A boy is not, by definition, a fool or a lout. If his living, and that of the master-actor whose apprentice he is, depends on his skill as an actor, he might certainly, given talent, be a very good actor indeed, in women's parts. In an age when Shakespeare's patron, the Earl of Southhampton, took his Cambridge degree at sixteen, and when the Earl of Essex took his Cambridge M.A. at sixteen and was commanding troops in the Netherlands at eighteen, the idea of a "boy" was different from our own. Life was shorter and there was little time to waste on a foolish immaturity.

What about the young actor's voice? The Elizabethans admired high voices, and we find much of their music scored for voices which are, by modern reckoning, demandingly high. Their voices were trained upward, unless they had uncompromisingly deep voices, in which case they were destined for tragedy. "I'll counterfeit the deep tragedian," says Buckingham in *Richard III*, meaning that he would speak as low as he could. But most actors, we may suppose, spoke in rather a high register, for most of them – and certainly all the boys – were trained musicians, and knew how to do it. Have you ever had the experience of speaking to somebody on the telephone without being able to say whether it is a man or a woman? The human voice is not as sexually characteristic as we often think, and if Shakespeare's young male players did not growl in the bass, they might well have been not merely convincing, but charming, as women.

I have seen *As You Like It* played with young men in the women's roles. That was in 1974 when the English National Theatre mounted such a production and Rosalind was played by Ronald Pickup, who was at that time thirty-three, and he played it very well. He was not the best Rosalind I have ever seen, but that was not because he was a man. Certainly he was graceful and winning and he did not find it necessary to strut and slap his thigh and do super-manly things, as some Rosalinds I have seen have done. He was feminine, but not effeminate. His voice never created any sense of unbelief. It was a most interesting experiment, but not one which is going to drive actresses from the stage. Good acting, male or female, is remarkably similar in its techniques and effects.

But that does not deal with the effect of *As You Like It* as its first audiences saw it. They saw a young man, who was supposed to be a young woman, putting on man's clothes and pretending to be a youth. I don't know how much farther you could continue the game of make-believe. But one thing is certain: the play was never meant to convey an effect of realism. It is a pastoral romance and the grace and charm of the text must be partnered by the grace and charm of the players. The poetry creates the magic.

There are always people who refuse to believe that, but I am convinced that it is true throughout the whole of Shakespeare; the poetry does the greater part of the work, and speaking it appropriately is the actor's first job. Years ago I saw a famous production of *Romeo and Juliet* in London, which was spoken beautifully and moved the audience as a great tragedy should. But the day after I met a young Canadian I knew in Piccadilly, and praised the production to him. He had seen it and he despised it. "They missed the whole point," said he; "what's the play about? It's about a coupla kids who got hot pants for each other, and you gotta *show* that. They didn't show it."

I understood what he meant. Much modern theatre, and even more modern cinema, is eager to *show* us the reality of sexual passion, and they think that sexual passion is all there is to love. That is why you see so many scenes of mauling, and face-chewing, and grunting and snorting, which is supposed to give us the reality of love. But that is not how Shakespeare does it. He gives us splendid poetry which awakens in us our memory, or our ideal vision, of love, and the actors do not have to wrestle and puff too much to make it clear to us what they mean. Shakespeare's method is subtle and indirect, but in the end its effect is more powerful than physical demonstration.

Why is that? Because it is not the theatre's task to show us reality, but to awaken a sense of reality, or a recollection of reality, in our minds and hearts. However we are engrossed in a play, we know it is a make-believe, and that the actors did it all last night, and will do it again tomorrow night. They are not suffering; they are making us suffer in a highly sophisticated sense. Have you never, at the movies, thought when some heated scene of sexual passion is being shown, and a pair of naked bodies are struggling in what is supposed to be the uttermost throes of sexual ecstasy – "I wonder how many times they rehearsed that? I wonder how many camera men, and directors, and scene-shifters and light focussers are standing within a few feet of this display of supposedly private passion?" We know it is an illusion, and when it strives to be something more than an illusion we know it to be a fake.

Opera makes us feel and believe in passion through music. Great theatre makes us feel and believe in passion through poetry, or great prose, which is much the same thing. We don't want "a coupla kids with hot pants"; we can watch that in the park. We want something that awakens deep and powerful feeling in ourselves. We want art, not nature, in fact.

And that brings us naturally to consideration of the last play in our group, *Love for Love*, by William Congreve. He was not born until more than fifty years after the death of Shakespeare, by which time women were fully established on the stage, and he wrote comedy parts for women which have rarely been equalled and never surpassed in their extraordinary charm. I do not suppose there are many men who would not give much to be in love with a Congreve heroine, and who would not run like a deer from the prospect of marrying one. So much wit, at close quarters for too long a time, would drive a man out of his senses, but to meet with it in the theatre is a wonderful experience.

Congreve belongs in a special category of English comedy, of which the other great exemplars are Sheridan, Goldsmith, Oscar Wilde, and Bernard Shaw. It is probably more than mere chance that four out of the five were Irish, and that Congreve, who may be called the greatest, was educated in Ireland. But you must not suppose that I am subscribing to the popular notion that Irishmen are especially witty; I am sure we have all known dull Irishmen. But when Irishmen are witty they have a very special way of showing it, and that is in their command of language. What they do with language differs from playwright to playwright: you might say that Congreve was a witty philosopher, for his comments on life and love have a reflective, almost contemplative air; Sheridan writes marvellous jokes, and points them with a brilliance that is unequalled; Goldsmith never makes obvious jokes, but his characters are so funny and say such characteristic things that we love them as we could not love the people in Sheridan; Oscar Wilde was the dandy of language, and his epigrams are so highly polished and perfected that they stand alone, and it is hard to remember which of his plays they come from. Why have these men such an extraordinary way with the language we all speak, and which we speak, it must be said, so carelessly that wit in this special sense is very rarely met with?

I have a theory, and it is probably indefensible, but I shall express it anyway. Here it is: English is always a foreign language to an Irishman. Deep in his heart, and at the root of his tongue, there lurks another language, and when he writes in English that very old language somehow colours what he has to say. Irish, like Gaelic and Welsh, is a medieval language and it has a medieval directness and clarity that is quite unlike the language of the Saxon or the Norman. The Scots boast that Gaelic is the ideal language in which to speak to God. The Welsh know that Welsh is the ideal language in which to speak to a crowd, and I shall never forget hearing David Lloyd George speak to a very large crowd – fifteen hundred people – and bring them to a pitch of enthusiasm that was like the audience at an opera. And Erse, the ancient language of Ireland, is certainly a language of poetry and very probably the ideal language in which to speak to women, and for women to speak in reply. Congreve and Wilde and Sheridan spoke not one word of the old Irish tongue – I cannot be so sure about Goldsmith – but its pattern and its elegance was in their minds and in their blood. I know that Congreve was English, but he first mastered English in Ireland. These Celtic languages, so direct in meaning, have the medieval dexterity in ornament – in metaphor and in choice of words – which makes them peculiarly effective when spoken. Literary English, written by wholly English writers, possesses unquestionable magnificence, and has a wit of its own, but this moonlight radiance seems to be a special possession of the Irish when they turn their attention to the stage, and write to be heard.

I am sure that some of you are from the United States, and perhaps you are wondering: What about us? Surely we too are a witty people? Of course you are, and I think your wit has gained much from the influence of the Jewish writers among you. Jewish wit has its own earthy exuberance, and it excels in what is called – I think rather dismissively and unfortunately – the wisecrack, the sudden encapsulation of a comic insight in colloquial speech. But the Irish writers do not go in for wisecracks in the same way. With them it is choice of words, of marshalling and parading words for unexpected effects, and imaginative deployment of words, that give them their particular greatness. When Congreve says: "I am always of the opinion of the learned, if they speak first," the words are simple, but the meaning catches us an instant after we have heard them – and that is a great function of wit at its highest. When he makes a man say to the woman he loves: "Ah, Madam . . . you know everything in the world but your perfections, and you only know not those, because 'tis the top of perfection *not* to know them," every man wishes he had thought of that, and every woman wishes it had been addressed to herself. And when he says:

Women are like tricks by sleight of hand
Which, to admire, we should not understand.

– every man knows exactly what he means, and every woman knew it first.

This sort of thing belongs to what is called Restoration Drama, though much of it was written long after King Charles had been restored to his throne, and had changed the face and mind of the English world. But it would be foolish to say that it is the common wit of the Restoration; it is obviously the best of it.

In my time, I have spent many hours trying to find out what wit is, and what humour is, and I have never succeeded. But I have at least learned that wit is rare, and that what most people consider to be wit is poor stuff. In pursuit of my hobby I have collected many jest-books, and studied them carefully, because they tell me what, at a particular time, people in general thought was funny. During the period of the Restoration Drama, which we might say extended from 1660 until about 1720, the popular idea of what was funny can be extremely depressing. Let me try this one on you; it comes from a jest-book printed in 1686, right in the middle of the period we are discussing:

A Notable merry soldier finding a louse one day on his sleeve walking to and fro for the benefit of the fresh air, took him between his fingers and said, Sirrah, take notice if I ever catch you out of your Quarters again, you shall dye, and so put him into his Collar.

Or how does this appear to you:

Two men walking through a Church-Yard one of them affirmed that Hell was nothing else but the Grave, for *Shoel* in the Hebrew signifies the Grave though it is translated Hell; the other one having lately buried there a shrewd curst wife, pointing to her Grave, said, Then one of the greatest Devils in Hell lies here.

Or here is one which used to be called "a rare rib-binder":

A Country Parson having bitterly inveighed against the Vices of his Parishioners in his Sermon, a silly woman who was present went to his Mother that lived hard by to complain of him, saying that her son had threatened them all with Hell and damnation if they did not speedily amend; for my part I have lived above threescore years, and was never told so much before, neither will I be taught now by one I am old enough to be his Grand-Mother. O said his Mother, he was a Lyar from his Cradle, I never whipt him but for telling an untruth, and you are mad if you believe him now.

Well, there you are. That is the sort of thing that passed for wit among people at large during the period of the Restoration, and you will agree that it does not sound like Congreve.

Another great matter in which Congreve is a past master is the tempo or timing of his dialogue. Because, as any of you who have had anything to do with stage work are well aware, the tempo of a play is of the highest importance, and if it is misjudged the play loses its effect, just as music does if you play it too fast or too slow. Congreve is careful to make this clear in the way he writes his plays, because he divides every act into scenes in the French manner; whenever a character comes on the stage, or leaves it, a new scene begins, and each scene is subtly different in tempo. This is not an imaginary matter; the relation between Baroque drama, which is what *Love for Love* is, and Baroque music is a real one, and you all know how painful it is to hear a piece of Baroque music played at the wrong tempo, even if the slowness of pace, or the unsuitable speed, is slight. Acting Restoration comedy, and Congreve as much as any, demands a very precise ear and a fine technique of speech. By far the finest production of *Love for Love* that I have seen was directed by Sir John Gielgud, who also played Valentine. The tempi were perfect from beginning to end.

Perhaps you wonder why, in discussing these four plays, I have taken so much care to emphasize the part of language in all of them – the bourgeois conversation of *The Merry Wives*, the dark, allusive, meta-phorical language of *Macbeth*, the goldsmith's filigree of *As You Like It*, and the silvery chiming of *Love for Love*. I have done so because in our day, which is neglectful of speech and when so much heavy, clumsy, dull writing is perpetually before our eyes, we often forget what a vital element language is in the structure of a play. When I was a boy, I used to hear people complain about the plays of Bernard Shaw: "They are so *talky*," they said. But now, when Shaw's ideas have either become commonplace or have ceased to be important, it is the talk that packs the theatre at the Shaw Festival and anywhere else that a Shaw play is well acted. Last year my wife and I went to Niagara-on-the-Lake to see *Getting Married*, elegantly presented, and although there was not an idea in it that was new, the magic with which those outworn ideas was presented was as fresh as it had ever been, and gave rich delight to the audience.

Is it not delight we seek when we go to the theatre? The delight of comedy, which refreshes and uplifts us, or the delight of tragedy, which carries us deep into ourselves and throws light into corners which are normally dark? While we watch a great play, we have a proprietary interest in the characters; we are as witty as Falstaff, or Valentine, as irresistible as Rosalind or Angelica, we are terrorized by the evil in Macbeth and his fiend-like Queen, we delight in the common sense of Ben the Sailor, or Touchstone the wise Clown. And what do we carry away with us? The memory of the players, of course, and there lingers in our ears the cadence with which they said a particular line – in fact, the language.

It is mankind's discovery of language which more than any other single thing has separated him from the animal creation. Without language, what kind of thought is possible? Without language, what concept have we of past or future as separated from the immediate present? Without language, how can we tell anyone what we feel, or what we think? It might be said that until he developed language man had no soul, for without language how could he reach deep inside himself and discover the truths that are hidden there, or find out what emotions he shared, or did not share, with his fellow men and women? But because this greatest gift of all gifts is in daily use, and is smeared, and battered and trivialized by commonplace associations, we too often forget the splendour of which it is capable, and the pleasures that it can give, from the pen of a master.

That is what we go to the theatre to rediscover.

5

———— ❧ ————

LAURENCE OLIVIER

WHEN LORD OLIVIER DIED on July 11, 1989, *Maclean's* magazine asked Robertson Davies to write an article about his life.

On July 11 Davies wrote: *Watch the news for word of the death of Laurence Olivier; they present clips from some films and say that he won two Oscars, breathlessly, as if that were the pinnacle of human achievement. Asses! The man was decorated by most countries in Europe, and a Life Peer in the U.K. – what are their trumpery Oscars? But it may be his fate to be remembered by his films, which were good but had not the dimension of his stage work . . . Maclean's calls and wants a thousand words on Olivier, which I shall do for $1,200. Could have got more, I suppose, if I had wrangled, but I am ill at reckoning; it befitteth the spirit of a tapster.*

In 1962 Olivier became the first director of the Chichester Theatre Festival and performed there many times. Robertson and Brenda Davies saw him in a production of *Othello* on August 4, 1964, and his impressions were recorded as follows:

Then Othello, *in the hottest theatre I have ever been in; audience sweating like coolies. Play began very slowly; not in full speed till Cassio's fight in Cyprus. Dull production; no illumination or ingenuity; Sir Laurence Olivier seems to have dominated the thing to its hurt. A Leavis concept – Othello a great, simple egoist, and Iago a mere malcontent. Frank Finlay played Iago just as he played Cockledemoy – arms spread, one toe cocked up, and the invariable bustling sore-footed walk. Maggie Smith a strong, whisky-voiced Desdemona and can't sing, which is death to a Desdemona. But Laurence Olivier is magnificent, all by himself. Assumes Negroid voice and walk admirably; blacks all over like Snittle Timberry; magnificent speech in a cast of mumblers and vulgar accents. Some good touches; wears a large cross and crosses himself a lot in a "Me good Christian boy" way, then, before the great oath, tears it off (and flings it into the audience) and prostrates himself like a Moslem. Odd pronunciations: "lieutenant" as "lootenant" and "ancient" as "ensign." At the end cuts his jugular with a ring. (No: a bracelet with a spike in it that could be lifted up: he threatened Iago with it earlier in the play, so it had been planted.) But I was never moved by any of this, as it happened in a void; no ensemble. Shabby costumes and a deadly pace. Laurence Olivier, like too many Othellos, would not get on from Desdemona's murder to his own death, and every moment weakened the tragic force. It wanted re-casting, re-dressing, and a strong director – Michael Langham, perhaps. But one had a notion of what Kean may have been like: magnificent, alone, and best pleased to be alone.*

———— ✎ ————

The past fifty years have been an age of great acting — as great, perhaps as any in the history of the English-speaking theatre. Three giants dominated the stage: John Gielgud, Ralph Richardson, and Laurence Olivier; and of the three only Gielgud survives, at the age of eighty-five. If, we say, as Byron did, "I am acquainted with no immaterial sensuality so delightful as good acting," they gave us that delight in its highest reaches.

Of the three, Olivier must be accounted the greatest because his range was greatest. As Romeo and as Hamlet he was not as fine as Gielgud, because he lacked Gielgud's extraordinary feeling for poetry; as John Gabriel Borkman he had not the grandeur of Richardson, who made us see that the heroic and the bourgeois life are not incompatible. But as Othello he was finer than either because the part demanded the flamboyance, the athleticism, and the delight in heaven-storming passion which were his strengths.

Nobody ever dared to call him an actor of the old school, but that was precisely what he was, and when the old school is the Great Old School it cannot be beaten. His Othello was essentially a nineteenth-century star performance: Othello first, the rest nowhere. His Richard III was diabolic and grotesque in a way that no one had attempted since the death of Irving. He loved what used to be called "a dual role" – Oedipus followed by Mr. Puff in *The Critic* in the same evening: Hotspur in Part I of *Henry IV* followed by the doddering Justice Shallow in Part II. He loved to *act*, to impersonate. He could be a matinée idol when occasion demanded, but what he liked best were the assumptions of extraordinary personalities, and the wigs, false noses, characteristic walks, and all that made the extraordinary seem not merely possible but inevitable.

He had no use for intellectual theories of acting, and was often derisive of The Method. There is a story that when once a Hollywood actor bored him about the difficulty he was experiencing in showing some particular nuance of character, Olivier said, "Why don't you just *act* it, cocky?" And by that he meant find the tone of voice, or the expression or the gesture, which will evoke the feeling you want in your audience, and stop fussing about what you feel yourself; your job is not to feel, but to make others feel. Tearing yourself apart with emotion is not acting. Acting is not photography, but painting in oils.

A story is told of Irving to the same effect. Visiting the American tragedian Richard Mansfield in his dressing-room after a performance, Irving found the actor drenched in sweat and drooping with fatigue. Mansfield harangued Irving about how much his work took out of him. "Well, Dick," said Irving, "if you find it unwholesome, m'boy, why do you do it?" Olivier did not find acting unwholesome. My wife, who was a student at the Old Vic at the time, remembers his 1937 performance of the uncut text of *Hamlet*. On matinée days there was barely an hour between performances and in that time Olivier, costumed and made up, gobbled a quick snack and was fresh and ready at the second curtain time of the day. His daily athletic workout and his singing lesson kept him in condition for eight hours of the most exacting work.

He was not a man of distinguished appearance or remarkable physique, and this was one of the many ways in which he resembled Garrick. He could, and did, look like anything at all. He said that he worked out his characterizations from the outside to the inside, trying varieties of make-up, wigs, false teeth, and costume until he got what he wanted. We may take this with a grain of salt, assuming that he found the inner character by developing the outer character – an application of Sheldonian typology of which he was probably wholly unconscious. But he was predominantly a technical actor, and in that respect a thorough professional who could play his part with precisely the same effect whether he was ill, or distressed, as he frequently was, for his private life was tumultuous. He owed it to his audience to be at the top of his form whenever he appeared, and he delivered the goods. That is what being a professional means, and all the three great actors of his era were professionals in this respect.

It was sometimes said of him, for he had his share of critical detraction, that he lacked pathos, but those who saw his superb Astrov in *Uncle Vanya* knew how false that was: not all the tragedy in the play was Vanya's. He could evoke pity even for a character of terrible egotism, like Coriolanus, or the stoic Titus Andronicus. One of his piercingly pathetic roles was that of Archie Rice, in *The Entertainer*; it was the pathos of the failed comedian. He had the distinguishing mark of the truly great player – a mark to be seen also in Gielgud and Richardson – for he was great in both comedy and tragedy, and could mingle both with lightning swiftness.

Spectators who saw him in his greatest roles sometimes assumed that he must be a man of great intellect, but that is not a necessary characteristic of the great actor. His autobiography was an experiment in another art from which he should have been dissuaded, but nobody could divert him from anything he had made up his mind to do. The story of his experience as the Founding Director of Britain's National Theatre, as we read it in Peter Hall's *Diaries*, is a sad tale of whimsical egotism and occasional deviousness; except when on the stage he was not a good colleague. But of his splendour as a great actor there can be no shadow of doubt.

Does his art remain for us in the films he made? They range from the triumphs of *Henry V* and *Richard III* to his embarrassing appearance in the remake of *The Jazz Singer*, and at their best they give us only a part of what made him one of the two or three greatest actors in the history of the English-speaking theatre. It was his arresting quality, his extraordinary ability to seize upon an audience and for the play's duration to hold them spellbound, that the camera could not wholly capture. To have seen him was a great experience, and to see his shadow on the screen is never more than a second best.

Peace to his ashes.

6

PROLOGUE TO
THE GOOD NATUR'D MAN

ROBERTSON DAVIES WAS ALWAYS accomplished in the art of parody. This entry shows one of his most successful imitations of another writer's style, on this occasion put to good, and undetected, use.

The following note was attached to the original copy of the prologue in Robertson Davies' handwriting: *Written for the Old Vic production in the Autumn of 1939 and spoken by Miss Marie Ney in the character of Mrs. Groaker. Dr. Johnson's prologue was thought too gloomy – this one seemed to create a proper mood for the comedy.* No one ever realized it was not part of the original play written by Oliver Goldsmith and presented at Covent Garden in 1767.

Since first Man was, the Drama's task has been
Aptly to mirror Life's fantastic scene;

In dances wild and crude, disgusting mime
The savage shewed the spirit of his time;
With strutting stilt and hollow, echoing mask
The Greeks gave grandeur to the actor's task,
While a lewd drama found a lewder home
In the round O's of great, but wicked, Rome,
'Til chiding priests crushed those libidinous stages
(For which their reign is known as the Dark Ages).
Then Thalia nodded by her dying fire
'Til roused to dance by daedal Shakespeare's lyre;
Strode by the Commonwealth, harsh and full of rage,
Great Charles returned, and cheered the fainting Stage
Playwrights appear'd, a wild, ungovern'd genus,
Who made a molehill of the Mount of Venus.

   Our modern writers, too, reflect a time
Chaotic, rude, unfit to live in rhyme,
Or ev'n blank verse (some slight excuse for those
Who wrap their thought in even blanker prose)
Pale and confused they flutter round Life's flame
Coining their fears, and shivering for fame;
By comic chance each wildly scribbling creature
Mistakes his limits for the bounds of Nature,
But yet exploits his complexes so ill
That things complex become more complex still.
Thus Drama, as successive curtains roll
Reflects the changing fashions of the Soul.

   Our play, though moderns find its theme amiss,
Reflects an age perhaps more kind than this,
When Wrong was merely Right that needed mending,
Love's path, though tortuous, sure a happy ending,
And justice, though inclined to some contortion,
At last was meted out in due proportion;
Abrupt Peripety cut the Gordian knot
And solved the jig-saw puzzle of the plot.

   Our fate lies in your *hands*, to you we pray
For an indulgent hearing of our play;

Laugh if you can, or failing that, give vent
In hissing fury to your discontent;
Applause we crave, from scorn we take defence
But have no armour 'gainst indifference.

7

——— ✦ ———

LEWIS CARROLL IN THE THEATRE

IN THE CELEBRATED WRITERS series at the Stratford Festival, Davies gave a lecture related to the production of *Alice Through the Looking Glass*, on July 10, 1994. The lecture was given in the morning with a production of the play in the evening. As you can see from the Theatre Diary entry that follows, Davies enjoyed the performance enormously, finding that it roused in him the Welsh sensation of *hiraeth*, or nostalgic longing.

Davies wrote on June 2: *Set to work on the Lewis Carroll lecture and find as I expected that the amount of material I have prepared must be handled with great care if the piece is not to be a mere jumble; I want it to be a pleasing causerie; no use bludgeoning a Sunday audience of holiday-makers, nor yet insulting them . . .*

And on July 10: *I give my lecture on Lewis Carroll in the Festival Theatre; very large audience, all downstairs sections filled except the two extreme sides, and a substantial number in the balcony. Lecture goes very well; great laughter and prolonged applause. But it was a bit too long, and as we began late it was noon when we finished and there was no time for questions.*

P.M. Alice Through the Looking Glass at the Avon, directed by Marti Maraden and very well dramatized by James Reaney. Sheer delight! Fine theatre art and accomplishment wedded. Splendid Alice (Sarah Polley); never put a foot wrong. A procession of greatly gifted actors in the familiar roles (e.g., Douglas Rain as Humpty Dumpty). Imaginative devices, after Tenniel but not slavish: e.g., a magnificent, alarming Jabberwock. Transporting. Roused in me hiraeth as the best theatre does.

———— ❧ ————

The English have long been famous for their eccentrics. I speak of the English particularly among the peoples of the British Isles because they recognize eccentricity and glory in it. The Scots do not admit that anything a Scotsman does is other than logical and inevitable. The Irish regard logic and inevitability as themselves evidence of eccentricity. Welsh eccentricity, like so much else that is Welsh, is apt to be dark and of the spirit. But the English are proud of their eccentrics because the centre toward which they face, spiritually, morally, and often physically, is different from that of their fellow countrymen, and the English people cherish them and indulge them because of their oddity and whimsicality. The English, we must remember, are very fond of pets of all kinds.

Eccentricity takes many forms. There are people who, like Dr. Samuel Johnson, are impelled to touch every post they pass in the street, or perhaps to avoid stepping on cracks in the pavement. There are people who cannot, or will not, sleep unless the head of their bed points toward the magnetic north. But these are trifles. There are other eccentricities that verge on madness, except that they do not inhibit the eccentric person from meeting the ordinary obligations of life. But the really great eccentrics are all inimitable; they are not possessed by a single oddity; they are, in their deepest selves, unlike the generality of mankind.

It is about one of these, Lewis Carroll, that I am to speak to you today. It is not part of his eccentricity that he is known to most people by a name that was not his own; that is because he chose to write under a pen-name, and Lewis Carroll is, by one of those logical tricks in which he delighted, a rearrangement of his own name, which was Charles Lutwidge Dodgson. He was, in fact the *Reverend* Charles Lutwidge Dodgson and his status as a clergyman influenced virtually every aspect of his life. He was not fully a priest of the Church of England; he chose not to advance beyond the rank of deacon because he had an inhibiting stammer which would have made the task of preaching very heavy for him and disagreeable for his hearers. He was known to many of his friends as Dodo, because he pronounced his own name as Do-do-dodgson. So, although he often assisted at church services, he was never a parish clergyman. He was, instead, a teacher of mathematics at Christ Church, Oxford, where he had been an undergraduate. All told, he spent something like fifty years in Christ Church, and a pleasanter place to live it would be hard to find if you were a retiring scholar, a bachelor, and – an eccentric.

Perhaps I should explain that, in the nineteenth century, it was necessary that he should be a clergyman to hold his position as mathematics don in the college. All those who ruled and taught in Oxford in those days had to be ordained, for the hold of the Church of England on both Oxford and Cambridge was still absolute, and Nonconformists and Jews were not admitted. Those of you who have visited Oxford know what a busy, crowded, noisy place it now is and you might perhaps not guess that it was a university town if it were not that, now and then, the traffic is halted while the Vice-Chancellor, preceded by his two mace-bearers, crosses the street. It must be one of the few places left in the world where self-assertion, covetousness, and the whole world of the combustion engine must come to a halt because somebody distinguished for his intelligence is going about his business. But in Dodgson's day it was a quiet university city where, it was said, grass grew through the cobblestones of the streets during vacation time.

Of course it was full of learned men who passed their time in teaching, study, and writing and in the evenings consumed extraordinary quantities of the excellent wines which were the pride of the college cellars. Dodgson, by the way, was extremely fond of sherry and was considered an admirable judge of it. If there are any of you here who have grown up under the barbarous illusion that sherry is a drink for old ladies, I advise you to drink a few glasses of the real thing, and learn better. Sherry is generously fortified with brandy. Dodgson, by the way, liked to drink his sherry while walking about the room. He never ate lunch, but at midday he got through a fair amount of sherry, while walking a quarter of a mile or so.

As a teacher he had the reputation of being dull. On the very few occasions when he preached, the report was that he was earnest, logical – and dull. A great many of his Oxford colleagues, where Common Room conversation was expected to be simultaneously learned and witty – which is by no means easy – found him dull. But was he dull? Dodgson seems to have been so, but why would you have come here this morning to hear me talk about a dull teacher of mathematics who lived from 1832 until 1898 and was dull every minute of it? No, you have come to hear about this eccentric man's *alter ego*, who was Lewis Carroll.

It is important, I think, to emphasize that he came of what used to be called "a good family," in Yorkshire. The Dodgsons could trace their ancestry back before Tudor times and they had always lived in the upper-middle range of society; since the early eighteenth century they had been chiefly clergymen, sometimes attaining to high office. They had large families, and a trick of marrying cousins, which was not so odd then as it might seem now, for when families were very large, and visits were confined to the distance a horse could travel in a day, cousins were the sort of people one met. Lewis Carroll had a positive army of cousins, uncles, and aunts and he knew them all and valued them as friends all his life. He himself had three brothers and seven sisters, and a lively and highly intelligent household they seem to have been. The photographs we have of them reveal an extraordinary degree of family likeness; there is a picture of Dodgson's seven sisters, every one of whom might have been taken for Charles "in drag." Not that he looked in the least effeminate; it was that the girls had the strong, rather distinguished features that marked him.

He was born into, and seems never to have questioned, that English "class system" which has been so much abused in the present century. Indeed, several governments have announced their intention of abolishing it, and the most recent prime minister to retire showed her egalitarian principle by accepting the title of Baroness Thatcher. Certainly it had its objectionable side, but it also had its virtues, and it is notable that in England it was possible to climb up the class ladder if you had the brains and determination to do so, and this was because the English always had a tender spot for anybody with money, which they associated, by no means mistakenly, with energy. This was not so in France, for instance, where rank was everything. Dodgson's family were gentlefolk, and never forgot it, but they had a high notion of what was expected of people in their position, and everybody who spoke of Dodgson's parents and his family, said how kind and generous they were to less fortunate people. The gentry did in those days what the state does now for those who cannot take care of themselves, and Dodgson was a generous man all his life long.

His childhood was very happy and – what is not always the case – his schooldays were reasonably happy. I mention this because so many writers have been unhappy at school, and in our century many have told us about their unhappiness at length and with bitterness. Of course nobody is *very* happy at school; if you meet anyone who says otherwise, you may know that you have met someone who is stuck in childhood, like a cow stuck in a swamp. Childhood may have periods of great happiness, but it also has times that must simply be endured. Childhood at its best is a form of slavery tempered by affection.

It is in Dodgson's childhood that we find the first traces of Lewis Carroll. The family of eleven children amused themselves with a magazine, most of which he wrote. They acted plays and presented puppet-shows, and these were his work. As a boy he showed the inclination toward light verse and nonsense verse which later made him famous. This sort of family invention and family entertainment was not forced upon the family of the Reverend Charles Dodgson by poverty, for they were privileged children; they were inventive because they were of more than average intelligence.

After schooldays at Rugby, Charles – so named after his father – Lutwidge, which was the name of his mother, who was his father's first cousin – went to Oxford, to Christ Church, as so many of his family had done before him, and in 1852 he achieved first-class honours in mathematics and was immediately appointed to a studentship – that is to say, a Fellowship in Christ Church – and in 1854 he took his B.A., proceeding in 1857 to an M.A., and assumed the duties of mathematical lecturer. In effect he never left Christ Church, which suited him exactly, until he removed to the home of some of his sisters in 1898, and died there, at the age of sixty-six. We do not think that a great age now, but he had begun in his fifties to speak of himself as an old man.

I don't want to bore you with biographical detail or load you with an account of everything Dodgson wrote. Because, as Dodgson, he wrote a considerable number of technical treatises on mathematics, which were received with respect, if not rapture, by the people who could understand them. One of these, called *Euclid and His Modern Rivals*, which he brought out in 1879, was a serious and excellent contribution to Euclidean geometry, but the mathematical world was offended by it because it contained a number of jokes, and the mathematical world does not admit the existence of jokes. This seems to have been a case in which Dodgson and Carroll became dangerously mingled.

So far we have talked a good deal about Dodgson, and said little about Lewis Carroll. Where did he come from and who was he? He came from an aspect of Dodgson's character that I must approach with caution, because I do not want to be misunderstood. He was extremely fond of little girls. Not of children in general. He detested little boys, and in one letter to a child friend he actually suggests that she should open the penknife which he has sent her for her birthday, and stick it up her brother's nose. In the present age, when everybody is an amateur psychoanalyst, and where the newspapers are filled every day with tales of horrible crimes committed against children and by children, such a suggestion as that must be jumped on and worried until some horrible secret has been squeezed out of it, but I do not propose to get into that sort of work this morning. I shall say no more than I have evidence to support, and that amounts to this: Lewis Carroll was enchanted by little girls, fell in love with little girls, and never laid a wicked hand on one of them. He was a gentleman and a Christian clergyman and it was on those principles that he lived his life.

We know who most of the little girls were, and there were a great many of them. The one of special interest to us was Alice Pleasance Liddell. She was the second of the three daughters of the Reverend Henry George Liddell, who was appointed Dean of Christ Church in 1855, at which time Alice was three years old. It was a family of intellectual distinction for the Dean was, with Robert Scott, then Master of Balliol, the author of the great *Greek Lexicon* which is still a standard work. Alice was a lovely child, and all the Liddell family had unusual good looks. She was a beauty – a *stunner* in the language of the time – even as a child, and she grew to be a beautiful young woman. But there is a revealing entry in Lewis Carroll's diary for May 11, 1865: "Met Alice and Miss Prickett [she was the child's governess] in the quadrangle; Alice seems changed a good deal and hardly for the better – probably going through the usual awkward stage of transition." Alice at that time would have been thirteen, and Carroll's judgement was right; she was becoming a young woman, and thus of no further interest to him.

Lewis Carroll was an expert photographer, at a time when photography was a vastly more complex pursuit than it is now. But all the drudgery of preparing the plates, and subsequently developing them, and of coaxing results from the huge cameras, whose focal length was determined by the most careful management of the extensible bellows, and the most exact adjustment of the heavy and very valuable lens, was a delight to his scientific, mathematical spirit. To make the work even more difficult, it had to be achieved by daylight, and this required very exact judgement and artistic talent as well as luck, to achieve a good result. We have great numbers of the photographs Lewis Carroll took, both of his child friends and of adults, and they show him to have been a man of quite unusual gift. Some of them, like his portraits of Tennyson, of Ruskin, of Christina Rossetti and her brother Dante Gabriel, of Ellen Terry and of Millais, are among the finest achievements of that early period of the photographer's art. And of course there were pictures of Alice.

They come as a surprise. We are accustomed to think of Alice as she appears in the accepted illustrations of the books by John Tenniel. There Alice is a self-possessed, charming little girl with long fair hair brushed back from a serious face, whose normal expression is serious, and sometimes darkens into a frown when something especially outrageous is happening. But the real Alice was not fair, but dark, and the dominant feature of her lovely face is the mystery of a pair of wonderful dark eyes, which seem to see far more than a child might be expected to see. This is certainly a face to fall in love with. Speaking for myself, and as the father of three daughters, I am not more than ordinarily susceptible to the charm of little girls, but when I look at the portraits of Alice, I can sense what it was that enthralled Lewis Carroll, and inspired two books that are undoubted classics, not simply of children's literature, but of that small portion of literature that is held dear by countless readers of all ages.

We know when the story first came into being. We have Dodgson's diaries, and on July 4, 1862, he records: "I made an expedition up the river to Godstow with the three Liddells; we had tea on the bank there and did not reach Christ Church until half-past eight." The Liddell children were Lorina, Alice, and Edith, and Alice at that time was just ten years old. The other member of the party was another young don, the Reverend Robinson Duckworth, who remained a friend of Carroll for the whole of his life. He says of the great occasion: "The story was actually composed and spoken over my shoulder, for the benefit of Alice Liddell who was acting as 'cox' of our gig. I remember turning around and saying, 'Dodgson, is this an extempore romance of yours?' I also remember well how, when we had conducted the three children back to the Deanery, Alice said, as she bade us goodnight, 'Oh, Mr. Dodgson, I wish you would write out Alice's adventures for me.' He said he would try and he afterwards told me that he sat up nearly the whole night, committing to a MS his recollections of the drolleries with which he had enlivened the afternoon. He added illustrations of his own and presented the volume, which used often to be seen on the drawing-room table at the Deanery."

It was not until 1865 that *Alice* appeared as a book. If you want to see what that original MS looked like, it has been reprinted in facsimile in a paperback; the later published story is a good deal enlarged and augmented. But if you have any ambition to possess a first edition of the printed book, I advise you to consider your next move very carefully, because Dodgson and his illustrator, Tenniel, were not satisfied with it, and recalled it, so that only about thirty of the first edition exist, and the last one to come on the market sold for one million, eight hundred thousand pounds. The second edition is also quite an expensive book. If you want quite a lot, but not all, of what Lewis Carroll wrote, you can get a fat book called *The Complete Works* (it isn't, but publishers have no shame) in The Nonesuch Edition, and I truly think it is all that any reasonable person could ask for, because Lewis Carroll was not always an enthralling writer, and I assume that you do not want his numerous mathematical writings.

He himself had no high opinion of *Alice's Adventures in Wonderland*, and was rather surprised when the first edition – which, as I have explained, is really the second – was a resounding success and quickly achieved the reputation it has since maintained as the finest book for children ever written. I will not weary you with the details of how many times it has been republished, and in how many languages. It made Lewis Carroll instantly famous, and it was characteristic of him that he maintained his privacy and his quiet life as an Oxford don in spite of all the admiration that was evoked by the book.

His popularity with children, of course, became almost overwhelming, and his children's parties were famous. They were very much along Victorian lines. Children came with their mothers or governesses, and there was always plenty to eat of the kind of thing children like – or liked in Victorian times – which seemed to mean a great deal of rich confectionery. The entertainment, which Lewis Carroll directed with total control, was likely to include conjuring, by the host, a magic lantern show, directed by the host, and games, led by the host.

These games give us most interesting information about Carroll himself. A great spinner of fantasy he might be, but he was a mathematician first and foremost, and one of the games he delighted to play with his child guests was called Symbolic Logic, and that was exactly what it was – but adapted to the child mind. The method is that familiar to Bertrand Russell and Alfred North Whitehead, but as Lewis Carroll uses it, the results are absurd. Was he demonstrating that logic is itself an absurdity? I don't know but I wouldn't put it past him. Here's an example: three concrete propositions are offered, thus – 1. Babies are illogical; 2. Nobody is despised who can manage a crocodile; 3. Illogical persons are despised. What is the logical conclusion? That babies cannot manage crocodiles. How do you like this one? 1. No one takes in *The Times*, unless he is well-educated; 2. No hedgehog can read; 3. Those who cannot read are not well-educated. What is the logical conclusion? No hedgehog takes in *The Times*. Can you stand one more? 1. Nobody, who really appreciates Beethoven, fails to keep silence while the Moonlight Sonata is being played; 2. Guinea pigs are hopelessly ignorant of music; 3. No one who is hopelessly ignorant of music, ever keeps silence while the Moonlight Sonata is being played. Logical conclusion – Guinea pigs never really appreciate Beethoven.

Would you like to try some of those when next you have a children's party? Or do you ever give children's parties? Or are you permitted to attend the parties your children give? But Carroll's parties were immensely successful and invitations to them were eagerly sought. He was keenly interested in everything relating to proper conduct and good manners, and even wrote some *Hints for Etiquette*. Here is one: "In proceeding to the dining-room, the gentleman gives one arm to the lady he escorts – it is unusual to offer both." As we read of those parties now, we must conclude that Victorian children were, in some respects at least, quicker in the wit than the children of today. But as I said earlier, much was expected of the children of the upper classes. Girls, I mean. Boys were expected to be rather thick in the head. Try some Symbolic Logic on your little Couch Potato, when you go home, and see what happens.

I have spoken of children's parties. When he was amusing a single child, Carroll was somewhat more exacting. One little girl, who spent a weekend with him, was driven almost to despair, because he insisted on teaching her to play chess. But not ordinary chess; it was a form of chess he had himself invented, in which all the rules were changed, and the moves of the pieces were determined by new rules. All children seem to have thought Mr. Dodgson delightful, but there is no record of any one of them who found him easy company.

Of course, Victorian children *were* bright. I am fond of the story about Carroll, who was entertaining a child friend of his who was visiting Oxford. She was a child actress, and she was appearing in the university city in a comedy now forgotten called *Bootle's Baby*. This is what Carroll records in his diary for June 12, 1889: "Again took Maggie about. We called on the Evans, Chapmans and Symonds and I introduced her to the Bishop of Oxford! The Bishop asked her what she thought of Oxford. 'I think,' said the little actress with quite professional aplomb, 'it's the best place in the provinces!' At which his Lordship was much amused." If that story puzzles you, remember that Maggie was a small actress, and that "the provinces" was a somewhat patronizing term used in her profession to describe any place that was not London, hub of the theatrical universe.

Lewis Carroll's popularity did not affect his work in Christ Church. Indeed many of his colleagues thought it somewhat below the dignity of an Oxford don to be associated with such frivolous stuff. But he showed a surprising practicality in dealing with his fame. He insisted on excellent contracts with his publishers, and he was quick to invent a number of games based on *Alice* which brought him in a lot of money. Indeed, he became quite rich.

Of course that did not happen at once. And Alice's family do not seem to have been overjoyed by the fame that had touched their small daughter. Indeed, Mrs. Liddell became cold and almost hostile toward Dodgson, who must have been rather a nuisance, for he hung around the Dean's house at all sorts of hours, and often visited the nursery without Mrs. Liddell's knowledge – though of course the governess was always present – and he wrote innumerable letters to Alice. These have not survived, for when she grew up Alice Liddell – who became Mrs. Reginald Hargreaves – refused to exploit her association with the popular book in any way. We assume that they were humorous love letters, such as might be written to a child, and we may be glad that they have not endured to be picked over and theorized about by insensitive scholars and psychoanalysts.

We understand Mrs. Liddell's concern. One of Dodgson's hobbies, which we must approach with care, was a passion for photographing the little girls he knew, sometimes in fancy dress, as fairy tale characters, but sometimes in the nude. None of these nude photographs have survived, for at his death his heirs distributed them to the ladies – now grown women – who were the subjects. We must try to understand this in Victorian terms; Dodgson repeatedly expressed his feeling that a naked girl child was the loveliest thing on earth, and from his other photographs we can divine that they were not erotically or provocatively posed. It was a fact, too, that he took these photographs always with the mother of the child present, and never a word of complaint was ever raised. But it remains an odd hobby for a bachelor clergyman, and we can understand the concern of Mrs. Liddell, who was by no means green. I have no doubt whatever that Dodgson never permitted a hint of adult sexuality to enter his mind, but such thoughts cannot be kept out of our twentieth-century minds. Nabokov's astonishing novel *Lolita* cannot be banished from consciousness. We are the inheritors for good and ill of what may be called the Freudian Revolution.

We must take into account Dodgson's extraordinary – one is tempted to say absurd – concern with female innocence. One of his projects – never achieved – was to produce a special edition of Shakespeare from which any reference that might even slightly blemish the innocence of a child had been deleted. This would have resulted in a somewhat ragged volume, for Shakespeare does not seem to have been aware of innocence as Victorians understood it, and even some of his most delightful heroines – Rosalind, for instance, or Beatrice – have very free tongues.

That purified Shakespeare was only one of the books for children that Dodgson wanted to produce, but did not do so. He had a plan for a child's Bible, from which any reference to God's anger or punishment for sin had been removed. It was pointed out to him that this would have meant cutting out Noah and his Ark, so popular with children, because Noah was escaping from God's wrath. The only departure from strict Christian orthodoxy of which we know Dodgson to have been guilty was his declaration that Jesus could not have believed in an eternal hell of punishment for sin, and that if he found that Jesus did entertain such a dreadful notion, he would declare himself to be no longer a Christian.

But this is all Dodgson. Lewis Carroll seems to have had extraordinary access to the imagination of a child and when he is writing the *Alice* books he never takes a stupid step.

What is even more astonishing is the hold that the *Alice* books have exercised over the minds of millions of adults. They have become what we may call "cult books," known to people who quote them slyly in conversation, hoping that someone else present will notice the quotation and perhaps offer another in return. This can be embarrassing. I recall an occasion in my youth, when I was at Queen's University in Kingston, when the English Club assembled one afternoon to hear the university librarian, a gentleman named Cockburn Kyte, address us on T. E. Lawrence's *Seven Pillars of Wisdom*. Mr. Kyte, who was immensely tall and thin and might well have come from one of Tenniel's illustrations for *Alice*, rose and with a smile of ineffable archness began: "'It was the *best* butter,' the March Hare meekly replied." And then he paused, plainly expecting us to fall about and slap our thighs at the aptness and witty allusiveness of his introduction to his subject. But we were a group of cornfed hicks who stared at him, thinking that he must have gone off his head, and his speech began with one very lame leg. We had read everything that was on the curriculum of the English Department, but I think I was the only one who had read *Alice* and I could not imagine how Mr. Kyte expected to make her relevant to T. E. Lawrence.

But since then I have been in company where the quotations and references to *Alice* flew about so swiftly that the oxygen in the air seemed seriously exhausted and we were in danger of ascending into what Shelley called "the intense inane." It is still – or it was so until quite recently – impossible to read a serious English newspaper or magazine without finding some *Alice* reference in it. Tenniel's illustrations have been a treasure-house to cartoonists, and particularly to political cartoonists, who have delighted to portray the Emperor of Germany as the Jabberwock, or various prime ministers as the Mad Hatter, and always with the solemn figure of Alice, making one of her sensible and taking-down comments.

It has remained an upper-class book. Let me read to you a passage from a play that was immensely popular between the two great European wars, called *Journey's End*; it first appeared in 1928, and was acted all over the world. The scene is a dugout on the Allied front, and an officer named Trotter enters from the trenches above, to find another officer, named Osborne, reading a book. Trotter is what was called a "ranker" officer, meaning that he had been an enlisted man who through his ability had been promoted to officer status; Osborne is a gentleman, formerly a schoolmaster. Trotter says: "What are you reading?"

OSBORNE: (*wearily*) Oh, just a book.

TROTTER: What's the title?

OSBORNE: (*shows*) Ever read it?

TROTTER: *Alice's Adventures in Wonderland*. Why, that's a kid's book!

OSBORNE: Yes.

TROTTER: You aren't *reading* it?

OSBORNE: Yes.

TROTTER: What – a *kid's* book?

OSBORNE: Haven't you read it?

TROTTER: (*scornfully*) No!

OSBORNE: You ought to. (*Reads*)

> How doth the little crocodile
>   Improve his shining tail
> And pour the waters of the Nile
>   On every golden scale!
>
> How cheerfully he seems to grin
>   How neatly spreads his claws,
> And welcomes little fishes in
>   With gently smiling jaws!

TROTTER: I don't see no point in that.

OSBORNE: (*wearily*) Exactly. That's just the point.

TROTTER: You are a funny chap!

Now, I think the author, R. C. Sherriff, has made a brilliant exposition of the charm and magic of *Alice* in that short scene. There is nothing in the world wrong with Trotter; he is a man of ability and great good sense, brave and good-natured in adversity. But his mind is not tuned to that curious pitch that is most frequently found in what used to be called the upper classes, which seems to hanker after an irrationality, a freedom from the chains of logic and reason, and a holiday in a world where the ordinary concerns of life have no validity. The English form of this cast of mind is brilliantly caught in the two volumes of *Alice's Adventures in Wonderland* and *Through the Looking Glass*, where unexceptionable logic gives rise to a totally inexplicable but logical chaos, and a freedom from the domination of dull reason. Why does this assert itself chiefly among the educated upper class? It would be politically incorrect to attempt any hint of an explanation.

People who do not know the *Alice* books, or have read them superficially, are apt to miss their poetry and also their dark side. There are portions of each book that can be frightening to a small child. As for poetry, I can only suggest that you study carefully the poems in the books, which are usually parodies of morally improving poems of the sort that Victorian children were expected to get by heart. But there is a gripping quality in some of the original poems that qualifies them, in my opinion, for identification as true poetry, which stirs the imagination and the emotions.

One of the finest of these occurs in *Through the Looking Glass*; it is called "Jabberwocky." You probably recall the first stanza:

'Twas brillig, and the slithy toves
  Did gyre and gimble in the wabe:
All mimsy were the borogoves,
  And the mome raths outgrabe.

What does it mean? Because it does mean something, and if you wish to make a close study of Lewis Carroll you can read his own explanation of what he called, in the beginning, *A Stanza of Anglo-Saxon Poetry*. He will tell you that "brillig" means "the time of broiling dinner, i.e., in the close of the afternoon." You will learn that a "tove" is a species of badger that has short horns like a stag and lives chiefly on cheese. It is "slithy" because it is smooth and active. What is a "borogove"? It is an extinct form of parrot which in its heyday lived on veal. And "outgrabe" is of course the past tense of the verb "outgribe" which means shrieked or creaked. The whole stanza, translated into modern English from Anglo-Saxon means, "It was evening, and the smooth active badgers were scratching and boring holes in the hillside; all unhappy were the parrots; and the grave turtles squeaked out." Are you still with me? And if so, are you edified and happy?

That first verse was written sixteen years before the heroic poem of the conquering of a monster called the Jabberwock was added to it.

"Jabberwocky" cannot be denied the name of poetry. It invites the imagination to explore a world that is complete within the poem. It arouses wonder. It tells a story which might easily have come from an Anglo-Saxon source or from one of the great German legends that inspired Wagner. A brave youth faces a dreadful monster, kills it, and returns in triumph to his father who is overjoyed. Perhaps we think of the hideous Grendel rising from the mere, slain by the dauntless Beowulf. But just a moment – there is something in the tone of "Jabberwocky" that tempts us, not to mock at the exploit of the heroic youth, but to see it somewhat askew; a child may feel terror on hearing the poem, especially if it is looking at Tenniel's splendid illustration of the creature, part prehistoric, part inspired by the wonderful paintings which show St. George slaying the dragon; but the triumph of the Jabberwock slayer is the triumph of a child, as we see him in the picture, valiant with his sword. What is the child slaying? The psychoanalysts have had their say, and some of what they say prompts us to assent. We share in the father's cry:

> "And hast thou slain the Jabberwock?
>> Come to my arms, my beamish boy!
> O frabjous day! Callooh! Callay!"
>> He chortled in his joy.

Have we all, at some time, slain the Jabberwock? Or, sad to say, have we failed to do so, or merely wounded the creature? I am not a psychoanalyst, and have no right to say, but I may be allowed my strong personal opinion. Lewis Carroll had seen something to which most of us are blind and had put it in a form of which only he knew the secret, and we can penetrate the secret – perhaps – by intuition.

The hold which this poem has had over countless readers is evidence of its power. Incidentally, it presents a pretty problem to those heavily burdened souls, the translators. It is the problem they face with James Joyce. But several of them have met it as bravely as the child-hero met the Jabberwock. I will not trouble you about many of them, but it may amuse some of you to hear how a scholarly diplomat, the late Lord Vansittart, rendered the tricky first verse in his Latin version:

Coesper erat: tunc lubriciles ultravia circum
Urgebant gyres gimbiculosque tophi:
Moestenui visae borogovides ire meatu
Et profugi gemitus exgrabuere rathae.

The rest is every bit as good, but I don't want to spoil your appetite for the play with too much pleasure now.

I promised somewhere, did I not, to talk to you about Lewis Carroll and the theatre? Apart from photography, it was his greatest pleasure and enthusiasm. It has been suggested – though I think wrongly – that he declined to accept full ordination into the priesthood because attendance at the theatre, though not actually forbidden, was not encouraged for the clergy of the Church of England. But whenever he could, there in the theatre sat Carroll, in his clerical dress, an enchanted playgoer and often a friend of some of the actors and actresses on the stage. (Perhaps I should say a word about clerical dress. He lived before the Roman collar was the usual wear for clergymen; in his day they wore white bowties with black clothes of clerical cut, which meant that they had no lapels. I can remember, when I was an undergraduate, seeing very old clergymen around Oxford, who still dressed like that.) So that is how you must imagine Lewis Carroll, as he sat in his favourite theatre, The Princess's, watching Charles Kean and his wife in Shakespeare, or perhaps a stirring melodrama. The pinnacle of his theatre experience, he wrote in his diary, was Kean's production of *Henry VIII* in the scene (it is act 4, scene 2) in which the much-troubled Queen Katherine falls asleep and has a vision of angel visitors of whom she says:

Saw you not even now a blessed troop
Invite me to a banquet, whose bright faces
Cast thousand beams upon me, like the sun?
They promised me eternal happiness

And brought me garlands, Griffith, which I feel
I am not worthy yet to wear: I shall, assuredly.

This is the Queen's vision before her death. Apparently the scene,
as Lewis Carroll saw it at the Princess's Theatre on January 22, 1855,
was a splendidly imaginative piece of stage illusion. This is what
Dodgson wrote in his diary:

Oh, that exquisite vision of Queen Catherine! I almost held my
breath to watch: the illusion is perfect, and I felt as if in a dream
all the time it lasted. It was like a delicious reverie, or the most
beautiful poetry. This is the true end and object of acting – to
raise the mind above itself, and out of its petty everyday cares
– never shall I forget that wonderful evening, that exquisite
vision – sunbeams broke in through the roof and gradually
revealed two angel forms, floating in front of the carved work
on the ceiling: the column of sunbeams shone down upon the
sleeping queen, and gradually down it floated a troop of angelic
forms, transparent, and carrying palm branches in their hands;
they waved these over the sleeping queen, with oh, such a sad
and solemn grace – So I could fancy (if the thought be not
profane) would real angels seem to our mortal vision, though
doubtless our conception is poor and mean to the reality. She
in an ecstasy raises her arms toward them, and to sweet slow
music they vanish as marvellously as they came.

Here's enthusiasm, indeed! I have seen *Henry VIII* several times,
and I have never seen anything to touch that; Dodgson was no simpleton who knew nothing of plays; he was a man of extensive
culture and a seasoned playgoer and this vision remained with him
as one of the great artistic experiences of his life. It reminds us, if
we need reminding, what splendours the Victorian theatre offered,
with its magnificent painted scenery and the magic of its gaslight.
Modern directors, of course, don't believe in angels. Indeed, one
often wonders what they do believe in. But this was Shakespeare
done for an audience who had few reservations about angels and it

was, it seems, splendid. So splendid that this playgoer cherished it all his life.

And yet it was stagecraft – a combination of art and illusion. Lewis Carroll knew a lot about that. He and his brothers and sisters had possessed two toy theatres, for which they wrote plays and performed them with great seriousness. Stage illusion was in Dodgson's blood and we miss something if we do not understand the dramatic qualities of the *Alice* books, the sudden appearances and disappearances, the transformations, and above all the rapidity with which the action takes place.

Dodgson's approval of the stage was not total, and he seems to have enjoyed farces and comedies of the most witless sort; I can speak with feeling because I have read some of them, and they speak of a theatre utterly gone, to be replaced by a witlessness agreeable to our own age. But there were plays to which he objected, and one of these was *Faust* – one of the many butcheries of Goethe's great play which he saw in 1857, and about which he wrote: "I think it is a play that should never have been put on the stage – it is too horrible, and too daring in its representation of the spirit world." The presentation of Mephistopheles "made my blood run cold." Yet, even here, great stagecraft and great acting could win him over. In 1886 he saw Henry Irving's version of *Faust* and wrote: "It is magnificently put on the stage and Irving as Mephistopheles is wonderfully good. Ellen Terry is of course exquisite as Margaret." You see, it was the great stagecraft that won him over. It was in the same year, 1886, that Lewis Carroll had the joy of seeing a stage version of *Alice*, the work of Henry Savile Clarke, opening on December 23, at the Prince of Wales Theatre. It was a great success, and Lewis Carroll's fame was extended in a new direction.

It would be beyond my powers to mention all the stage versions of *Alice* that have appeared since that triumph, and you would quickly be bored by the recitation. Some have been very good: there was one, with the text adapted by Clemence Dane, in 1944, with a cast that included Sybil Thorndike as the ferocious Queen of Hearts and Rima Beaumont, who was a splendid reminder of the beauty of Alice Pleasance Liddell. Not surprisingly, it is in the casting of the central role of Alice that so many productions have come to grief. The desire to make her cute, or pert, or a giggler, or a wisecracker, or sexy, is the downfall of countless actresses and their directors who are convinced that they need to make Alice more interesting than she appears in the book – which is, of course, to mistake what Alice is really like, for Alice is a very serious, self-respecting little girl. It appears that the first stage Alice, whose name was Phoebe Carlo, filled the bill perfectly and won the admiration and gratitude of Alice's creator.

Alice has been made into a ballet – more than one, indeed. And of course *Alice* has inspired countless films, not one of which has been really satisfactory. They include a complex version devised and directed by Dr. Jonathan Miller, in which was explained – for Dr. Miller is nothing if not an explainer – that all the figures in the stories represented Victorian adults, as they appeared to the eyes of a child. I have never been able to track it down for it did not enjoy wide distribution, but I am sure it was interesting, as everything Dr. Miller does is interesting, and I fear that it may have been too clever for its own good, which is a trap into which Dr. Miller has occasionally fallen.

At the opposite end of the intellectual scale lies the Hollywood film of 1933, which was made accessible to the kind of people for whom everything must be blatant and vulgar, and its success was thought to be assured by a cast that included Cary Grant as the Mock Turtle (why?) and Gary Cooper as the White Knight (somewhat more credible) and W. C. Fields as Humpty Dumpty, which was total disaster to all except those who thought Fields funny whatever he did. This was a thoroughly illiterate film, made by people who had never been children, and perhaps had never seen a child. Their worst choice was in casting Charlotte Henry as Alice. I must guard my tongue, but perhaps I may say that she was a thoroughly democratized Alice. But one movie critic wrote of her, "she's as pert a piece of jailbait as ever fell down a rabbit hole." *Alice* has been filmed performed by puppets. It has been filmed as a musical. There was a version made in 1951, with a fine cast, but somehow the story went askew and turned out to include Queen Victoria as the Queen of Hearts. A film called *Dreamchild* showed us Alice, grown old, remembering Dodgson and the story at Oxford. *Alice* has been very well done on the stage, but the movies have never come near it.

As Lewis Carroll and the Reverend Mr. Dodgson grew older – they never grew very old in modern terms for he died when he was sixty-six, convinced that he was an old man – the split between the two became more pronounced. Inevitably his success in the theatre was deplored by very serious people who thought it was unfitting in a clergyman. He was not to be shaken, and defended the theatre boldly – but not without reservation. Consider this passage, which he wrote in 1889 when he was fifty-seven:

> Let me pause for a moment to say that I believe this thought, of the possibility of death – if calmly realized and steadily faced – would be one of the best possible tests as to our going to any scene of amusement being right or wrong. If the thought of sudden death acquires, for *you*, a special horror when imagined happening in a *theatre*, then be very sure the theatre is harmful for *you*, however harmless it may be for others; and that *you* are incurring a deadly peril by going. Be sure that the safest rule is that we should not dare to *live* in any scene in which we dare not *die*.

That passage occurs in the preface to Lewis Carroll's last work of imagination. It is a novel called *Sylvie and Bruno* (1890). I am sorry to say it is a very bad novel but it is of great psychological interest because in it the Reverend Charles Lutwidge Dodgson and Lewis Carroll are struggling for supremacy. Neither emerges as the winner. It is a broken-backed novel, for the plot leaps dizzily to and fro over the abyss that divides two stories. The one is about two children; Sylvie, a delightful little girl but obliged much of the time to adopt a maternal or perhaps governess-like attitude toward her little brother Bruno. Sylvie is sweet as Alice never is; indeed she becomes cloying all too easily. As for Bruno, I find it hard to speak with moderation.

Evelyn Waugh said of him that he was "a creation of unique horror." If you think that harsh, let me give you a sample. Impersonating children is not one of my gifts, but I shall try my best.

"Really, Bruno, you must come and do your lessons."

"I *wiss* oo wouldn't say '*really*, Bruno!'" the little fellow pleaded, with pouting lips that made him look prettier than ever. "It *always* shows there's something horrid coming! And I won't kiss oo, if oo's so unkind."

"Ah, but you *have* kissed me!" Sylvie exclaimed in merry triumph.

"Well, then, I'll *un*kiss oo." And he threw his arms round her neck for this novel, but apparently not *very* painful, operation.

"It's very like *kissing*," Sylvie remarked, as soon as her lips were again free for speech.

"Oo don't know *nuffin* about it! It were just the *conkery*," Bruno replied.

There is really an extraordinary amount of kissing in this book, and we know that Carroll was a great kisser. He might well have been more reserved in print.

It would take too long to tell you the tale of these two children who dwell most of the time in Elfland, where their father is King; they also spend some time in Dogland, which you will not be surprised to hear is full of dogs. But by means of elephantine contortions their story is intermingled with that of some adult humans — because Sylvie and Bruno seem unable to determine whether or not they are fairies. The other story is about an impossibly beautiful, pious, and refined girl called Lady Muriel, who has two lovers. One is a doctor who thinks he is too old for her, and thus disqualifies himself, and the other is a Captain Eric Lindon who is a heroic, splendid fellow, who has one grievous defect in the eyes of the lady. He is a convinced atheist. The author wrote, "Whether it is better, or worse than the *Alice* books, I have no idea; but I take a far deeper interest in it, as having tried to put more real *thought* into it." But thought, alas, is no substitute for genius. The careful planning of

Sylvie and Bruno cannot match the inspired improvisation of *Alice*. The book is filled with painful religious arguments, in which Lady Muriel tries to bring the atheist Captain into a better frame of mind. But it won't do, so she marries the doctor, who thereupon destroys his health by heroically fighting an epidemic of some unspecified illness in a nearby town. It is Captain Eric who nobly brings him home, a wreck, and Lady Muriel settles down to one of the happiest fates that could befall a Victorian heroine – that of devoting herself to a hopeless invalid. Endless love but no hint of sex. If you want to find how Sylvie and Bruno become involved in this high-minded affair, you must read the book yourself. It is sad that after the genius of the *Alice* books, and of *The Hunting of the Snark*, Dodgson should have fallen to this, but nothing can take those splendid works from us, nor should we suppose that even as Dodgson gained strength in his latter years, Lewis Carroll became a shadow of what he had been. It was Lewis Carroll, the inspired mathematician, who replied, when he was asked to contribute to a philosophical symposium –

And what mean all these mysteries to me
Whose life is full of indices and surds?
x squared plus seven plus fifty-three
equals eleven-thirds.

8

—— ∾ ——

An Allegory of the Physician

ROBERTSON DAVIES WENT TO Johns Hopkins University in Baltimore, Maryland, to lecture on several occasions; two of these lectures have been included in the selections in *The Merry Heart.* They are "Can a Doctor Be a Humanist," given on November 18, 1984, and "A View in Winter, Creativity in Old Age," given on November 14, 1993. In this lecture, which was part of a symposium called "An Allegory of the Physician," he talks of the role of the physician in drama. Two of the plays he mentions are *Macbeth* and *The Doctor's Dilemma,* so we have included Theatre Diary entries for productions of these plays.

July 12, 1995: *Wednesday, Festival Theatre* [Stratford, Ontario]: Macbeth. *Have I ever seen a really good* Macbeth? *Not in my eighty years: This one skilfully and perceptively directed by Marti Maraden: good understanding and respect for the supernatural, good witches and the best Masque of Kings I have ever seen – black-robed figures in white masks carrying on long wands the crowns of Banquo's line, from early circlets to heavy and*

begemmed crown of the Double Kingdom – a good Cauldron
which hissed as the nasty things were thrown in. A good Severed
Head at the end. BUT: Macbeth (Scott Wentworth) physically
good but vocally disastrous. Lady Macbeth (Seanna McKenna)
lightweight and a very "modern" personality: bad, hysterical
sleep-walking scene: obviously never seen a somnambulist. Dixie
Seatle as Lady Macduff very good and Scots: made Lady Macbeth
look as if she has been transferred from some society play of the
'20s. Very good Banquo (Benedict Campbell) and his Ghost all
bloody, a splendid apparition. Good Macduff (Wayne Best) and
the last fight a real thriller. Macduff's small daughter played by
Ellen Ross Stuart, Moira Whalon's god-daughter and child of my
student Ann: charming and very moving when the Murderers
moved toward her. But all these good things could not prevail
against a pair of dull leads.

July 24, 1991: *Wednesday, Shaw Festival, Evening:* The
Doctor's Dilemma. *Well done except that Jennifer was wanting
in charm and mystery for the role. Could not hear her nor could
Brenda, so it was not my deafness. The doctors were admirably
cast and played and* spoken: *it was a feast of splendid dramatic
prose. Some discreet cuts and even so it ran till 11:05. Benson as
"B.B." – MacGregor as Walpole – Farrell as Cullen – Medley as
Schutzmacher – Ball as Ridgeon: a very strong team and a deeply
refreshing evening.*

———— ∽ ————

It is my task to speak first in this
symposium, and when I was thinking about what I should say to you
this afternoon I could not get out of my mind the striking illustration that appears on the public notices of this event, and which I
presume you have all seen. At the bottom of the page is a pageant-
like depiction of four figures – an Angel, a Man, a God, and a Devil,
and it bears the title "An Allegory of the Physician." It is a brilliant
choice, and I have made it the foundation of what I am about to say.

I suspect that before the symposium is over the distinguished sym-posiasts will have presented you to yourselves in all four guises – Angel, Man, God, and Devil – and you will be pleased with the identification. You will not mind being likened to angels or gods, you suppose yourselves to be men of various kinds, but you will be most pleased to be equated with devils. There is something about having devilishness attributed to oneself that is rather jaunty and stylish – a hint of unsuspected depths – and among no classification of mankind is that feeling stronger than it is among doctors. Why is that so? I shall tell you something about that this evening, after dinner, when your nerves have been calmed by food, and possibly even by drink. At this moment, however, I am going to face you with what happens when you are considered merely as men.

This symposium is called "Medicine in the Mirror of the Stage." The title is an echo of some words of Shakespeare's. In the tragedy of *Hamlet*, the Prince of Denmark, who is an actor, a critic, a play-wright, and a scholar – in fact a whole symposium in a single man – gives some advice to a group of actors, and he tells them what acting and theatrical illusion is. He speaks of "the purpose of playing, whose end, both at the first and now, was and is to hold as 't were, the mirror up to nature: to show virtue her own feature, scorn her own image, and the very age and body of the time his form and pressure." A sym-posium, as you all know, was originally a drinking-party, where the guests delighted themselves with amusing but by no means trivial conversation. If there is no drink here this afternoon, do not blame us; we never said a word against it. But amusing conversation – well, I hope we may provide that. I assure you that we have thought of little else but this occasion for several weeks past.

As you have discerned, I am trying to put you in a good mood, to soften you up, just as a doctor does when he is about to reveal a disagreeable diagnosis. I may as well tell you at once that in my inves-tigation of the role played by the medical profession on the stage – that is, as you are reflected in the Mirror of Nature – you have not, until comparatively recent times, cut much of a figure. Why this should be so I cannot explain; writers, and playwrights as much as any, are all hypochondriacs, continually fretting about their health, rushing to the doctor at the slightest twinge, and consuming pills and potions in extraordinary quantity. Why, then, have they not been kinder to you? Why have they not put you in a flattering light at centre stage? Why, indeed, when you are obviously the character most relevant to the action, have they not called you in? I have raked the great tragic drama of Greece from end to end, and in all those tragedies I have not discovered a single doctor. Yet, to choose but one familiar example, think what a doctor might have done for Oedipus! A few words from a Priest of Aesculapius, explaining that although incest is inadvisable it is by no means fatal, and that tragedy might have had quite a happy conclusion. Of course, about twenty-five hundred years later, Dr. Sigmund Freud would have had to find some other field of work. The Greeks, as reflected in their tragedy, were a violent people, and where violence rages the surgeon thrives. But in the whole range of classic drama I could find only one doctor and he is in a Roman comedy by Plautus; he diagnoses a patient as insane, and prescribes gigantic doses of hellebore. The Romans thought of that sort of thing as excruciatingly comic because, as I am sure you know, hellebore is a violent purge, and the notion of some poor creature being purged almost to extinction was surefire comedy to the toughs who made up the audience in a Roman theatre.

Things are not much better two thousand years later. Shakespeare has a few doctors in his plays. There is a purging doctor – you see how long the joke lasted; in *The Merry Wives of Windsor* one of his patients says, "He gives me the potions, and the motions." One gets the impression that in past ages people had bowels of brass or they could not have withstood the horrors of heroic purging. And Shakespeare has a doctor in *Macbeth* who is asked to treat the Queen of Scotland, who walks in her sleep – but he throws up the case: "More needs she the divine than the physician," he says. Macbeth himself appeals to him:

Canst thou not minister to a mind diseased,
Pluck from the memory a rooted sorrow,
Raze out the hidden troubles of the brain,
And with some sweet, oblivious antidote

> Cleanse the stuffed bosom of that perilous stuff
> Which weighs upon the heart?

Obviously Macbeth is asking for chemotherapy. But the doctor was a pre-chemotherapy physician, and the best he can say is:

> Therein the patient
> Must minister to himself

a suggestion so horrendous that the King cries

> Throw physic to the dogs, I'll none of it.

Not a happy doctor-patient relationship, I am sure you will agree. But Shakespeare, who was always ahead of his time, does offer us one splendid portrait of a woman doctor in *All's Well That Ends Well*. Her name is Helena, and she is one of the most charming of Shakespeare's heroines. Her specialty is an odd one, for her time and her sex; she is a proctologist. The King of France is gradually succumbing to a stubborn fistula of the anus; Helena has a sovereign ointment, and after a few dabs of this magical substance, the King is up and dancing, and offers Helena any husband she chooses as her reward. I should like to meet Helena. Not that I would have anything to offer her in her professional line, but as a general physician – witty, compassionate, and learned – she meets all my most optimistic medical requirements.

It is not long after the death of Shakespeare that we encounter a very great playwright who positively hated doctors. That was the French genius Molière. Characteristically of his profession, Molière was a hypochondriac, and his neurosis was as great as his genius. Perhaps I am wrong to say he hated doctors; he wanted his daughter to marry one, so that he would have a physician constantly in attendance. In several of his best plays doctors appear, usually armed with those huge, ominous brass squirts with which they administered enemas, for medicine was still in the grip of that obsession with enemas which it has not wholly shaken off to this day. The doctors usually converse in the bad Latin which was part of their mystery at that time. Your profession made a grave mistake when it discarded Latin. Did the medical brotherhood like Molière? No, they disliked him only slightly less than the clergy, who loathed him. I might present Molière's death as a warning to all men of genius but faulty discretion. It was on the night of February the 17th, 1673, when he was himself acting the leading role in his most ferociously mocking anti-doctor play, called *Le Malade imaginaire*, that Molière suddenly became ill, and died. Now – was it the malign power of an outraged medical profession that brought about his end? A poisoned enema, perhaps? I think it by no means impossible: you all know how dangerous it is to thwart the medical brotherhood. Certainly the doctors and the priests had the last word. Molière was refused Christian burial and had to be huddled into his grave at night, unhouseled and unaneled, like Hamlet's father.

Now, lest you should become unduly proud of your feat in having killed Molière, I should point out that the greatest theatrical enemy of your profession in recent times, Bernard Shaw, wrote a play called *The Doctor's Dilemma* in 1906, and although some of your professional forebears hated him as fiercely as ever they hated Molière, he lived in robust health for another forty-four years, succumbing at last at the age of ninety-four. Of course I should point out that Shaw was an Irishman, and thus not subject to the common rules that govern mankind. In justice I must say also that a great number of doctors admire Shaw's play without reserve, for they have understood the truth that lies behind the brilliant comedy. And that truth is that medicine, like everything else, is subject to fashion, the form and pressure of the time; the best of doctors are still men, and their medical practice is strongly coloured by what they themselves are.

Perhaps you are becoming a little restless. Were there no doctors, you may ask, who were presented as serious characters in the greatest drama? Oh yes, indeed there were, and if you want to study a splendid example I recommend you to Henrik Ibsen's great drama *A Doll's House*. Most people remember it as a protest against the psychological subjection in which women were held in nineteenth-century society. But in the character of Dr. Rank there is another protest that should not go unnoticed. Dr. Rank is that pitiable object, a sick physician, and there is no cure for what ails him. He has inherited syphilis, a disease very common in 1878, when the play was written, and not unknown in our own time. Some of you who have a literary cast of mind will recall that this was the disease that brought such tragedy to the life of the Baroness Karen Blixen, who wrote under the name of Isak Dinesen. She did not inherit it; it was a wedding present from her husband, but there is a link between her suffering and that of Dr. Rank. In *A Doll's House* Rank puts a question which may be familiar to some of you from your own clinical experience: Why should I suffer for the pleasures and sins of my parents? Why should I pay another's debt with my life? I offer you Dr. Rank as a splendid, artistically controlled portrait of a physician mercilessly reflected in the Mirror of Nature – the Theatre.

But it is not in Comedy or Tragedy that the doctor appears most frequently or most compellingly, in theatrical art of every kind. But theatrical art has found new forms in our century and the most widespread and most popular are film and television. There, on the large screen and the small one, you may see the doctor presented in the fullest range of character, every day of your life.

In film and television the doctor appears in full Technicolor as the Hero. Of course Ibsen, who saw everything and seems to have known everything, had a Doctor-Hero before anybody else. In *An Enemy of the People* (1882) Dr. Stockmann is engaged in the classic doctor struggle against the stupidity and corruption of society. He discovers that the mineral springs on which the fortunes of his town depend are in fact polluted by the local sewage disposal and he wants everybody to know about it. But he is beaten by the entrenched interests; he is told to keep his mouth shut. He is represented as an enemy of society, and he loses his fight. So Dr. Stockmann, though a Hero, is a loser, and that is not what movie and TV audiences want to see. They want their heroes to be winners, and it is as winners they appear in a hundred popular films – *Arrowsmith*, *The Citadel*, *Magnificent Obsession*, *Men in White*, *Doctor Zhivago*, and in all those films about Louis Pasteur, Paul Ehrlich, and Albert Schweitzer in which we see Edward G. Robinson or some other powerful actor triumphing, after a heroic battle, over the stupidity of people who have

the impertinence to oppose him and his infallible scientific knowledge. Anybody who opposes the great doctor is a villain, and is naturally played by some lesser-paid actor with a nasty face. The lesson
of these extremely popular movies is that the doctor is always right.

In television this lesson is greatly simplified, but it is even stronger.
Who but a villain would dare to contradict handsome young Dr.
Kildare? He is certainly the Angel in the Allegory of the Physician
which you have all seen. Who would dare to contradict good old Dr.
Gillespie, who is Dr. Kildare's guru, and who is certainly cast in the
mould of God, another figure in the Allegory? Of course these characters have their faults; now and then Dr. Kildare is flirting with a
pretty nurse when his attention ought to be on some ugly old man,
obviously a trouble-maker. Now and then Dr. Gillespie loses his
glasses, or his temper, but in medical matters he can conquer anything but Death and one is led to think that he regards Death as a
fellow doctor, who has a cure for everything. And as well as Dr.
Kildare we have Ben Casey, who is such a regular guy, as well-up in
medicine as he seems to be illiterate in everything else. And we have
probably made the acquaintance of that charming group who
appear in *The Nurses*, and *The Doctors and the Nurses*. We, the television viewers, understand from these programs how hard you work,
what splendid people you are, how little you care for money, and
what a lively, eventful life you lead! We envy you, and though we
realize that we are unworthy to be doctors, we vow that we shall be
humble, unresisting patients. You are our heroes.

That is not the whole story, of course. There are evil doctors,
whose character is the complete opposite of dear old Dr. Christian,
whom we remember as a saintly man, living only for others. These
evil doctors are likely to be great medical discoverers, like the villainous Dr. Mabuse, who will be remembered only by those of you
who are well into middle age. But you have probably encountered
Dr. Cyclops, whose specialty it is to reduce human beings to midgets,
and then to subject them to fearful humiliations. There are lots of
evil doctors, and it is psychologically significant they are virtually all
foreigners. Now why could that be, do you suppose? You are all profound psychologists, and I leave the problem to you. These doctors,

of course, are related to the figure of the Devil in the Allegory of the Physician.

But there is one doctor who is the most popular of all – so popular indeed that no less than sixteen films have been made about him – and he is not a foreigner, unless you regard Englishmen as foreigners. He is Dr. Henry Jekyll, and he first appeared in Robert Louis Stevenson's brilliant short story "The Strange Case of Dr. Jekyll and Mr. Hyde" (1886). It is such a thrilling story that sometimes we miss its psychological comment, and I am afraid most of the sixteen movies have done so. Dr. Jekyll is an admired London physician, famous for his upright character, his kindness of heart, and his charity toward all mankind. But he has one fault; he *will* tinker with his chemicals and he finds a formula which, when he drinks it, changes not only his character but also his physique, and he becomes the repellent, hateful Mr. Hyde, a malign dwarf whose urge is to do whatever is evil. Dr. Jekyll is horrified; can there be such a monster repressed within his own blameless – no, his noble – character? Indeed it is so, and in the end Mr. Hyde triumphs. What the story is telling us, of course, is that to seek to attain perfection is to try to be more than a man; not perfection, but wholeness, should be our aim. Be angel, be God if you will, but never forget that you are a man, or you will have an ugly encounter with your devil. If Dr. Jekyll had taken the trouble to make the acquaintance of the horrible Mr. Hyde without having Hyde forced upon him by scientific accident, he could have made allowance for Hyde, and without yielding to him, he could have recognized him as a dangerous possibility, and made some sort of moral reconciliation with him. The lesson of the story – all Stevenson's stories have lessons, though they are so charmingly disguised – is the old Greek injunction, "Know thyself." I wish every doctor had that mighty counsel written in large letters over his desk. But the striving for perfection is a professional hazard of the medical profession, and one of your hardest tasks is to resist it. Never forget Mr. Hyde.

Even Robert Louis Stevenson was not immune from the popular desire that doctors should be perfect. You notice that his hero is DOCTOR Jekyll, but his villain is plain MISTER Hyde. Or have I forgotten something: in England surgeons are addressed as Mister – perhaps Hyde was a surgeon.

Do you wonder what I am getting at? Perhaps you have forgotten that I promised to talk to you about your profession as it appears in the Mirror of Nature – that is to say, the Theatre in all its forms.

I assure you that I have not forgotten. I said that portraits of doctors are comparatively rare in Tragedy and Comedy, but we cannot forget that other, huge category of dramatic entertainment which must be called Melodrama, for it too is a Mirror of Nature. When doctors appear on the stage, on the large screen or the small one, they are most often bathed in the lurid light of melodrama.

What is Melodrama? The word has bad connotations in common speech. People think it means plays and films in which impossible situations and crude emotions are exploited – shows quite unworthy of the attention of such sophisticated persons as you and me. Not at all. I have spent a great deal of time studying melodrama, and I have come to the conclusion that it is the dramatic depiction of life as most of us wish it to be, and indeed as, in our personal experience, it is.

Few of us live in a dimension of Tragedy, for Tragedy demands a nobility of feeling and a depth of suffering, which is not ours, though we take great delight in it when we see it in the theatre. Few of us live in a dimension of Comedy, for Comedy is only funny when you are an observer; to be involved in a truly comic situation can be as demanding and exhausting as living in a situation of tragedy. What both Comedy and Tragedy share is a strong spirit of Inevitability; the situation is going to work itself out as the gods wish it, not as we ourselves desire it. But in Melodrama our wishes are supreme; the good are rewarded and the wicked punished; the heroes and heroines win their battles and win each other; the villains and villainesses are crushed beneath the weight of their own unworthiness. And the Heroes and Heroines have no faults – or only small, lovable faults.

That is why, in the popular plays and films and TV programs about doctors, you always appear as heroes – a little flawed, but only enough to be cosy. That is what we, the public, the great group whom you refer to as "laymen," want you to be. After all, we trust you with what is most precious in ourselves. We have, I think foolishly, banished many of the heroes we used to admire, and we have forced the heroic image on a few professions, and the medical profession is our favourite. So there you are: if your professional image is heroic, and if in consequence you are sometimes impatient when you are questioned, or if you immodestly assert your preeminence in society, and if you demand rewards that seem excessive, it is because you are what we have made you.

I have been talking about your profession in terms of the theatre. Let me conclude by giving you some sound theatrical advice: don't believe your own publicity. Don't succumb to the desire of wretched, suffering mankind to see you as angels or gods or – when you make dreadful mistakes as now and then you do – to see you as devils.

The most important figure in the allegory of medicine is the Man. It is your quality as men that is the real truth about you, and what ought to be reflected in the Mirror of Nature. If, from time to time, the reflection should be unflattering, perhaps we are both at fault.

9

— ❧ —

THE LURE OF FANTASY

ROBERTSON DAVIES WAS A great admirer of George Bernard Shaw and thought the first two volumes of Michael Holroyd's biography to be excellent. Therefore, when he was asked to review volume 3, *The Lure of Fantasy*, for the *Washington Post Book World*, he was delighted to accept. This review, written on September 4, 1991, was published in Volume XXI, Number 40 under the title "The Playwright of the Western World." He made the following short entry in his diary while reading the book, doing "a mass of signatures" to assist his publisher in the launching of his new novel *Murther & Walking Spirits*, and writing the review.

August 22: *I finish reading Holroyd's* Shaw *and am ready to do the 1,000-words-plus the* Post *wants*... August 26: *Do a mass of signatures and plan my GBS review.* August 30: *Complete GBS piece; not bad, not extraordinary.*

— ❧ —

Michael Holroyd has now completed his three-volume life of Bernard Shaw; it will rank with the finest biographies of this century. A great life deserves a great Life; Shaw provided the first and Mr. Holroyd has hit the bull's-eye with the second. There will be other books about Shaw; scraps and crumbs of detail will emerge and be recorded; the critics will chew him over for centuries. But this book will be the point from which they all start and to which they must constantly recur.

The lot of the biographer is not an easy one. He would like to create a work of art, like every other writer worth talking about. But he cannot indulge his imagination; he must not suppress facts or invent them and he must determine the relative importance of all the facts that confront him. He must have an opinion about every circumstance that concerns his subject, but he must not be idiosyncratic, as is Hesketh Pearson in his good but cranky book about Shaw; he must not fall into the abyss that claims Pearson, Frank Harris, and Chesterton, who were determined to know best in political and aesthetic arguments with Shaw, and were not up to the work. He must not play the rival Irishman to Shaw, a fault that sometimes asserts itself in St. John Ervine's valuable but opinionated biography. But on the contrary he must not suffer the fate of the biographer who falls in love with his subject and excuses his every failing. Indeed, the biographer walks a tightrope.

As a tightrope-walker, Mr. Holroyd is in the Blondin class. Blondin, as some people remember, crossed the Niagara Gorge several times on his rope, often stopping midway to cook an omelette, eat it, and enjoy a glass of champagne; once he crossed the Gorge with a man on his back, and this is the feat Mr. Holroyd has so successfully completed. The man, of course, is Bernard Shaw. And what an Old Man of the Sea!

The problem is that Shaw was so chock-full of "that immense energy of life which we call genius," to quote his own words about Shakespeare. He spread his energy unstintingly over a wide variety of enthusiasms, not all of equal importance, and not all of which have worn well. But his biographer must cope with them all. Rational dress, an improved alphabet, vegetarian diet, all remain much as they were; Shaw lavished countless hours on the Irish Question, the imbecility of war, and particularly the Fabian advancement of socialism, and there has been some progress here; he determined to make the British public look at the theatre in a new way, and although he was not alone in that movement he was the most conspicuous leader. As he grew older he yielded to a craving for strong men in government and ignored the faults and praised what seemed to him the virtues of manifest villains, such as Stalin, Hitler, and Mussolini. He was the most persuasive of polemicists, and in pursuit of a phantom he could ignore the most obvious facts, so that he frequently put weapons in the hands of those who thought him mad, or a traitor.

His life was full of contradictions and ironies. He and his wife, while professing the most advanced socialist opinions, saw nothing absurd in requiring five servants to look after two old people. While Adam delved and Eve span, Bernard Shaw rode in a succession of splendid motor cars, and drove to the public danger. I have myself observed that when they attended a concert he and his wife took four seats, and sat in the middle two, in order not to be troubled by intrusive humanity. A socialist in politics, he was as shrewd and exacting as the most purblind capitalist when he drew up his contracts and exacted his fees.

A man of impeccable nineteenth-century manners in his dealings with strangers, Shaw could be abrasive and seemingly cruel in his relations with his friends, as witness his dreadful jocosity at the funeral of H. G. Wells's wife. His opinions on religion are probably best expressed in *The Adventures of the Black Girl in Her Search for God*, but this did not stop him from seeking eagerly for the friendship and approval – to say nothing of the prayers – of Dame Laurentia McLachlan, Prioress of the Stanbrook Abbey, an "enclosed" Benedictine nun, as rigid in her Catholicism as any of the "Papishers" with whom he had been forbidden to play in his Dublin childhood.

Of course, he had to come to terms, as we all do, with the fact that our most cherished convictions cannot always be made to jibe with the realities of life, and so does Mr. Holroyd. No doubt about it, in the slang of the nineteenth century in which he was born, Shaw was a rum old party.

Nowhere was he more rum than in his dealings with women. He married Charlotte Payne-Townshend, who feared and detested sex, and St. John Ervine believed (though it is not the sort of thing that anyone can now prove) that the marriage was never consummated. But Shaw did not fear or detest sex, and, though a late beginner, he was a very active lover in the days before his marriage. He is reported to have once said that he did not know how a couple who had slept together could face one another at breakfast, but perhaps he did not remain for breakfast.

His most celebrated love affair, with Ellen Terry, was principally an epistolary wooing; he did not meet her until the fire had cooled. His affair with Mrs. Patrick Campbell, after his marriage, appears never to have been a fully sexual involvement, and once again the letters are far more interesting than any amount of pillow-talk. In his seventies, he had a fling with a young American, Molly Tompkins, who sought him out and threw herself at him, but, although he flirted and enjoyed a certain amount of sexual brinkmanship, he appears never to have reciprocated her rather foolish infatuation. Once he had married Charlotte, Charlotte came first and Charlotte knew it, although she felt some understandable jealousy of more beautiful, younger women. He asked Ellen Terry's advice about marrying her, which was not perhaps in conventional good taste; he tormented Mrs. Pat by breaking away from their bedroom dialogues because Charlotte would be expecting him at home; he made Molly Tompkins behave politely and considerately toward Charlotte, which Molly was not naturally inclined to do. And when Charlotte spent her last years in the toils of a deforming and wasting form of arthritis, he was touching and exemplary in his consideration, spending many hours every day attempting to divert and amuse her even when, in his own phrase, "she had survived her wits."

Love, to Shaw was, like virtually everything else, a matter of the mind, and of words. But what did he think the mind was?

We do not know. The names of Freud and Jung appear rarely in Mr. Holroyd's three volumes and not at all in St. John Ervine. Mr. Holroyd says that *Too True to Be Good* is a response to the challenge of Freud's world, but one could read or see the play without an inkling of it. Shaw appears to have ignored one of the most revolutionary movements of his time, that of psychoanalysis, the infiltration of virtually every aspect of modern life by a new way of approaching and valuing the processes of the mind. However misinterpreted, vulgarly misunderstood or shallowly applied, nobody today can escape that influence. But Shaw seems to have done so. Seems, yes; but he was far too discerning a man not to have been aware of this movement, and to have given some thought to its relevance to his own experience and work. He was too confirmed an Ibsenite not to have understood that great precursor of Freud.

We might know a little more about Shaw's ideas on the link between mind and body if Mr. Holroyd had chosen to explore Shaw's involvement with F. M. Alexander, who cured him of his disabling migraines; Alexander and the philosopher Dewey had ideas about education which at one time interested Shaw deeply.

So – we now have Mr. Holroyd's three admirable, extraordinary volumes, making up a great biography. Why do we hasten to read it? What makes Shaw important now, when so many of his ideas have become outworn, so many battles have been won, and so much high-minded bunkum about politics, economics, and sociology has been dispersed into air? We read Shaw eagerly, and we support productions of his plays because he remains the greatest dramatist writing in English since Shakespeare, and a prose stylist able to stand beside Swift and his admired Bunyan. He is certainly among the greatest wits in our language, or in any language, and his criticisms of long-dead musicians and actors are delightful because they make us laugh, and also because they suffuse us with a high-spirited enthusiasm which is always rare and which we seek with an unappeasable hunger. Shaw is great because he was a great artist, and it is as an artist that he endures and will endure. His art was language, in which he clothed the irrepressible, flaming spirit and the reviving wit that captures and strengthens us still. For language is, after all, the most astonishing attribute of mankind, and it takes a Shaw to remind us how grossly it is undervalued.

10

— ❧ —

TANYA MOISEIWITSCH

GEORGE BERNARD SHAW PROVIDES an unlikely link with this next piece since it was he who attracted most – but not quite all – of the attention at the party in 1933 when Davies first set eyes on Tanya Moiseiwitsch. As this piece explains, their paths were to cross many times thereafter.

In 1994 a delightful exhibition of theatrical designs by Tanya Moiseiwitsch toured in Canada and the United States. It was organized by the David and Alfred Smart Museum of Art, at the University of Chicago; The Stratford Shakespearean Festival Foundation of Canada; and the Parnassus Foundation. When the catalogue of the exhibition was being planned, Davies was asked to write An Appreciation for it, and was pleased to pay this tribute to his old friend.

When Davies started his Theatre Notes, he wrote short entries about productions he had seen before 1957, including this short note about the 1949 production of *Henry VIII* which Miss Moiseiwitsch designed: *Henry VIII at Stratford, England a fine*

121

production by Tyrone Guthrie in 1949: A.[nthony] Quayle the Henry and Diana Wynyard, Katherine, Harry Andrews, Wolsey.

Miss Moiseiwitsch went on to create designs for productions at The Stratford Festival for many years and the Theatre Diary entry which follows describes the 1962 production of *Cyrano de Bergerac* by Edmond Rostand, which was adapted and directed by Michael Langham, designed by Tanya Moiseiwitsch and Desmond Heeley, with music by Louis Applebaum. The production of *Macbeth* referred to here is the same one about which the following selection "A Letter From Friar Bacon & Friar Bungay" was written.

July 30, 1962: *Monday:* Cyrano de Bergerac *opens: great expectation in the house beforehand: applause after Lou Applebaum's seventeenth-century arrangement of* The Queen. *Cheers after first act. All this rather overheated enthusiasm I think because many wanted* [Christopher] *Plummer to have a triumph after the* Macbeth *fiasco. And he had it: a standing ovation and five calls, mounting to a storm when he was left alone on the stage. – Handsome production: would not have thought so many variations on brown and grey possible: only colours were Roxane in deep red on the battlefield, and de Guiche in Prussian blue. A bang-up production: Langham at his best with the great crowds. But I found the play less moving than I had hoped: Plummer's style is dry and ironic and he cannot suggest* adoration: *in act one Roxane gave him a white rose which he later gave to the orange-girl! What gallantry is that! Wished he might have some of the quality Martin-Harvey possessed – he treated women like camellias. And in* Roxane's Kiss *the bittersweet was lacking. But in all that was grotesque, humorous, and daring he was admirable.* [John] *Colicos fine as de Guiche: he understands and believes in villainy.* [Douglas] *Rain a fine Ragueneau, a minor Cyrano. Toby Robins never suggested distinguished intellect as Roxane and was a bit Forest Hill, though very pretty, as always. Miranda* [Davies] *a pré-cieuse and a nun and did well what she had to do. But the play –! They adored this bauble as they have never adored Shakespeare.*

Cynics are wrong to say that when wishes are granted they invariably prove disappointing: I was nineteen when first I saw Tanya Moiseiwitsch and longed to talk to her, and I was thirty-nine when at last I did so. It was anything but a disappointment and has indeed been a delight ever since.

The first encounter was in Malvern in England, at the summer festival of unusual and new plays that was offered in 1932 by the late Sir Barry Jackson. I was there because my parents wished to indulge my love of the theatre, and I was being edified by one of Sir Barry's chronologically designed seasons; not only great classics, like Jonson's *The Alchemist*, but rarities like *Ralph Roister-Doister* and Southerne's *Oroonoko* were deployed before my astonished eyes. But one did not spend all day in the theatre; as well as more strenuous pleasures, one walked in the beautiful public gardens, and it was there that I saw the fascinating girl who I later learned was Tanya Moiseiwitsch.

Of course I wanted to make her acquaintance, but that was out of the question. One saw all sorts of notable people in the gardens, taking the air. Many of them were the stars of the theatre, like Ralph Richardson (Oroonoko and Face in the Jonson), Ernest Thesiger (Ralph Roister-Doister and Dazzle in *London Assurance*), and Cedric Hardwicke (brilliant as Abel Drugger in *The Alchemist*). But the cynosure of all eyes was the group that surrounded Bernard Shaw and his wife: Barry Jackson, John Drinkwater, the poet and playwright, his wife, Daisy Kennedy, the Australian violinist, and, standing modestly a pace or two behind these great ones, the amazing girl.

Amazing because of the fixity and solemnity of her expression, as if she were listening to something beyond the fireworks of Mr. Shaw, who seemed to do all the talking. Amazing also because of the beauty of her eyes which were large and dark and looked like the eyes one sees in Russian ikons. A girl obviously far and away above the girls I knew, who were pleasant enough but who giggled and chattered and never seemed to see or hear anything very interesting. There was no question of approaching her.

So I stared, and wished, and at last met Tanya when she came to Canada in 1953, to supervise the building of the thrust stage which she had designed as the permanent background for Stratford productions.

She was the daughter of her mother's first husband, Benno Moiseiwitsch, the pianist, and with the passing of years that seems to me to be of increasing importance, for he was a great artist and a wit, and so is Tanya. Benno Moiseiwitsch was, until his death in 1963, one of the greatest pianists of his day, and of a distinguished musical line, for he was a pupil of the mighty Leschetitzsky, maker of many artists of the first rank and himself a pupil of Czerny, whose teacher had been Beethoven. Benno – if I may be excused that familiarity in writing of a man with a long name – was distinguished for his soaring approach to music, governed by elegance of taste and a superb technique. He was, critics agreed, primarily a lyric player of great fluency and subtlety, extraordinary in the romantic repertoire from Chopin to Rachmaninoff (who declared him to be his artistic heir) and of an impeccable musicality. A romantic firmly grounded in the classics, as is his daughter.

She tells of an occasion in her childhood when she played the piano for her father. He gave her a big hug, followed by, "But that's not for your playing, darling." Her art was to lie in another direction. But her wit may well be like her father's which was, as his friend James Agate says, cat-like – not unkind, not wounding, but playful and ambiguously caressing. Agate tells of an occasion at the Savage Club, of which he and Moiseiwitsch were *habitués*, when Agate said, "Mark is playing in Edinburgh tonight." Mark was Mark Hambourg, another Club member and a bridge companion of both men. "If someone would open a window," said Benno, "perhaps we could hear him." Indeed, Hambourg was a pianist whose playing could make embarrassing descents from heaven-storming greatness to mere rowdiness, and he had a fine disregard for wrong notes. His presence accorded with his artistry; Tanya has a childhood memory of a time when she was brought from her bed to meet Mark; she stood at the top of the stair gazing down on the corpulent man, wild of hair and thick of spectacles, who looked like Beethoven seen in a distorting mirror. "What is it?" she cried in fright, and rushed back to the nursery. This was her childhood background, a world of musicians, poets, theatre folk, but none of them, so far as I know, painters.

It was her stepfather, John Drinkwater, who urged her in the direction of the theatre. He was a poet and a playwright whose influence on the speaking of Shakespearean verse was manifest for many years in the outdoor productions in Regent's Park in London. As a schoolboy I listened many times to the lecture "On the Speaking of Verse" which he had recorded for the guidance of just such hearers as I. His taste was impeccable, but never precious, his feeling for rhythm as refined as that of any musician, and his pronunciation seeming to go back through Forbes-Robertson to the beginning of the nineteenth century, before the coming of that accent, now almost past, which was called "English" but was really the speech of a rather small group. It was he who introduced Tanya to the practical work of backstage and the scene-dock where she learned those realities of her craft, which underlie all her splendid inventions.

She would not call herself a painter. She denies that she can draw. But she is contradicted by the romantic grace of her line and a sense of colour that has not been approached by any other designer. These things did not come at once, but after long apprenticeship at the Abbey Theatre in Dublin, at the Oxford Playhouse, the Old Vic, and the Memorial Theatre at Stratford-upon-Avon. It is stupid to speak of an artist's name "being made" by a single work, but her designs for *Henry VIII* at Stratford in 1949 attracted very serious attention. Her work became associated with that of the great director Tyrone Guthrie. It was as though his own strong, but not sophisticated, visual sense found its outlet in greatly enlarged form in the designs that Tanya Moiseiwitsch made for many of his finest productions. Nor was she simply a canvas and paint designer; the permanent setting at Stratford in Ontario tells all that needs to be told of her fine architectural sense, and it will stand for long in the history of the theatre as a new concept, rooted, as always, in a deep understanding of the past and a feeling for materials.

Materials, and craftsmanship. She once came upon my eldest daughter giving a hand in sewing costumes for a Stratford production (the students were expected to help where they could) and she observed that Miranda was "felting" a seam. "It's been a long time since I've seen anyone do that," she said, in a tone that, to a student, was an accolade. She has worked in poor theatres, where it was necessary to look at both sides of a penny, so she knows the value of economy, but never economy that meant bad work or second-best. When she came to Stratford in Canada she astonished the management by saying firmly that she liked to work with genuine materials – real leather, real silks and wools, palpable things which, as she put it, "once had lived." What this means is apparent in any play that she designs and dresses; they have a reality, a depth, which is directly opposite to the common meaning of "theatrical."

Not, of course, that she is lacking in theatrical expertise. There is not a trick of the trade she does not know. Perhaps her only non-theatrical venture in establishing an atmosphere is her decoration of the chapel in Massey College in the University of Toronto. The architect had created large panels in the walls that were composed of rounded pebbles stuck in plaster, and painted a dark red which proved, when completed, to be too aggressive a colour. What was to be done? Paint them with buttermilk, said Tanya, and it was done, producing just the right effect, and in the course of time the smell, which would not have caused much comment in a scene-painter's *atelier*, wore off.

The exhibition which you are about to see gives much, but cannot give all, of the quality of her work, because it is immobile and her costumes are all meant to be seen in movement and in changing effects of colour as they encounter one another on the stage. But if you will look imaginatively, much of what makes all of the plays that Tanya Moiseiwitsch has designed as truly dramatic as the acting, is that her work is never obtrusive but seamlessly integrated with that of all the other theatre artists. These are the robes of Thespis, freshly imagined for every play, by the inheritor of a great tradition of strength governed by impeccable taste.

11

—— ∽ ——

A LETTER FROM FRIAR BACON &
FRIAR BUNGAY

ROBERTSON DAVIES LOVED A JOKE and was known to indulge in
some elaborate pranks. When he noticed that the scene in
Macbeth involving the three witches and their unappetizing cauldron had been omitted, he sensed an opportunity:

I wrote this letter to Tanya in 1962 when Macbeth *was first presented at Stratford, directed by Peter Coe – and a sorry mess it was!
I thought this spoof would cheer her and also the company, which
it did as she posted it on the notice board in the Green Room.*

*I tried a similar spoof on Tony Guthrie in 1955, when I wrote
to him in the character of an historian, deeply learned in Scythian
lore, offering to direct the make-up of Tamberlaine's warriors
with special attention to ornamental painting which threw the
male nipple into angry prominence. Tony was bewildered by it,
and it was Tony Quayle – who played Tamberlaine – who smoked
it as a hoax.*

—— ∽ ——

FRIAR BACON & FRIAR BUNGAY
Necromantic Suppliers and Supernatural Warehousemen
(Founded 1594)

Miss Tanya Moiseiwitsch,
Festival Theatre,
Stratford, Ont. Canada

Dear Miss Moiseiwitsch:

It has been brought to our attention that in the current production of *Macbeth* at Stratford, the first sixty-eight lines of Act Four, Scene One have been omitted, doubtless because of the difficulty of securing the properties necessary to its apt performance. As a very old-established firm, who had the honour of victualling this extremely effective scene for Mr. Shakespeare himself in 1606, may we quote you the following attractive bundle, which we can supply on receipt of a cable, our telegraphic address being Paddockanon.

"Toad, that under cold stone
Days and nights has thirty-one
Sweltered venom sleeping got . . ."
    Immediately available in unlimited quantity from our own gardens. True *Bufo vulgaris* as supplied to Mr. Shakespeare. $3 per doz.

"Fillet of a fenny snake"
    Blindworm, from the Norfolk Broads, $3 per doz., filleted and shipped in ice. We recommend, however, fillet of adder, as each order includes the "fork," thereby effecting a pleasing economy. Fillet of adder, $8 per doz. shipped in ice.

"Eye of newt and toe of frog"
    Pleasing minor items, shipped dry; soak for two hours before curtain time. Our MERLIN'S MIXTURE $2.50 per lb.

"Wool of bat"
Per generous hank, unwashed, $6. Washed, $12.

"Tongue of dog"
Recent difficulties with the R.S.P.C.A. make this formerly reasonable item somewhat expensive. Mongrel: $1 per tongue. Pedigreed: $5. Shown at Crufft's: $8.

"Adder's fork"
See above. Separately $6 per doz. dried. Exercise care in handling.

"Blindworm's sting"
A very attractive dried bunch, comprising approximately fifty stings, $5.

"Lizard's leg"
Our South American special. Large: $1. Small: 25 cents.

"Howlet's wing"
Genuine English howlet, warranted from churchyard or belfry, "not a wing is sold till it is five years old." $12 per wing.

"Scale of dragon"
From Continental China, *guaranteed*, $18.50 per scale. From Formosa, no guarantee, $5 per scale.

"Tooth of wolf"
Best Canadian timberwolf, $9 per tooth.

"Witch's mummy"
Increasingly difficult to obtain, and we must limit orders to one pound per customer per month. Best quality, from the Carpathians, $250 per pound. SPECIAL – While she lasts! – Dracula's Aunt Sybilla! A steal at $750 per pound, packed in her

own skin! Many personal hairs in each package! A MUST for the large operator!

". . . maw and gulf
Of the ravined salt-sea shark"
    Fresh daily from Newfoundland. $35 per set.

"Root of hemlock digged i' the dark"
    Per root, $4. In powdered form, $3.50.

"Gall of goat"
    From Wales, packed in "slips of yew." Open with care as the fumes
    have been known to overcome experienced Stage Managers. Per
    gall, $28.

"Finger of birth-strangled babe
Ditch-delivered by a drab."
    From a Salvation Army home for Repentant Magdalens.
    Guaranteed ditch-delivered, as the Chief Obstetrician is Dr.
    Duncan Ditch, M.D., FRCP, per dozen, $4.

"Add thereto a tiger's chaudron . . ."
    An item rarer than it was in the great days of the Empire, but
    still available. Royal Bengal Chaudrons, $80 each. A cheaper class
    of chaudron, from zoos and circuses, at $50 each. Delivered in
    ice, C.O.D.

"Cool it in a baboon's blood"
    True baboon, per carafe (approx. 1 litre) of superior bouquet and
    body, $15. Canadian native baboon, bottled by a Canadian Winery
    (screw-top returnable bottle) $3.

We undertake contract work, supplying your Stage Management
nightly for the duration of your run, at an inclusive price of $38.50
each night. We have many letters on file attesting to the effectiveness

of this service, and extraordinary manifestations are by no means uncommon in theatres where it is used.

Awaiting the favour of your esteemed order, madam,

for: Bacon and Bungay

12

— ⁌ —

STRATFORD FORTY YEARS AGO

IN NOVEMBER, 1991, Davies was asked to write an article for the Stratford Festival Souvenir Program of the following season, the Festival's fortieth. The anniversary was a great cause for celebration and Davies was just the person to write the piece, having been involved with the Festival for many years as a Member of the Board of Governors, a lecturer, and an always enthusiastic playgoer.

After the first year of the Festival in 1953, Robertson Davies and Sir Tyrone Guthrie wrote, and Grant Macdonald illustrated, *Renown at Stratford*, which was encouraged and published by W. H. Clarke of Clarke Irwin & Co. of Toronto. Davies had not yet begun keeping his Theatre Diary but in the book he wrote of the original 1953 production of *Richard III*:

On the first night, and at more than one subsequent performance, the audience rose to its feet and cheered when Alec Guinness appeared to acknowledge their applause at the end of the play. Had we seen a great Richard? Or was this a tribute to a player who had cast in his lot with an unproven venture, as a gesture of encouragement to the theatre in a new country?

There can never be any final judgement on this matter. Both emotions – gratitude for a fine performance, and gratitude for a fine gesture – were mingled in this applause, and there is no means of sorting them out. But it may be said that this production of Richard III had a noble sweep and produced upon the audiences that completeness of effect which is possible only when the theatre has worked its truest magic; the crown of this production was Alec Guinness's performance as Richard. Experienced lovers of the theatre, and playgoers to whom Shakespeare came quite new, united to applaud him, and therefore we may say that his performance rose far above any accumulation of critical points. It was a fully rounded artistic creation, and auditors of every condition yielded to its enchantment. Let those who reserve the adjective "great" for performances which take place in capital cities describe this one by what term they please – we know what we saw and felt at Stratford.

After another production of *Richard III*, Davies wrote in his diary, Wednesday, July 13, 1988: *Thirty-fifth anniversary of the opening of the Stratford Festival. "Survivors" are invited and Brenda and I go. Some of the survivors are that indeed. There are even pseudo-survivors, including one who reproaches me because he was not mentioned in* Renown at Stratford: *mad, perhaps? The play is of course* Richard III *and of the four Richards we have seen here – Alec Guinness, Alan Bates, Brian Bedford – Colm Feore is the dismal forty-fourth. No sense of aristocracy or even of command – simply an Italian bandit. One recalls Guinness's fine, reserved dignity, and the sense of class that pervaded Tony's [Guthrie] production [Stratford, 1953]. As Gielgud said, directing* Richard II *at Oxford: "Never forget, these are tremendous swells!" Feore did the deformity by adopting a paraplegic walk – knees together and legs straddling outward like a trivet. Astonishing to begin but a bore as the play progressed for it was grotesque rather than menacing and made the fight an absurdity as one good push would have put him on the ground. The production dull and slow*

and one heard – the words were clear – but no meaning came with
them, for the actors too plainly did not care. Amateur faults:
snowy hands on murderers and churls: the usual ecclesiastical
boners – a bishop carrying his own cross! The children boisterous
and bad. A dull evening and symptomatic of what is wrong with
the Festival: needs shaking up from top to bottom. Alf Bell died
July 12 and his name is affectionately heard everywhere.

———— ∽ ————

Stratford fifty years ago is easily
described; what does the infallible Karl Baedeker have to say in his
Handbook for Travellers in Canada? . . . "a divisional point and important railway centre . . . an agricultural and industrial city . . . prettily
situated on the Avon . . . its schools include a Collegiate Institute
and a Provincial Normal School." But in 1953 Stratford underwent
a transformation which nobody had foreseen, not even Tom Patterson,
who brought it about.

Stratford forty years ago suddenly became a theatre town, and saw
the beginnings of what is now generally admitted to be the foremost
centre of classical theatre in North America. Nobody forty years ago
thought that would happen or had a clear idea of what it might mean.
I well recall my own early visits to Stratford, for I was one of the few
non-Stratfordians to be a member of its earliest Board of Governors.
Why I was so honoured I cannot truly say, except that I was a friend
of Tyrone Guthrie's, who knew that I liked long chances and would
do anything to give the theatre in Canada a lift. My personal expectations for the infant Festival were high, because I had great faith in
Guthrie, whose organizing ability and theatrical wizardry I knew
well, but as I sat at those early Board meetings, I knew that I was an
outsider and carried little of the real responsibility for what was happening; the Stratford citizens who sat there with me were undertak-
ing a venture which could cost them dear in reputation and good
hard cash. They hadn't much notion of what a theatre festival might
be, but they knew that their town was no longer an important railway

centre and something must be done if it were not to lose significance. They were prepared to take a very long chance – for chances don't come longer anywhere than in the theatre. So they listened with caution to Tom Patterson, and very soon they were listening in astonishment to Tyrone Guthrie.

His impact on Stratford was immediate and extraordinary; the town had never seen anything like him before. He was not like anybody's idea of a great theatrical director. With his height, air of command, and informal dress he was often described as looking like a policeman off duty. And indeed there was something of the policeman about him – his gimlet eye, which awoke a sense of guilt in the sluggard; his remarkable physical strength, which showed itself in immense endurance and an ability to absorb malt liquor without visible consequence; his sometimes rough and peremptory dismissal of arguments he did not choose to consider. This was his Scottish side. But he had an Irish side, which showed itself in a light-hearted approach to difficulties that looked insurmountable, a brilliant wit, and very often in a sort of inspired silliness, which confused people who had, a moment before, heard him uttering what sounded like the thunderings of Jove. Not an easy man for the sober citizens of an Ontario community to understand.

He was, however, irresistible, or almost so, for there were Stratfordians who resisted him and did so until they had reluctantly to admit the success of what he had done for the town. But everybody associated with the Festival venture was hypnotized by him. To be with him was to breathe a finer air, to be swept into a world where life was strenuous but entrancing.

So, the Festival came into being with Tony as its inspiring spirit. And how lucky that was for Stratford, because he was, in all things that related to the theatre, a man of unimpeachable probity, and he recommended nothing, insisted on nothing, that he was not prepared to support with every ounce of his remarkable energy.

Suddenly, there was the Festival, and that story has been told many times and need not be repeated here. Tony's enthusiasm spread through the town and the town responded in ways that were both characteristic and admirable. Actors had to be housed; people found houses and overcame the fears of those who thought actors must be fly-by-nights and fallen women. Visitors had to be housed, and people were found who threw open their homes, charging minimal prices for excellent beds, and breakfasts of astounding variety and quantity. Churches undertook to provide hot meals for the playgoers who could not squeeze into the town's few hotels and cafés. The Festival was a town festival and everybody with an ounce of daring wanted to get in on the action. It was thus that the town made the Festival its own, and not an exotic visitor.

As a dweller in Eastern Ontario I watched this development with astonishment, for, though Eastern Ontario has virtues of its own, enthusiasm and bounteous hospitality are not among them. Was it a matter of heritage? The people of Western Ontario tend to be descendants of English settlers, from the gentler parts of the Old Land, and from Germany. The Scots and Irish of Eastern Ontario are a different breed.

Not everything went smoothly, of course. The press was not pleased that Guthrie would not admit its representatives to rehearsals. What could he be hiding? He was, of course, protecting artistic creation on a high level, which is something the press has never been quick to understand. But when the uttermost is being demanded of Canadian actors who have never been so stretched before, it is not fair to invite reporters to watch them. Nor, if reporters had been present, could Guthrie have spoken in the combination of extravagant rhetoric and quarter-deck profanity which was his rehearsal mode.

The actors were a puzzle to some Stratfordians. "What do you do in the daytime?" was a question often heard, from people who had never known what hard work make-believe can be.

There was turbulence. The local newspaper did not, at first, favour the Festival, and it had its following. *Maclean's* magazine, a national publication, carried an article which was somewhat jocose and patronizing about Stratford's presumption in attempting a Festival of the first rank, as big-city papers tend to be when writing about smaller places. The writer went so far as to say that Alec Guinness who was, with Irene Worth, at the head of the acting company, was cold and standoffish and kept the local people at a distance. This was trivial and untrue, but for some reason Guinness was deeply offended and wanted to sue the magazine for libel. He was not to be deflected from this determination, and because I knew something about the press, I was deputed by the Board to reason with him. It was not easy, but when I pointed out that such a suit would be a long time coming before the court, and would simply give further circulation to an inept article, he withdrew, without being wholly appeased.

The public could not peep at rehearsals, but it could, and did, take the keenest interest in the digging of the hole, and the pouring of the cement, for the amphitheatre. Most of all, it loved the huge tent. The master of the tent was Skip Manley, a circus man, gaudy in dress and richly be-ringed; he worked with his crew for sixty hours without a break to raise the poles, the guy-wires, and the canvas. It was such a tent as sultans dream of, for inside the heavy canvas shell it was hung with cloth of royal blue, establishing an atmosphere of opulence and distinction which Canadians do not associate with tents. Manley slept in the tent, and managed it through winds and storms like the captain of a great galleon, for there was unceasing and unrelenting need to ease it here, tighten it there, and adjust the stress on the four huge cedar poles that bore the greatest strain.

All this was to be seen, and Stratford saw it. What could not be seen, but which hung like a storm cloud over the Board, was the terrible financial responsibility, for demands were daily – hourly – and there was never enough money. But great acts of faith were called forth, courage was demanded and shown, the people who had decided to back the venture bent – sometimes distressingly – but they did not break. This was municipal heroism, a virtue we seldom hear celebrated.

At last came July 13 – not a date of happy omen – and the opening performance. A few minutes before *Richard III* began, my wife and I were standing with Tony and Judy Guthrie between the canvas and the blue inner tent, far down on the right side of the amphitheatre. It was the only time we had seen them a prey to nerves. They were deeply apprehensive, for they knew how much hung on what

happened in the next three hours. They were not fearful for themselves, but for the troops of friends they had made in Stratford. Could
this absurd adventure succeed?

If it had not done so, you would not be reading this recollection
now.

13

---- ∽ ----

INTRODUCTION TO AN ANTHOLOGY OF CANADIAN PLAYS

THE MAN WHO WAS TO BECOME known as a world-famous novelist was an accomplished playwright, and was always a great supporter and encourager of Canadian theatre. When Richard Perkyns asked him to write the foreword to the book of plays he had selected and edited called *Major Plays of the Canadian Theatre, 1934–1984*, Davies was delighted to oblige. It was written on April 19, 1984, and the book was published later the same year. The selection includes Davies' play *At My Heart's Core* and plays of eleven other Canadian playwrights. One of these was James Reaney with his play *The Canadian Brothers*. As so often happens in Canadian theatre, Davies and Reaney were involved in another project some years later, when *Alice Through the Looking Glass* was staged at the Stratford Festival, with James Reaney adapting the book for the stage and, as we have seen, Robertson Davies lecturing on the book and its author at the Celebrated Writers Series. Having read Reaney's play he also wrote an article about Rev. Charles Lutwidge Dodgson, for the

Souvenir Program of 1994. There he said of Dodgson: *The theatre was one of the great enthusiasms of his life and he delighted in stage versions of his Alice books. The highest praise that could be accorded to Stratford's version is that it would have pleased his spirit.*

——— ⌀ ———

Byron recorded that he awoke one morning and found himself famous. One presumes that it was an enjoyable discovery. What would have been his feelings, I wonder, if he had wakened to learn that he was historical?

Of the twelve playwrights represented in this anthology all save one are still living, but there are some of us who belong to a primitive era of Canadian drama. We wrote plays when there was no strong likelihood that they would ever be performed, and we knew that if we were so lucky as to achieve performance it would be possible to describe the performance as professional only by considerable generous extension of the meaning of that word. In our lifetimes our work has taken on the patina of history, if one does not wish to be disagreeable and say that it has become old-fashioned.

Perhaps I would be wise to speak only for myself. It never occurred to me when I began writing plays that I was contributing to the growth of a Canadian drama; my self-esteem did not extend so far. I simply thought that I was doing what I wanted to do, in the hope that some people, somewhere, would like it well enough to give it a trial on a stage. I was one of the lucky ones, for several of my plays did achieve production, and I am grateful to those who took a chance on my work. I must also say that the productions my plays received were not of the standard that the younger dramatists represented in this book may expect, and to which new work of merit is entitled, if it is to reach the public in the guise the author intended for it.

To begin with, theatres were few and most groups that were interested in new plays were handicapped in their playhouses and their finances. Audiences were not warm toward Canadian plays. What they wanted from the theatre, understandably, was popular entertainment, a good night out, and they had only limited confidence that a Canadian writer and Canadian actors could provide it. There were hopeful souls who found their way to improvised theatres to see new plays by fellow countrymen done on inadequate stages; there were a few critics who were as encouraging as they felt they could decently be. But a common attitude was that expressed by a man whom I overheard going into a performance of my play *At My Heart's Core* at the London Little Theatre: "I suppose this is another of these damned Canadian plays that we have to encourage." But people have to see a lot of damned plays before a country has a body of good plays of its own.

Sometimes the experience of the playwright was humiliating. I have spoken elsewhere of attending a performance by a Little Theatre group of my play *Fortune, My Foe* in which I beheld with astonishment a character on stage which had certainly not been put there by me. When I spoke about this later to the director he said, cheerily: "Oh, your character was a newspaperman, and I didn't think he was illiterate enough to be a newspaperman, so I rewrote it entirely." As I was a newspaperman at that time I was rather cast down, until I was told that the same director had rewritten the whole third act of a play by J. M. Barrie (who was still living, and one hopes, learning) because he did not like the way Barrie had ended it. This sort of rewriting was not uncommon. I have had a play of mine rewritten by the director as far away as Australia.

These inventive directors, however, never shared their talent with the playwright, and that was one of the problems of Canadian playwrights in the forties and fifties. In the modern theatre, which is so much more complex than the theatre of an earlier day, a playwright has the chance of working with his director and his actors, and unless he is totally convinced of the rightness of what he has done he is wise to listen to them. The theatre is now a co-operative art, and the writer who is not wise enough and humble enough to listen to his fellow artists would do better to write in some other form. They are not always right, but sometimes they are, and their contributions demand serious consideration.

The development of the Stratford Festival, which has been abused for its mild interest in native plays, has, nevertheless, done more than any other single factor to make Canadian theatre truly professional in its attitudes. When I was writing plays the Dominion Drama Festival offered the only place in which a Canadian play could expect criticism from somebody who was occasionally a first-rate man of the theatre, as opposed to a critic who knew what he wanted, but could not be expected to know how that result was to be achieved. From DDF adjudicators I sometimes received high praise and encouragement, and sometimes such scorn as was hard to endure. To have one's play condemned as rubbish within fifteen minutes of its performance and before the same audience which had seen it and often applauded it, was the equivalent of being pelted with rotten eggs. Good for the soul, perhaps, but was it good for one's future work?

That is behind us, fortunately. The modern Canadian playwright is taken seriously, is given the co-operation of theatre artists, and is criticized pretty much as if he were a part of the English-speaking or French-speaking theatre, and not an overexcited child demanding attention. And things will be better.

They will be better, however, only if the playwrights remember that large audiences are gained only by plays that give real theatre delight as tragedies or comedies to people who are looking for a good night out. That does not mean that such audiences want trashy farce or sentimentality; they want to be purged with pity and terror, and they want to be made to laugh without being ashamed of themselves for laughing. What they want, indeed, is real theatre and not a coterie theatre offered as propaganda for some fashionable mode of thought, and accepted with the implicit proviso that the play is not meant for the public at large.

None of the plays in this anthology is coterie theatre. They are the real thing, so far as it lay in our twelvefold power to give it. Though what you hold in your hand is a textbook, it is not essentially so; as Laurence Olivier has said, the theatre is a matter of the heart, and what is best in these plays comes from the heart. I am honoured to have been asked to introduce them to you. If some young readers do not find them all to their liking, let me remind them that the history of the theatre in Canada has moved with extraordinary swiftness, and that some of these plays are already historical. But what comes from the heart is not diminished by time.

14

—— ❧ ——

INTRODUCTION TO AT MY HEART'S CORE AND OVERLAID

IN 1990 THE PUBLISHERS Simon & Pierre of Toronto decided to begin a project of republishing Robertson Davies' early plays. The first volume included *Overlaid* and *At My Heart's Core*, and the author's introduction gives us greater insight into the plays.

At My Heart's Core was written in early 1950, when Michael Sadlier, the Manager of the Summer Theatre, asked Davies to write a play to mark the Peterborough Centennial. He decided to write about three of the area's exceptional pioneers: the botanist Catharine Parr Traill, author of *The Backwoods of Canada: Being Letters from the Wife of an Emigrant Officer, Illustrative of the Domestic Economy of British America* (1836); her sister, author Susanna Moodie, author of *Roughing It in the Bush; or, Life in Canada* (1852); and the letter-writer Frances Stewart. The play opened first in Niagara Falls on August 22, followed by the official première in Peterborough on August 28, 1950. Mrs. Stewart was played by Brenda Davies, a role her husband wrote for her; Mrs. Traill by Kate Reid, and Mrs. Moodie by Clarine Jackman. The

play takes place at Auburn, the home of the Stewarts in Douro
settlement, on a December day in 1837.

At My Heart's Core spoke positively to contemporary Canadians. Culturally impoverished Canada might be, but the challenge of staying to make things better was, in Davies' view, worth
accepting. The play was very well received and by 1952 it had been
performed more than fifty times. It was televised in 1953 and was
performed across Canada into the 1960s.

———— ∽ ————

The two plays offered in this book
have been performed many times in Canada, and I have seen several
of these productions. The ones I liked best were those which recognized that Overlaid and At My Heart's Core are in no way realistic, but
are theatrical in their nature and are best when performed with full
theatricality.

What do I mean? Many theatre people are committed to what they
call realism, and their aim is to persuade the audience that it is looking
at something that might occur in precisely the same way in daily life.
Plays presented in this manner often have long passages in which real
objects are employed to further the illusion of reality. Taken to its
highest pitch this sort of theatre finds its pinnacle in a production by
David Belasco (1859–1931) who astonished New York audiences in
1912 by representing an exact replica of a Child's Restaurant on stage,
complete with real food! But the outward trappings of life are not the
innermost secrets of life, and these are, in my opinion, best presented
in a heightened form of theatre in which the dialogue, acting, and
setting are somewhat larger than life. Thus poetry of speech, histri-
onic accomplishment, and fine designs can combine to speak to the
audience of the deepest truths of life as it is in its most intense
moments. This is painting, as opposed to photography.

Consider the short play Overlaid. To present it realistically misses
its point entirely, for it is a protest about what people of imprisoned
mind think of as "real." To Ethel reality is the outward appearance of

respectability, to be careful never to give the neighbours anything to criticize, to aim toward the day when the whole family will be under total control, incapable of any wrong or absurd action, under a tombstone of uncompromising solidity and obvious expense. Contrasted with her is Pop, who yearns for a larger life than his farm has ever brought him, and who catches a whiff of it in the Saturday afternoon broadcasts from the Metropolitan Opera in New York. These two embody the opposed attitudes that Bernard Berenson called "life-diminishing" and "life-enhancing." If I had wanted to be fancy, I might have written a play in verse which was an argument between Eros, the spirit of life and love, and Thanatos, the spirit of Death. But that would not have been as much fun as setting the argument in a Canadian farmhouse kitchen, and embodying Life and Death in an eccentric old man who is determined to get everything out of his life that it can be made to yield, and his daughter, who is his superior in education, but not as brave a spirit, whose strongest desire is for the safety and respectability of the graveyard.

The best production of *Overlaid* that I have seen showed the farmhouse kitchen, tiny and very much distorted, against a wide panorama of the Canadian winter landscape, bleak and uncompromising. That was certainly not realism, but it was a thrilling aspect of theatricality, and it did much to assist the actors.

Nobody in real life speaks like Pop; he is a vaudeville farmer. But for that reason he is all farmers everywhere. And Ethel is like all life-haters everywhere. The play must be read as an abstraction from life and not as an attempt to depict life realistically. It is meant to make you laugh, but it will not be a foolish laugh.

This applies also to *At My Heart's Core*, a more elaborate treatment of the same theme, which is the cost in pain and bitterness of intellectual starvation.

Very often, when we are offered our pioneer ancestors by playwrights or novelists, we are shown very humble people who have left Europe because of painful necessity, and whose enemies are want and starvation. There were others, and their troubles were different. They were educated people, usually with some money of their own, who came to Canada in search of adventure in a new land, or else in the hope of rising above whatever the old land seemed to offer them. The Stewarts are of the first group; Irish people of distinguished family and education, they want the excitement of a new life. That is to say, Thomas Stewart did so, but he did not give much consideration to his wife; indeed, he forbade her to bring her piano to Canada because he said that she might play Irish songs on it, and feel homesick. If he thought homesickness needed a piano to evoke it, he must have been a very simple man. The Moodies and the Traills came because they had little money and Canada seemed to offer chances that were more encouraging to two retired army officers than life in England. This was an illusion, for Moodie and Traill were not men of much ability, and the height of their ambition was a safe government job, as the play makes clear.

It was the women who suffered. If there was any adventure, it was probably the men who enjoyed it. The women had to work as they had never worked before, and if their minds were not to rust and all the accomplishments that entitled them to think of themselves as ladies were not to wither away, they had to struggle, and often their pain must have been grievous. This is the theme of the play. At the heart's core there lingers the image of the dear native land and the position that they had held in it. Mrs. Moodie and Mrs. Traill could not forget Reydon Hall, where they were raised, nor could Mrs. Stewart forget that she had once been a belle of the vice-regal court in Dublin, with distinguished suitors. If they had not chosen the husbands they did, might Mrs. Moodie and Mrs. Traill have found distinction in the literary and scientific worlds of London? Might Mrs. Stewart have been Lady Rossmore, with a husband who would not have denied her the piano or the luxuries of a refined life? This is what lies in the heart's core: the yearning for What Might Have Been.

These are not trivial discontents. They have to be faced and conquered if they are not to destroy the life that has been chosen.

The ladies are tempted, by the insidious Mr. Cantwell, who may perhaps be the Devil, for, as Hamlet assures us, the Devil may assume a pleasing shape. Indeed, the ladies are seduced. That word is often used as if it meant sexually possessed, and nothing more, but there are worse kinds of seduction than that. Cantwell does not tempt them into a brief infidelity to their marriage vows; he tempts them to be discontented with the choice they have made and the life it has brought them, and such a temptation could ruin their lives, poison their marriages, and turn them into bitter, wretched people forever. This is a terrible temptation, and Mrs. Moodie and Mrs. Traill do not fully escape it. Only Mrs. Stewart escapes, because of her real and deep love for her husband, who is a good man if not a particularly brilliant one.

Contrasted with the ladies and their husbands and their seducer are the Irish characters. Because this is an avowedly theatrical play they are funny and highly coloured, but they are not simple hooligans. Honour is of the stuff from which new countries are made; she is courageous, strong, and undefeatable. Phelim is quite another thing. As he makes clear to Mrs. Moodie, he is descended from the great Irish line of bards and storytellers; his heritage is mythical and indestructible. Compared with the popular stories she writes for magazines, his heritage is glorious and hers is simply commercial and popular. Like many true artists he is a disreputable creature, but there are depths of nobility in him which shame Mrs. Moodie's genteel pretensions. Like Pop in *Overlaid*, Phelim is too big for the life in which he finds himself, and like Pop any escape he finds must be in tall talk and dreams.

All the talk in *At My Heart's Core* is tall talk, and it is the tall talk of 1837 when the accounts we have of conversations among Byron's friends, or the speeches politicians made to the public, tell us of a world where talk was of a copiousness and literary distinction that our age of radio and TV has wholly lost. Nowadays such talk is in the highest degree unrealistic, and good performances of the play have convinced me that I was right to make it what it is, for it convinces the hearer that these are truly people of 1837, and gives pleasure by its apparent artificiality and extravagance. A play is, after all, a work of art, or should be one, and artificiality and extravagance are accompaniments of art in many of its most pleasing forms.

Sometimes critics have rebuked me for making the theme of Canada's intellectual poverty the theme of several of my plays. But if I may speak in my own defence, critics normally live in big cities and mix with sophisticated people, whereas I have lived in places that were small and culturally undernourished, and I know what that does to the people who live in such circumstances and have nothing upon which to hone the mind. The things of the spirit are fully as necessary as the things of the flesh, and where they do not exist a serious disease appears which I have called Cultural Rickets. And of course it must be remembered that these plays were written many years ago, and that things in Canada are changing, and intellectual isolation is not as severe as once it was. But I will not be moved from my conviction that what I have shown in my plays are certain aspects of truth, and the task of the playgoer, and the reader, is to find the truth wrapped in the theatricality.

15

---- ❧ ----

INTRODUCTION TO FORTUNE, MY FOE AND EROS AT BREAKFAST

IN 1993 SIMON & PIERRE of Toronto republished two more of Robertson Davies' plays, *Fortune, My Foe* and *Eros at Breakfast*. In this Introduction he explains the circumstances of writing the plays and what they are about. *Fortune, My Foe* is notable for a frequently quoted speech in which Nicholas Hayward tells Szabo:

> If you stay in Canada, I can, too. Everybody says Canada is a hard country to govern, but nobody mentions that for some people it is also a hard country to live in. Still, if we all run away it will never be any better. So let the geniuses of easy virtue go southward; I know what they feel too well to blame them. But for some of us there is no choice; let Canada do what she will with us, we must stay.

Even though this was written in 1949, it still speaks to Canadians today.

Davies' last experience of being involved in a theatrical production that related to his own work was when Elliott Hayes adapted his book *World of Wonders* for the stage. It was produced at the Stratford Festival in 1992. This entry from his Theatre Diary describes the first night of the play:

June 3: *To Stratford on Tuesday in the evening, the first night of* World of Wonders – *Packed house and very receptive. (Our party were Jenny and Tom, Christopher, Piers, Cecilia and Virginia.) All the cast at concert-pitch. Pennell in total control, Atienza as Tresize brought back Martin-Harvey uncommonly: he had never seen him but had seen Forbes-Robertson. Thus, at last, I have paid my homage to John Martin-Harvey and Lady Nell, who enlarged my life forever in my youth. Pat Galloway much improved: Leon Pownall (said to look like me) impressive. Willard's death and Sir John's death very moving. – Standing ovation. I spoke in the John Martin-Harvey manner – "a play a collaboration between players and audience . . . without you we are nothing, and without us you are incalculably less . . . we are your very humble, obliged, and obedient servants." Went splendidly and several people commented on it. I was most generously received at the call and given flowers – yellow roses! How unlike the first night of* Love and Libel!

———— ∾ ————

When *Fortune, My Foe* was first produced by Arthur Sutherland's International Players in Kingston, Ontario, in August 1948, there was little that might be called professional theatre in Canada. Since the latter days of the eighteenth century there had been touring theatre in the young colony, and companies, often of excellent quality, had visited Kingston from the United States and England, but the war of 1939–45 had put an end to that. Sutherland, who was an adventurous and charming man, thought that a professional company might survive in Kingston, and he called it International because it did indeed attract a good many visitors from the United States; they could come to Kingston from Watertown across the lake, have dinner at the Frontenac Hotel, in the ballroom of which the theatre was accommodated, see the play and be home by midnight. He gave them a diet of American and English comedies, as suitable summer fare, but he longed for something a little more daring – a Canadian play, in fact, at a time when Canadian plays were rarities – and he turned to me for one.

Arthur and I had been contemporaries and friends at Queen's University, in Kingston, and had often worked together in the students' Drama Guild. From his earliest days he was stage-struck. People often use that expression contemptuously, but I am not one of them; to yield to the beauty, the charm, the excitement, and the profound psychological insight the theatre offers, is not to be a lightweight, an inconsiderable creature, but very possibly to be an artist, a creator, a person who enlarges and illuminates the lives of others. Even a simple run-of-the-mill comedy may offer charm and some excitement; beauty and psychology are less common, but that was what Arthur wanted. He knew it was risky, but he wanted a play about Canada.

It was risky because Canada has for a long time been thought a dull country, with dull people. But there was a time when Norway was thought dull, and Ireland was thought absurd, yet both of them brought forth plays which have been acclaimed as treasures by theatres around the world. I don't suppose for a moment that Arthur had any such ambition as that, but he thought Canada might have something to say, and he asked me for a play. I had written a few one-act plays, because those were what Canadian amateurs wanted, but something in three acts was a new venture for me.

What should it be about? When Arthur approached me I had already begun a play on the theme I have mentioned above – the supposed dullness of Canada and its poverty of artistic expression. We had poets, novelists, painters, and some of them were very good, but they seemed not to be accepted by Canadians as a whole in the way that other countries accept their artists. It was notorious that university teachers were poorly paid; perhaps it was thought that learning was its own reward. So there was my theme, and my hero was a young professor who loved his country and loved a girl, and received rather a frosty response from both of them. The character of the puppet-master, who brought the artistic feeling of the Old World to the New World, and met with indifference and sometimes incredulity, was everywhere to be observed in Canada at that time; the war had brought us many refugees, and we had not always understood what they could do or what they were that was important. The old professor, who had worn himself out at a university which he thought was beneath his deserts, and who projected his personal failure on the new country, was a familiar figure also, and not one to be wholly condemned, for Canada had not given him understanding. Oh, indeed, there was lots of material for a play; the problem was not to overcrowd the stage and load the play with that fatal thing, A Message.

Message was very much on the lips of Canadians like [Davies' characters] Philpott and Tapscott, the do-gooders who took up the puppet-show, without having any understanding of its special quality or its cultural background, but who were convinced that the task of art was to teach – to offer A Message, in fact, and to offer it in terms that the stupidest listener could understand. Canada was, and still is, full of such people. They think of art of all kinds as a sort of handmaid to education; it must have A Message and it must get it across.

The truth is that art does not teach; it makes you feel, and any teaching that may arise from the feeling is an extra, and must not be stressed too much. In the modern world, and in Canada as much as anywhere, we are obsessed with the notion that to *think* is the highest achievement of mankind, but we neglect the fact that thought untouched by feeling is thin, delusive, treacherous stuff.

A circumstance that lent distinction to Arthur's production was that the setting was from a handsome and imaginative design by Grant Macdonald. It is now in the Macdonald collection in the Agnes Etherington Art Gallery, at Queen's University in Kingston.

The play fulfilled Arthur's trust; it had an extended run, which was extraordinary, a theatrical wow, in Canadian theatre at that time. And it has been acted many times in Canada since, and I know that it has made a lot of people feel differently about Canada, because they have told me so. And that has been my reward and a very welcome one.

The little play that appears also in this book [*Eros at Breakfast*] has an odd history. When I was a small boy in rural Canada, schools were expected to get up a concert at Christmas, and no concert was complete without a "dialogue" or two. "Dialogue" was the word used to describe a play suitable for children, always profoundly instructive, crammed with Message and just the sort of thing Philpott and Tapscott could understand and encourage. I was much impressed with one "dialogue," the scene of which was a human Stomach. The Stomach was offered a variety of foods, and responded eagerly to Miss Piece of Cake (in those days the term had no ambiguous significance) and Mr. Slab of Pie, but these two characters proved false, and the Stomach suffered from their treachery. The Stomach found salvation with Mr. Apple and Miss Glass of Milk, highly virtuous characters, who brought peace, growth, and improved intelligence with them to the owner of the Stomach.

Even as a child, I found this ghastly affair very funny (which was very wrong of me because dialogues were not meant to be funny in that way). And when I began to write plays I thought that something that took place inside a human creature – in his solar plexus, for instance, where an astonishing complex of nerves at the base of the stomach does so much to influence our feelings and our minds – would be amusing. What would love do to the solar plexus of a young man newly in love? It would fill him with joy, and insane rapture, obviously. From there it was easy to conceive of the solar plexus as a government office, filled with civil servants who directed the affairs of the young man who incorporated it in his being – without really knowing that it existed.

This play also has had a wide acceptance, but it is a delusive little piece. It requires delicate comedy acting, and I have seen it done by actors who handled it too roughly. It is a fantasy, not something for Stunt Night at camp. I must add that I have also seen it performed in the spirit in which it is offered, and then it had its full effect, which is gently, and never unkindly, satiric.

16

————— ∽ —————

INTRODUCTION TO HUNTING STUART
AND THE VOICE OF THE PEOPLE

WHEN JUSTIN GREENE WROTE to Robertson Davies of his plans to produce *Hunting Stuart* at the Pitlochry Festival Theatre in Scotland in July 1994, Davies was delighted to help. In a letter written in May 1993 he wrote: *"When matters are further advanced I would like to look over the text again and possibly suggest a few alterations so that the play does not seem too dated. I have seen it done two or three times and it plays very well indeed, but perhaps a few nips and tucks would not be amiss. We can talk of this when matters are more settled."*

As the time drew nearer and the production was in rehearsal, Davies wrote in May 1994: *"The question of accents is tricky and my scalp tingles a little bit when you speak of making Stuart speak with a Canadian accent. To my personal knowledge there are at least 500 Canadian accents and I think that the best thing would be for him to speak in a good clean English speech without attempting to identify himself as a Canadian, for he is sure to put his foot in it somewhere. In the best Canadian production that I*

have seen both Stuart and Aunt Clemmie spoke quite ordinary
English with here and there the faintest touch of foreignness and
this established them as not as completely Canadian as Stuart's
wife and daughter. The wife and daughter I suppose, if you want
to get into the question of accents, would speak with an Ottawa
Valley accent, which is perfectly clear and straight-forward
except that it has a strong dash of Scottish about it; I grew up in
the valley and remember it very well. What I think must, at all
costs, be avoided is the sort of raucous speech like a circular saw
striking a knot which so many actors in the U.K. imagine to be
the characteristic of this continent, Canada included. It always
sounds phoney."

The introduction which follows was specially written for the
Simon & Pierre edition of the plays published in 1994, a time
when the marital misadventures of Prince Charles and Princess
Diana, and of Prince Andrew and Sarah Ferguson, were attracting
disapproving notice.

———— ∽ ————

As I write this, there is a great
deal of indignation in the United Kingdom, and possibly an even
greater amount of prurient interest elsewhere in the world, con-
cerning the rowdy behaviour of some members of Britain's royal
house. A headline in the London *Times* reads "Can the Royal Family
Survive?" and articles and letters everywhere proclaim the opinions
of anti-royalists who declare that the money spent on maintaining
the royal family might better be spent on government committees,
pensions for parliamentarians, more trade commissions and goodwill
visits by elected persons to countries outside the U.K., support for
backward countries, and all the other things that delight the hearts
and raise the spirits of politicians. The substantial amount of money
that Britain receives from the royal family, from the Crown estates,
is rarely mentioned.

Here in Canada, where we spend no money whatever on the royal family, except when they visit our shores (and the demands of hospitality are, after all, binding), we can be more philosophical about this crisis. But we are a country with a monarchical form of government, the Queen is Queen of Canada, and we may fittingly be interested in what the institution of royalty means in our time, and whether it is worth maintaining.

In a government like ours, the Crown is the abiding and unshakeable element in government; politicians may come and go, but the Crown remains and certain aspects of our system pertain to it which are not dependent on any political party. In this sense the Crown is the consecrated spirit of Canada. The embodiment of the Crown is the monarch, who has virtually no personal political power, but whose personal influence may be very great, as an adviser to whatever government may be in power. And in addition to this, millions of people have an affectionate regard for the monarch, as somebody above politics who stands for rights and values which the majority of people cherish.

Understandably, when members of the royal family kick up their heels and play the fool (exactly as ordinary people do all the time without exciting any special remark) people who do not separate the constitutional aspect of monarchy, and its mystical significance as an embodiment of cherished rights and beliefs, from the fallible human beings who are born into the royal family, or marry into it, think that the monarchical system is tumbling down.

Because I do not think that this is so, and because I think that monarchy has a psychological significance for the countries that maintain it, I wrote the play *Hunting Stuart* some years ago. It deals with the matter in terms of comedy, but not mindless comedy – not just for giggles. In it an ordinary man discovers that he is of royal blood and has a very slight claim to the throne of Britain. He is what is called a Pretender, in the sense of the word which means a claimant, one who advances a right to something which is in the possession of another. When for a time he embodies the spirit of one of his ancestors, he shows tendencies that shock his wife, who has the not uncommon idea that the monarch is precisely like herself, though richer. But the pleasure-loving, woman-chasing pseudo-king is something else; he shows himself truly royal when he cures a suffering woman by the Royal Touch, which was widely believed in as late as the reign of Queen Anne (1702–1714), who was the last ruler of Stuart blood. There is, it appears, something more in kingship than ancestry and privilege; there is a trace of divinity, as well.

Of course the play is a fantasy and a comedy, but I do not think it is trivial. It was written for the Crest Theatre, in Toronto, where it was produced in 1955, with Donald Davis as Henry Benedict Stuart, and his sister Barbara as Dr. Maria Clementina Sobieska. They splendidly realized the saturnine physical distinction of the Stuarts. The play was well received by its audiences.

Perhaps a brief historical note may be of interest to readers who have forgotten about the Stuarts. They were famous in the history of Scotland from the twelfth century, and from the fourteenth century were kings of that country; it was through the marriage of James IV of Scotland with Margaret, daughter of Henry VII of England, that the Stuart claim to the English throne became a reality in 1603, when James VI of Scotland (son of Mary, Queen of Scots) succeeded Queen Elizabeth I as monarch of both Scotland and England as King James I. He was not at all a bad king and we remember him as having inspired the translation of the Bible into English, which has not since been surpassed for literary worth. But the Stuarts were an unlucky family, intelligent and refined, great lovers of art and letters, but absurdly blind to political reality, and it was this that brought James's son Charles I to the headsman's block. After an interval (1649–1660) during which England and Scotland tasted to the full the delights of puritan democracy, the monarchy was restored and King Charles II ruled – and although opinions vary he seems to have ruled pretty well – until his death in 1685, when he was succeeded by his brother James II, a disastrous king who had all the pig-headedness of the family with none of its charm, and who was forced into exile in 1688. After that the Stuarts were wanderers, and pensioners of the French court, though still asserting their right to the throne of Britain. James III, son of James II, is remembered as "the Old Pretender" (to that throne) and his eldest son, Charles Edward Louis Philip Casimir, best remembered as "Bonnie Prince Charlie" by the Scots, was "the Young Pretender."

The pleasantest of this latter group was the Young Pretender's younger brother, who became a Cardinal, enjoyed substantial wealth from the King of France, until the French Revolution left him penniless and the much-abused King George III of England granted him a pension of four thousand pounds a year. He was a charming man and it is told that on one Christmas day, one of his guests at dinner complimented him on serving a real English plum pudding. "Alas," said the Cardinal, who knew the limitations of his Italian chef, "I fear it is only a Pretender."

Relations between the exiled Stuarts and their successors, the House of Hanover, were amiable. The Cardinal bequeathed the crown jewels which had been carried off by James II, to King George IV of England, and in 1819 George IV contributed generously to the erection of the fine monument by Canova, which you may still see in St. Peter's in Rome. It proclaims itself the tomb of James III, Charles III, and Henry IX, of England.

There are still people who regard the Stuarts as the true English monarchs. When I was at Oxford (1935–1938) there was a quite flourishing White Rose Society in the University, the sole purpose of which was to proclaim and support the pretension of an obscure European prince to that dignity. To find out how the Stolbergs and the Sobieskis come into this complex story (and into my play) you must look in books of reference.

Hunting Stuart may be taken as a play about Canadian snobbery, though I hope that will not be your chief interest in it; after all, snobbery, even at its meanest, is an acknowledgment of something worthy of admiration; if that object is something fine, is the snobbery thereby redeemed? But I intended the play as a reflection on the nature of kingship, and the strong likelihood that royal blood may turn up in unexpected places. There may be an element of nobility in any one of us, and we should be careful not to betray it.

Nor should we be too sure of our opinions. Fred Lewis, the know-it-all young psychologist, discovers that part of the origin of his present-day belief included the discredited quackery of the phrenologist. Not that we should be incredulous about everything, but we should avoid becoming cocksure, especially in matters labelled "Science," which tends, at the moment, to discredit the idea of heredity.

Hunting Stuart, by the way, is the name of the dark tartan worn by the Stuarts and their clansmen; it is not the gaudy Royal Stuart, worn on dress occasions. The pun in my title will not go unnoticed. Both tartans are said by some Scots authorities to be nineteenth-century inventions, but on such a vexed topic I decline to comment.

The little play, *The Voice of the People*, is a *jeu d'esprit*, not meant to be taken very seriously, but to touch on a human foible familiar to every newspaper man. Indeed, this play has been a favourite with many newspaper people, all of whom are familiar with the subscriber who regards the paper's letters column as his megaphone and his platform. Newspaper people know that writers of Letters to the Editor, who are unaccustomed to the pen, often need protection against themselves, when indignation has triumphed over common sense.

17

A PROLOGUE TO THE CRITIC

THIS PROLOGUE WAS WRITTEN in two parts: the first, for a production of Sheridan's last play, *The Critic* (1779), at the Studio Theatre, University of Toronto, directed by Herbert Whittaker. The second part was added when it was spoken by Robertson Davies at a tribute for the same Herbert Whittaker on September 17, 1990.

On January 9, 1978, Davies wrote in his Theatre Diary of the production for which the prologue had been written originally: *At the experimental theatre, Herbert Whittaker's production of* The Critic: *not a bad production, full of good ideas, but a bad theatre and lack of money dragged it down. – I wrote a special Prologue for it which was well received.*

Twelve years later, on September 11, 1990, Davies wrote: *Settle to the tribute to Herbert Whittaker for next Monday, and complete it. I am no poet, but I am not a wholly inept versifier.*

On September 17: *At eight* The Great Bespeak for Herbert Whittaker *which we had somewhat feared but which turned out*

to be a roaring success, admirably carried through by a large
group of friends who spoke sincerely, amusingly, and with
moving warmth. Brenda says I read my verses very well, and my
voice was in no way inferior to [Richard] Monette, who came
before me, and was very good. Chris Plummer was there, a
picture of elegance, with a gold-knobbed evening stick – a thing
I have not seen in many a day.

———— ✧ ————

*E*nter Mrs. Dangle, a copy of the play-
bill in her hand.

THE CRITIC – what a title for a play!
Dear SHERIDAN, you don't mean what you say!
What outrage to our feelings do you plan
Thus to cry "Rope!" in the house of the hanged man?
As children, by good sense and instinct sound,
Insist a bogey's to the churchyard bound,
Players wish that bogey they THE CRITIC style
Securely chained to "two seats on the aisle,"
From whence he scrambles at the curtain's fall
(Like CINDERELLA dashing from the ball)
To meet his "deadline," type his censure burning,
E'er midnight sounds and sets the presses turning. –
Mad SHERIDAN, whatever can you mean
To bring THE CRITIC thus upon the scene?

  Ah, but methinks I fathom your intention;
This is a Critic of your own invention,
Some understanding, amiable good fellow,
Gentle of mien, of learning ripe and mellow,
Wise to instruct, just and discreet in blame,
No slave of Calumny, a friend to Fame,
Of Fancy quick the author to engage,

Of wit as deft as any's on the Stage –
I see it now, this is the Ideal Critic, or
To put it in two words, 'tis HERBERT WHITTAKER!
Our own for long, though born in Montreal,
But heedful to our Stage, where'er it call;
No critic of the sour Toronto line,
Sired, by Nate Cohen, on a porcupine,
But a true godson of Melpomene,
Committed to the Drama, as are we.

No, I'm mistaken, 'tis some other kind
Of critic that our author has in mind.
Whom, in our farce The Critic may we call?
Surely not DANGLE, stage-struck friend of all;
Nor could we name SIR FRETFUL PLAGIARY
('Tis the vexed scribbler in that role we see);
Nor MR. PUFF, mistake his trade who can,
That finished, brisk, audacious PR man;
Don't say it's SNEER, he's far too indolent –
No, plainly, there's some other Critic meant.

Of course, I see it! Bless me I'm so slow –
THE CRITIC, right before me, row on row!
All you, the drama-loving Sons of earth,
Who pay your fee, and call on us for mirth –
Yes, and for tears, when Tragedy is toward,
And the high boot strikes hollow on the board.
THE CRITIC – yes, the AUDIENCE is the one
That quite eclipses *Globe*, or *Star*, or *Sun*;
You are our judges, when we mount a play,
Run, or stop dead – the word is yours to say:
The stage's life the Stage's patrons give,
So – Bless THE CRITIC, ever while we live!

———— ∽ ————

In nineteen seventy-seven 'twas thus I wrote
And do not ask your pardon thus to quote
That's what I thought, and that's what I think now
I'll emphasize it, if you will allow –
So, here's a postscript, a poetic leaven
To lift e'en higher my words of seventy-seven.

As a deft goldsmith, with his subtle skill
Shapes base and precious metals to his will,
Heating his fire just hot enough, but never
So hot as to destroy his whole endeavour
So the true CRITIC'S art is to engage
In one creation, both the stalls and stage;
Nudging the dull who in our frosty land
Sit low and lumpish, slow to understand,
Scorning the new and grumbling at the old
And thinking CRITIC means "a common scold";
And at the same time twitch the player's bridle
Curbing the skittish, urging on the idle,
Cheering the playwright, seeking still to guide
The writer's Muse, but not to flay her hide;
Thus to meld audience and stage in one
And bring forth his own work of art when done.
Done! Yes and done in forty minutes flat –
How many of *your* readers thought of that!

So, HERBIE, as we fête you here tonight
What may we call you? I must get it right –
No high-strain'd rhetoric can your work embrace
– Blarney, to bring the blood up to your face –
There's one apt word we stage-folk offer though –
Our highest accolade: Herbie, you are a Pro!

18

---- ❧ ----

MELODRAMA: THE SILVER KING

DAVIES ALWAYS HAD A great affection for melodrama ("not a form of drama that appeals only to simple people") and so was pleased to have an opportunity to speak about it at the Shaw Festival at Niagara-on-the-Lake. The lecture was part of the July Seminar of 1993 and took place on July 17. The play under discussion was *The Silver King*, which he had seen a few days before. As always, he recorded it in his Theatre Diary.

On June 11 he wrote: *Set to work on the Shaw piece on* The Silver King; *it moves trudgingly, but I have begun so early I will have time to tart it up – want to stress melodrama music.* On June 12: *On with my melodrama piece and do somewhat better, but I am conscious of having said it all many times before, and having nothing much that is fresh to add. . . .* July 17: *My lecture goes very well and Ron* [Bryden] *is very pleased. Lots of laughs and prolonged applause.*

July 14, evening: *At the Festival Theatre,* The Silver King, *done well and imaginatively with no trace of tedious guying of its deeply melodramatic substance. As Denver, Stuart Hughes acted well, but lacks the splendid presence the part calls for: but as Nelly, Sherry Flett was true and moving. Barry MacGregor a fine Spider and as Mrs. Spider Jan Alexandra Smith was unexpectedly powerful. Robert Benson a fine Coombes, rather like Perkins Bull – a sinister Santa. Splendid setting and exemplary production by Christopher Newton. The audience (full house) received it with enthusiasm. As Jaikes, Jack Medley very nearly stole the show and topped the applause in the call. – How splendid to see a play with substance.*

———— ❧ ————

My task this morning is to talk to you about *The Silver King*, the play by Henry Arthur Jones that is offered to you in this Festival as an example of the drama of the nineteenth century. We are very lucky that this Festival offers, every year, something from the nineteenth century, because it gives us an opportunity to enjoy playgoing as our great-grandparents knew it, and thus we are able to peep into the past and discover, in the pleasantest way, that the past has much to be said for it. It is impossible to talk about this year's play without revealing a great deal about the story, and I am sorry for that, because it would be much better if you could simply attend the play and let its thrills and its moments of high emotion come to you freshly. Such plays as *The Silver King* were never meant to be lectured about; they belonged to the theatre and to a world of romance which a great many people suppose is now dead – I mean the world of melodrama. But I hope I may persuade you that melodrama is by no means dead and that it is not a form of drama that appeals only to simple people. I am certain that all of you here have been experiencing melodrama during the past few weeks, but it never occurred to you to give it that name. And you are not simple people, are you? No, of course not. You are the kind of people who attend drama festivals, and seminars; you are sophisticates, and nobody could pull the wool over your eyes. I don't know what you expect from *The Silver King*, but it is my job to talk about a few of the things you are going to get.

Let us look at the story, to begin. The chief character is a young man named Wilfred Denver; he is a good fellow at heart, a thoroughly decent sort, with a country background – and for some reason a great many people believe that country people are more moral and upright than city people. But Denver drinks heavily and he gambles recklessly, and he is in a bad way when first we meet him. That is in a skittle alley, which is also a betting shop and a place where liquor is sold. Denver has had heavy losses at the races, and he is drunk; he meets a man named Ware, who hates him, because Denver has won the love of the girl whom Ware wanted for himself. Ware taunts Denver with having dragged his wife down by his dissolute habits, and Denver unwisely allows himself to be heard saying that he will kill Ware. A drunken extravagance of speech, but dangerous talk. Denver rushes after Ware, in spite of Nelly's attempts to dissuade him.

Now we meet the second most important character in the play, the villain. He is a very smooth villain, who moves in very respectable circles under the name of Captain Herbert Skinner, but to the underworld he is known as The Spider, and he is planning a big jewel robbery, in which Ware's clerk is implicated, because he is going to make it possible for the thieves to get into the vault where the diamonds are. By ill luck Ware returns to his flat, finds The Spider and his accomplices at work, and in a moment of bad judgement The Spider shoots him. Denver arrives, drunk and furious. The Spider arranges that the drunken Denver should be chloroformed and left on the scene while the robbers escape. When Denver recovers consciousness he finds that his revolver is in his hand, and one shot has been fired – the shot that has killed Ware, whose body lies before him. Denver is horrified, naturally enough, and determines to escape if he can.

Now we meet a vital character in the drama, Denver's wife, Nelly. She is everything a wife should be – faithful, true, noble of spirit and ready to stick to her man through thick and thin. She lives with their two delightful children, Cissy and Ned, and another very important character indeed; this is Daniel Jaikes, an old servant who has remained with the family from better days, and who is noble and self-sacrificing as only a stage servant can be; he keeps the Denver family going with his savings, and never dreams of being paid. Denver comes home to his wife, confesses to the murder he has not committed, and she helps him to escape. He takes a train to a distant place and then seeks to cover his tracks by jumping from the train as it speeds north. But he learns very shortly after that the train has been wrecked, and several passengers destroyed in the resulting fire.

In his anguish, Denver has prayed in words that became famous: "Oh God! put back Thy Universe and give me yesterday! Too late! Too late!" But it is not too late; he realizes that his prayer has been answered in a very subtle way. The Wilfred Denver who is being pursued as a murderer has, so far as the world knows, been killed and burned in the railway accident. God has, in His own fashion, given Denver the yesterday, and the second chance, he craved.

Now there is an interim of three years and six months. Nelly Denver is in deep trouble, for her cruel landlord, who is The Spider under his respectable guise, is determined to evict her and her children. They are nuisances on his property. Even the faithful Jaikes has no solution; because of his age he is unable to get even the odd jobs that might have brought in a little money. The children are ostracized at school, because it is known that their father was a murderer. The boy is seriously ill, and if the family are evicted he will surely die. Things could hardly be blacker.

But then little Cissy comes home with a purse full of money which has been given to her by a mysterious stranger, a man with silver hair. Of course this stranger is Will Denver, who has returned from Nevada, where he has made an enormous fortune in the silver mines, winning the name of the Silver King. But although he can get money to his family, and reveal his identity to Jaikes, he dare not be too bold, for as Will Denver he is still wanted for murder. He must clear his name before he approaches his wife and children. He manages to intrude himself into the riverside warehouse where The Spider's gang congregates, disguised as a simpleton called Deaf Dicky, and there he learns the truth about the murder, and his own innocence. The Spider is brought to justice, the exile is at last free to disclose himself to his wife and children, and after desperate trials all is well; at last we see the Denver family kneeling in their now luxurious home, to give thanks for God's mercies.

I have done my best to put the story before you without making fun of it, and when you see it I think you will admit that the play-wright has given it a seriousness that convinces, and has used lan-guage which is for most of the time acceptable as ordinary speech. Of course it is not ordinary speech; the stage has no use for ordinary speech. All stage speech is heightened and distilled and given a certain sort of suitable eloquence. Even the supposedly allusive, cryptic speech of Harold Pinter is very carefully constructed. We could not bear to listen to a play which was in the speech of ordi-nary life because it is too loose, too repetitive, too uninteresting to hold our attention. But what you hear in *The Silver King* passed very well as ordinary speech when the play first appeared at the Princess's Theatre in London, on November 16, 1882. The speech of The Spider's gang deserves particular attention; they are criminals, hardly literate and of limited intelligence, and that is how they sound, but there is no exaggeration. The Spider and his wife speak like people in any one of a hundred plays about good society in the latter part of the nineteenth century. It is when we come to the Denver family that we hear speech that is not precisely that of every day. Theirs is often of heightened speech.

This is owing to the skill of the playwright, Henry Arthur Jones, who was an innovator in his time. After his early melodramas he wrote a number of plays about society and upper-class life which were very successful in their own sphere and which put forward some ideas that were advanced in their time. But we may perhaps reflect that Jones had bad luck, of a kind that happens to playwrights and indeed all writers. If there had been no Shakespeare, we should now think of Ben Jonson more generously as the very great dramatist he undoubtedly was. But throughout history Jonson has had to play second fiddle to the greater man. Henry Arthur Jones might appear to us as a more important innovator in drama if he had not been at his peak contemporaneously with two formidable rivals – Oscar Wilde who was wittier, and Bernard Shaw who was cleverer.

Jones was a figure familiar in many areas of nineteenth-century life – the serious-minded, intelligent, industrious man who rose above humble beginnings and made the world pay attention to him. He was born in 1851, the son of a small farmer and his wife who were both deep-dyed Nonconformists. It is difficult to convey to a modern audience what that means, and some of you who are from the United States may not even know what a Nonconformist is. To what did these people refuse to conform? To the doctrines of the Church of England, which dominated the religious life of England in the nineteenth century as it had done since the Reformation. And if any of you are so remote from the history of thought that you do not know what the Reformation was, I shall see you in the vestry after the service. To be a Nonconformist was not simply to go to a place of worship other than the parish church; it was a social class, a climate of thought, and a political colour that encouraged rebellion against the seeming laws of society; the Nonconformist did not believe that he had to live out his life in the station in life in which it apparently pleased God to call him. If he had what it took, he could rise in the world, and thousands of ambitious people did precisely that. One of them was Henry Arthur Jones.

Nonconformity, however, is something which appears to be bred in the bone. It imposes a seriousness about life which very few people are able to shake off; it also, unfortunately, gives an impression of Knowing Best to those who adhere to it. Their philosophy is: I have succeeded in the world and made circumstances bow to me, and this is evidence not only of my own ability but also of God's favour toward me; therefore I am able to advise and rule people who come under my influence with the assurance that what I say is probably God's word and what I want is God's will. Sometimes this worked as a benevolent force, but very often it led to a kind of moral tyranny, and a harshness toward anybody who dared to disagree. To me, Nonconformity rose from the later plays of Henry Arthur Jones like the smell of burned cabbage in a middle-class home.

An important aspect of Nonconformity was its cult of the Bible as the fount of all wisdom. But the Bible takes much of its colour from whoever is reading it, and it provides a text to support almost

every shade of opinion, however preposterous. Jones was an enlight-
ened Nonconformist, but a Nonconformist for all that.

All of Henry Arthur Jones's plays – and he wrote something like
sixty plays altogether – have a strong moral foundation. This does not
mean that they were goody-goody plays or simple-minded plays or
that the morality stuck out of the fabric in an obvious and irritating
fashion. When he hit his stride he wrote plays that appealed to fashionable audiences who took them seriously. He was, far more than
Shaw, accepted as a leader of popular opinion. But the trouble was
that he had not Shaw's intellectual scope, and his morality was that
of the great majority of people who, without being stupid, rarely
questioned anything that appeared to be an accepted fact of moral,
or economic, or social life.

He was, for instance, contemptuous of Ibsen. He thought Ibsen a
man of ability who simply didn't understand his job or the ways of
the intelligent world. He wrote a play called *Breaking a Butterfly*, which
was in fact an adaptation of Ibsen's *A Doll's House*, and in it he showed
Ibsen how it should be done. Ibsen, thought Jones, didn't understand
women, and he, Jones, most decidedly did. But Jones, like so many
Nonconformists, seems to have known only two kinds of women –
good ones and bad ones; the notion that a woman was a human being
with an incalculable mixture of good and bad in her nature simply
did not enter his head. He seems to flirt with such a dangerous idea
in one of his successes, called *The Case of Rebellious Susan*, but Susan
is not really very rebellious when compared with a Shavian heroine.
Perhaps it was because Jones rose from humble beginnings into good
society, and never quite ceased to take good society at its face value.
But of course that was long after *The Silver King*.

The play we are discussing was highly praised in its day as a
refinement and improvement on melodrama as it had previously
existed. It won acclaim in no less influential a journal than the *Pall
Mall Gazette*, and the critic was Matthew Arnold, who was by no
means an easy man to please. And while we are talking of Arnold it
may not be amiss to say that what we call melodrama was enjoyed
and praised by people whose opinions we cannot lightly dismiss –
writers such as George Eliot, Anthony Trollope, Charles Dickens, and

Lewis Carroll. Arnold particularly praised the production of the play, by the popular star Wilson Barrett. He said: "Instead of a company with a single powerful and intelligent performer, with two or three middling ones, and the rest moping and mowing in what was not to be called English but rather stagese, here was a whole company of actors, able to speak English, playing intelligently and supporting one another effectively." The play had a long run, in terms of the nineteenth century, and after the hundredth performance the London *Times* said that Barrett had worked to raise "what for want of a better word is called melodrama into the region of literature and poetry, and natural tragedy." This is high praise from a most respected source and it must have made Barrett's heart glow. In the words of *The Times* we recognize the yearnings for refinement, for improvement, for lifting of public taste, which was characteristic of the nineteenth century. But enduring, living stage work has sources that might astonish and dismay such serious-minded souls as Matthew Arnold and writers for *The Times*; refinement is a surface quality, not the enduring substance, of theatre, which is an art that sinks under the burden of too much refinement and which must have a saving quality of coarseness in order to please and endure.

To begin, the play was a disputed collaboration; Jones worked not only with the star, Wilson Barrett, but with another playwright, Henry Herman, who, when *The Silver King* became a great success, complained that Jones had robbed him of his share of the credit. To this Jones replied that Herman had written only one line – "An angel from Heaven has sent it!"; he also said that Herman could not write correct or colloquial English, as he had not a drop of English blood in him and could hardly speak English correctly. Such disputes were not uncommon. When Henry Irving had an extraordinary success with *The Bells* in 1871 the translator and adapter, Leopold Lewis, complained that he had not been given enough credit, though Irving continued to pay him for the use of the play as long as Lewis lived. The complexities of writing for the stage in the nineteenth century were not resolved, and a proper royalty system established, until the century was almost at an end, by which time a playwright of Jones's stature could rely on a very reasonable return for successful work.

To return to the genesis of *The Silver King*, the story is told by Chance Newton, a much-respected critic and man of the theatre at the time, that Wilson Barrett approached Herman – who was his business manager – and Henry Arthur Jones, who was just beginning to make a name, saying, "Look here boys, the sort of play I want is *East Lynne* turned around. That is, with a man in the position of Isabel Carlyle; lost to the world for a while – reported to be killed, like her, in a railway accident, if you like – and returning secretly in disguise, well-off though totally unable for a time to see or succour his suffering wife and children." What Barrett wanted was a play in which he could exploit the popular theme of self-accusation and tortured conscience.

Why? Because that was very much to the taste of the last quarter of the nineteenth century. Self-accusation was "in." Did you enjoy meat? The vegetarians were down on you as an eater of carrion who was coarsening and destroying his body. Did you smoke? You were poisoning yourself and everybody around you. Drink, of course, was old stuff, but still a strong form of reproach. Among the highbrows Swinburne and Ernest Dowson proclaimed the joy and anguish of sin in many of its forms but chiefly in its sexual aspect. Does any of this sound familiar? Is there something about the close of a century which provokes the perverse passion for guilt? Are we not at this moment in just such a situation where everybody, in some form or other, is a sinner, weighed down with guilt? It's enough to make one believe in astrology.

Barrett's reference to *East Lynne* is of great interest. It was one of the most popular of the nineteenth-century melodramas, rivalling even *Uncle Tom's Cabin*. The chief character, Lady Isabel Carlyle, is by any ordinary standards a dubious figure. She is an adulteress, and rather a sneak and eavesdropper, but the story is so loaded on her side that she provokes pity in everyone who sees the play or reads the book – if anyone still reads it. And how she repents! Her repentance and eventual death would draw tears from a grizzly bear. *East Lynne* is a very crudely written play, which Jones's play most decidedly is not. But beauty combined with penitence is a sure card in the theatre, and Wilson Barrett knew it.

Who was Wilson Barrett? To begin, he was a magnificently hand-some man who thrilled both men and women with his splendid mas-culinity. I stress that, because the nineteenth century demanded of a leading actor either that he should be a male beauty, like Barrett and a score of others (of whom Johnston Forbes-Robertson was an espe-cially gifted example, with looks that made him a Pre-Raphaelite saint on the stage) or else the actor must be a man of compelling magnetism and distinction, like Henry Irving. People went to the theatre to gape at these handsome figures, and probably to lust after them; that was certainly the case with Lewis Waller, a great male beauty whose performance in *Monsieur Beaucaire* marked the top of his career; he had a gigantic fan-club of gallery-girls, who called themselves the KOWs – Keen on Wallerites – and who came night after night to worship him. It must be said that he was a modest man; this sort of acclaim embarrassed him and he depended on his wife to defend him from other women. But I must emphasize that these actors were more than male beauties; they could really act, and good judges declared that their performances were thrilling.

The demand that actors should be handsome and dress well is very much a thing of an earlier day. It lent a romance and glamour to the theatre that has quite disappeared. If you met a member of the theatre company on the street in this town, would you recognize him? A hundred years ago you could have spotted him at a hundred yards. But nowadays the demand for fine looks has been transferred to the movies, which are the popular theatre of our time. I shall have some-thing to say about this later.

To begin with, then, Wilson Barrett was very handsome and he had a magnificent, muscular physique which he delighted to expose on the stage. He particularly liked Roman parts, such as that of Marcus Superbus in his famous play – he wrote it himself – called *The Sign of the Cross*. Its success was triumphant, and in our own century a silent film and two talkies have been made from it. In it Barrett was able to exploit to the full one of his principal attractions. I refer to his breast. And I mean his breast, not his chest. The masculine bosom has not often surpassed in splendour its female counterpart, but in Barrett's case it decidedly did so, to the rapture of his female fans, and to the despair and derision of his male contemporaries. Not only had he a splendid bosom – or buzzem, as it was called in those days – but he had a magnificent neck, strong and pillar-like. How did he acquire these beauties? The answer is simple; as a boy he had been apprenticed to a blacksmith and he forged his figure, so to speak, at the anvil.

You see, I am giving you a considerable amount of anecdote about the nineteenth-century stage, not only because it gives me pleasure, but because I want to counteract a tendency in modern theatre historians to make the nineteenth century too solemn, too loaded with deep artistic significance. Of course it was artistic – splendidly so – but artistry is not a solemn, dead thing that flourishes in universities and seminars on solemn subjects. Art is alive, or it is nothing, and the people who create it are highly coloured. Even Henry Herman, of whom I spoke earlier and who has a peripheral place in the history of *The Silver King*, was an interesting character; he had a glass eye, which replaced one he lost in the American Civil War. He was a great chaser of women, though he himself lacked attraction, being grotesquely fat. He had a pretty wit: once he refused to pay a cab-fare, accusing the cabby of having cut out his eye with a flourish of his whip – he held out the glass eye in proof before the astonished onlookers. He called himself a dramatic author, but he hated the labour of writing, and so he liked to confide his dramatic ideas to aspiring young men who didn't mind putting pen to paper, allowing him to take the larger share of the profits. He met his match in Henry Arthur Jones, whose Nonconformist outlook on life would have no truck with such double-dealing.

A theatre that contained figures like Wilson Barrett and Henry Herman was splendidly alive, but it liked to play dead when there was anything to be gained by it. When clergymen and serious-minded critics acclaimed *The Silver King* or *The Sign of the Cross* as a great force for good, Barrett was delighted, but he always kept his feet on the ground; moral values must arise from strong dramatic situations; the theatre might at times walk hand in hand with the church, but it must never make the mistake of following it.

Why, you may ask? You are probably thinking of modern clergy who have no dread of the theatre. In the nineteenth century the theatre was still regarded by millions of people and virtually all Nonconformists as a place of dubious moral standing. Lewis Carroll, the author of *Alice in Wonderland* and *Through the Looking Glass*, was a keen theatre-goer, and had many friends among the theatre folk, of whom Ellen Terry was the most eminent. But he refused to take a young lady who was a friend of his to meet Ellen Terry because no unspotted (unspoiled) girl should make the acquaintance of an actress, however eminent.

He was a clergyman, because if he had not been one he could not have held his position as a don at Christ Church in Oxford. Certainly the clergyman rather than the fantasist was on top when he wrote this: "Let me pause for a moment to say that I believe this thought, of the possibility of death – if calmly realized and steadily faced – would be one of the best possible tests as to our going to any scene of amusement being right or wrong. If the thought of sudden death acquires, for *you*, a special horror when imagined happening in a *theatre*, then be very sure the theatre is harmful for *you*, however harmless it may be for others; and that *you* are incurring a deadly peril by going. Be sure that the safest rule is that we should not dare to *live* in any scene in which we dare not *die*."

It was this attitude, among people of the intellectual station of Lewis Carroll, that impelled Henry Irving's long struggle to make the theatre respectable. Perhaps he overdid it; the theatre in our day has become a place of complete respectability allied to a numbing intellectuality, but consider the situation that Irving faced. We know now that for some time Ellen Terry was his mistress, but when they lived only a very few people knew it, and not all of them could be certain.

I have already spoken to you of Matthew Arnold's warm praise for *The Silver King*, and I have contrasted it with Wilson Barrett's insistence that the young Jones and the old Herman should concoct for him something founded on one of the most popular and artistically unchaste melodramas of the time – *East Lynne*. The contradiction is an interesting and fruitful one – apparent refinement and restraint balanced against coarse sensationalism and tear-jerking pathos. Melodrama was the drama of the people, and they loved it hot and strong; but the movement toward general education in the nineteenth

century was having its effect, and there was a place for a kind of melodrama which did not produce pathos and sensation with such unre-
strained vehemence and coarseness. But the elements which made
melodrama what it was remained unchanged. A sensational plot,
strongly drawn characters, and no time wasted on psychological
explorations or emotional niceties – that was the recipe.

Was it as coarse and vulgar as the highbrows insisted, and as they
still insist? Indeed it was, but it was something else; it went straight to
the depths of feeling which are common to all mankind. If a play
touches deep feeling, it need not worry too much about improbabilities of plot, far-fetched coincidence, and characters who seem to have
but one dominating characteristic or emotion. The refinement of *The
Silver King* is on the surface. If we look below we find the archetypal
situations and characters that have served melodrama since the days of
Shakespeare, who was a master melodramatist as well as being a psychologist and a poet of blazing genius. And though Shakespeare had
his faults, extreme refinement was never one of them.

The characters – where shall we begin? With the hero, of course.
Wilfred Denver has a touch of complexity in his character; when the
play begins we see him as a man given to drink and gambling. But
is he a weak man? No, at the slightest hint of a reflection on his wife
he shows himself a true Hero, chivalrous and bold. He is tricked into
a false situation; he thinks he has committed a murder, and immediately he comes to himself – to his true self – and he prays: "Oh God!
put back Thy Universe and give me yesterday," he begs, and that is
precisely what God seems to do. He is given that inestimable gift, a
Second Chance. The grateful Denver is a reformed man, and he
devotes the new life he has been granted to industry – and the nineteenth century, and particularly its Nonconformist element, had the
deepest reverence for industry – and when he has made his great pile
he becomes a benefactor of the poor, as well as restoring his family
to respectability – another Nonconformist fetish – and affluence,
without which respectability is somewhat restricted.

He is the Melodramatic Hero in a particularly fine aspect. Noble,
chivalrous, a lover of children, and a man redeemed by trial, we see
in the latter part of the play a man who has put behind him the booze

and the gambling mania and become a spiritual and financial success. The Baptist Church, in which Henry Arthur Jones was raised and from whose maternal breast he never fully weaned himself, would have been proud of Wilfred Denver. The scene in which he listens to the children singing their simple hymn in the school, packages up and delivers to us the whole impact of the play;

> What though my sins as mountains rise
>   And reach and swell to Heaven,
> Yet Mercy is above the skies
>   I may still be forgiven.

You see? Denver, sinner and headed for ruin, has been forgiven and reclaimed by Divine Mercy.

> Then let me stay in doubt no more
>   Since there is sure release,
> For ever open stands the door,
>   Repentance, Pardon, Peace.

I have not been able to trace this hymn, and I wonder if Jones may not have written it himself; it fits the play so exactly. "Repentance, Pardon, Peace" – surely at some time or other most people have experienced the longing for cleansing and the bliss of a new life. You, ladies and gentlemen, does your mind never stray back to the old family farm, where your white-haired mother wept over your youthful misdemeanours, and you, joining your tears with hers, knelt in the dear old kitchen to pray for help in living a better life? It doesn't? Shame on you! But perhaps, as you have come away from your psychoanalyst's consulting-room, having paid him almost a hundred dollars for – Repentance, Pardon, Peace? – you experienced the emotion that lies at the heart of *The Silver King*. Somewhere in most of us there is an image that looks very much like Wilfred Denver. It is the image of the Good Man Falsely Accused, and which of us has not at some time played that role?

The Good Man, yes, but what about the Good Woman? When we look at Denver's wife, Nelly, we see a figure common to a thousand melodramas, but do we recognize her as what she is? She looks rather a spiritless creature, unequal to the trials that life heaps upon her. But considered psychologically, she is something quite different. She is what some psychologists have called the External Image of the Soul of the Hero; she is his better nature, she is the Eternal Feminine that draws him upward; if you know the old play of *Everyman*, you recognize in Nelly Denver the character called Good Deeds, who at last assures the Hero of his salvation. As a part for an actress, it is pretty dull; but as a peg upon which the audience can hang its ideas of all that is good, faithful, and pure, and as an appurtenance to the Hero, she is invaluable.

What about the Villain? You can't have a melodrama without one, because he is the architect of the Hero's trials and misfortunes. Melodramatic villains are an interesting study; they are rich, they seem to wear evening dress more often than is normal, they are great rhetoricians and speak in a fancy lingo that nobody has ever heard from lips that were not villainous. Further, they are rotten to the core. Now here *The Silver King* breaks some new ground, and in The Spider we meet one of the earliest manifestations of the Gentleman Crook, who has been as popular a figure in our century as the Gentleman Detective. How we love those figures who bring gentility and a whiff of High Life to otherwise mundane occupations! The Spider wears evening clothes, but only in the evening; he lives a life of luxury but not of vulgar opulence; he has an assured place in society but he is not an ostentatious swell. He speaks politely to his wife, he seems to have no lustful interest in Nelly Denver, but he is hard-hearted; he will evict Nelly, not out of sheer malignance but she must be got rid of because she is a reminder of Denver. The Spider is the Villain of this melodrama sure enough, but he is not a vulgar waxwork of a Villain; there are lots of Spiders in every society.

Now we come to a figure vital to melodrama, and he is the Comic Man. Tragedy is not supposed to have Comic Men in it, and French critics have been very severe with Shakespeare because he wiggles a

Comic Man into every one of his tragedies – and the tragedies are vastly helped by the contrast the Comic Man affords. He is an assurance that outside the world of misfortune in which the tragic figures live, there is another world, inhabited by simple people of good and simple nature, where tragedy has not blackened the skies. The Comic Man in *The Silver King* is Daniel Jaikes, the old family servant, who remembers Denver's father, "the Old Squire," and Denver as a daring, lovable boy, and Daniel is determined to stick with Denver and Denver's wife as long as there is breath in his body. His savings are all spent to help Nelly in her distress and he wants no payment; indeed, he does his feeble best to earn money for them by doing odd jobs. And he is full of jokes and happy inspirations. Indeed, in skilled hands he is almost the best part in the play.

Why is this sort of character so popular? Because melodramas at their best are fairy tales, and as I don't need to tell an audience of your degree of sophistication, fairy tales embody the dreams, the wishes, the traditions of mankind, and one of those wishes is for a Helper who can be relied upon to come to our aid when we seem almost to sink under the blows of Fate. In fairy tales this Helper is often an animal, a clever cat, or a donkey who can find the path when the Hero has lost it. In Melodrama the Helper is most often a Comic Servant, who possesses a sagacity that saves the day time and again. Of course he is not the social or spiritual equal of the Hero, or the External Soul of the Hero. No, no; he is happy in his humble station and asks nothing better than to be of service. Have you never longed for such a helper? We all live in a world where fairy tales are not so irrelevant as we might suppose.

So, there you have the principal ingredients of melodrama: the Hero, the Heroine, the Villain, and the Comic Servant. But *The Silver King* gives us a glimpse of another character who was soon to take the stage, and a whole genre of fiction; he is Samuel Baxter, the detective. As detectives go today, he isn't up to much. He does not dominate the action and has no great scene in which he unfolds the mystery and denounces the Villain. But he is remarkably like a *real* detective; he hangs around in the places where criminals meet, and he keeps his eyes and ears open. He knows who the crooks are, and he is waiting for a chance to catch one of them in the act. He is, in fact, believable.

But we don't want detectives to be believable; we want them to be omniscient and unnaturally clever. Jones was probably aiming at realism when he created Baxter, but the unrealistic and thrilling detective had already been seen on the stage nineteen years earlier in a play called *The Ticket-of-Leave Man.* That detective's name was Hawkshaw. I can still remember actors who, when they felt the impulse to do so in private conversation, would make motions – the left hand removing an imaginary cap, the right hand seeming to remove the wig, and the third is for the hand with the cap in it to remove an imaginary pair of false whiskers – while they spoke the magic words, "I am Hawkshaw, the Detective" – this having been the culminating line of the play. Samuel Baxter is no Hawkshaw; he has not given his name to a profession, as Hawkshaw has done.

Having talked thus far about *The Silver King,* it may be well to conclude with some general comments about melodrama. The Jones play was praised by people who did not generally concern themselves with the theatre, and won for the author, and for Wilson Barrett, reputations that grew with the years. Barrett was hailed as "a thoughtful, refined, and scholarly man," which was coming it rather strong, for although Barrett was undoubtedly a good fellow, he was a man of the theatre first, last, and all the time. Mr. Gladstone praised him and praised Jones and unless Queen Victoria had so far condescended as to offer a few words of encomium, there was no nineteenth-century praise that carried more conviction. Serious people wanted the theatre to appear on the side of whatever was serious, and as comedy could not be depended on, and tragedy did not appeal to a wide enough public, melodrama was the theatrical form that carried the greatest intellectual and moral weight. And it was that burden which would have destroyed it, if melodrama had not been indestructible.

What is it, really? The name tells us all. At the beginning of the nineteenth century it was a romantic and sensational stage-play, with interspersed songs and a musical accompaniment which was either continuous or frequent. It was also expected to have a happy ending, but that did not necessarily mean the uniting of lovers. One of the most continuously successful of melodramas was *The Corsican Brothers*, which ends when the ghost of one of the brothers appears to the other, who has avenged his death, speaking the words: "Weep not, dear brother, we shall meet above." Indeed, death concludes many of the most popular melodramas, including the deathless *Camille*, where the great-hearted courtesan expires saying: "All the pain is gone! Is this Life? Now everything appears to change. Oh, how beautiful! Do not wake me – I am so sleepy," while her lover Armand cries, "Camille! Camille! Dead! Dead!"

It is of great interest, by the way, that death which was so common on the Victorian stage in this form of transfiguration and peace, is virtually never seen thus in modern drama, where death is violent and final. Are we more realistic than our forebears, or merely more afraid of death? But that is not a theme that can detain us now.

The musical content of melodrama was made necessary in the early part of the nineteenth century because the law still forbade the presentation of what were called "legitimate plays," meaning the classics and plays of serious literary worth, in any theatres except those which held royal patents, which were Covent Garden and Drury Lane. This was the law until 1843, by which time a tradition of drama with music had gained acceptance for the best of reasons: the music supported the drama in a way that words alone could not do. The writers for the popular theatre were not gifted men of letters; they were hacks, and their hack dramas, written quickly and for poor pay, were not able to stir the emotions of a simple audience unaided, and were greatly strengthened by assistance from the orchestra.

As melodrama gained in stature, the writing became better, and the music became better, as well. Instead of being anything that the orchestra leader thought might fit a dramatic situation, music of good quality was especially written for specific plays.

Consider *The Bells*, which Henry Irving played over a thousand times during his career as unchallenged leader of the British stage. (Incidentally, Irving would not permit *The Bells* to be described as a melodrama, but it was unquestionably a drama with music.) I have Irving's own copy of the music for *The Bells* and it is a splendid example of the way in which music was used to heighten, without overwhelming, the action on the stage. The music was written by a French composer, Etienne Singla, for the first production of the play in 1869, and he was asked to London to conduct when the play opened in London at the Lyceum Theatre on November 25, 1871. The score is elaborate: twenty-six players are required, including strings, woodwinds, brass, and drums. There is an Overture, and twenty-seven passages of music of varying lengths to accompany scenes of special dramatic importance, and to mark the entrance of crucial characters. The music, which relies heavily on Alsatian folk-songs, to partner the setting of the play, is used in a fashion very much akin to the leitmotivs of Wagner. It is very respectable music, without being in any way obtrusive, which Irving would not have permitted. Indeed, the story is told that when Sir Arthur Sullivan wrote music for his production of *Macbeth*, Irving was unsatisfied with the music that accompanied one of his soliloquies, and at last demanded that the orchestra play it without the melody – and that proved to be exactly what he wanted. *He* was the melody, and no rivalry was permissible. It is worth adding that Sullivan concurred without complaint; he knew very well that music to accompany a play must not seek to dominate.

In passing, I must take note of a use of music to accompany melodrama which will be within the recollection of many of you who are here present. During the era of the silent films, they were accompanied in hundreds of the lesser movie houses by a piano, played by an artist of what we must now recognize as extraordinary versatility. Every feature film was accompanied by a thematic cue-sheet for the pianist, and it gave the cue for every scene in the film, the length of the scene, and the music that was to be played to support it. I am lucky in having a collection of these cue-sheets, and they are of the greatest interest. Consider that for the 1923 filming of *The Green Goddess*, in which George Arliss starred, every phase of the action has its musical accompaniment defined, with reference to the compilation of popular music in which it could be found; the music ranges from very popular airs, to what the film people called "classical" – as, for instance, Saint-Saëns' "Funeral March of a Marionette," which supports the scene where the wicked Rajah of Rukh pursues the dewy English maiden round and round a table, determined to plant his loathsome kiss upon her pure lips. There are thirty-six music cues, in all. As a boy I sat transfixed during dozens of such films, and always aware that Mr. Harrison, who played the piano, was adding immeasurably to the thrill of what I saw. From time to time in very serious films, like *The White Sister*, starring Lilian Gish, Mr. Harrison would slide almost imperceptibly from the piano stool to the bench of a parlour organ, upon which he played music suitable for religious scenes. These movie pianists were as adroit as cathedral organists in the way they could change ("segued" was the technical term) from key to key, from mood to mood, without unseemly breaks. They are a vanished race but memory holds them in respect and affection. In them the spirit of a thousand melodramas lived well into our century, not in the sophisticated form of such scores as that for *The Bells*, but as orchestra leaders in humble theatres glued them together for plays now forgotten. If you want to find out what those orchestras were like, and what sort of musicians played in them, I suggest that you read Balzac's splendid novel, *Cousin Pons*.

Melodrama is not dead. It lives in the movies, where every film has a score specially written for it, and sometimes of high quality. It lives in television: next time you watch, observe how your response is being nudged in the desired direction by the music. Melodrama lives in our opera houses, for dozens of the most popular operas – *La Traviata*, *La Bohème*, *Madama Butterfly*, *Rigoletto*, *La Tosca*, one could go on for a long time – are musical versions, by acknowledged masters, of plays that were melodrama successes before they became operas. They create excitement and often draw tears, just as did the stage versions because, as E. T. A. Hoffmann so finely said, "the lyre of Orpheus opens the door of the underworld," and music touches us as only the finest words of the greatest poets can do. Music releases emotion directly, and it knows no barrier of language.

When I was a boy, living in a somewhat primitive community, it was my good luck to see *Uncle Tom's Cabin* twice, and I assure you when Little Eva died, while a choir of her loving slaves sang "Nearer, My God to Thee" at her bedside, an audience of lumberjacks and millhands wept unashamedly. Do we ever dash away a tear when

Violetta in *La Traviata* dies to exquisite music? I know we do. The degree of sophistication and the level of art are far divided, but the effect is achieved, surely and firmly.

That is what melodrama means. It appeals not simply to the intellect, but to the heart, and even in our own seemingly harsh days audiences still have hearts to be touched. And I hope your hearts will be by *The Silver King*.

19

———— ❧ ————

SOME REFLECTIONS ON RIGOLETTO

THE FOLLOWING ARTICLE MOVES us from the world of melo-drama into the overlapping world of opera. As Davies notes in his first paragraph: "Melodrama reached its peak in the nineteenth century and its greatest practitioner was Giuseppe Verdi. *Rigoletto* is one of his finest melodramas." Written for the Canadian Opera Company's Souvenir Program on April 27, 1992, this piece was used during the 1992 season when *Rigoletto* was directed by Nicholas Muni, and was reprinted in 1996 when the production was revived, directed by Frank Matthus.

September 30, 1992: *To Canadian Opera Company: Rigoletto: well sung and played under Richard Bradshaw. But a wilful visual production, à la Moscow 1930, by George Tsypin, all Magritte flat walls and vistas but without Magritte's genius. Eccentric production by Nicholas Muni: Rigoletto in a whirling, darting wheelchair which became a bore and inhibited his action. Stupid sets, and one sees the Duke mauling a woman on a staircase while singing of his infatuation with Gilda: the Duke*

*presented as an unappeasable womanizer, like J.F.K. – The storm
very wild and hard on the singers: Sparafucile's inn transparent
and seemed to be made of Meccano. Poor Jean Sitwell as
Maddalena appeared in a see-through nightie (her work-clothes,
one presumes) in the pelting storm. Absurdities of this sort
abounded but the excellent cast somehow rose above them.
Young Ok Shin a splendid coloratura as Gilda. Brent Ellis was
Rigoletto and good, though the singer pleads in vain for pity for
that evil cretin.*

———— ·◊· ————

Ｆor many people, melodrama is still
a dirty word, a word used to deride whatever is too strong in feeling
and too weak in thought. Applied to plays or novels it suggests too
much high-coloured incident, characters of unconvincing virtue or
vice, a happy ending in circumstances where such an outcome is
unlikely. But melodrama deserves a better reputation. Austere people,
who are by no means modest in asserting the excellence of their taste,
treat drama like wine; they are pleased only with comedy that is dry
and sharp to the palate, and tragedy that humbles you with its aristocracy of age. Melodrama offers none of that; it is hot and strong
and often rough and it stuns you into acceptance. That is why melodrama is so much truer to life as most of us experience it than either
comedy or tragedy. Melodrama reached its peak in the nineteenth
century and its greatest practitioner was Giuseppe Verdi. *Rigoletto* is
one of his finest melodramas.

It has its origin in a play by Victor Hugo, *Le roi s'amuse*, which
appeared in Paris in 1832, and was immediately suppressed, for a
reason not uncommon in the history of censorship: it seemed to
reflect unfavourably on the rights and privileges of monarchy. By the
time Verdi's opera, called then *La Maledizione*, made its appearance
in 1851, that had blown over, doubtless because it had struck through
even into the intelligence of officialdom that the play and the opera
were not about a corrupt court, except as it provided a background

for a drama about the workings of Fate. Verdi had, with his unerring instinct for a strong plot, seen what was at the root of Hugo's play, and his libretto by Piave goes straight to the point and sticks to it until the last curtain falls.

Verdi was not an easy man to satisfy with a libretto, because he knew what he wanted, and could doubtless have dispensed with a literary collaborator if that had been necessary. He himself decided what scenes he wanted, and gave his librettist a detailed scenario, indicating where emphasis was to come. The librettist then provided him with a version of the drama in which all the speeches were written out in prose. It was only when that had been approved that the librettist set to work to compose the verse for the opera, and here Verdi was extremely demanding, cutting and hacking until the essential points were as clear as they could be made without becoming positively telegraphic. Verdi did not ask for poetry of any distinguished order. Indeed, he disliked it because it distracted from his music. The inferiority of what he made his librettists produce from the bleeding ruins of *Macbeth* and *Othello* is proof of his musical genius, but certainly not of his literary taste. To read the libretto of a Verdi opera can be a shocking experience, for its crudity and the pell-mell speed of its action are worse than in the most unpolished prose melodrama of the period.

But Verdi knew what he was doing. He was composing a melodrama, which literally means a play conveyed in melody, and it is the music that establishes the emotion, determines the speed of the action, and carries the weight of the drama. Verdi was no Strauss or Benjamin Britten, who brought a fine taste and a deep respect for literature to their work as composers. We know that he liked to read classical poets, but he did not permit them to come between him and his work.

Nevertheless, there had to be a story, and words. The story of *Rigoletto* is about the working out of a curse. Monterone, a greatly wronged nobleman at the court of the Duke of Mantua, lays his curse first upon the Duke, and then, with greater emphasis, on the court jester and parasite, Rigoletto, who had mocked his wretchedness. Rigoletto is a wit (or at least so we are given to believe, though he never says anything funny that we hear) but he is not a man of strong intelligence; he is a superstitious man, whose court place he owes to his deformity, and the curse strikes coldly upon him. We watch the working out of the curse with fascination, as the jester's daughter is abducted with his own assistance, because he is made the fool of the Duke's courtiers; we know that Gilda has accepted an invitation which can only mean death. The curse strikes Rigoletto down because he has allied himself with an evil master, and because his own nature is base, when he might have sought to live more decently. There is nothing extraneous in the opera; everything moves inexorably toward the achievement of Monterone's curse.

How does Verdi achieve a work that is still one of the most popular in the standard repertoire of opera with such crude materials? By the brilliant deployment of his dramatic musical sense, which is powerful rather than subtle. Why do we, 140 years later, find ourselves gripped by *Rigoletto*? Do we believe in curses? In our age of sexual liberation do we worry about a girl who has been brought up to be simple (or innocent if you prefer) and who falls headlong for a wooer whose wish is to enjoy her and then get rid of her, as he has done many another? I think the answer must be in the affirmative. When we are under the spell of Verdi, we believe these things, and not because we have suddenly become stupid. Quite the contrary: through his art Verdi has given us uncomfortable enlightenment.

The human mind is an affair of many layers. However sophisticated we may be on the surface, we are usually aware that our sophistication is shallow and that deep in our hearts we believe many things which we might not wish to talk about to strangers. In most of us there is a strong hankering for what is sometimes called Poetic Justice, which may be interpreted colloquially as "Everybody, sooner or later, gets what's coming to him," or if we prefer a more classical turn of phrase: "Be not deceived; God is not mocked: for whatsoever a man soweth, that shall he also reap." Rigoletto chose to serve an evil master, and paid the price.

There is no point in snuffling over the jester's fate. We are not asked to consider that in his infancy the hunchbacked baby was probably sold to somebody who sold him as soon as possible to another wretch who dealt in such goods, supplying cripples and idiots to people who liked that kind of fun. If this were all there is to Rigoletto he would not have a lovely and innocent daughter. We have to look at the drama psychologically, and not realistically – which is to say, strictly on the surface. Gilda is the best of Rigoletto; she may be said to be his soul, which at last comes to ruin because of the degradation of his life. Verdi lays the blame solely on the jester himself, who has chosen to ally himself with evil and who pays the price. Who destroys the girl who is Rigoletto's soul but his evil master? But is the Duke really evil, and not just a man devoted to the pleasures of the senses? Is not the evil in Rigoletto himself? Is he the victim or the architect of his fate? We are gripped because, in some sense, we are all Rigolettos; we have done those things which we ought not to have done, and we have left undone those things that we ought to have done, and there is no health in us. In each of us there is a sinner, and when we see a sinner on the stage struck down in his pride, we feel the weight of the blow. Verdi is a severe moralist, like many another great artist. He does not preach from the pulpit, but from the playhouse. And like so many great preachers, it is not our overt actions, but the desires of our hearts for which he holds us accountable.

You did not think when you booked seats for *Rigoletto* that you were coming to a sermon? Of course not; you are quite right. But art on a high level – and Verdian opera is a pretty high level – is rooted in morality, and Rigoletto is a demonstration of the inexorable workings of Fate. What Rigoletto has sown, we see him reap. Here is the master of melodrama in his finest form.

20

— ❧ —

OPERA FOR THE MAN WHO
READS HAMLET

IN THIS LECTURE ABOUT "Opera as Related to Literature" (he used both titles for this talk), Davies has given many examples of operas whose libretti were based, however loosely, on books. We have selected three pieces from his Theatre Diaries to give you his reactions to productions of these operas. *Wozzeck* was chosen because it was the first time he saw it, and *Sir John in Love* and *Falstaff* because they are based on Shakespeare's *The Merry Wives of Windsor*. The lecture was first given at Roy Thomson Hall in Toronto on March 15, 1989, and again at the St. Louis Opera Festival on June 18, 1989. Colin Graham, who is referred to in the Diary entry, is the Artistic Director of the St. Louis Festival.

October 29, 1977, Saturday: *Alone to* Wozzeck *by the Canadian Opera Company at O'Keefe: Had never seen it or heard a note of it before. Captivated. Deep pathos approaching tragedy. Could not have been achieved except by Berg's atonalism, which totally won me. Fine performances by Allan Monk as Wozzeck, Lynn Vernon as Marie, and Ara Berberian as the Doctor and all the others congruous. Very good simple production by Lotfi Mansouri, and sensitively conducted by Raffi Armenian. As I left a woman I did not know seized me: "Didn't you think that last scene was just awful? It left the whole thing flat." I had found the last scene deeply moving, and said so. Many old-guard opera people won't go to* Wozzeck. *And it was written in 1925!*

March 2, 1984: *Friday: at the Macmillan Theatre, the Opera School,* Sir John in Love. *Have known this opera since Mazzoleni discoursed on it at U.C.C.* [Upper Canada College] *nearly sixty years ago: I believe he did some study with Ralph Vaughan Williams while it was being written, or produced. Have greatly admired it from the score and the recording but have never seen it before. Pretty well acted, though costumes were unimaginative except for the children in the forest. Settings bad, feebly coloured and Olde Shakespearean in the weak sense – though the forest in Act 3, Scene 2 was good. Lighting disastrous: purple skies and pastel "effects." But the singing was good and the orchestra under James Craig good though often too loud. Tempi right and sense of the texture of the music right. What a fine score! I prefer it to Verdi's* Falstaff, *which lacks tenderness and of course Englishness, and reduces the plot to Mediterranean sniggering about cuckoldry and Falstaff to a mere schemer. But Ralph Vaughan Williams gives it fine English dimension and opens up the silly plot with magnificent, truly Shakespearean music. We were delighted, as was the full house.*

April 14, 1992: *Tuesday: Canadian Opera Company* Falstaff *well directed by Jonathan Eaton and conducted by Richard Bradshaw. The* Globe and Mail *slated this production but I found it excellent, though it does not reconcile me to Italianized Shakespeare. Timothy Noble a spirited, witty Falstaff and Nancy Gustafson a charming Mrs. Ford. What a good artist she is as well as an excellent singer. Sheila Nadler as Mrs. Quickly has a fine voice and presence but is too pleased with herself as a comic – though Verdi tempts the player to overdo. Bardofo and Pistola admirable – Bardofo a gnome and Pistola a giant – and they were truly actors who can sing. Enjoyed the evening and dismissed*

The Merry Wives of Windsor *from my mind for its duration. But what an Italian mess Boito has made of Shakespeare's warm bourgeois play – even dragging in a Trappist monk: he and Verdi had no conception of anyone who was not either a Roman Catholic or a Freemason, and cuckoldry was their one joke.*

Davies wrote in his daily diary at St. Louis on June 18, 1989: *Lunch with Colin Graham at the Botanical Gardens. Fine gardens: indifferent food. A storm comes up and torrential rain falls. I fear there will be no one at my talk, for the streets are flooded, but upward of a thousand make it and the lecture goes well. Much applause and the sponsors are very pleased. Encounter the campus bag lady – a learned woman who lives with her brother, a former member of the faculty, in a derelict car: they haunt the campus, are at all refreshments, go to all the free lectures and concerts and wash in the public loos. In fact, real medieval university hangers-on. University opinion about them is understandably divided.*

———— ❦ ————

Ibelieve that you have been told that I am going to speak about "Opera as Related to Literature." That is indeed a portentous title for a speech, and if I remember correctly it came into being some time ago when the lady who was preparing publicity for these talks demanded a title for my speech, and wanted it without delay. On such occasions I am likely to panic and say the first thing that comes into my head, and I suppose I said "Opera as Related to Literature." But when I felt today drawing nearer, and I had to work on my speech, I realized that I had bitten off far more than I can chew. "Opera as Related to Literature," indeed! It would take a long scholarly book to begin to come to grips with that subject, and it would have to be written by somebody else. It is quite outside my abilities.

I know a little bit about literature, though it seems to be less every day. But literature has been the great joy of my life, and the unresting pursuit of my life, even when I have had to give much of my energy to other things. Opera is another matter: I am devoted to it, I go to the opera wherever I am whenever I can. But in what relates to opera I am, in the true sense of the word, an amateur. And I assure you that in opera I do not look for the kind of pleasure that comes from literature. Opera is a wholly different satisfaction. I recently made a count of operas I have seen, and the figure is something between eighty and ninety, which astonished me, for I thought it would have been much higher. Of course I have seen several of those operas many times, and under all sorts of conditions. If I heard that *The Magic Flute* was to be performed by polar bears, on an iceberg, I should immediately hasten to book a ticket. At the other end of the scale, I had the luck to see many splendid productions of rarely performed operas, one of which was Weber's *Oberon* at the Paris Opera with the original, dreadful libretto by J. R. Planché. That was an experience to cherish, for *Oberon* is surely one of the most ill-used, messed-about great works in the operatic repertoire. But as you see, my experience of opera is not great, though it has certainly been enthusiastic. I am not the man to pronounce learnedly on "Opera as Related to Literature." I can only give you a few personal opinions, and when I have finished you are free to contradict me and despise me as much as you please.

Several years ago an excellent book was published called *Music for the Man Who Reads Hamlet*; perhaps a suitable title for what I am going to say would be "Opera for the Man Who Reads *Hamlet*," and I wish I had thought of it when a title was asked for. Perhaps some of you wonder if I have ever seen *Hamlet* as an opera. Indeed I have. There are, so far as I can discover, something like fourteen operatic assaults upon *Hamlet*, and God forbid that I should see them all. I have never seen Ambrose Thomas's *Hamlet*, which first appeared in 1868, but I have strummed the score on the piano, and I found that at times I could hardly see the music for tears – of laughter. It concludes with Hamlet ascending the throne of Denmark amid the cheers of his admiring courtiers; Hamlet does not have soliloquies, in which he opens his heart – no, he has a Drinking Song, in which he opens his throat. The genius of the French people has never been receptive to Shakespeare, and Thomas was very, very French. But his opera has this to be said for it; it is funny. None of the *Hamlet* operas I have seen were in the least funny.

Why has *Hamlet* never been made into a great opera? The answer is simple; it is too complex; its mingling of political and dynastic arguments with the spiritual agonies of the deeply introverted, philosophical hero cannot be accommodated to the chief necessity of an opera libretto, which is simplicity. Verdi knew all about that. In a letter in which he refused an invitation to write a new work for the Paris Opera, he said: "If the work is an organic whole, it is built on a single idea, and everything must contribute to the achievement of this unity." There is no single idea in *Hamlet*: its extraordinary power lies in the opposition of several irreconcilable ideas; the opera has never found a way to do that. Irreconcilable forces and ambitions, yes: irreconcilable philosophies, no. Consider that wonderful opera *Wozzeck*; we are shown the wretchedness of Wozzeck, who is tragic because he stands for the great mass of the ignorant and the oppressed, and the opera is terrifying in its range of pathos. But of the philosophical implications of Büchner's play we hear nothing, because that is not the sort of material with which opera can cope. If we want philosophy or profound reflection in music we must find it in whatever is aroused in us by the work of the great symphonic masters. We cannot have it imposed on us from the stage through the medium of that most evocative, stirring, and emotionally powerful instrument, the human voice. If it were otherwise, the Dialogues of Plato would be the finest operatic libretti in existence.

This is not to say that opera is a mindless form of art. I am saying rather that the region of the mind that is engaged in opera is not the same as the region of the mind that brings forth philosophy or profound discussions of abstract topics. But as soon as I have said that I am reminded of an opera which contradicts me; it is Benjamin Britten's *Death in Venice*, in which the reflection on the nature of art that is basic to Thomas Mann's wonderful story is manifested in musical form with astonishing success. It is achieved, however, in a long central passage of ballet, not in operatic action of the usual kind. Britten is particularly gifted in his ability to handle difficult themes

and unresolved problems, and in *The Turn of the Screw* and *Billy Budd*
we have examples almost unparalleled in the history of opera of
musical subtlety matching literary subtlety. Although I would not go
so far as to say that Britten extends the range of the literary sources
of his work, he certainly does them no damage – and that is much
more of a compliment than you might at first suppose. Perhaps time
will show that Britten has given opera a new direction.

Who do you consider to be the supreme master in operatic
composition? Many will say Mozart. Many more, perhaps, will say
Verdi. There will be a few voices for Strauss. There may be bold
spirits who will say Puccini – though we have all been so beaten by
the critics who say he is vulgar that we may hesitate to declare our
preference. There may be some who will agree with me that
Tschaikovsky is usually underrated and, although we would not put
him at the top of the tree, we think he deserves a higher place than
he is usually given.

Let us take a slightly lowbrow point of view and say: who fills the
opera houses most often? A great director of opera, the late Tyrone
Guthrie, once told me that for his money, *Carmen* was the greatest
opera of them all. He called it "the perfect opera." He spoke from a
director's point of view, of course. In *Carmen* there is something happening all the time; even that tedious girl Micaela does not succeed
in holding up the action for long. It is drama from start to finish and
there is no nonsense about complex psychology or ambiguity of
purpose to be found anywhere.

I think this may be true, or as true as such brief judgements are
likely to be. But let us look at the short novel by Mérimée on which
Carmen is founded. In it we find a great deal about the predicament
of Don José, who has to sacrifice his adored mother, his country
sweetheart, and his loyalty to his soldier's calling in his hopeless
pursuit of a heartless gypsy slut, Carmen. In the story José is a very
young man and his sudden seizure by overwhelming sexual passion
is more than he can handle. But when did you last see a really young
José on the stage? The reason is an excellent one in operatic terms:
a very young tenor cannot successfully cope with the music, and what
we demand is Placido Domingo or somebody close to him, who can

thrill us when the opera demands that we should be thrilled, with a mature voice.

The same thing applies to Carmen. How old is she supposed to be? Under twenty, in all probability, and still a stranger to the compassion which might come in another ten years. She ruins José because she is a bitch, no more, no less. But on the stage we cannot afford that, because we want a Carmen who can knock us out of our seats, and if that means that we are watching a drama of mature cruelty opposed to apparently retarded masculinity, we are glad enough to pay the price. But the flavour of Mérimée's story has gone, and has been replaced by something quite different. Not inferior, I insist, but certainly not the drama as it was conceived by its author.

Mérimée's story is not a great work of literary art, and it survives the simplification the opera makes necessary without too much being lost. And this is where I reach what is, I suppose, the substance of what I wish to say: great literary art cannot be transferred to the opera stage without the loss of virtually everything that gives it greatness. I am not speaking simply of style, and the masterly use of language, although, of course, that is important. Apart from style, great writing carries the colour and texture of the writer's mind. What is left of the great work of literature, after the operatic composer has finished with it, is the plot, and the boldest depiction of the characters. Literary art is not enlarged or complemented by music; indeed, second-best is often best for musical settings. When opera turns to great drama or great narrative for its libretti, dreadful rapes are likely to result.

Such a rape, which never fails to astonish and amuse me, is the libretto for *Lucia di Lammermoor*, prepared for Donizetti by Salvatore Cammarano. It is reputedly based on Sir Walter Scott's novel, *The Bride of Lammermoor*. One might say, without exaggeration, that every dramatic stroke Scott has provided, Cammarano has ungratefully snubbed. The leading character in the book is Edgar of Ravenswood, who is a fine example of the Byronic hero, the Fated Man, for he lives under a curse. Understandably, perhaps, Cammarano wanted his heroine, Lucy Ashton, to be the leading role, but he need not have robbed Edgar of virtually all character.

In the novel, by the way, Lucy is presented to us as a girl so sensi-tive, so delicate that at one point Scott describes her as almost imbe-cilic, but her beauty of form and character was so great that Edgar could not resist her. In the novel the impediment to the marriage of the lovers is not solely the greed of her brother Henry; Lucy is socially inferior to Edgar, for he comes of a great house, and her people are *nouveaux riches* and what is worse, a low kind of Presbyterian; Edgar, of course, is very High Church Anglican. This is what makes it hilarious when, in the opera, we see Lucy's wedding procession. I have seen it done, at the Met, no less, with enough nuns and monks and priests and bishops and even a Cardinal to fill a stage; I have seen Henry Ashton, that low Presbyterian, prostrating himself before a huge Cross in his private chamber. The chaplain Raimond, who is of course a Presbyterian – perhaps even a Wee Free – is usually represented as some sort of priest, or at least an abbé. And thus the psychological background of the drama is thrown away, pre-sumably to please Italian audiences who could not conceive of anybody with a fixed income being anything but a Roman Catholic. After the great Mad Scene the opera runs downhill, culminating in a dull last scene, with only the dull Edgardo to carry it. But as I told you, in the novel Edgar of Ravenswood is a Fated Man, conscious of a prophecy uttered by one of three magnificent old witches who are cut out of the opera. This is the prophecy:

When the last Laird of Ravenswood to Ravenswood shall ride,
And woo a dead maiden to be his bride,
He shall stable his steed in the Kelpie's flow
And his name shall be lost forevermoe!

Imagine that last scene! Edgar rides his horse out into the quicksand until he disappears, and only the eagle's feather on his Scottish bonnet is to be seen above the cruel waters! There's drama for you! But not for Salvatore Cammarano, who enjoyed a great reputation as a con-triver of operatic libretti.

Let us look at another obvious example. Goethe's *Faust* is one of the great dramas of Western civilization. But when Gounod decides to make an opera of it, and turns to Barbier and Carré for a text, what happens? The awesome theme of the philosopher who sacrifices his hopes of immortality for earthly power becomes a tale of a silly old man who asks for the return of his youth and then throws everything away in pursuit of a village ninny; he has not even the common prudence to ask the Devil to sterilize her before he seduces her. You remember the Devil's cynical comment in the play? "She's not the first!" Goethe's great creation of Mephistopheles becomes a sideshow conjuror and we are treated to the ballet, the Soldiers Chorus, and the Drinking Song without which a French opera of the nineteenth century would have been unthinkable. Goethe's mighty warning against materialism is turned into a trumpery tear-jerker.

What is the outcome? I am devoted to the genius of Goethe but I will go to see Gounod's *Faust* any day, because I love a good third-rate melodrama, wedded to some excellent second-rate music. I leave all thoughts of the real *Faust* at home, knowing that it has no relevance whatever to what I am going to hear at the opera.

It is not for nothing that the book of the words of an opera is called a libretto. You know what the word means: a little book, and books don't come littler than they do when they enclose the words, and the words alone, of an opera. Who reads a libretto simply for literary pleasure? There have been musicians, men of refined literary taste, who have sought to change this situation by a simple means of setting a fine play to music, without change. Debussy's *Pélleas et Mélisande* is such an opera; virtually every word of Maeterlinck's magical play is set to music. Another example is Ralph Vaughan Williams's *Riders to the Sea*, in which he has followed J. M. Synge's text faithfully. But philistine that I am, I wonder when I hear these works if it would not have been better simply to act the play, and avoid all that tedium of slowness which is involved in setting prose dialogue – even when it is prose dialogue of great poetic resonance – to music? A great play is not a great libretto, for the excellent reason that it is not a little book. It is a great book, and music can do nothing to enhance it.

Some of you are probably dying to shout, "What about Verdi and Shakespeare?" Sorry, I am not to be moved. *Macbeth* and *Othello* leave me cold. What Piave and Boito did to Shakespeare offends me deeply; they have turned these mighty tragedies into nineteenth-century melodramas, with the full agreement, and indeed under the remorseless demands, of Verdi. I know that Verdi adored the playwright, whom he called Papa Shakespeare, but to be an object of adoration is not always a happy fate. Too often the adorer is convinced that the adored one is a mirror image of himself, and Verdi, who knew little English, did not know Shakespeare nearly so well as he thought he did.

I do not accuse Verdi of wilful vandalizing of Shakespeare. But he was a man of the nineteenth century, and it was a time when Shakespeare was roughly treated. When, indeed, has Shakespeare not been roughly treated? Soon after his death dreadful versions of his plays were prepared for the stage in which inferior writers had corrected what they thought of as his Gothic crudities and his want of art. I have read many of them: *Lears* that end happily, *A Midsummer Night's Dream* reduced to a pantomime, *Romeo and Juliet* in which the lovers recover from their suicide. In the nineteenth century it was usual for leading actors to perform versions of Shakespeare's plays in which the leading roles were made attractive to a distinguished actor and an actress of high quality, and thrown into high relief by remorseless cutting of the text, rearrangement of the scenes, and sometimes by rewriting. This was shameless and rough in Britain and the United States, but at least most of what was spoken on the stage was the work of the poet; on the Continent translators rendered Shakespeare in the fashion most suited to their language and added whatever pleased them. The German translations are the best; the French were drastic; the Italian translations were, in the worst sense of the word, operatic. What Verdi knew of Shakespeare were his plots – which are not always Shakespeare's best work – and the characters, and the strongly defined situations. We know what the resulting libretti were like. We in Toronto are accustomed to reading the white type above the proscenium during *Macbeth*, when something not far removed from this is likely to appear, having been translated first into Italian, and then back into telegraphic English:

Let's kill the King.
Good idea. He's in the guest-room.
Somehow I don't like the idea.
That's you all over! Give me the daggers!

Of course when this is sung, splendidly, in Italian, we may yield in some measure to the spell, but not if our loyalty to Shakespeare is profound.

I must restrain my urge to talk too long about Shakespeare, but there is one thing I must say. A distinguishing quality of his mind, as reflected in his plays, is his sense of another world which lies behind his use of ghosts, witches, fairies, monsters, and other uncanny creatures in order to rouse our sense of the workings of Fate in human life. Those of you who know something of Verdi's personal life know how remote such thinking was from his mind; he would doubtless have agreed with those who insisted that this element in Shakespeare's work belonged to an earlier, superstitious age, and to beliefs which the nineteenth century – so remorselessly rational in its thinking – had outgrown.

One such belief was in the mystical quality of kingship. When Macbeth killed King Duncan, he not only committed murder; he violated something in the order of nature, and nature and the super-natural – the supernatural is simply that portion of nature herself we do not care to accept freely – exacted its penalty. Verdi, who was inclined to think that all rulers were tyrants, was not in tune with any mystical ideas about monarchy, and he was strongly opposed to the concept of Fate Tragedy which appealed to so many theatre artists of his time. Verdi's kingdom is very much a kingdom of this world. A gorgeous, thrilling world, but nevertheless a palpable world.

I have not yet said anything about *Falstaff*, which many people consider Verdi's supreme achievement. In *The Merry Wives of Windsor* Shakespeare wrote his only play of bourgeois life, and the sense that this play gives us of Elizabethan England depends on its variety of characters – village types, the doctor, the clergyman, the magistrate, the well-to-do merchants, the innkeeper, the domestic servant, the young man with more money than brain, the loafers and rousta-bouts − and it is for this panorama of a charming complete community, not pastoral, but certainly not of the court or the city, that we turn to the play for refreshment. The central plot, in which Falstaff is made a village joke by two charming, faithful wives, serves to hold the play together, but it is not the essence of the play, for that is a delightful Englishness of good humour and warm domestic feeling.

But when Boito is let loose on the English charm of the play, he ruthlessly cuts out everything except the fooling of Falstaff, and he turns that into the favourite joke of the Mediterranean world − the joke of the deceived husband. Sometimes one is driven to feel that it is the only joke Mediterranean people can really understand. Certainly Italy, which had no bourgeoisie in the English sense, was not a fertile soil for this extremely English comedy. The result is some very coarse characterization, disguised by some very fine music, and a dismally thin plot. Vaughan Williams wrote a much better opera as *Sir John in Love* and perhaps some time you will do it here.

Very fine music − that explains it all. In *Otello*, when the villain, Iago, takes his place centre stage and confides to us that he believes in a cruel God, we put up with his nonsense because what he is singing is so much more expressive than what he is saying. We forget the subtlety of Shakespeare's Iago, who is a superb and baffling study of many-coloured malignity, and settle for Verdi's puppet with the golden voice. So, in *Falstaff*, we put up with Verdi's funny fat man, though we cannot forget Shakespeare's superb portrait of the triumph of wit and undefeated intellect over the indignities of age and poverty.

Have I offended you? How many people have walked out, as I have blasphemed against Verdi? Do not think I do not revere his greatness. But the exactions of opera made him, to my way of thinking, at his best in such works as *La Traviata*, the last act of which would draw tears from a gorilla. Here, you see, Verdi is dealing with a novel, later a play, by the Younger Dumas. It is not a great novel, but it is finer than Verdi lets us know. The author tells us how cheap, how ill-mannered and grasping Violetta was, and yet, for all her harlot's vulgarities, she was irresistible because she could charm a bird out of a tree and her beauty was transporting. But Verdi has given us one of art's great portrayals of that archetypal figure, the Lost Lady, and Alfredo has none of the Younger Dumas's double-mindedness about her.

Now, at last, I am getting to what it is about opera that makes me its slave – though, like most slaves, I am not wholly uncritical of the slave-master. Opera in a splendidly direct way takes us into the world of archetypes, and music has its own overmastering way of making archetypes palpable to us. Music is the language of feeling, not of thought, and when it meets literature – as it does in opera – it is the language of music which must prevail. In great opera it does prevail and silences, or almost silences, criticism of what it does to its sister-art, literature. As E. T. A. Hoffmann put it, "The lyre of Orpheus opens the door of the underworld," and the underworld is the home of the archetypes.

What is an archetype? The word is thrown about nowadays in a careless way, but most of the people who use it would be stumped if they were asked for a definition. Indeed, a definition is not easily formed, but I am going to try.

The word has been given currency because it is important in the analytical psychology of C. G. Jung. He defines it, in part, in these words: "In my view, it is a great mistake to suppose that the psyche of a new-born child is a *tabula rasa* in the sense that there is absolutely nothing in it. In so far as a child is born with a brain that is predetermined by heredity . . . it meets sensory stimuli coming from outside not with *any* aptitudes, but with *specific* ones . . . These aptitudes can be shown to be inherited instincts and performed patterns . . . They are the archetypes, which direct all fantasy activity into its appointed paths and in this way produce . . . astonishing mythological parallels such as can also be found . . . in the dreams of normal persons. It is not, therefore, a question of inherited *ideas*, but inherited *possibilities* of ideas." In other, and much cruder terms, we respond to ideas about the world and about our lives which are part of our inheritance as human beings. In great opera, as in great painting and great literature, we meet these possibilities of ideas given an immediate and incomprehensive form, and we are seized by them because what we see and hear from the stage speaks directly to things that lie very deep in our nature.

Shall we try another example? One of the operas which is a staple of the popular repertoire is Puccini's *La Bohème*. What lies at the heart of it? The overwhelming nature of youthful love, which comes to us when we have not fallen utterly into the grip of anxieties about a career, about money, indeed about anything that puts a cold hand on the marvel of the present. Young love is not love that will endure forever; frequently it is utterly impossible and ill-advised and it will certainly die. Usually it is supplanted by a love which has more hope of endurance in a world where love does not conquer all; we know perfectly well, if we pause to think about it, that Rodolfo and Mimi would never make an enduring and happy marriage, just as in *La Traviata* we know that Violetta and Alfredo haven't a chance, because she is a harlot and he is a poet and even one of those elements in a single union may be too much. But the beauty of what these lovers feel in the present strikes directly into the hearts of the audience at the opera, because there are very few people who have not, at some time, experienced something of what Mimi and Rodolfo feel. This all-subduing love is an archetype, a possibility, and we are swept up by it emotionally, however we may question it intellectually. But if you read Murger's novel with its bald Rudolphe and its silly Mimi, you may not weep, but your ideas about the pathos of life will be enlarged, for that book has not the music of Puccini, but what Wordsworth calls "the still, sad music of humanity."

We recognize these archetypes throughout the operatic range. The archetype of Power is plain as day in *Boris Godunov* and in *Macbeth*, as is also the archetype of Fate, for God is not mocked and the usurpers are brought low. The operas of Wagner, about which I have said nothing, are built upon a complexity of archetypal ideas which were the spiritual baggage of that extraordinary genius and dreadful crook, Richard Wagner, who must surely have had as wide a range of accessible archetypal material in his personal psychology as any genius of the operatic world. If Verdi had little apprehension of the unseen world in his nature, surely Wagner has enough for two. Britten and Tschaikovsky speak through their music of things that they would probably – Tschaikovsky certainly – have denied in any written discussion of their lives. The great operatic composer speaks to us from the archetypal roots of his own psyche, and we respond from what we share with him in that shadowy but immensely powerful realm. It is here that Wagner stands alone and untouchable by any other composer.

It is easy to make fun of opera. The people who say that they cannot understand why anyone should sing what he thinks and feels when he might more easily speak it, have missed the point completely; the singing possesses an authority which many people do not feel in the greatest poetry, because with poetry there must be some intellectual quality in the hearer's understanding, but with singing there need be none. To express the overmastering passion of love Shakespeare writes a sonnet, but when at the end of act one of *La Bohème* Mimi and Rodolfo go out of the door of their garret singing "Amor, Amor," the same archetype is evoked in us. Let us not haggle foolishly about which is the greater art. They are not susceptible of comparison, though they draw their strength from the same depths.

There are people who insist that opera is a vulgar art, and personally I do not mind that at all. Vulgar simply means "of the people" and great opera is of the people to a far greater extent than is great literature – though on the Shakespearean level literature is vulgar in the same sense and appeals to the same wide audience.

I am aware that I have said nothing about Mozart, who has in our day been accorded the highest acclaim as an operatic composer. It was not always so. I remember a few years ago talking about *Cosi Fan Tutte* with a relative of mine, who was a fine musician, trained in Germany at the time when Brahms was the God of all right-thinking musical people. He could not understand my enthusiasm. "It's accomplished, it's pretty, but it's so *trivial*," he said. And I know what he was talking about. It was Da Ponte's libretto, which is all those things, but in which Mozart found a vehicle for the expression of a wonderful acceptance of human frailty, which turns a cynical playlet into a masterpiece of Comedy. For Comedy, I assure you, is one of the most powerful of all the archetypes, for it enables us to see folly and beauty intermingled, and to love them both.

So, I was to talk about "Opera as Related to Literature," was I not? And because the subject is so vast, I have wandered here and there, trying to illuminate, as if with a candle, a vast chamber full of fascinating corners, mysterious with mirrors, and echoing with some of the loveliest music ever written. I have not succeeded on any high level, but then, I never expected to do so. But perhaps I have thrown out an idea or two which you would like to consider for yourselves.

21

---- ⌛ ----

OPERA AND HUMOUR

THIS LECTURE WAS GIVEN as the Prince of Hesse Memorial Lecture at the Aldeburgh Festival, Aldeburgh, England, on June 11, 1991. The Festival was founded in 1948 by the composer Benjamin Britten and the singer Peter Pears. Aldeburgh is a small fishing town on the east coast of England, made famous largely because Britten lived there for many years and because of the existence of the Festival. The lecture series was started in memory of Prince Ludwig of Hesse and the Rhine, and his widow was, at this time, the President of the Aldeburgh Foundation.

Davies noted in his travel diary: *Give the Hesse Lecture in the Town Hall: a decided success and indeed I think I stunned them, but delighted the Princess who said that many previous lectures had been short-weight – "wanting in content," she put it. Jokes went well and eased them painlessly into the Jungian-Heraclitean part. So that is done, and well done. Lunch after with the Princess: a party of thirty and a large and luxurious luncheon beginning with chilled vodka. The Princess is a Scot, eighty and*

*determined, charming and very much on the beam: liked her
immensely.*

In the lecture that follows Davies draws on the Strauss opera
Ariadne auf Naxos for examples of humour in opera. He wrote in
his travel diary of a production he saw on October 3, 1995: *The
Canadian Opera Company* Ariadne auf Naxos *very well done
under Bradshaw: sensitivity but not to the point of degeneracy.
Fine cast: Isabelle Vernet, as Ariadne, partnered by David Rampy
as Bacchus; they both sang admirably and* intelligently:
*Zerbinetta was Tracy Dahl who sang brilliantly but was cruelly
costumed. Kristine Jepson as the Composer sang splendidly and
made the Composer's yielding to Zerbinetta touching and beautiful. So – a great evening for the ear and one forgave what one
saw. The Nymphs were very personable and sang finely. Only the
comedians were under par, and their roles are impossible: acro-
bats and great mimes do not sing: their costumes were messy.
Produced by Tom Diamond, tactful and funny in the right places,
and noble when nobility was called for. Monty Wood played the
Prima Donna's pet: twenty seconds of glory. David William was
the Major Domo: a fine actor but failed here: inaudible. What
happened. – This opera is one of my great favourites: a great and
daring theme of Tragedy and Comedy mingled, superbly worked
out. A theme very dear to me for I value Tragedy less than
Comedy, for it exalts in so many cases a noble stupidity. Not, of
course, in Shakespeare except in* Othello.

———— ❧ ————

Let me begin by dispelling any
impression you may have received that this is going to be a funny
lecture. As soon as I had imparted my title – "Opera and Humour"
– to Miss Sheila Colvin, I began to regret it, but the word had been
given, and there was no way in which I could recall it. You know
why: the programs and brochures for such a festival as this must be
printed early in the season, and once they have been given to the

printer, there is no room for second thoughts. So – "Opera and Humour" it must be, and if anyone has come this morning expecting one of those side-splitting talks about the performance of *Lohengrin* when the swan made its entrance backward, or the time when Tosca could not find the knife and had to murder Scarpia with a candlestick, I beg that person to feel free to leave at once. I shall not take offence. I intend to be serious about my subject, and as you know, when someone undertakes to be serious about humour, the result is certain to be of the uttermost gravity.

Having thus warned you, let us talk for a while about humour. I assume that we shall get to opera in good time, but not at once.

Humour is extraordinarily hard to define, and even the meaning of the word is in dispute. Everybody claims to have a sense of humour; at least, I have never met anyone who would admit to having no sense of humour. But when this "sense of humour" is examined, it usually proves to be sharply limited and often – though not invariably – it is conditioned by considerations of class, of education, and of nationality. The theatre audience which is convulsed by *No Sex Please, We're British* is certainly not that which is delighted with *The Way of the World*; the man who reads and rereads the romances of P. G. Wodehouse is not the man who is enthralled with the complex humour of *Finnegans Wake*; the fun of Martin Amis is certainly not that of Jane Austen. Yet all of these works may claim to be humour of one sort or another. There are people who wince at a pun, and people who cannot resist a pun. There are people who confine humour to funny stories and do not acknowledge it in any other form. A Russian friend of mine once told me that the Russians had no sense of humour, apart from an elaborate facetiousness. A French friend assured me that the French have the most acute perception of humour of any nation in the world about everything but themselves. As for the English sense of humour, it is widely celebrated. I wish I had time to offer you some examples of Canadian humour, which tends to be ironic, but I do not wish to dispel the widely held notion that Canadians have no sense of humour. I once had a dispute with a group of Swedish professors at the University of Uppsala as to which country, Sweden or Canada, was the dullest in the world. It was a draw; they claimed superiority because of their long history, and I claimed it because of Canada's immense land mass, which gives us space for tremendous expansion, even of such things as dullness.

Humour has been pursued by many distinguished scholars, who have attempted, with the uttermost seriousness, to say what it is. I have read the chief works in this field, and I can say of them, as the schoolboy said of the Complete Works of Matthew Arnold, that they are no place to go for a laugh. One of the most famous is *Le Rire, Essai sur la signification du comique*, by the philosopher Henri Bergson; Bergson's proposal, very roughly, is that comedy arises from the rigidity, the failure to adapt to circumstances, which makes a person behave like a mechanism, and society seeks to correct this defect by its laughter. But unquestionably the most famous book on the subject is *Wit and Its Relation to the Unconscious* by Sigmund Freud; it is a brilliant book and not an easy book to master, and its psychoanalytical discussion of what is funny, and why, is illuminating without being, to me at least, wholly persuasive. Incongruity, relief of tension, and resolution of conflict are all observable in humour, but something prevents me from accepting Freud's explanation as a wholly satisfactory one. The reason is that, like virtually all of Freud's thinking, it is reductive in tendency, and his ideas about humour support his deeply pessimistic view of life. I have never been convinced that pessimism is the only possible philosophical attitude for a thinking person; it is notable in some of its aspects, but it is not all-inclusive. I had a friend, a deeply learned man, who used to assure me from time to time that what he called The Tragic Attitude was the only one possible for anyone who was not foolishly deluded about the nature of life. I cannot accept that because it exalts the mind of man as the measure of all things. In the great tragedies of the Greeks it is the suffering of an individual which is supposed to darken the sun for everybody who is aware of it. That is an egotism I cannot admire. The mind of man, though perhaps the most splendid achievement of evolution, is not, surely, the answer to every problem of the universe. Hamlet suffers, but the Gravediggers go right on with their silly quibbles. Hamlet is great but he is not the only creature under the sun.

So, brilliant as Freud is, I would hesitate to apply his theory of humour to opera, or indeed to any manifestation of the creative spirit. He was not at his best when he approached the world of creative art. To his credit it must be said that he admitted as much.

Of course the academic critics have had their say about the nature of humour, though not about its origins. Indeed, in my own country the University of Ottawa publishes twice yearly a compilation called *Thalia; Studies in Literary Humour*, and in it you may read carefully thought-out studies called "William Cowper as Mock Epideictic Elegist," and "Social Myth as Parody in Jack London's Northern Tales." These discussions are in themselves interesting, but the light they shed on the nature and origin of humour is not blinding.

Not only the philosophers and the psychoanalysts have presented us with theories of humour, of course; the scientists have been at work as well. Their experiments are often fine examples of unintentional humour. We cannot go into this subject at length, but I should like to present you with the finding of some scientists who claim to have discovered that women find jokes funniest when they hear them with the left ear, because this ear relates to the right hemisphere of the brain, which processes information more holistically than the left hemisphere, which is analytical.

Think of the work that must have gone into this discovery! Call up in your minds the silent laboratory, in which the white-coated experimenters are gathered around a steel chair, in which a woman sits; she wears a hospital gown and electrodes are attached to her wrists, ankles, and diaphragm, which in turn lead to a device that measures her responses. Her left ear is filled with a medicated wax, and is covered by an earmuff, which has a lead plate inside it, to exclude all sound. A total hush prevails. The most important of the investigators approaches her, and leaning forward speaks slowly and clearly into her right ear. He reads very distinctly from a book, and we can see that the title is *Joe Miller's Jests*. "Why does the chicken cross the road?" he reads. An interval of a full minute passes before he reads the answer, "To get to the other side." The woman's eyes cloud over; her response, if anything, is an expression of disgust. But now there is a half hour's break, while the subject is given a cup of tea, and her right ear is blocked, while the left ear is syringed out and restored to full usefulness. When silence has been restored, the chief investigator approaches her once again. "Why do firemen wear red braces?" he asks. A minute passes and he gives the answer, "To hold up their pants." Eureka! The woman is immediately convulsed, slaps her thigh, tumbles out of the chair and rolls upon the floor, helpless with laughter. The attendants give her a tranquillizer and she is wheeled back to bed, to recover. It is thus, you see, that science enlarges our lives and expands the boundaries of human knowledge.

You may well protest that it is easy work to make fun of these deeply serious people who have tried to explain something of the nature of humour, and you may well ask me if I can do better. I do not know, but I can try. I have no unshakeable confidence that I shall succeed wholly, but perhaps I may open another approach to this elusive subject, and someone following me may smooth the path that I have hacked through the undergrowth.

Let me begin by brushing aside all simple jokes, wisecracks, and journalistic or television drolleries. They are well enough in their way but they are poor substitutes for what I take humour to be. *The Oxford English Dictionary*, defining humour, calls it "that quality of action, speech, or writing which excites amusement; oddity, jocularity, facetiousness, comicality, fun. The faculty of perceiving what is ludicrous or amusing, or of expressing it in speech, writing, or other composition; jocose imagination or treatment of a subject." Of course a dictionary must record educated usage, not opinions, and I think that indeed educated usage banishes humour with such grandsire terms as jocular, facetious, comical, jocose. But all these words suggest something that is done to us by a determined funnyman, to which we lend ourselves with a sense of having for the moment set aside our accustomed gravity; in such circumstances humour is imposed upon us; it is not something that is evoked from within us. I think that we all have, in some measure, a quality within us that may be termed humour, which asserts itself independently of the determined work of the clown, the gagman, or the sophisticated wit. After all, the word "humour" used to mean something that was characteristic of a human creature, and I think that indeed it is so still.

To explain what I mean, you must bear with me during a brief venture into the psychology of the late Carl Gustav Jung. Not that Jung wrote about humour; so far as I know, no speculative thinker in the psychoanalytical world save Freud ever did so. You will search in vain in the indexes of works of philosophy or psychology for any references to humour. For centuries it was considered an unworthy, undignified quality. My guess is that because humour always suggests uncertainty, or ambiguity, the wise men feared it. But Jung gives us hints as to where to look for humour. Indeed, the search for it recalls those medieval legends, where we set out to find a sacred spring in a tangled wood. We meet with many dragons and misdirections on the way, but we hope to get the better of them, because we know that the water of the spring brings magical transformation. I do not exaggerate in my use of the metaphor of the magical spring. Schopenhauer was unusual among philosophers because he declared a sense of humour to be a "divine" characteristic, because it made it possible for a man to maintain his soul in freedom and to seek that ultimate joy in life which lies in the creation or cherishing of what is beautiful. *Possible for a man to maintain his soul in freedom.* Freedom from what? What puts him in chains? This is where our Jungian exploration leads us into a very dark wood indeed.

Jung was a deeply learned man, and one of the bases of his thinking derives from the writings of Heracleitus, a Greek philosopher who lived long before Plato, and of whom we know little. But he said some things of enduring worth, and chief among them is a declaration that there is unity in the world, but it is unity formed by the combination of opposites. From this comes his most famous declaration that "Everything flows; nothing stands still." And with this goes the belief that anything, if pursued to its farthest extent, turns into its opposite. In our world, where so many things are pursued without moderation we see this principle at work: charity, driven as hard as it can go, becomes a vast organization which seems to exist to support itself; so it is with research, which demands vast funds to support the research, creating a structure which would fall to the ground if the aim of the research were ever achieved. (A friend of mine, an ironical scientist, says that if a cure for cancer were ever found, it would create disastrous unemployment.) We see this principle in the pursuit of pleasure, which eager, craving, tormented people pursue to a point where it becomes a weariness. Moderation, the Golden Mean, the Aristonmetron, is the secret of wisdom and of happiness. But it does not mean embracing an unadventurous mediocrity: rather it is an elaborate balancing-act, a feat of intellectual skill demanding constant vigilance. Its aim is a reconciliation of opposites.

Nowhere, I think, is this task more difficult than in preserving a balance between the contrasted attitudes toward man's fate, the Comic and the Tragic. The Comic, pursued without discretion, runs into a shallowness which brings in its wake a triviality of mind and spirit which produces results that may be tragic; the Tragic, as with my friend who declared it to be the only endurable intellectual stance for an intelligent man, produces in its farthest reaches a gloomy egotism which impresses the onlooker as comic. But in seeking the Golden Mean we cannot be content with a bland rejection of both the Tragic and the Comic until life becomes a kind of vanilla custard, fit only for spiritual and intellectual invalids. No, the Golden Mean is not a sunny, untroubled nullity, but a deep awareness of possibilities, with one eye cocked toward Comedy and the other eye skewed toward Tragedy, and out of this feat of balanced observation emerges Humour, not as a foolish amusement or an escape from reality, but as a breadth of perception, and what Heracleitus called "an attunement of opposite tensions, like that of the bow and the lyre." A reconciliation of opposites, indeed.

Such a duality of vision may make us sad at the great party which is given to a colleague who is about to retire, his usefulness having expired; in the midst of the jollification we are aware of the eyes of his younger colleagues, fixed on his professorial chair, or his seat at the head of the boardroom table; this is the duality of perception which made Bernard Shaw laugh uncontrollably at his mother's funeral, as he thought of what she would have said about the obsequies. A sense of humour, in the true sense, is not always a comfortable possession.

What I have been saying, of course, offers only examples and instances – very commonplace and simple ones – of the way in which the sense of humour may work. But examples do not say anything about the nature of the sense of humour itself, and here I must return again to the thought of Dr. Jung. It is my belief that humour is, in fact, an archetype, and one about which very little, if indeed anything, has been said. You will understand my diffidence as I pursue my argument; I make no claim to being a deeply learned Jungian, and in what I am going to say I may go wrong, but I do not think I shall be wholly wrong.

I have used that tricky word "archetype," which has gained a good deal of popularity and is used loosely to describe any complex of ideas, or any situation that may come up in discussion. But an archetype, in the sense that Jung used it, and in which he inherited it from the thought of Plato, is not so easily defined. It has been called "a hypothetical entity irrepresentable in itself and evident only through its manifestations." In other words, you know it by its effects, but cannot grasp its cause. A familiar archetype is that of First Love, of which most people have some knowledge. It seizes upon its subject, bringing about changes both mental and physical and provoking actions which seem inevitable to the subject, but which may be inexplicable to the lookers-on. Not all archetypes work so obviously or, as a usual thing, so briefly. Any of us, at any time, may fall under the spell of an archetype, for good or evil.

Why do I suppose that humour is archetypal in its manifestations? (Because, as I hope I have made clear, an archetype may be known only by its manifestations; its essence cannot be pinned down.) I think so because humour seeks a balance in what is perceived – a balance that lies between the comic and the tragic, aware of both but not wholly committed to either. It is an archetype that seems to face both ways, and therefore we might call it the Janus Archetype, after the Roman god *Janus Bifrons* – Janus with Two Faces. Janus who looks both East and West; Janus, who is thus constantly aware of possibilities. Janus, who might therefore be taken as the God of Humour.

You may well be wondering when I am going to get to opera, and how do I propose to associate this theory of humour that I have been talking about with music. Simply by telling you how compellingly such humour seems to me to assert itself in some of the greatest operatic works, and in some which are not usually thought of as great but which cannot be ignored in any such talk as this.

Virtually all operas, including many that seek tragic stature, contain some humorous element, and during the nineteenth century the inclusion of some comedy was thought to be obligatory in the melodramatic plots that served as the basis for opera libretti. Such operas abound with comic labourers, or absurd notaries, or elderly widows who give an opportunity for *buffo* singers to appear briefly and amuse the kind of people who thought them funny. We think of the Sacristan in *Tosca*, for instance, or that remorselessly funny monk in *La Forza del Destino* who appears when Leonora seeks sanctuary in a monastery. Anyone who ever saw the late Salvatore Baccaloni in any of these roles knows the kind of funny-walking, eye-popping, funny make-up performance I mean – unlike anything on earth, or in the heavens above, or in the waters under the earth. As we survey these characters – and they are numberless – we form a poor opinion of the comic invention of nineteenth-century librettists. Of course they were working in the atmosphere of a melodramatic theatre where comedy had to be shoved into the action with a shoehorn, because it did not arise naturally from the plot; in melodrama there are the really important people, whose high seriousness and splendour of character never waver, and there are lesser folk – comic servants in many cases – who are allowed to make jokes and do absurd things. There are really two worlds; the world of drama and the world of comedy, and they mingle uneasily. The notion that the two might ever unite in one person is unthinkable; in *Rigoletto*, for instance, the jester is a tragic figure and, although his profession is that of a clown, we never hear him crack a single joke; when he jeers cruelly at Monterone we know that irony is intended and that the evil at which he jeers will recoil on his own head. If we permit ourselves such irreverence, we wonder how on earth Rigoletto ever got, and held, his job as a funnyman.

Even Mozart, who had comic genius of a high order, never permitted it to appear in any of his avowed tragedies. When lesser composers were at work, they were inhibited by the lack of comic perception in their librettists, and one suspects also in themselves.

Consider as an example Donizetti's *Lucia di Lammermoor*; I choose it because it has held the stage for 150 years and never fails to draw an audience when a great soprano plays the title role. To compare the libretto by Salvatore Cammarano with the novel by Sir Walter Scott is a depressing business. I do not speak of Cammarano's determination to make the plot comprehensible to an Italian audience by throwing aside Scott's careful descriptions of Scottish degrees of social standing; nothing is made of the fact that Edgar of Ravenswood is vastly superior to the common Lucy Ashton; Cammarano cannot define religious sympathy within the Scottish Church; it is nothing to him that Edgar is an Episcopalian and a ritualist, whereas Lucy is a stark Presbyterian. What would that mean in Roman Catholic Italy? (I have seen a production in which so many crucifixes adorned the ancient Presbyterian home of Lucy Ashton that Walter Scott would have died either from rage or laughter.) But I do think that Cammarano, if he had more than a schoolboy's command of English, might have made use of some of Scott's fine humorous characterizations, such as the splendid Caleb Balderstone, and not have changed the chaplain Bide-the-Bent into the characterless Raimondo, a sort of half-priest half-secretary whose principal duty seems to be to provide a fine bass in the celebrated Sextet. There is room in a novel for humour, but not in an opera, it appears. If it were possible for us to question Cammarano about what he thought he was doing, he would certainly reply that he was providing a simple dramatic scaffold on which the composer might hang some melodious upholstery, and that subtlety of character had nothing to do with it. As for humour, such dramas as *Lucia* and *Il Trovatore* afford no place for such triviality.

It is the concept of life, you see. Tragedy and comedy can never meet. Not, that is to say, in opera. Not in the classical theatre of France. Why, we may ask? Quite simply because to introduce tragedy into comedy and vice versa is work for a great master, and great masters are few.

The supreme master in this line, of course, is William Shakespeare. None of his great tragedies is without its comic relief. Hamlet meets the Gravediggers at Ophelia's funeral; when the tension of the knocking at the gate in *Macbeth* is at its height, in comes the Porter, full of drink and dirty jokes. The examples could be multiplied but I do not wish to bore you by telling you what you already know. And what is the result of these comic intrusions? It reminds us that the world is wide, and that although Hamlet is in deep distress, there is another world just over the castle wall; Macbeth is deep in evil, but to at least one of his servants life is a thing of lewd merriment. The tragedy is made more poignant by being made more personal. The city of Thebes was ravaged by plague when Oedipus was King, but Prince Hamlet suffers alone. This is a recognition of the wholeness, the infinite variety, of life, and of the dominance of Janus, who faces two ways.

Does Shakespeare bring tragedy into comedy? Again and again he does so, and the comedy is more effective for it. An example I particularly cherish comes in *Henry IV, Part II*, when Falstaff is jesting with the harlot, Doll Tearsheet, and she bids him to begin to patch up his old body for Heaven. Falstaff replies: "Peace, good Doll! do not speak like a death's-head, do not bid me remember mine end" – and it is as if a shadow fell suddenly over the whole rowdy, scabrous scene.

Can this happen in opera? Perhaps, but I do not know of any powerful instance of it. One of the most tragic operas of our century is Berg's *Wozzeck*, in which the misery of a wretched man is presented, frequently in farcical terms; but a whole scene is needed to achieve each example. The shot-silk, Shakespearean effect of comedy or tragedy intervening to deepen a dramatic effect is not part of the genius of music.

Here I may tread on some toes. All my life I have been devoted to music and have taken enormous pleasure in opera. But my principal love is the theatre, and it is impossible to spend a great deal of time with both without being aware that music is a comparatively slow means of expression. Spoken dialogue makes a joke in three words. Music must take its time.

Consider again the entrance of Falstaff in any of the Shakespeare plays in which he appears – the two parts of *Henry IV*, and *The Merry Wives of Windsor*; as soon as Falstaff steps on the stage we know him to be a great comic creation because of what he says. But compare the entrance of another notable comic, Baron Ochs in *Der Rosenkavalier*. How many bars it takes to get him onstage, and establish him as who he is! Music, however rapid the tempo, is deliberate in offering its message. And when the Baron is to be reduced in self-esteem by a series of practical jokes, what a time it takes and what a deal of shrieking and scampering about! With Falstaff the Prince has but to say, "I know thee not, old man," for us to feel the chill. Drama rises like an eagle; it sometimes seems that music has to do a great deal of flapping its wings before it gets off the ground.

My task, however, is not to talk about what opera cannot do, or does unwillingly, but to offer examples of humour of the profound, archetypal sort that I have described that appear in opera and which, in my opinion, lift such operas as have it into a special category of masterworks. They are not in every case operas that serious musical critics put high on their lists. Let me begin with one that rarely meets with serious discussion, but which has held the stage since 1728, and after the First Great War achieved an extraordinary London run of 1,463 consecutive performances. I refer, of course, to *The Beggar's Opera*.

Why do I introduce this feather-light ballad opera into a supposedly serious discussion of operatic art? Because I think it has never been given quite the sort of recognition it deserves, and which goes far to explain its unfailing freshness and popularity. It demonstrates in the clearest terms the combination of comic and tragic elements into a work that produces the particular sort of pleasure, what perhaps I may call "the glory in the breast," which is humour.

We all know that *The Beggar's Opera* had its beginning in a suggestion made to John Gay by Jonathan Swift that a Newgate pastoral "would make an odd, pretty sort of thing." And how right the Dean was! The combination of a plot which is a tapestry of villainy, betrayal, and infidelity with tunes – many of them folk-songs – of the uttermost charm and delicacy has produced a work of unique quality; every roguery, every cynicism and bitterness of heart is turned to innocence and simple beauty by the music. When we see it well done, in the true spirit of its origin, we come out of the theatre delighted, not forgetting the harshness of the story, or the duplicity of the politicians it originally caricatured, but possessed by that deep serenity which I take to be the ultimate effect of the truest humour.

I have said "when we see it well done," and I mean done as Gay intended it – simply and prettily, allowing its darker themes to assert themselves without emphasis. But many musicians of high attainment have been unwilling to permit that, and Arthur Bliss, and Benjamin Britten, and Kurt Weill in his German version, have been determined to rub our noses in the dirt of the plot, as if we had not wit enough to see it and judge it for ourselves. They have utterly missed the point of the work which is a splendidly ironic juxtaposition of the prison filth of plot with the hedgerow sweetness of the music. Serious musicians, unable to understand the magic of Gay's simplicity, have striven mightily, with huge orchestras, crying, "Look! Look! This is the tragedy of life! Macheath is a scoundrel and Polly is a sad slut; look on their works, spectators, and despair!" But we don't want to despair; we want to relish the irony, the absurdity of the thing, and be enlarged by its true humour. The best version of the original is still that of Frederick Austin, who never wrote a bar that a hundred other accomplished orchestrators might not have written, but who nevertheless never put a foot wrong, because he had seen the true nature of his material. He had simply seen what makes *The Beggar's Opera* a masterpiece of musical and theatrical humour, and took care not to spoil it.

Let us turn now to a very different acknowledged masterpiece of operatic comedy, Verdi's *Falstaff*. I confess that it is not a favourite work of mine, and that as a treatment of Shakespeare's *The Merry Wives of Windsor* Ralph Vaughan Williams's *Sir John in Love* is far superior. It is the libretto that I cannot like. *The Merry Wives* is the one play of Shakespeare's in which he has given us a comedy of contemporary life; this is the bourgeois England in the reign of the first Elizabeth, and the real hero of the play is not Sir John Falstaff, but the town of Windsor with its merchants, its spirited women, parson, physician, innkeeper, busybodies and gossips, roustabouts and children, all linked in a community. Vaughan Williams has given us all of that in a work of great lyric beauty and happiness, but for these very reasons his opera lacks the powerful impact of Verdi's. Verdi demanded of his librettist, Boito, a strong plot about a single character and a single joke – the favourite joke of the Mediterranean world – which is cuckoldry. Boito delivered the goods, and Shakespeare went into the dustbin. Verdi's opera, wholly Mediterranean and Catholic, has no hint of England about it. It contains some splendid music and a star part for a great *buffo*, but Vaughan Williams's opera has made a brave attempt to convey something of the spirit of Shakespeare in music, and has come admirably close to doing it. In his music we sense much of the tragedy and depth of feeling that lie behind the comedy. I do not feel any of that in Verdi, where Falstaff's reflections on his increasing age seem lacking in shadow. Perhaps we should remind ourselves how much the *commedia del arte* had contributed to the theatre, and remember that it came from Italy; Falstaff becomes a splendid *commedia* figure, but much of the buffoonery still clings. The *commedia* was fun without shadows, and I hope I am making clear my point that the deepest humour never lacks for shadow.

How admirably this is shown in the operas of Mozart. It is easy to lose one's balance in talking about Mozart, as it is about Shakespeare, but I do not think anyone will contradict me when I speak of the shadowy quality, the bittersweetness, which is so often an element in his comedy. *The Marriage of Figaro* is full of it. We are not so strongly aware now as were its first audiences, of the impropriety of suggesting that a servant may be a cleverer man than his master, but most decidedly when this opera first appeared that was looked upon as questionable humour. Perhaps this is the place to say that much of the finest humour *is* questionable. The people who fear humour – and they are many – are suspicious of its power to present things in unexpected lights, to question received opinions and to suggest unforeseen possibilities. They are people whose world is, they think, founded upon rock. Such people think of humour as an emollient, a balm for sore feelings, an oil for troubled waters; and indeed it may be all of these things, and it may also be their precise opposite. And of the deepest humour a reconciliation of opposites is the strongest quality.

It is in this area that Mozart moves with masterly assurance. It is not astonishing that in our century, when psychoanalysis has wakened us to the ambiguity of so many human emotions and actions, Mozart has taken so prominent a place in the world of art. In *The Marriage of Figaro*, when the Count, an inveterate philanderer, is moved to ask pardon of his Countess, we find, in a musical phrase, what it would take a psychoanalytical writer an essay to express – the complexity of feeling of a man whose self-doubt drives him to empty infidelity, while his innate moral sense makes him ashamed of himself. Time and again in this opera we find musical comment that illuminates and deepens Da Ponte's by no means trivial libretto, and this musical comment is made with a sure but light touch – something which cannot be said for every genius, as, for instance, Wagner. In passing, I may say how frequently composers do not seem to credit their audiences with ordinary common sense and agility of perception. Music, like all arts, readily becomes tediously didactic.

No comment of this sort about Mozart could avoid some reference to his metaphysical masterpiece, *The Magic Flute*. When I was a boy, receiving my first instruction in music, I was assured that *The Magic Flute* was an incomprehensible muddle, in which the divine composer had wasted his time with a cretinous librettist whose playlet was a botched Christmas pantomime. We know better now. Schikaneder was a thoroughly competent librettist when we understand what he is doing, but when I was a lad people were not so familiar with the concept of the Hero-Struggle in life, or the significance of initiations and rites of passage in establishing a human creature as an individual in the true sense of the word – a complete and unified human being. Schikaneder and Mozart work within a Masonic frame, which derives from the initiation ceremonies and rites of ancient times, and doubtless the adventures of Tamino have resonances for Masons that escape the rest of us. But we do not need Masonry now to tell us that for a young man to come face to face with life, and win his soul – personified by the heroine Pamina – he must undergo trials that will prove or disprove his worthiness. We are aware also that lesser trials await the less psychologically developed Papageno. This is offensive to some modern democratic thinking, which would like to believe that all souls are the same size and develop in the same way. Fortunately we have no time at present to discuss this fascinating theme.

In *The Magic Flute* the conflicting opposites are the Queen of the Night, who is all evil, and the sage Sarastro, who is all good, and the tension between them gives its energy to the opera. But we must remember Heracleitus and his theory of the regulatory function of opposites. The Queen is the shadow of Sarastro, and thus there is a link between them. We are assured that the Queen is evil, but we may think that the evil that sings like that is so attractive that we might very well mistake it for good. Nor are we wholly won by the nobility of Sarastro; we may disloyally think that after a few years of his company one might have had enough of unremitting wisdom and goodness. In the opera we happily enjoy the best of both worlds. That is one of the most splendid gifts of art, where we are enabled to have our cake and eat it, too. When the curtain falls and we have enjoyed the splendid balance between Good and Evil, where the Janus god is casting an eye in both directions and we are wrapped in the serenity of a glorious, and probably precarious, balance. This is humour at its pinnacle. It is here that we are aware of what G. K. Chesterton finely called "the mysticism of happiness."

It is out of the question, of course, in so brief a survey as this, to go deeply into the question of which operas may be said to achieve this highest form of humour and which do not. But there is one that tackles the problem head-on and, in my opinion, achieves a splendid balance; it is Richard Strauss's *Ariadne auf Naxos*.

You recall the circumstances of that work. It was originally meant to serve as an afterpiece for Molière's *Le Bourgeois Gentilhomme*. The richest man in Vienna is giving an entertainment for his friends, which is to include the performance of an opera, a show by a troupe of Italian comedians, and – much the best of all – a great show of fireworks. The young composer of the opera is outraged that his deeply serious work in which, he declares, "the mystery of life is revealed," is to be followed by some comic trash called *Fickle Zerbinetta and Her Four Lovers* – "a merry comedy with dancing, light, tuneful music and a plot as clear as daylight." But worse is to come. The order goes out, from the great rich host himself, that in order not to delay the fireworks the harlequinade must be performed simultaneously with the tragedy. And in spite of extraordinary displays of temperament, that is what happens, because, although art is art and must be served without thought of self, artists must live, and if the opera singers and the comedians are to have their fees, they must obey the command of their employer.

What follows is a masterwork of profound psychological penetration, as well as a splendid piece of music. Strauss had as his librettist Hugo von Hofmannsthal, who was extraordinary among librettists in being a fine poet and literary man apart from his work with the composer. And so he intertwines the tragic tale of Ariadne, the maiden who saved Theseus when he sought out the Minotaur in the labyrinth by giving him a guiding thread; Theseus, ungrateful wretch, abandoned her on the island of Naxos, and it is there, in the company of three nymphs, that we see her, grieving for her lost love and longing for Death.

The circumstances of the rich patron's entertainment, however, mean that she has to do this under the observation of the Italian comedians – the fickle Zerbinetta and four comic, lively, ebullient suitors. Zerbinetta is astonished that Ariadne is taking things so hard; to be thrown over by a lover is certainly disagreeable, but another and perhaps a better one will come along soon. And anyhow, is a girl who really exerts herself to charm ever short of lovers? Zerbinetta cannot understand it at all.

Ariadne is resolute for Death, and begs him to appear and be her last and longest lover. Zerbinetta determines to give her some sound, woman-to-woman advice, which she does, in an aria of astonishing brilliance. Men, she says, are faithless, but irresistible. Women are not faithless but often, when she believes she belongs to one man and to him alone, a new love steals into her heart, and she finds herself both true and false at once. She deceives one man – and yet she loves him truly; it is never a matter of caprice, but of compulsion, and is it not marvellous that the heart should have so little understanding of itself? But every lover comes like a new god, and she surrenders without a word.

Zerbinetta and her lovers find that Ariadne cannot comprehend what the charmer from the comedy is telling her. But Zerbinetta has hope; in time Ariadne may come to speak the language of love she has been so eloquently expounding.

And indeed it is so, for in the distance are heard cries of triumph which Ariadne interprets as the approach of Death. But it is nothing of the kind; it is Bacchus, who has escaped from the love of Circe, and who is immediately enthralled by Ariadne. He is not the captain of the sable ship that sails a dark course; he is the lord of Life, and in rapturous music he declares his love; Ariadne yields to him, so that we last see them entering the enchanted cave on the island which she thought was to be her grave.

So Zerbinetta's prophecy that one lover succeeds another has come true, but not precisely in the terms of Zerbinetta's own delightful and essentially comic understanding.

The effect of this opera when it is no more than adequately performed – and I have seen it under circumstances that were not of the best – is to make manifest humour in the form that I have been attempting to describe in this talk. It would be absurd to describe the means used by Strauss and Hofmannsthal as obvious, but certainly it is crystal clear. The comic approach to life and love is directly opposed to the tragic approach, on the same stage and simultaneously, for we are aware of both the comedians and the creature of mythic nobility at the same time. The comedians are sprawled out on the beach of Ariadne's island, watching her every move, and listening without comprehension to her tragic utterance. The effect is magical. Here we have that bringing together of the opposites of which I spoke earlier; here we have the union of comedy and tragedy to produce a splendid synthesis, with a very strong hint that everything depends on the way you look at it – which is the wisdom of the street, but not for that reason contemptible. If you must have it in a handsomer package, remember Hamlet's observation that there is nothing either good or bad, but thinking makes it so. And what is the effect on the audience?

It is enlarging, delighting, contenting. It sends us out into the world more deeply aware, not of simply the opposites of comedy and tragedy, but of the fluidity that brings them together. It moves us not precisely to optimism, because that word has been abused and suggests a shallow refusal to see and take heed of the dark side of life. Perhaps the word for the feeling I mean is serenity, a high acceptance, a recognition that Heracleitus's doctrine of eternal flow is a great truth, and while we may not, in ourselves, find the moment when the one element changes into the other, that moment will come and the consciousness of its inevitability may give us courage in adversity, and balance in good fortune.

That, I suggest, is humour in its highest form. In our century we have known dreadful tyrannies and fearful inhumanities, and of these by no means the least have been the sufferings of prisoners, confined in circumstances of degrading cruelty. From the stories that have come out of those prison camps we know that the survivors were those who had a faith, or a philosophy, that gave them a vision of life that rose above their fearful sufferings. Nor, we learn, were such people grimly pious, or wrangling philosophers. Rather, they were possessed of a serenity at the root of being, which sustained them. In the extremity of adversity they did not lose sight of the Golden Mean.

It would be remarkable if this serenity, this extraordinary human possession, did not manifest itself in art. In the highest art it does so, and as I hope I have persuaded you, we sometimes meet with it in opera.

22

——— ✧ ———

A CONVERSATION ABOUT
DR. CANON'S CURE

IN JUNE OF 1996, The Canadian Children's Opera Chorus staged a wonderfully inventive production of *Dr. Canon's Cure* under the direction of John Tuttle, in the theatre at Toronto's Harbourfront. The music for this children's operetta was composed by Derek Holman and the libretto written by Robertson Davies in 1981. The first production was in May 1982 and the following fictional conversation is a piece that Davies wrote for publication in *Opera Canada* in the spring of 1982, which came out before the operetta opened.

On Wednesday May 19 he wrote in his diary: *Jenny and Tom arrive during the afternoon. We have a meal at Harbourfront with Rosamond and the children and then see* Dr. Canon *in its initial production; all performances now sold out. It went splendidly, and the audience was held and often laughed and applauded. The score improves greatly with hearing. Several people complained they could not hear the words; but do they ever hear words in opera? I could have wished many things better done, but am*

*grateful it was as good as it was; the broad outlines very well drawn
in. Already Ruby Mercer ravens for another. During the night I
woke and sketched out an idea for that other, if she ever gets
around to it – an idea about the Zodiac coming to life for some
children at a Midway.*

*On Sunday May 23: At 7 to Harbourfront for the final perfor-
mance of* Canon. *House overflowing; extra seats brought in.
Splendid audience getting all the jokes. Performance has improved
greatly since the first night, and Dodington acts admirably; the
kids have developed nuance in some cases – and Columbine is
delightfully gentle and sings her coloratura prettily and funnily,
but with proper restraint. Great applause at the end.*

—— ❧ ——

On December 24 the Secretary of
Opera Canada telephoned Robertson Davies, and the following is a
transcript of the conversation that followed.

OPERA CANADA: Is that Professor Davies?

ROBERTSON DAVIES: As much of him as has survived the festive
season until this moment. What do you want?

OC: The article. You know – the one you promised to Ruby Mercer
on December 15.

R.D.: You speak of Dr. Ruby Mercer, the linchpin, the life and soul,
the animating spirit of opera in Canada?

OC: That's the one.

R.D.: I yield to no one in my admiration of Dr. Mercer, but what's
all this about an article?

OC: She says you promised her one when you met at a cocktail party on December 15, and it is due now, and where is it?

R.D.: It is lost, lovely child, somewhere in the ragbag that I laughingly refer to as my memory. What was it to be about?

OC: About the opera you and Derek Holman are writing for the Canadian Children's Opera Chorus. Don't tell me you've forgotten that!

R.D.: No such thing. But you are mistaken, you know. Dr. Holman is writing the opera. He is the composer. I am merely the librettist. I am to him as Schikaneder was to Mozart, or Da Ponte to Mozart, or Hickenlooper to Rossini, or Meilhac and Halévy to Who-Ever-It-Was. A librettist is a mere drudge in the world of opera. Why don't you get Dr. Holman to write something?

OC: Dr. Holman says you are the man of words.

R.D.: I see. And when is this piece expected at the palatial offices of *Opera Canada*?

OC: Yesterday.

R.D.: You rob me of speech.

OC: Oh no I don't! You'd better tell me what you can on the phone, and I'll make the best of it I can.

R.D.: May God reward you, as we librettists say.

OC: How far is the opera toward being completed?

R.D.: The libretto is completed, insofar as it can be while Dr. Holman is still working on it. But I am poised to make alterations,

rewritings and excisions as he wishes. A librettist must be totally
at the disposal of the composer. You know how Strauss used to
kick Hofmannsthal around and demand new material? Even so,
between me and Dr. Holman.

OC: Is he very cruel?

R.D.: Not so far, but at times I see a red light in his eye.

OC: Couldn't that be the light of inspiration?

R.D.: The divine fire? I suppose it could. I never thought of that.

OC: Enough of this trifling. What's the opera about?

R.D.: Well, it's rather complicated, but essentially simple, like all
noble creations.

OC: Where is the setting?

R.D.: In northern Italy. I see a charming roadway, beside an inn. In
the background are splendid romantic mountains. Derek and I
both hope the scene-painter is going to excel himself.

OC: Sounds very pretty. But what happens in this charming spot?

R.D.: Turbulence! Furious dispute! The innkeeper has just expelled
a travelling opera company from his inn because they can't pay
their bills! He has seized all their orchestral instruments until the
debt is paid. The opera company is torn between rage and despair!

OC: Aha! What next?

R.D.: The company cannot function without its orchestra. It has
singers but no instruments. What are they to do? They think of

various expedients, and try one or two but they simply won't do. The innkeeper is adamant and they are on the rocks. Until —

OC: Yes — don't leave me in suspense! Until what?

R.D.: Until a strange figure appears, an immensely tall, top-hatted man of demonic appearance, accompanied by his blind daughter. He asks what the trouble is; they tell him; and he laughs and says he can put everything right.

OC: How?

R.D.: The strange gentleman is the great Doctor Canon, friend of all the mighty musicians of the day, who has helped Mozart, Haydn, and countless others out of difficulties. He says that the problem presented by the travelling company is duck soup.

OC: Duck what?

R.D.: It is a musical term meaning "simple of solution." He knows just what to do.

OC: Yes, yes — and what is it?

R.D.: Ah, that would be telling! You must wait and find out when Dr. Holman completes his score. But it is a solution, and a splendid one, and the company is able immediately to perform a new opera it has had in preparation. And that opera is a beauty.

OC: What kind of beauty?

R.D.: It is an opera suitable to the period of the piece, which is very early nineteenth-century Italian. It is about young lovers who are prevented from marrying by a tyrannical father. The hero, Harlequin, is a magnificent tenor, and the heroine, Columbine, is a coloratura of a sort to make Joan Sutherland decide to take up some other career. The Basso Buffo is just the sort of role that the late Salvatore Baccaloni delighted in. And of course there is a Chorus, which is very prominent, and there are some other characters.

OC: Sounds as if it might be funny.

R.D.: It *is* funny. And when it is over, the innkeeper is so moved that he restores the instruments to the opera company. But they no longer need them, because of the great secret Dr. Canon has imparted to them. The whole thing ends with a paean of praise to Dr. Canon, the Ingenious Virtuoso. That was to have been the title of the opera, you know.

OC: Was it?

R.D.: Yes, I wanted to call it *Il virtuoso ingegnoso*, or *The Happy Intervention of Doctor Canon*.

OC: And isn't it being called that?

R.D.: No. That is too long to go up in lights, and you know that an opera with a title too long to go up in lights works under a special disadvantage. So it is going to be called *Dr. Canon's Cure*, which will just fit on the front of La Scala, the Met, Covent Garden and other good houses, but especially Harbourfront.

OC: You sound full of confidence.

R.D.: I am. Confidence in Dr. Holman, in the Canadian Children's Opera Chorus, in the audience, and in Dr. Ruby Mercer and all her assistants, among whom I rank you very high, my dear young friend.

OC: Are there going to be lots of good tunes?

R.D.: It is all tunes. Dr. Holman has hummed me some of his best –
you know how well he hums in four parts – and I can assure you
that it is a splendidly tuneful opera.

OC: How long will it take to do?

R.D.: We are aiming at forty to forty-five minutes. The audience will
want it to go on all evening, but it is best to put great gifts in small
parcels, as we say where I come from. And now do you think I
might ring off? I hate to keep people waiting, and up on my roof
I hear the pawing and prancing of many a little hoof. Reindeer,
you understand. Christmas is very near.

OC: Well – I can't think of any more questions at present. I must say
you seem to have said a lot.

R.D.: We librettists are professionally gabby. Good-bye.

23

— ❦ —

CHILDREN OF THE MOON

An Operetta for Young People

AS WAS MENTIONED IN the diary entry in the previous selection, Robertson Davies had the idea for this libretto at the time of the production of *Dr. Canon's Cure*. He began writing it in December 1982 and finished in early 1983 because Ruby Mercer of the Canadian Children's Opera Chorus had requested another libretto to follow the success of *Dr. Canon's Cure*. The project was never completed; the music to date remains unwritten. But for the reader this glimpse of Davies the librettist is a rewarding one.

His final libretto is *The Golden Ass*, commissioned by the Canadian Opera Company for production in their 1998/99 season. This more mature work shows his understanding of the theatrical power of opera. Over many years he had studied the story by Apuleius, written in the second century A.D., and thought it would make an excellent theme for an opera. When Richard Bradshaw, Artistic Director of the Canadian Opera Company, asked him if he had an idea for a new opera, he was ready to write the libretto he had been visualizing for so long.

As for his operetta for a younger audience, *Children of the Moon*, on December 4, 1982, Davies wrote: *Settle to my libretto, about which I have been fretting for weeks, and get a surprising amount done, as so often happens after a term of unnatural retention.*

———— ✑ ————

CHARACTERS

MISS ROSE PRIMM, a beautiful teacher
BARNEY O'GRADY, a handsome farmer
ZADKIEL, a Gypsy

A GOOD GIRL
A RICH BOY
TWO ORPHANS (m. & f.)
BABY GENIUS
FILLPAIL a cow (two singers)
SECOND–SIGHTED SAMMY
VENTRILOQUIST BOY

CHORUS of the Children of the
Pumpkin Centre Public School

(THE STAGE is empty save for a large banner overhead which reads PUMPKIN CENTRE COUNTY FAIR 1901. At the back on the horizon is a cut-out of tents, and a Ferris Wheel; it should be possible when night falls at the end of the Opera for the Fair to be seen in silhouette, and show a few coloured lights, and for the Ferris Wheel to revolve.)

(WHEN THE OPERA BEGINS the Chorus of Children and all the Young Principals march onstage, singing heartily F. H. Torrington's patriotic song "Canada, the Gem in the Crown"; they carry small flags, some the Union Jack and some the Canadian Red Ensign, and as they march and countermarch in wonderful patterns they wave their flags, directed by their teacher MISS ROSE PRIMM, who is young and beautiful, but consumed by her desire to seem efficient, disciplinary, and wholly absorbed in her office as an instructor in learning and morals. She is soberly dressed but cannot help looking delightful and desirable.)

CHORUS: Canada, the Star and Dominion,
          That shines in the beautiful west,
    Where the Sun in a robe of vermilion
          Sinks softly and sweetly to rest;
    The land of a great federation,
          Which time will never untie,
    Till it swells to a glorious nation,
          With a charter that nothing can buy.

    Then cheer, cheer, for Canada,
          For her sing loud and long
    We will defend dear Canada
          In battle and in song.

    The Gem in the crown of Britain
          The fairest it ever shall be;
    A cross in the glorious banner
          That floats upon ev'ry sea;
    The pride of our fathers we'll ever
          Defend and claim as our own,
    And we know that old England will never,
          Her Canadian daughter disown.

    Then cheer, cheer for Canada,
          For her sing loud and long;
    We will defend dear Canada
          In battle and in song!

MISS PRIMM: Class! – at attention:
                 Grades four to ten – Right turn!
                   Now, stand at ease!
                   All of P.C.P.S.
                 You, Pumpkin Centre Public School, are here
                 To enjoy our Pumpkin Centre County Fair.

CHORUS: O, the Fair! Our Fall Fair!
                 We are here for the fun of the fair!

MISS PRIMM: No! Who said fun?
                   I will not hear that word said:
                 Put the idea of fun out of your head!
                   The only true enjoyment
                   Is in the mind's employment.
                   So – concentrate instead
                 On rural culture, and what follows suit –
                   The Bottled Fruit,
                   The tender Squash,
                   The succulent Beet Root:
                 Home Cooking Arts
                 The jellying and the potting,
                 The pickles, chutneys, jams,
                   The knitting, and the knotting;
                 The subtle crochet, and the skills that lurk
                 Behind the lovely brow of Fancy Work!

CHORUS: How daedal the needle!
                   O macramé, O matting!
                 O multi-beaded bags,
                   O many-splendoured tatting!

MISS PRIMM: Then turn your wondering eyes
                 Upon the great surprise;
                   Our glorious Provincial Government –

CHORUS: O bounteous friend! O force benevolent!

MISS PRIMM: Well may you say so –
                 Our Provincial Government
                 Turns us from kitchen-culture
                     To serious agriculture;
                 And in a special darkened tent
                 The inmost secret of the Egg betrays
                     (Using electric rays
                     Without the egg's consent);
                 (O revelation ne'er to be forgotten!)
                 And shows us in a trice
                     If an egg's fresh or rotten!
                 Class – on your toes!
                 What is this called?
                     Who knows?

GOOD GIRL: Such miracles of handling
                 Bear a simple name –
                     Egg-candling.

CHORUS: O wonderful! Egg-candling!

MISS PRIMM: First lesson of the Fair
                     Is the lesson of thrift;
                 Class, I urge you, beware
                     Of wastefulness and drift;
                 Though your parents may choose
                     To use any bank,
                 Your School Board offers you
                     The Penny Bank!

GOOD GIRL AND RICH BOY:
                     O the Penny Bank
                     Is the children's friend;
                     Put a dollar in the Penny Bank

      And at the year's end,
      Your interest is immense –
         You've a dollar and three cents!

CHORUS: Shun every urge to spend,
      Never, never, never lend –
         Your reward will be immense!
         Three cents for nothing!
            Three free cents!

THE ORPHANS:

      The path of the investor
         Is forever closed to me:
      I'm an orphan, a pore orphan,
         And never will I be
      A store-keeper, a farmer
         Or a landlord with rents,
      'Cause I haven't got a penny
         So I can't dream of three cents.
      If the Penny Bank is Heaven
         I am Lazarus at the door,
      And the Penny Bank is closed to me –
         Pity the Wretched Pore!

BABY GENIUS:

      If the Penny Bank is Heaven
         Salvation's path is stoney;
      I've a very superior intellect
         But I can't hang on to money!

CHORUS: But money, money, money,
         Is the children's friend;
      Put a dollar in the Penny Bank
         And at the year's end
      Your reward will be immense –
         You've a dollar and three cents!

It's money for nothing!
  Three –
    Absolutely free –
  Cents!

MISS PRIMM: No, don't say free,
Say the reward of Prudence.
Prudence, sister of Providence,
  Brings assured success:
Wasteful, uncharted living
Spells poverty and distress.
Egg-candling, household arts, the Penny Bank,
These are the agencies good people thank
For making life wise, and thus long, and healthy;
  Certainly solvent, and – it could be –
    WEALTHY!

BABY GENIUS:

        Is wealth the goal?
        Is Wealth the Vision Splendid?

CHORUS: Yes, for wealth feeds the soul,
            Wealth is what Fate intended!

(Enter BARNEY O'GRADY, a handsome young farmer.)

BARNEY: Good-day, good-day, good-day to you all,
              Pupils of Pumpkin Centre!
            And a special good-day to you, Miss Primm,
              Sure, and this is a happy encounter!
            For today is the day of my mightiest venture –
              I offer my finest cow
            To the searching gaze of the judges' eye,
              Ah, what will they make of her, now?
              Fillpail the Queen, my butterfat queen,
                My glorious champion cow!

CHORUS: Hail, hail to Fillpail!
               Fillpail, the champion cow!

(Enter FILLPAIL, obviously a very superior cow, but modest.)

BARNEY: Fillpail, mavourneen, I see thee before me,
                   Decked for the Fair, and as fresh as the dew;
               Master, you call me, and yet I adore thee,
                   Sweet as your butter, as cream good and true.
               What will the night bring of triumph or sorrow,
                   Love's Dream for me, and blue ribbon for you?
               Butterfat champion, Queen of my dairy
                   Fillpail mavourneen, my hopes rest on you!

GOOD GIRL: A song of love!
               My heart goes out to him!
                   Fillpail, he sings,
               But, oh, he means Miss Primm!

MISS PRIMM: (aside as the others caress FILLPAIL)
               If Fillpail wins the prize,
                   I know he'll pop the question!
               I see the lovelight in his eyes
                   As he hints at the soft suggestion!
               O Love, you hang on Fillpail's horns
               And swell in her splendid udder!
               Triumph, O Fillpail, win today,
               The alternative makes me shudder!
                   Fillpail, dear Fillpail,
                       Yours be the victory!
                   Love rides upon your horns
                       And love is all to me!

CHORUS: If Fillpail wins the prize,
                   He'll surely pop the question;
               We see the lovelight in his eyes

As he hints at the soft suggestion!
Oh, how we love Miss Primm!
We dote on Barney O'Grady!
If you do not win,
Their future is grim –
Triumph, O Butterfat Lady!

BARNEY: Now, if you please, I'll take Miss Primm with me;
And you, you rogues, get on with your holiday!

MISS PRIMM: Oh, no –
Oh, yes –
What do I mean to say?
I should remain,
But long to be away!
Torn between Love and Duty, as you see –
O Love, O Duty, can't you two agree?
Pupils, I go – I must –
O heart, be brave!
You, class, be still,
Be quiet,
Above all –
Behave!

(She goes with BARNEY: immediately the children change their
demeanour, becoming much more at ease.)

GOOD GIRL: Oh, how I love Miss Primm's severity,
Her affectation of extreme austerity;
Her lightest word gives me a shameful thrill:
I love Miss Primm till I am nearly ill!

ORPHAN GIRL: That's all salt-taffy,
Rose Primm is daffy
About Farmer Barney
And his Irish blarney!

CHORUS: Here's a fine thing!
           Our teacher's in love!
       She flushes, she blushes,
          O Heavens above!
       Here's a fine thing!
          Our teacher's in love!

RICH BOY: Aw nuts! Miss Primm is not like that;
         She's straight as a cedar stick!
           Would she kiss and cuddle
           And get in a muddle
        With a simple country hick?
       Aw no! Miss Primm will hold right out
         For a rich man with a castle
          'Cause her head's screwed on,
          And her brains are plumb,
        And she'll give old Cupid a rassle!

ORPHAN BOY: She pretends to be tough,
         But she's sappy enough;
       She's dawny and faddy
         For that cow-happy Paddy!

CHORUS: Here's a fine thing!
       Our teacher's heart soars,
       She flushes, she blushes,
         Sews lace on her drawers;
       And that's a sure sign
         That teacher's in love!

       Second-sighted Sammy
         Tell us true –
       What's our teacher
         Going to do?

SECOND-SIGHTED SAMMY:

    Just gimme a minute –
      Oh boy, I feel the Power!
    Come on, let's go the limit!

(Some strong boys hold him upside down, and shake him; he prophesies while standing on his head.)

    Upend me, somebody,
    Put me in my trance –
      I see a pair of overalls –
        Yep, blue denim pants!
    And sewed all over 'em
      Are lovely posies –
    Wait – now I've got it –
    They are – yes – Primroses!

CHORUS: Primroses!
      Oh, Rose Primm!
    Primroses!

SECOND-SIGHTED SAMMY:

    And wait – above 'em
    Floating in the air,
    Is a Mystical Presence,
    A Being Rare!
      O Gee, it's smiling!
      O Gee, it's smiling!
    Wait a minute – Wow!
    I see it clear, and Hokies –
      It's a Cow!

GOOD GIRL: Fillpail for sure!

RICH BOY: Has it a giant udder?

SECOND-SIGHTED SAMMY:
               Yep, it's a whopper!

CHORUS: Oh, with joy we shudder!
               Cupid, embark your ship of love
                  And Fillpail, guide the rudder!
               Sail on, sail on, Rose Primm,
                  To a land of milk and honey,
               Where dwells a tender Irish heart
                  And a farm and lots of money!

CHORUS OF GIRLS:
               Lucky, O lucky Rose,
                  Headed for wedded bliss!
               Say Fortune, do you hold for me
                  Such a romance as this?
               We know that telling fortunes
                  Is very, very wrong,
               But where is the girl
                  Who finds no hint
               In this innocent old song?

               Monday's child is fair of face,
               Tuesday's child is full of grace,
               Wednesday's child is full of woe,
               Thursday's child has far to go,
               Friday's child is loving and giving,
               Saturday's child works hard for a living,
               And the child that is born on the Sabbath Day
               Is blithe and bonny and good and gay!

ALL GIRLS: Monday's child is fair of face —

SOME GIRLS: And that's me! That's me!

BOYS: No, you're not, you're ugly and freckled!

ALL GIRLS: Tuesday's child is full of grace –

SOME GIRLS: And that's me! That's me!

BOYS: No you're not, you're nasty and cranky!

ALL GIRLS: Wednesday's child is full of woe –

SOME GIRLS: And that's me! Poor me!

BOYS: Always crying! Use your hanky!

ALL GIRLS: Thursday's child has far to go –

SOME GIRLS: And that's me! Wayfaring me!

BOYS: The farther the better, through rain and snow!

ALL GIRLS: Friday's child is loving and giving –

SOME GIRLS: And that's me! Generous me!

BOYS: Boo! You're as tight as the bark to a tree!

ALL GIRLS: Saturday's child works hard for a living –

ORPHANS: And that's me! Orphans are we!

GIRLS AND BOYS:
          You've only your rotten parents to thank,
          You know you were born
          The wrong side of the blanket!

ORPHANS: Picking on orphans! picking on orphans!
          You can't go to Heaven
          If you pick on orphans!

GIRLS: And the child that is born on the Sabbath Day —

GOOD GIRL: I'm a child of the parsonage! That's me!

GIRLS: Is blithe and bonny and good and gay!

BOYS: You're a pain in the neck
                  Whatever you say!

GIRLS: Hateful, nasty dirty boys!
                  Shut up your horrible
                  Ignorant noise!

BOYS: Girls are silly and girls are stupid!
                      Hurrah for the Penny Bank!
                          Down with Cupid!

Melodrame   (There is a fight; some very daring girls run at the
                  boys and slap them. The boys slap back, where-
                  upon the girls fall to the ground and weep as if they
                  had been stabbed. There is some pulling of hair.
                  The ORPHANS dodge about egging on the fighters
                  and making whatever trouble they can . . . Enter
                  ZADKIEL, A Gypsy Peddler, fantastically dressed,
                  with a plumed hat and all the toys and souvenirs
                  he sells hanging about him.)

ZADKIEL: Souvenirs, souvenirs —
                  The best in the Fair!
                  Buy my souvenirs!

                  Here! what's amiss?
                      Boys and girls fighting?
                  What a way to behave
                      At a fairday outing!

Now my missies and masters,
Open your pockets;
Boys, buy my pony-whips,
Girls, buy my lockets.
See my fine whistling-birds,
See my kaleidoscopes,
Rare Phenakistoscopes
Telescopes, gyroscopes!
Girls, see my rings,
Cut to a prism;
Boys who love magic,
Here's Ventriloquism:
Your name, young master?
John, do you say?
Look, with this in my mouth,
My voice flies away!
Listen – John! John! John!

VOICE FAR AWAY:
John, John, John!

BOY: It must be an echo!

VOICE FAR AWAY:
No, I'm calling for John!

ZADKIEL: It's a wonderful secret –
Now, take my advice
Here's the book that tells all
And includes the device
And it's wonderfully
Gloriously,
Cheap at the price!

(The Boy buys, as the children have been buying all through his song.)

ZADKIEL: Now here is a friend
                    You can always call on,
                        When money is short
                        And desires are many:
                    Fortunatus' Purse –
                        Someone lend me a penny –

(Several do so)

                    See – I drop it inside,
                    Turn the purse a few times,
                    Then – what have we here?
                        All the pennies are dimes!
                    Here's a fortune for sure,
                    And you'll have me to thank.

RICH BOY: That's a thousand per cent.
                    Golly! Now where's your Penny Bank!

(He buys.)

ZADKIEL: Buy from Old Zadkiel
                      The Romany friend;
                    Here is good fortune
                      That knows no end!

CHORUS: Charley has a dollar!
                      He can buy for us all!
                    Come on, now, Charley,
                      Don't be stingy and small!
                    Take Charley's dollar,
                      He has plenty more;
                    Charley's made of money –
                      His father owns the store!

ORPHANS: Soak the rich! Soak the rich!

ZADKIEL: No, Charley's dollar
                    Pays for Charley only;
              You all must pay for yourselves
                    If you've only a penny.

ORPHANS: Gimme a penny!
                    I haven't any!
              Pity the wretched pore!

BABY GENIUS:

              Bang goes my dime!
              Oh, ain't it a crime?

SECOND-SIGHTED SAMMY:

              The cost of living,
                    Increases ever,
              But it isn't a patch
                    On the cost of pleasure!

ZADKIEL: Empty your purses,
                    Buy my bargains rare!
              Buy Zadkiel's treasures,
                    Finest in the Fair!

              Lay out your money
                    For pleasure unending;
              Learn the great lesson
                    That pleasure comes with spending!

BABY GENIUS:

              All my money's gone –
                    I'm skint, I'm broke;
              Have I spent wisely,
                    Or sent it up in smoke?

GIRLS: Please, do you tell fortunes?
                    Please, do you tell fates?

ZADKIEL: Aye, that I do. I know
                        Where Destiny originates!
                    Tell me your hour of birth,
                    The month, the day,
                    And from my Zodiacal Chart
                        I'll prophesy, I'll say,
                    All that will come your way!
                        But first —
                            You must pay!

(Now the CHILDREN disclose their secret stores of money —
inside pockets, the tops of stockings, in the heels of boots,
braided in hair: this is their most secret, long-hoarded treasure.
Meanwhile Zadkiel sets up a large brilliantly painted Wheel of
the Zodiac, which he can spin easily to each sign as he names
it. He has grown even more mysterious, and has put on a many-
coloured cloak.)

ZADKIEL: (he speaks above evocative music)
                    All creatures born are children of the Sun
                    Whose hour of birth shows how their fortunes run:
                    See here my Mazzaroth, my Zodiac,
                    My starry wonder, my Genethliac,
Melodrame   My Fortune's Wheel, my Round of Life and Death,
                    That tells the infant from his earliest breath
                        What Span of Years,
                        What meed of Gold is his:
                            His Loves, his Kindred, Opportunities,
                            His bounden Task, his Mate, his Enemy,
                            Death's Hour,
                        And what Inheritance may be;

His God, his Soul, his Ruler and his Friends
What be his Ills, Betrayals, Shameful Ends:
   All are revealed,
    Don't miss your lucky chance –
     Old Zadkiel speaks –
      Your silver –
     Now . . . The Dance!

ZADKIEL: (sings now)
     For this is the Dance
      The old, old Dance,
    The Dance of the Children of the Sun!

     See, the Ram begins the year,
      Adventurer and Pioneer:
    First of the Children of the Sun.

CHORUS: And the Wheel goes around and around!
      Adventurer and Pioneer –
    And the Wheel goes around and around.

ZADKIEL: Next the Bull, with patient tread,
      Gold and silver deck his bed:
    Second of the Children of the Sun.

CHORUS: And the Wheel goes around and around!
      Gold and silver all the year,
      Adventurer and Pioneer:
    And the Wheel goes around and around!

ZADKIEL: Now the Twins, clever and fickle,
      Cold in love, tongue sharp as sickle:
    Third of the Children of the Sun.

CHORUS: And the Wheel goes around and around –
      Quick of wit and cold in love,

> Gold and silver all the year,
>> Adventurer and Pioneer:
> And the Wheel goes around and around!

ZADKIEL: Now the Crab, the Moon's dear daughter,
>> Born to bathe in spirit water
> Fourth of the Children of the Sun.

CHORUS: And the Wheel goes around and around –
>> Bathed in waters of the Moon above,
>> Quick of wit and cold in love,
>> Gold and silver all the year,
>> Adventurer and Pioneer:
> And the Wheel goes around and around!

ZADKIEL: Now the Lion, molten-gold,
>> King of all, the young and old:
> Fifth of the Children of the Sun.

CHORUS: And the Wheel goes around and around –
>> Molten gold and born to reign,
>> Bathed in waters of the Moon above,
>> Quick of wit and cold in love,
>> Gold and silver all the year,
>> Adventurer and Pioneer:
> And the Wheel goes around and around!

ZADKIEL: See the Maid amid the grain,
>> Golden harvest, silver rain:
> Sixth of the Children of the Sun.

CHORUS: And the Wheel goes around and around:
>> Lo, the Maiden of the Grain,
>> Molten gold and born to reign,
>> Bathed in Waters of the Moon above,
>> Quick of wit and cold in love,

    Gold and silver all the year,
    Adventurer and Pioneer:
   And the Wheel goes around and around.

ZADKIEL: See the Scales of Harmony,
    Justice, Reason, Courtesy,
   Seventh of the Children of the Sun.

CHORUS: And the Wheel goes around and around:
    Justice, Reason, Harmony,
    Lo, the Maiden of the Grain,
    Molten gold and born to reign,
    Bathed in Waters of the Moon above,
    Quick of wit and cold in love,
    Gold and silver all the year,
    Adventurer and Pioneer;
   And the Wheel goes around and around.

ZADKIEL: Now the Scorpion, rashly bold
    Draws his power from Pluto's hold;
   Eighth of the Children of the Sun.

CHORUS: And the Wheel goes around and around:
    Born a Pirate Bold to be,
    Justice, Reason, Harmony,
    Lo, the Maiden of the Grain,
    Molten gold and born to reign,
    Bathed in Waters of the Moon above,
    Quick of wit and cold in love,
    Gold and silver all the year,
    Adventurer and Pioneer:
   And the Wheel goes around and around!

ZADKIEL: Now the Archer, sure of aim,
    Strikes to the hottest of the flame,
   Ninth of the Children of the Sun.

CHORUS: And the Wheel goes around and around:
             Marksman hits the fiery mark,
             Born a pirate bold to be,
             Justice, Reason, Harmony,
             Lo, the Maiden of the Grain,
             Molten gold and born to reign,
             Bathed in Waters of the Moon above,
             Quick of wit and cold in love,
             Gold and silver all the year,
             Adventurer and pioneer;
        And the Wheel goes around and around!

ZADKIEL: Now the Goat, the witty, subtle –
             Spirit sad, but quick rebuttal:
        Tenth of the Children of the Sun.

CHORUS: And the Wheel goes around and around!
             Sonsy face but spirit dark,
             Marksman hits the fiery mark,
             Born a pirate bold to be,
             Justice, Reason, Harmony,
             Lo, the Maiden of the Grain,
             Molten gold and born to reign,
             Bathed in Waters of the Moon above,
             Quick of wit but cold in love,
             Gold and silver all the year,
             Adventurer and pioneer:
        And the Wheel goes around and around!

ZADKIEL: Next the careful Water Carrier,
             Thinker, Scientist, and Inventor:
        Eleventh of the Children of the Sun.

CHORUS: And the Wheel goes around and around –
             Maker, doer, and inventor,
             Sonsy face but spirit dark,

Marksman hits the fiery mark,
Born a pirate bold to be,
Justice, Reason, Harmony,
Lo, the Maiden of the Grain,
Molten gold and born to reign,
Bathed in Waters of the Moon above,
Quick of wit and cold in love,
Gold and silver all the year,
Adventurer and Pioneer:
And the Wheel goes around and around.

ZADKIEL: Last the Fishes, going nowhere,
                   Facing both ways, sworn to Jupiter,
              Are the twelfth of the Children of the Sun.

CHORUS: And the Wheel goes around and around!
                   Facing both ways, holds to centre,
                   Maker, doer, and inventor,
                   Sonsy face, but spirit dark,
                   Marksman hits the fiery mark,
                   Born a pirate bold to be,
                   Justice, Reason, Harmony,
                   Lo, the Maiden of the Grain,
                   Molten gold and born to reign,
                   Bathed in Waters of the Moon above,
                   Quick in wit and cold in love,
                   Gold and silver all the year,
                   Adventurer and pioneer,
              And the Wheel goes around and around –
                   For this is the Dance –
                        The oldest Dance –
              The Dance of the Children of the Sun!

(The Children dance in a round.)

(MISS PRIMM returns and is horrified — or perhaps it is truer to say she is terrified — to find the Children liberated, happy, and, as it certainly appears to her, "out of hand.")

MISS PRIMM:
What's this? What's going on here?
Who is this stranger?

ZADKIEL: Old Zadkiel, pretty lady,
Fear no danger;
A humble Gypsy, and a starry messenger —

MISS PRIMM: A fortune-teller?

ZADKIEL: Please, no anger!
   I only read
What's written in the sky:
I did not write it there —
Innocent am I
   Of any harm
   I speak but what I know
That which is written above
Shall be below!
'Twas from on high
   The word was given —
"Be it on earth,
   As 'tis in Heaven."

MISS PRIMM: Blasphemy! Superstition!
Children, come away!

CHORUS: Oh, please, Miss Primm,
Hear what he has to say!

ZADKIEL: Hear me, pretty miss –
                Hear me, Miss Primm,
                Who shall be Rose O'Grady!

CHORUS: She's to be Rose O'Grady!

(MISS PRIMM faints dead away, into the arms of the Children.)

BOYS: Rub her hands!
                Loosen her stays!
                Burn feathers under her nose!

GIRLS: Boys, stand back!
                This isn't for you –
                Off with these awful tight clothes!

(They strip off MISS PRIMM's tight outer garments, so that she
is in her white shift: they let down her hair, which flows over
her shoulders; she now looks her real age, and her real self.)

GIRLS: See, in her shift,
                She looks like a bride!
                O glorious, lovely white Rose.

ZADKIEL: What is above,
                Must be below –

(BARNEY O'GRADY enters, and is transported at the sight of ROSE,
who has now recovered and stretches out her arms to him.)

BARNEY: ZOE MOU, SAS AGAPO!*
                – Now, what have I said?
                Sure, I'm speaking in tongues!

---

* A classical Greek endearment: O my Life, I love thee!

ZADKIEL: Greek, sir, is the language of love!
                     In victory's hour, sir,
                     Greet your bride, sir,
                  And praised be the Heavens above!

CHORUS: Praised be the heavens above!

BARNEY: Rose Primm, mavourneen,
                     I see thee before me,
                  Decked for a bridal
                     And fresh as the dew!

MISS PRIMM: Barney, my own one,
                     Oh, what has befallen me?
                  Barney – oh, dare I
                     Surrender? I do!

BOTH: .   Blest be the day
                     That brings triumph and gladness
                  True love requited,
                     And Blue Ribbon, too
                  Fillpail's the triumph
                     And ours the dear madness,
                  Oh, what a Fair Day that leads me to you!
                  Triumphant Fair Day, that leads me to you!

(Enter FILLPAIL, modest but conscious of triumph, wearing a
splendid blue rosette and a ribbon saying FIRST IN CLASS. She
now reveals that there are two voices concealed inside her, and
she sings a duet with herself, in delightful harmony.)

FILLPAIL: Though but a cow I be,
                     Rich thoughts arise in me,
                  And when they do –
                  O-le–O-lahee-hoo!
                     I yodel.

The Cow Cabaletta

> Yodelling's a bovine art,
>> That sets us cows apart,
> And as a yodeller,
>> I'm a model.
> So, on this lucky day,
>> Join me boys and girls, I pray,
> Bliss, on this happy day,
>> Be total!
>>> So –
> Let's yodel!

(The CHORUS and all PRINCIPALS join with FILLPAIL in a Tyrolienne Yodelling Chorus, at the discretion of the Composer. Night has fallen, the lights on the distant fair begin to twinkle, and the Ferris Wheel begins to turn.)

BARNEY: See, darkness brings in
>> Its own rich treasure,
> The secret delights
>> Unbefitting the day;
> Then off to the Midway,
>> You children, and measure
> Its joys to the bottom,
>> For Barney will pay!

CHORUS: (girls)
> O, the pink candy-floss,
>> O the dolls, O the ribbons,
> The rings green and red,
>> The brooches, the scarves!

CHORUS: (boys)
> The monkeys, the Fat Woman,
> The Human Skeleton,

The perilous rides,
O, the giants, and dwarves!

CHORUS: (both)
The weight-guesser's chair,
The games and the prizes,
The whispers in darkness,
The merry-go-round,
The hot, thrilling blisses
Of hasty, snatched kisses,
The fun of the fair,
And Calliope's sound!

ZADKIEL:
As above, so below,
There is wisdom in night-time
When the bright stars above
Urge us on to delight;
Let the wisdom of day
Be confined to its right time,
But now, let the heart
Learn the wisdom of night!

When the full blaze of day
Into darkness has run
It has great words to say
To the Child of the Sun;
For here is the dance –
The Night-time Dance –
That is danced by the Children of the Moon!

VENTRILOQUIST BOY:
Are we also the Children of the Moon?

(Voice in reply):
Of the Moon –
Yes, Children of the Moon!

VENTRILOQUIST BOY:
          So the Wheel really does go around?

(Voice in reply):
          Yes, the Wheel goes around, and around!

CHORUS: The Wheel goes around and around

   (The Moon rises in the Sky.)

BABY GENIUS:
          Day-time thinker, night-time dreamer,

SECOND-SIGHTED SAMMY:
          Light-time prophet, dark-time schemer!

GOOD GIRL: Tame to woo, but wild to marry!

RICH BOY: Fortune haste, and sorrow tarry!

ORPHANS: Bad beginning brings great ending –
               Woe betide the condescending!

FILLPAIL: Daily be the bucket brimming,
               Nightly work the stripping, skimming!

MISS PRIMM: Chalk and ruler, long farewell,
               Music is the wedding-bell!

BARNEY: Richest land and fairest wife,
               Children be the crown of life!

ZADKIEL: Fates to read, and fates be sold,
               There's the Gypsy's fortune told!
                  From on high

The word was given,
Be on earth
As 'tis in Heaven
The word is given none may unsay –
ZOE MOU SAS AGAPÓUME!*

CHORUS: ZOE MOU SAS AGAPÓUME!
And the Wheel of the Night goes around and around
For the Children of the Moon!

For this is the Dance,
The oldest Dance –
Of the CHILDREN OF THE MOON!

(Round dance in which all join except ZADKIEL who waves to them and steals away.)

The End of the Opera

---

* Greek: O Life, we love thee!

24

———— ❧ ————

WHEN IS OPERA REALLY GRAND?

RUBY MERCER ("the linchpin, the life and soul, the animating spirit of opera in Canada") was the moving force in *Opera Canada* for many years, and often asked Robertson Davies to contribute to it. This piece was written in 1993 and was included in Volume XXXV in 1994.

Davies cites the opera *Les Troyens* as an example for opera being really grand, and when he saw a production in New York in 1994 he wrote:

January 8, Saturday: *Long rest in afternoon and at six to the Opera, and at 6:30* Les Troyens *until 11:30. Magnificent! Up to highest expectations! Superb to hear (Levine conducts finely) and wondrous to behold. Admirable ballet. We were to have heard Paul Frey as Aeneas but he was ill and Gary Lakes sang the role well but was too fat for Aeneas. Dido was Mira Ewing: top-notch. Transporting rendition of Hylas's song by Philip Creech. Cassandra – Françoise Pollet, good but not Jesse Norman. A great evening and Brenda, despite flu, enchanted. – Our bus*

was late afterward and we stood for twenty minutes in a howling
storm while David Stanley-Porter sought for it. – A picnic of bran
muffins, apples, and chocolate, washed down with brandy, in our
room afterward.

———— ❧ ————

When I was a child opera was
known to our village through the gramophone. The few people who
had one of these things – it was usually called a Victrola – included
in their pile of records a few Victor Red Seal discs in which were
trapped the voices of great stars of the Metropolitan – Caruso singing
Celeste, Aida, or *M'appari* from *Marta,* or joining some celebrated
soprano to give us the *Miserere* from *Il Trovatore* with the opera chorus
grumbling reverentially in the background. There were other great
singers, but Caruso was by far the most admired, and in the ear of
memory I can still hear his silvery tenor, much diminished by the
primitive recording technique of the time, and with the orchestral
accompaniment positively ghostly.

All of these records, whether Caruso singing Faust's apostrophe
to Marguerite's humble dwelling, or Alessandro Bonci singing the
Vaquero's Song from Victor Herbert's *Natoma* – "Who would the
bronco wild defy? / Who look the mustang in the eye?" – were
spoken of as "grand opera." It was not until I had grown up that I
discovered that this term had a much more limited application.

The idea of opera – all opera – as an art of surpassing grandeur
was further emphasized in my childhood by a moving picture of
extraordinary power called *The Phantom of the Opera,* from the novel
by Gaston Leroux (1868–1927). The same title has been used for the
modern work by Andrew Lloyd Webber, but any resemblance to the
thrilling book or movie is slight. Leroux was a prolific writer of
romances, and he deserves a place in memory for *The Phantom,* just as
Bram Stoker does for *Dracula;* I reread it recently and it thrills me still.

The movie was one of the triumphs of Lon Chaney, a fine actor
and a master of make-up (he applied it himself, instead of relying on

a make-up man) who appeared as the composer-monster-madman
Erik. This unfortunate genius had sequestered himself in the lowest
basement of the Paris Opera, where he had luxurious quarters and
passed the time playing the organ and composing an immense musical
work, when he was not haunting the huge building and frightening
everybody out of their wits. Among other accomplishments he was
a great singer, a splendid teacher, and a master ventriloquist, so it is
hardly surprising that he gained the slavish devotion of a beautiful
soprano, even after she had boldly torn off his mask and revealed his
surpassing ugliness. (Poor Erik had been born partly dead, and he had
a skeletonic body, a skull-like head, and flesh which could be torn
off like plasticine; despite his genius he was not attractive to ladies.)

Erik was the Opera Ghost, and I still have a sneaking belief in him.
So splendid a building as the Paris Opera needs a ghost, and some of
our Canadian opera theatres would be better off if they had one to
bring a whisper of enchantment to their dull interiors. I cannot
imagine that the new opera house in Paris has a ghost – not yet.
Perhaps Son-of-Erik will move there.

Erik's favourite opera was *Faust*, and *Faust* is a truly "grand" opera
in the sense in which the Paris Opera uses that term, which is its own
invention. To be "grand" an opera must have a thrilling plot, allow
for a spectacular physical presentation, use the Chorus effectively,
require a ballet, and provide showy roles for the Great Opera Five:
Heroine (Marguerite), Hero (Faust), Confidante (Martha), and Villain
(Mephistopheles) – of course not neglecting the Fifth Business
(Valentine). Critics liked to use such words as "monumental" to
describe the works of composers like Meyerbeer, Auber, and Halévy.
Increasingly they called for stunning great opera-pantomimes like *Le
Prophéte* (1849) and *L'Africaine* (1865) and *Faust*, which has long been
one of the most popular operas in the repertoire. Meyerbeer was
oppressed by "the public's incredible expectations of magnificence in
production and originality in the music," but he filled the bill, and
Gounod did so even better.

I have seen *Faust* many times, and it was not always "grand"
in the Parisian sense. But that sort of grandeur, which rules out

Rosenkavalier, and *The Marriage of Figaro*, and *The Magic Flute* and *Fidelio* and *Elektra* and *Peter Grimes*, and dozens of others which are unquestionably great, offers too restrictive a definition. Nevertheless, there is something to be said for the Parisian sort of grandeur.

But it must be allied to a great work. One of the "grandest" operas I have ever seen – and it was at the Paris Opera – was Weber's *Oberon*. Here is a sad instance of a splendid score being set to an imbecilic libretto; ever since its first appearance in London in 1826 hopeful opera companies have struggled to overcome Planché's dreadful script, but none has ever really succeeded. The Paris production was superb; chorus, ballet, singing, and design were all magnificent, but the best efforts of Henri Busser had been unavailing against Planché's dire English original. The result was a superb show suggesting an English Christmas pantomime as it might be performed in Heaven.

That was in 1954. In 1951 I had seen, at Covent Garden, Sir Thomas Beecham's valiant attempt to give a "grand" production to Balfe's *The Bohemian Girl*; this was in celebration of the hundredth anniversary of the Great Exhibition, and England was putting her best postwar foot forward. It was wonderful; it was a thrill; it made Balfe's by no means insignificant score sound as well as it ever could possibly sound. But once again the libretto betrayed the work; the text by Alfred Bunn was tosh, and no amount of grandeur in performance or design could save it.

The lesson, for me, is that an opera to be truly "grand" must have a grand script, and upon the whole composers have preferred second- or third-rate men of letters to provide them with opera texts. Gounod knew better than to pit himself against Goethe, and got Barbier and Carré to prepare him a sweetly pretty text. But there are exceptions, and one of them came my way recently.

Last January I saw, at the Metropolitan, Berlioz's *Les Troyens* – and in it Berlioz drew his inspiration from Virgil, and allowed Virgil to speak. Result: a work of astounding dramatic impact, in which music and words (which Berlioz himself prepared) were a noble unity. Perhaps composers ought always to prepare their own texts. I am one of those who thinks that Wagner, heavy though his texts sometimes are, was far better off than if he had employed some hack to do, as well as a hack can, his bidding. This was Verdi's method, and some of Verdi's libretti make one blush.

Les Troyens is truly grand, in both the French and English senses of the word. It is also murderously demanding, on both the company and the audience. Five hours is a long session, even for undoubted grandeur. But when the final curtain falls, you know that you have experienced greatness. And how often in your life are you able to say that?

25

—— ❧ ——

SCOTTISH FOLKLORE AND OPERA

DAVIES WAS INVITED TO LECTURE at the St. Louis Opera Festival on June 18, 1992, about the opera *Highland Wedding*, a new work by Judith Weir. He took great delight in his subject and invited the audience "to ramble on the moors of Scottish folklore, undertaken with a poor map and an enthusiastic but not wholly reliable guide."

In his diary he wrote about the event: *I am very nervous and have a persistent frog in my throat. Fuss and fret backstage before my lecture. Good house and it goes well but I am conscious of not being in my best form. About two minutes before I conclude a fire alarm sounds: I am frozen, fearing I have done something stupid with the mike. (It proves later that some scene-shifters in the basement had struck a signal point.) The house empties, aborting my speech. Very disturbed. But people were complimentary and the composer Judith Weir liked it greatly and was most complimentary. Several people after the opera said it helped them to get some grip on an elusive work.*

Elusive because dramatically ill-conceived: lacked clarity and relied on much make-believe – but we didn't know what we were to make believe. Music often delightful and evocative: it was the drama which was amateurish: she needed a good theatre person to help her.

After the lecture was written, Davies was asked to cut it to forty-five minutes. It is presented here at full length. The point when the fire alarm sounded is marked with an asterisk *.

———— ∾ ————

When I was asked a long time ago – I think it was in January – to talk to you today about Scottish folk-lore, I accepted with alacrity and thought it would be a pleasure to put together something that would divert you. But Scottish folklore began to haunt me, and I realized that I must take great care or I would disappoint you, because the subject is a vast one, and this really ought to be the first in a series of lectures offered by somebody vastly better qualified than I am, to very serious-minded people under the gloomiest possible circumstances – it really ought to be winter today rather than June – and, when the series was finished, some very learned and solemn people ought to take the platform and contradict everything the speaker had said. Because folklore, you see, like so much else in our gloomy time, has been pushed and compressed into something almost resembling a science, and a speaker should not say anything about it that he cannot prove.

But that takes all the fun out of it, and we do not come to the St. Louis Festival to be instructed and bullied and bored, but to be pleased and, if possible, delighted. So I have decided that what I say today shall be simply what I think, and what I have put in quite a lot of my lifetime thinking, and if you want science and certainties you won't get them from me. I invite you to ramble on the moors of Scottish folklore, undertaken with a poor map and an enthusiastic but not wholly reliable guide.

What are my credentials that justify my speaking to you about Scottish folklore? None at all that would satisfy a university department of ethnology, but I have a few that I think justify my presumption. The Scots – at least the Highland Scots whose folklore informs the opera we are going to see called *Highland Wedding* – are a Celtic people, and I am a Celt myself. Not a professional Celt, I assure you (they can be terrible bores), but a Celt in that I have a great deal of Welsh ancestry and somewhat less Scottish ancestry, though of the true Highland variety. But I am something else, which I consider important: I am a North American, and thus I am able to look at the Celtic world with a certain objectivity. I am not drowned in it, not a whole-hearted partaker in its innumerable grievances, and though truly sympathetic to its powerful cultural inheritance and its insidious charm, and though I can grieve over the wrongs the Celts have suffered through the centuries, I am aware, as so many Celts are not, that the verdicts of history cannot be reversed.

Who are these Celts, of whom I speak? Well, a professor of ethnology would tell you that they were the ancient people of Northern Europe, who have since become inextricably mixed with Germanic neighbours. But the Celts I am going to talk about are the ones who live in the uppermost reaches of the British Isles, and on the Western Coast of those islands, and in Ireland, and who constitute what is sometimes called in Britain the Celtic Fringe. It is typically English to call it a fringe – a somewhat insubstantial and rather amusing adjunct to the solid stuff of the island, which is, of course, the English themselves. Indeed, one of the sour jokes of the Celtic world is that the Anglo-Saxons, having driven the ancient Celtic inhabitants of the island westward into the mountains, called them Welsh, or as they pronounced it, Wealas – and that word means "the strangers." To grab somebody's country and then call them The Strangers requires a self-confidence that is breath-taking.

Of course the Welsh lost that series of battles because, like all the Celts, they are brave and daring fighters but disastrously poor strategists. The Celts in the Scottish Highlands demonstrated this weakness sadly when they mustered the clans to defend the claims of the

Stuarts and put Bonnie Prince Charlie on the throne of England. They were ready to fight to the death, and fight they did, but too often they fought one another, allowing some clan rivalry to take precedence over the principal campaign. They were splendid guerilla fighters, but hopeless regular troops. Discipline and co-operation have never been strong Celtic characteristics.

The Celts are the northern and western Britons. They are the Highland Scots, the Welsh, the Cornish, the Manx, and the Irish. They are all much of a muchness, though they violently protest their individuality. But in their hearts they know better. It is one of the great Welsh jokes that the Irish are simply the Welsh who knew how to swim. Of course there are regional differences, but the Celtic peoples are more alike than they are divergent.

Before the Roman conquest (between 50 and 60 B.C.) the Celts held sway in Britain, and resisted the Roman invasion bravely, under such leaders as Caractacus and also Boadicea, whose influence as a leader is evidence of the very high estimation that Celts have always had of women. Many of their gods were women and women had rights under Celtic law that they have only just begun, during the past century, to regain under modern law, which was so decisively shaped by Roman, and by Mediterranean, ideas of law and the position of women. Celtic civilization was tribal, but by no means savage or uncultivated. People who regarded the theft of a harp from a bard as a crime second only to an attack on the tribal chieftain cannot be regarded as wanting in cultivated feeling. Their organization, though liberal, was markedly aristocratic, which should be understood in the ancient sense of the word – meaning the rule of the best. Bards were certainly high among the best, for bards were poets and musicians, and to this day it is a Celtic people – the Welsh – who maintain the oldest annual festival and contest of poetry and music of which history gives any record.

What sort of people are they, these Celts? By their English neighbours they have, from time to time, been mocked, or despised as thieves and liars, or extravagantly admired for supposed qualities of imagination and other-worldliness in which the English (in my opinion quite wrongly) believe themselves to be lacking. But to people who know them they are none of these things. They are not thieves – or not more than the human race in general – but in medieval times they were vigorous border raiders, carrying off cattle and sheep from their Saxon neighbours. They are not liars – or not more so than the human race in general – but they are boastful and mischievous, and dearly love to confuse anyone who approaches them in a spirit of patronage. They also have a fatal desire to please, and any of you who have asked for a direction in Ireland, and have been told that the house you are looking for is just down the road, have found out to your sorrow how great a distance an Irish mile can be. Celts are very good at examinations, because they will always say what they think the examiner wants to hear, and this accounts for their great success in the civil service. As for their supposed imagination and other-worldliness, that requires a rather longer look.

Anybody who has lived at close quarters with any of the Celtic peoples will know that in worldly affairs they are hard-headed and extremely practical. They are essentially an agricultural people and they know how to accommodate to the weather, to the peculiarities of animals, and the endless make-and-mend that is part of the farmer's and shepherd's life. They have a disposition toward religion, and the Scots and Welsh who live in the hills have the real hill-person's sense of the God who dwells on the mountaintop; as for the Irish, their island has for long been one of the foremost strongholds of the Church of Rome, and a sense of religion seems to be built into their very nature, even when they declare themselves irreligious. Where else can you find a writer like James Joyce, a professed atheist, whose work is, nevertheless, steeped in Catholicism? But it is widely believed that the Celts are very superstitious.

We all know that superstition is something that somebody else believes; our own notions are never superstitious. The Celts are supposed to believe in fairies, and if you ask one of them if he or she so believes, you will probably receive a smile that seems to rebuke you gently for imputing any such nonsensical belief to them. They certainly do not believe in fairies – that is to say, the sentimental, pretty little creations that emerge from the rose-scented paintbox of Walt Disney. If you have seen the currently popular film *Hook* you will recall the fairy Tinker Bell, a very pretty girl with lots of swelling bosom and alluring leg, who seems to promise a fairyland of eternal sexy fun. But when Sir James Barrie created Tinker Bell he knew, like a true Celt, what a fairy was, and those of you who know the play or the book of *Peter Pan* remember what a malicious, devious little creature she appeared to be. And even then, Barrie sweetened his fairy for the non-Celtic taste.

The fairies, as the Celts have described them, dwell in the land of Eternal Youth, and they are not little things like mayflies, who sport in flowers. A few of them are of normal human size, and unlucky mortals may be trapped into marriage with their women, who possess great beauty. Quite a few are of a small growth, being between three and four feet in height, of fair complexion and delicate form. Even smaller ones tend to be goblins, trolls, kobolds, gnomes, malicious underground workers of ugly nature.

Sometimes the fairies entrap mortals by promises of a delightful life of music and dancing and feasting; the mortal who goes with them may return many years later, to find his friends and his family grown old, though he – who has been in the Land of Eternal Youth – is unchanged. In the second act of Judith Weir's opera, which we are to see, one of these stories is the foundation for the libretto.

The fairies are vengeful and resentful of any slight. I have an account, dating from 1883, of a Welsh servant girl who mischievously gave the fairies urine when they had asked for milk, and the fairies told her that forever after she would have a fool among her offspring; that was not much more than a hundred years ago, yet you may judge the weight of this curse by the number of fools you meet with every day. Fairies were great ones for tying up anyone they met on the hillside with fairy ropes, where they remained until the next cock-crow. In Wales to this day someone may say of a child who is asleep – "Ah, he's in the ropes of the fairies."

Another fairy trick was to rob people of their wits. The last time I heard of that was less than a year ago, and I heard it, not from some illiterate peasant, but from a university professor, a Ph.D., who told me of an aunt of his who had been, he said, "away with the fairies" for several years. Professor he might be, and apparently a North American, but the Scots Celt was not dead in him.

Of course, fairies are all imported in North America. We have no native fairies. The Little People do not long survive importation – unless they go to California and grow large and beautiful, but haven't much flavour, like the fruit and the film stars.

There are many collections of stories about the fairies, made by folklorists, and they are of great interest because they speak, not of a Disneyized world of insufferable cuteness, but of a world that seems almost tangible, in which wholly human characteristics appear, slightly askew. If you want to read what is unquestionably, to my mind, the best work of modern fiction that concerns fairies, I strongly recommend *Kingdoms of Elfin* by the late Sylvia Townsend Warner. It is a little-known classic. As a guarantee that the stories are in no way cute or sugary, I assure you that most of them first made their appearance in *The New Yorker*.

If the facts about the fairies are so hard-headed, so rooted in earth, how did the foolish world of the Disney fairy gain such ground among non-Celtic peoples?

It was the Romantic Movement in literature that did it, without meaning anything of the kind. That movement was a strong protesting reaction to the cool classical rationalism of the eighteenth century. The human mind can only stand so much rationality, and in our own day we can observe a strong reaction which has given our century its characteristic flavour. If science is supreme, why do people hanker after science fiction (which is itself an imaginative parody of real science) and if the unseen world is a dream why are the astrologers and palm-readers doing a roaring business within a few blocks of Wall Street? Why are there so many popular evangelists, exploiting the new scientific marvel of television? Why does a world that seems to have rejected the strong creeds and intelligently argued theologies of an earlier day go, in the sturdy Bible term, whoring after pseudo-faiths like Scientology? Why do people who have been slack-twisted, half-awake Christians believe that they will make splendid Buddhists? Man cannot live by bread alone, and the sawdust bread of Rationalism will not content the hungry spirit. Let those who deplore this fact reflect for a few moments on the stupidities, cruelties, gross errors, and downright follies that have been foisted on us during the century past under the name of Science. The truth is, it seems to me, that the hard-boiled businessman, the tough trade unionist, and the angry feminist of our day are not so remote as they seem from the country folk of a couple of centuries ago, and as they have lost their folklore, they have had to improvise something – something which is somewhat fragile and flavourless – to take its place. You cannot wipe out centuries of country life by two or three generations of town life.

To return to the Romantic Movement, it was almost an industry in the period between 1770 and 1850 and its strong influence persisted until at least 1914. The Romantics seized upon folklore and decked it out in new finery for the sophisticated public. Consider those two undoubted Celts, Robert Burns and Sir Walter Scott.

I call Burns a Celt, though at first appearance he seemed to be a Lowland Scot. But he was born in an area of Scotland not far from Glasgow, of which the early inhabitants were Welsh. (Glasgow is itself a Welsh word.) By inclination and education, Burns was very much a man of the people, and their culture and beliefs are constantly to the fore in his poetry. Some of that poetry relates to the three themes of the opera we are going to see. Act one – *The Inheritance* – is rooted in the morality of a country people, and their reliance on a local wise man to arbitrate in disputes: Acts two and three – *The Disappearance* and *The Stranger* – are about the fairy folk, who carry off mortals to the Land of Eternal Youth to return them at last, unchanged, to their families and friends, who have grown old and grey in the meanwhile; *The Stranger* tells of that widespread folklore theme, the appearance of the Devil among mortals, and how he is foiled by mortal cunning. This story is heard everywhere; in my own country, Canada, it lives in the legend of *Rose Latulippe* who swore that on Shrove Tuesday she would dance with the Devil if he came to her party – which he did, and she did, and she had the narrowest of escapes.

Nobody believes in the Devil nowadays. That is one of the Devil's favourite jokes.

Burns's best-known tale of the supernatural world is *Tam O'Shanter*, many of you, I am sure, recall it. Tam has been drinking with his friends in the town of Ayr – which was Burns's own town – and when he has had rather too much he sets out to ride home in the dark, mounted on his grey mare, Meg. It is storming, but Tam is too drunk to mind it.

> Inspiring bold John Barleycorn!
> What dangers thou canst make us scorn!
> Wi' tippeny we fear nae evil;
> Wi' usquabae, we'll face the devil!

And that is precisely what Tam does, for he and grey Meg happen on a witches' dance, and who was supplying the music?

> There sat auld Nick, in shape o' beast
> A tousie tyke, black grim and large,
> To gie them music was his charge:
> He screwed the pipes and gart them skirl
> Till roofs and rafter a' did dirl –

And on the refreshment table was laid a proper witches' feast – a murderer's bones in gibbet-irons, two unchristened infants (very dainty eating, those are), a rapist just cut down from the gallows, and a variety of other goodies, waiting to restore the dancers when they were weary.

What of the dancers? Witches, old and ugly, and dancing in a fashion unsuitable to their age.

> The dancers quick and quicker flew,
> They reel'd, they set, they cross'd, they cleekit,
> Till ilka carlin swat and reekit,
> And coost her duddies to the wark
> And linkit at it in her sark!

Nothing to delight the eye there; a sweating, smelly pack of old hellions in their undershirts –

> . . . wither'd beldames, auld and droll
> Rigwoddie hags wad spean a foal,
> Loupin' and flinging on a crummock
> I wonder did na turn thy stomach.

Ah, but there is one, "a winsome wench and waulie" who has done enough evil things to make her acceptable at the witches' frolic, young though she is, and the dream of the thing is that her undershirt is very short indeed, and Tam stands like one bewitched as she leaps and prances, until he forgets that he must not be seen and cries out, "Weel done, Cutty-sark," and before he knows it the witches are after him, full pelt. Tam remembers that witches cannot cross a running stream, and that is his hope. But just as his faithful horse Meg is about to jump the stream, the terrible young witch in the short shirt catches her by the tail, which comes off in her hand.

> The carlin claugh her by the rump,
> And left poor Maggie scarce a stump.

This is a merry story, but witches were an important and fearful part of Scottish folklore. I do not want to go too far into that because it is a horrifying record and has nothing to do with the opera which is the reason for this talk. But a few words must be said if only to make the point that of the Celtic countries Scotland has by far the worst record for persecuting witches. It seems to have been a matter of religion. In Ireland, firmly Catholic, witches got into trouble but were rarely tortured or burned. This was also the case in Wales, which was not Catholic, tending toward Quakerism. But in Scotland, under the severities of Presbyterian rule, the torturing and burning make a sickening record; in 1938 a reputable historian estimated that something like 4,400 witches were burned in Scotland, to say nothing of those who underwent prolonged persecution and torture before they were released. A curious detail of these witchcraft trials was that the witch was expected to pay all the costs of her destruction. Of course, as most of them were poor old women, they had to die in debt to their government, which nowadays would be far worse than being a witch.

What were the witches? It is now the opinion of scholars who have gone deep into the matter that they were women who continued practices that belonged to the early religion of the British Isles before the coming of Christianity. The nature of that religion is not well understood because there are no written records of it; its lore and its rituals were handed down by word of mouth through a priestly caste – which included women – whose credit was directly involved in handing on belief and knowledge without variation. We must remember the extremely long and accurate memories that people without written language possessed. The Christianizing of Britain was well advanced in the first century A.D. There is a legend that St. Joseph of Arimathea came to Britain about 60 A.D., bringing with him the Holy Grail. He built the first Christian church at Glastonbury. What is called the Celtic Church remained the Christian faith until the arrival of St. Augustine in 597, who secured the allegiance of the Celtic church to the Bishop of Rome (not without much heat and argument, be it said) and set about that organization for which the Church of Rome has always been famous. The Old Religion, which appears to have been a complex Nature cult, seems not to have had too bad a time with the Celtic Church, but the Church of Rome set to work to suppress it.

It is not a simple task to root out a very old belief and put a sophisticated new one in its place. To tell British peasants who had never been further from their homes than they could walk that their lives must be lived after the precepts of a wonder-worker who had lived in a far-off country of which they had no notion whatever, is uphill work, and the missionaries took the simple course of Christianizing the British chieftains, and then telling their followers – that is, the Celts – that they were all Christians henceforward, and must be baptized and begin paying their dues. Of course they preached the Christian faith, but how much the people understood, and how much they kept their mouths shut and clung to their old beliefs, we cannot know for sure, but we can guess from the fact that scraps and shreds of the Old Religion persist to this day. I have myself seen that in Wales a goat frequently runs in the fields with sheep or cows, and although nobody quite likes to say so, everybody knows that it is to keep the animals safe from witchcraft. I have myself seen a witch, a male witch, who dispensed charms and cures, very much on the quiet, to rural people who had a faith in him that they did not extend to the local doctor.

It would be a mistake, I think, to assume that the witches and wizards who maintained the last remnants of the Old Religion were harmless eccentrics. Oppressed and displaced persons rarely are and they revenge themselves when they can. The faith they served had had its ugly side, and human sacrifice was part of it. They were abortionists and undoubtedly they dealt in poisons, as well as herbal cures. They knew how to prepare hallucinatory drugs. There is at present a movement on this continent to revive their cult, and every now and then we may see a picture in a newspaper of some healthy, determined-looking woman, whose innocent appearance belies her assertion that she is the head of a modern witches' coven; these modern asserters of the Old Religion are very ready to insist that the witches were in fact primeval feminists, perpetuating women's values in a hostile male world. One does not have to look very far into the records – and there are plenty of records – to see that this is as wide of the mark as were the judgements of those courts which, a few hundred years ago, sent witches, who were in fact heretics, to the flames. The witches were not just nice old herbalists.

That must be all, for the moment, about witches. What about the fairies? There has been a great deal of speculation, which does not command much historical support, for the notion that the fairies represent a dim recollection of people of small stature who lived in Europe even before the Celtic and German races. Archaeologists tell us that some of our most remote ancestors lived in caves in the earth, or in dwellings built on piles over lakes, and fairies certainly had their Land of Eternal Youth deep in the earth, and many stories tell of fairy wives who came from, and returned to, lakes. It is true that in Lapland very small people continue to live in a culture of their own. And if you visit some of the lands where that ancient race the Picts have left remains – places like the Shetlands, for instance – you may see dwellings which only very small people could possibly have used. But to build an ancestry for the fairies on such evidence requires unusual credulity. Modern man has a tendency to either over- or under-estimate our earlier ancestors; sometimes they are villains, sometimes wondrous folk whose wisdom and way of life we envy. Most such ideas are without any convincing evidence to support them.

Let us return to the Romantic Movement of the early nineteenth century, when there was a strong revival of interest in folklore all over Europe. The Brothers Grimm in Germany collected hundreds of tales from peasants in their work of establishing the roots of the German language, but most of us now remember the great stories, and take the language for granted. And in Britain, from the end of the eighteenth century, antiquarians collected tales and beliefs which were evidence of what life had been very much earlier. Because, among the peasantry, life continued on pretty much the same lines from generation to generation, until the nineteenth-century revolutions in agriculture and daily life suddenly thrust the old beliefs and the old wisdom into the past, and people neglected it. There is no sense in grieving romantically for that way of life; much of it was brutal and disgusting. But it had its own culture, its own foundation of belief, and its own attitude toward life, which has been preserved, to some extent, as folklore.

One of the most influential figures in Europe in preserving and casting a romantic cloud over ancient belief was Sir Walter Scott. He is neglected today, but there was a time when he was a profound and far-reaching influence on what people thought about life. Indeed, Mark Twain makes it clear in *Huckleberry Finn* how strong was Scott's romantic influence in establishing the culture of the American South, where extraordinary ideas of chivalry lived side by side with what can only be called stupidity. With chivalry went a belief in the supernatural, and one of Scott's most illustrious descendants was Edgar Allan Poe, who carries the Romantic commitment to the uncanny to the point of decadence.

Walter Scott is remembered as a novelist, but he began his career and established his fame as a poet. Scotland had three great poets during the Romantic period; there was Burns, the poet of the people who pretended to be a great deal less sophisticated than, in fact, he was; there was Sir Walter, who embraced tradition and folklore and moved in that world like a king; and there was the greatest of them all, who is not often remembered as being Scottish, though he most certainly was so. I speak, of course, of Lord Byron. But Byron was not interested in folklore.

I wish that one of the brilliant actors who nowadays delight us with one-man shows would devote himself to the poetic romances of Walter Scott. They cry aloud for declamation and theatrical splendour. They are delightful to the ear and, though they are not by any means simple-minded, they are not hard to understand. Best of all, they tell wonderful romantic stories, full of marvels, noble love and chivalrous combat, beautiful girls, wizards, dwarfs, and everything the romantic heart could ask. We cannot linger over them today, but if this sort of thing interests you, I urge you to dust off your grandfather's copy of *The Lay of the Last Minstrel* and settle down for two hours of heart-lifting splendour.

It is relevant to our subject – because I assure you that, though I appear to have been rambling, I have not forgotten our theme – because Scott offers it to us as a tale told by an ancient minstrel, the last of his kind, and its story springs from an old legend of the Scottish Border, including the goblin Gilpin Horner. The story is full of reminders of the beliefs of an earlier day, and vital to the plot is the recovery of a wondrous magic book from the tomb of the wizard Michael Scott, in Melrose Abbey. Michael Scott was an historical character, born in 1214, and so famous, or infamous, as a magician that Dante thought him worthy of banishment to the Fourth Circle of Hell – and to have incurred the displeasure of Dante is undoubtedly to have "made it big" in the annals of infamy.

I have spoken of Walter Scott's passion for folklore. To *The Lay of the Last Minstrel* he appends 124 pages of fascinating notes, which you should not miss.

Another of Scott's poetic romances is even nearer our theme, because it served as a springboard for two operas, one by Rossini, so we should be especially aware of it this year, the bicentenary of Rossini's birth. But *La Donna del Lago* (which is, of course, *The Lady of the Lake*) gets an awfully long way from Scott and Scotland, as indeed do all of the more than thirty operas which have been based on Sir Walter's work. And here we come directly to the opera we are about to see, which is as true to Scotland as it is possible to be.

The trouble with most of the thirty-four operas – which is as many as I have been able to count – which are based on the work of Sir Walter Scott, is that the composers know nothing, and seem to care nothing, about Scotland. This is part of the extraordinary blinkered attitude which so many musicians reveal when they seize upon a work of literature. They do not, truly, seem to think of literature as an art, and they ravage and strumpet their original in search of musical advantages. Of course the results are ineffective; well, let us call them Operatic. It is when the sensitivity and truly literary good taste of Benjamin Britten is brought to bear on a fine piece of writing that we get a fine opera. But most of the operas written on the work of Walter Scott are brutal.

Take that brass-bound old favourite of the big opera houses, *Lucia di Lammermoor*. If you like that kind of fun you can have a merry evening comparing its libretto with Scott's novel, *The Bride of Lammermoor*. Scott's novel is complex, and rooted in truly Scottish concerns, two of which are religion and social standing. Edgar of Ravenswood wants to marry Lucy Ashton, but he is a High Church Anglican, and she is a lowly Presbyterian: he is a nobleman of long descent, and her family are newly rich and tainted with trade. Obviously such a match is bound to cause trouble. Does this mean anything to Salvatore Cammarano, who was Donizetti's librettist? Not a thing. He assumes that anybody who is anybody must be a Catholic and that a family feud must necessarily be an affair of honour and not, as so often has been the case, a matter of politics or money. Psychologically, Cammarano is a barbarian. He cares nothing for Walter Scott's splendid peasant characters – Caleb Balderstone, the

dour defender of the dignity of the Ravenswoods, and Aulsie
Gourlay and her two companions, who are very much like the
witches in *Macbeth*, and the Presbyterian minister Bide-the-Bent,
who is changed for the worse into the feeble Raimondo, who seems
to be in the opera only to provide a bass in the famous Sextet.
Nothing is made of the chilling Curse of the Ravenswoods –

> When the last Laird of Ravenswood to Ravenswood shall ride
> And woo a dead maiden to be his bride,
> He shall stable his steed in the Kelpie's flow
> And his name shall be lost forevermoe!

Indeed, Cammarano seems intent only on cobbling up a conventional story which will provide a soprano heroine with a showy Mad
Scene. Result: the production of a durable opera and the degradation of a fine book.

If you know Scott's novel, a production of *Lucia di Lammermoor*
can provide you with some good laughs. I remember one at the
Metropolitan in New York, with the redoubtable Dame Joan
Sutherland as Lucia, where every interior scene had at least one
crucifix on the wall, and Lucy's wedding was attended by more
monks and nuns and bishops of the Roman faith than can have ever
existed in Scotland before the Reformation. Every element of the
supernatural or the workings of Fate have been banished in *Lucia* and
in most of the other operas based on the works of Walter Scott, to
serve the vulgarity of nineteenth-century Italian taste. There are no
fairies in the Mediterranean countries.

Later in the nineteenth century – very near its close, indeed – there
was another important manifestation of the Romantic Movement,
when the poet W. B. Yeats published, in 1893, his collection of stories
called *The Celtic Twilight*. It was about the mysticism of Ireland, and
belief in fairies, ghosts, and spirits of all sorts. It was at this time, also,
that the English, who regard themselves as great experts on the nature
and psychology of their neighbours, decided that the Irish were no
longer to be regarded as a nation of cheerful half-wits and were to
be considered, instead, a people of great sensitivity and other-worldly

insight. It was at about this time too that the English, under the wizard-like influence of J. M. Barrie, decided that the Scots were henceforth to be looked upon as a witty, deep people with a dark background of spirituality.

They never really changed their minds about the Welsh, because the Welsh stubbornly clung to their ancient language, which made their literature inaccessible to English readers. It was not until the coming of Dylan Thomas that the Welsh began, so to speak, to come out of the closet. Or perhaps I should say, the Welsh dresser.

The interest in, and exploitation of, Celtic lore and even the Celtic languages had an earlier beginning than W. B. Yeats and his colleagues. It was in 1876 that the University of Oxford – always sensitive to spiritual currents – established a Chair of Celtic Studies, strongly influenced to do so by Matthew Arnold's influential lectures on *The Study of Celtic Literature*, which, as Professor of Poetry, he delivered in 1867. Balance, measure, and patience, said he, are the eternal conditions of high success, and balance, measure, and patience are just what the Celt has never had. But the Celt, said Arnold, was always ready to react against the despotism of fact. Here speaks Arnold the Englishman, who cannot regard a psychological fact as a genuine fact. But for the Celt the unseen world is a psychological fact, and it is only in our own century that we have come to recognize the significance of such facts. A thing may not be demonstrably, measurably true – consider the whole matter of religion, as an instance – but if large numbers of people think it true, and agree to its truth, and act as if it were true, it is a psychological fact, and will have its influence as such. Every year, at Easter, we celebrate something which is not demonstrably true, which flies in the face of all science and human experience, but which is beyond doubt a psychological fact. Is there anyone so bold as to say that it has had no influence on the spirit and history of mankind?

The Romantic Revival is not exhausted. In the world of opera there was a remarkable demonstration of this fact in the early years of the present century, when an extraordinary opera called *The Immortal Hour*, by the English composer Rutland Boughton, was presented in London in 1922. It had an unprecedented success for a new opera, because it was performed for 216 consecutive performances to enthusiastic audiences. It was seen in New York in 1926. It has since fallen out of favour, though a good recording of it is available and its musical worth and its undoubted charm may be experienced by anyone who hears it. It is an opera of the Celtic world, in which the theme of the misfortune which attends the marriage of a fairy and a mortal is finely treated. The fairy princess Etain and the mortal King Eochaidh are to be married, but the fairy prince Midir intervenes and carries Etain off to the Land of the Ever Young. Calua, the god of shadows, touches Eochaidh, and he falls dead. Throughout the opera the fairy world is hinted at, but not seen, and the fairies are referred to as "the lordly ones," and are superb, beautiful and pitiless. My dictionary of opera declares that "the work's whimsy and naivety are outmoded," but the editors of the dictionary are mad for Verdi and I do not take what they say as gospel. I wish that one of the many opera festivals that now abound on this continent would give it a try.

Because, as this year's St. Louis festival proves, the public for opera, rooted in folklore of the Celtic world, is not dead. The opera which we are to see, *Highland Wedding*, offers us aspects of that folklore which are not familiar to those who think that folklore is entirely a matter of ghosts and fairies. Consider the first episode in *Highland Wedding*, which is called *The Inheritance*.

The story is simple. An old farmer who is dying calls his three sons about him, and tells them that when he is dead they will find, in the drawer of a dresser, in an inner chamber, a sum of gold. They are to divide it fairly and honestly among the three. After his burial, the sons open the drawer, and it is empty.

Mark carefully the response of the three sons. The youngest says, "There is no knowing if there was ever any money at all." The second son says, "There was money surely, wherever it is now." The eldest says, "Our father never told a lie. Come, let us go to our father's friend who is our godfather, and who knew our father better than any other man. Let us ask his advice."

That is what they do. The wise old man keeps them for ten days, watching them closely, and then he tells them a story which revolves around a moral principle. Which of the three men in the story is the best character? The eldest says, the man who behaved with generosity. The second son says, the man who showed a fine sense of property right. But the youngest son says, the wise ones in the story were the robbers who got the money. Then the old man says, it was you who stole the inheritance. And so it was.

This is not a tale of fairies, but of folk wisdom and Celtic hardheadedness – the quality which so many of those who write about the Celts seem to miss.

The story on which the second act of *Highland Wedding* is based is about a man who goes with a friend to buy a keg of whisky to celebrate the birth of a child. On the way home they sit down near the mouth of a cave and, hearing music inside, the father goes to investigate and does not return. His friend is accused of having killed him, but he begs a year and a day in which to clear himself, and on the very last day he thinks he sees the father's shadow in the cave. He goes in, seizes the father by the sleeve, and begs him to come outside. The father says: "Why could you not let me finish my reel, Sandy?" and the friend replied: "Have you not had reeling enough this last twelvemonth?" and drags him into the outer world. The father will not believe he has been away so long until he reaches his home and finds his wife with a year-old child. He has been away with the fairies.

The third tale is about a shepherdess who meets an entrancing young man on the hillside, who begs her to come away with him. To show what he can offer he tells her to pick up a handful of sheep droppings, and when she does so, she finds that they are pellets of gold. But she is fearful, and promises to meet the young man again, and runs home to her parents, who summon the priest. So, when next the young man comes to meet her, he cannot enter the holy circle the priest had drawn about the girl and her parents and himself, and, in a rage, the young man bursts into flames of fire * and flies away, cursing. And when the girl looks at the gold in her hand, it is filth again.

These are the three tales on which our opera is founded. I am not going to tell you how the composer, who is her own librettist, has put them together to make her story, because I do not myself like to be instructed too carefully about something I am going to see, and hear. But I think you will find that you are being invited into the real world of the Celt, and that is a very different place from the world of *Brigadoon* and *Finian's Rainbow* and other fake Celtic offerings that appeal to people who have no seriousness of spirit.

That's the nub of the thing, you see — seriousness of spirit. It doesn't mean heaviness of heart, or a lack of fantasy, but it does mean an awareness of influences that touch our lives, sometimes in ways that seem cruel and unfeeling, and sometimes in ways that open up a glory which can never be forgotten. In our nervous, fretful time we are possessed by the illusion that anything which we cannot explain is somehow an injustice, and that any splendour of spirit which is enjoyed by some fortunate soul must surely be available to everybody. Because we are all superficially democratic and often really believe that all men are created equal. We believe in Disney Land, where we can all possess the fairy world and the land of fantasy simply by paying our admission at the door, and carrying our dull, superficial selves inside, to be welcomed by Mickey Mouse, the Fairy King of our brave new world. We cry pitifully for perpetual youth as our population grows older and older, but we have forgotten the Land of the Ever Young, the land of the Lordly Ones, who may put out a finger to us or may, perhaps, decide to leave us to age and decay. We suppose — God help us! — that the Land of the Ever Young is Florida.

Our age has lost its sense of wonder, and with it a sense of Fate. Or does it only seem so? Tonight's opera brings us wonder and the workings of Fate, and it is perhaps through art that we preserve for our time the riches of the past.

26

———— ⌀ ————

MY MUSICAL CAREER

ROBERTSON DAVIES FELT THAT MUSIC, which turns the thoughts inward and is conducive to contemplation, was a route to self-knowledge; a journey he described many times as the most important of all. He loved many forms and styles of music and had done so from his youngest days. Therefore, when the Royal Conservatory of Music at the University of Toronto invited him to become a Fellow, he was very grateful for the honour, being acutely aware that he was not an accomplished musician. He made this speech at the ceremony on November 26, 1994, and noted the event in his daily diary:

Rest in p.m., and set out to dine with the Principal of the Royal Conservatory (Peter Simon) and his wife at a restaurant high up Yonge Street which we had great trouble finding, as the numbers on that miserable thoroughfare run both ways – one up and one down! Pleasant dinner and the Simons are both charming. To the Recital Hall at the Centre, and greet Lois Marshall. The ceremony well managed, and my speech goes admirably, for they had not expected to laugh, and I had determined that they should, and succeeded in the highest degree. Enjoyed the affair, which I had not expected to do. But Simon is reviving and putting new dignity on the Conservatory, and is succeeding very well . . . A young man and his father both received degrees; the son, a Canadian, had the characteristic Canadian pie-face; the older man, a European, had a well-formed and distinguished face. This so often happens. Why? Can it be a matter of climate?

—— ❧ ——

I am more grateful than I can express for the honour which you have done me; it is totally unexpected and it comes from a source which I have long held in awe. My admiration for this institution goes back to the days of Sir Ernest MacMillan who, among other accomplishments, made Canadians a perceptive and sophisticated audience for music. That I should, on this occasion, be linked with Miss Lois Marshall, whose art has been one of the great pleasures of my musical experience – as indeed it has been to hundreds of thousands of others – is to me a truly wonderful experience. I thank you warmly, and I wish I could say that I shall strive to be worthy of this distinction – but I know that will be utterly impossible.

Let me explain. It is not that I am ignorant of music, or that I have no career in music. But alas, that career has been so obscure, so ignominious that it hardly deserves to be regarded as a career at all. You are all of you this evening receiving awards that mark your musical achievement, in some degree; doubtless music will be your profession, and doubtless some of you will achieve great things in the musical world and bring refreshment, and perhaps enchantment, to a new generation of listeners. I could never have been included in such a group as yours, because I have, all my life, been among the very worst musical performers in a profession which is not lacking in failures.

I come from a family that was devoted to music and I was brought up in an atmosphere in which music was a very special interest.

Everybody sang. Everybody played something. My father played the flute; my mother the piano; one of my brothers was a by no means inglorious performer on that now almost forgotten instrument, the cornet. We were a Welsh family and song was as familiar to us as speech. It was decided that I should excel all the rest as a musician, and as soon as I could sit on a piano stool without falling off I was set to work on that appallingly difficult instrument, and I was kept at it for years, and years and years.

It was obvious to me from the beginning that I had no talent, and the piano, with its array of grinning teeth, was my tormentor. But simply by the process of growing older, I made something that looked like progress, and in my teens I was despoiling the works of Beethoven and Chopin and Schumann. I had, you see, no scrap of that quality which psychologists call "the sensation function." I never knew where anything was. I would place myself at the piano, and bring my hands down on what ought to have been a commanding opening chord, and foozle it every time.

My mother's idol among pianists was Paderewski. I knew that I would never be a Paderewski, so I searched among the other great pianists of the day, looking for a model, and I found one at last who seemed to be just right for me. He was Vladimir de Pachmann. His style was refined, and so was mine. He was distinguished for the fact that especially in the works of Chopin he struck a great number of wrong notes. It was here that I knew I could rival him, and perhaps even excel him. You see, he struck his wrong notes in extremely rapid passages: I worked at my technique until I was certain that I could strike great numbers of wrong notes *in very slow passages*.

Nobody appreciated my style. I remember the dark day when my teacher, who was a very kind and patient man, but also a musician of a high order, said to me: "You know, Davies, it's perfectly clear that you will never be able to play the piano acceptably even if you live to be a hundred. Why don't we stop wasting time and settle to some serious study of musical literature, and it's just possible that after a while you might make some mark as a music critic."

You will understand my dejection. A critic! Could any greater ignominy befall someone so devoted to music as I was? It was as if I were an aspiring tennis player and had been told that some day I might be a ball-boy. But I did as I was told. I tried to understand what I could never hope to perform.

Not, mind you, that I did not have my triumphs. When I was an actor in my young days I was often asked to provide music for plays in which I appeared, and I did. I suppose nobody listens critically to such music. My finest hour came when I was working in a play which was set in the time of Henry VIII, and some offstage music was required on an instrument called the virginal. I expect you all know what a virginal is: it is a young and inexperienced piano. I twangled out a few easy pieces, some of them written by Henry VIII himself, and all went well. Then, suddenly, the British Broadcasting Company decided that it would like to have some parts of our play broadcast over the air, and again I was required to provide the musical accompaniment.

I cannot forget my dismay when I went into the studio and was confronted with a large harpsichord. It was a huge affair, with two sets of teeth and a bewildering variety of pedals. I assumed an air of nonchalance, and tinkered with the thing until I had subdued it to, roughly, the status of the virginal to which I was accustomed. And I got away with it! Nobody found me out and I listened to the subsequent broadcast with a good deal of satisfaction.

And what do you suppose happened? The play was scheduled to go on for an hour, but when it ended there were still ninety seconds before the end of the hour. My guardian angel was hard at work, because some kindly soul at the BBC filled in the time with a record by Yella Pessel, who was one of the great harpsichordists of the day! Afterward, several people said to me, "I never dreamed you could play like that."

I am not a liar. But I am not a fool, either. I always replied, "I'm glad you liked it."

That was the high point of my musical career. After that, I did indeed become a critic, but I wasn't much good because I couldn't bear to write nastily about some wretched performer who had played far better than I had ever been able to do myself. If you can't spray the acid around you are no use as a critic, so I had to take to other forms of writing in which I was able to say what I really felt about music, without having to provide personal examples.

There it is, you see. I stand before you as a failed musician, upon whom nevertheless this kindly institution has bestowed an honour. You are not failed musicians. You are the real thing. Speaking, as it were, from the sidelines, I wish you every success and happiness in a career to which I was never able to aspire.

27

—— ❦ ——

DICKENS AND MUSIC

IN 1995 WHEN THE PENGUIN publishing group in the United
Kingdom wanted a story for their sixtieth-anniversary celebration,
Davies gave them a story he had in hand called "A Christmas
Carol Re-harmonized" (which was included in *The Merry Heart*).
As it was a little short for Penguin's purposes, he offered to write
an additional article or short epilogue about Charles Dickens and
the music mentioned in his novels. We have included it here, as
it is more at home with other selections that deal with the subject
of music.

When Davies sent the original story to Penguin U.K. he wrote
his editor, Mr. Peter Carson: *Here is the story. I am concerned
that it may be somewhat short for your purpose, so if you agreed
I thought that I could produce a short epilogue about Dickens
and Music, which, so far as I know, is a subject that nobody has
written about. The songs he mentions in his books are an interesting study and I must be one of the very few people in the world
who knows the music for his operetta,* The Village Coquettes. *It*

may interest you to know that the music for this piece was written by John Pyke Hullah, whose name I borrowed for the hero of The Cunning Man.

On March 1 Davies wrote: *To the College to do some research in the library for the piece on Dickens and Music to flesh out the "Carol Re-Harmonized."* On March 3: *Finished the Dickens "coda" and it is not bad but I would have liked to make it longer.*

———— ✧ ————

Anyone who has read widely in Dickens knows how often he refers to music and how plain it is that he took great pleasure in the kind of music he knew. But what was it? His sister Fanny was an accomplished musician and received her education at the Royal College, so Charles must have been aware of what was considered the best music of the time. But his own taste seems to have been for the popular music of the genial, domestic world in which he grew up – not quite street and pub music, but the songs and ballads sung at dinners for journalists and theatre people, and at such gatherings as Scrooge's nephew offered their friends on that famous Christmas night.

Even the music of Fanny's world was not demanding in modern terms. Incidental pieces of trivial quality were interposed at concerts between the movements of symphonies and concerti, so that the hearers might not be too heavily taxed. The great virtuoso Paganini, who enchanted England when Dickens was a youth, was greeted in the press with such comment as –

Who are these who pay five guineas
To hear those tunes of Paganinis?
Echo answers: *pack o' ninnies.*

– and the feat of Paganini's that attracted the greatest applause from the general public was his imitation of farmyard noises on his fine Guarnerius. The music of England in Dickens's formative years was the music of ballads (not always sentimental but always strong in sentiment) and comic songs. As a child little Charles sang comic songs for the delight of his father's friends.

Comic songs! They seem to have vanished from our world. They were the vessels through which high spirits were shared and encouraged during most of the nineteenth century. It appears that virtually everybody sang – so very unlike the age in which we live when nobody sings except for money – and in Dickens's pages the most unlikely people *do* sing. The villainous dwarf Quilp sings; his attorney Sampson Brass sings, and in a moment of high glee declares that "the still small voice" is a-singing comic songs *within* him. How comic were these songs? In *Great Expectations* we are given the first verse of what might have passed as a comic song in a remote village.

When I went to Lunnon town, sirs,
Too rul loo rul!
Too rul loo rul!
Wasn't I done up very brown, sirs?
Too rul loo rul!
Too rul loo rul!

and the hero of that book tells us that though he did not question its merit, he thought that the amount of Too rul was somewhat in excess of the poetry. But in London things were brisker and a song like *Sich a-gittin' upstairs* enjoyed a long popularity. There were indecent songs, too, and in *The Newcomes* Colonel Newcome is deeply offended when a singer in a London tavern strikes up such a song in the presence of his schoolboy son. But Thackeray was by no means caught up with the music of his time; for Dickens it was one of the elements in which he lived.

Its range is wide. Songs by Dibdin like "The Waterman," "Tom Tough" and "Tom Bowling" were immensely popular in an age when the British Navy was the greatest seaforce in the world and the memory of Nelson was still alive. The songs of Tom Moore were Dickens's favourites, and in particular "The Woodpecker," charmingly set to music by Michael Kelly.

I knew by the smoke that so gracefully curl'd
Above the green elms that a cottage was near,
And I said "If there's peace to be found in the world
A heart that was humble might hope for it here."

Ev'ry leaf was at rest
And I heard not a sound
But the woodpecker tapping the hollow beech tree

– and the woodpecker goes on tapping through a charming variety of musical phrases. Rollicking songs and pathetic songs were numerous, and we recall that Mr. Micawber confided to David Copperfield that when first he met the lady who became his wife she was famous both for "The Dashing White Sergeant" (a rollicker) and "Little Tafflin" (a weeper) and that when he heard her sing the first one she attracted his attention in an extraordinary degree but when it came to "Little Tafflin" he resolved to win that woman or perish in the attempt.

What was the manner of performance? Of course it varied with the ability of the singer, but there was a style toward which even undistinguished amateurs aspired and it had been set by the great Charles Incledon whose tenor singing was amplified by ten charming notes in falsetto, with which he ornamented his renditions, we are assured, with volubility and sweetness. His "shake" (which we should now call a trill) was especially admired. Not every guest at a literary dinner who was called on for a song sang like Incledon; some we know were roarers and some were not in tune, but they did their best, unaccompanied but encouraged, in all probability, by drink. Sometimes the company sang together, and a favourite for such choruses was "Away with Melancholy," adapted from a tune in Mozart's *Magic Flute*; this was the air that Dick Swiveller played so sadly on *his* flute.

Dickens's most ambitious musical venture was a "burletta" called *The Village Coquettes*, with music by John Hullah, written in 1836 when *Pickwick* was becoming the rage. It is sad stuff; Hullah was a conventional composer, and although Dickens could extrude lengths of technically correct verse he was no poet, and the songs in this little work are pleasing but nothing more. I have myself heard it well performed, but little lingers in the memory. Later in life Dickens disowned it. Several of his songs, such as "The Ivy Green," were set to music and sold respectably during his lifetime, but he took no pleasure in them.

Perhaps he realized that his musical vein, though deep, was not broad: was indeed *sui generis*. It is observable that in the later books the musical references are less frequent. He knew little of music of any complexity, and in *Edwin Drood*, where a cathedral and its choirmaster are vital to the plot, he tells us nothing of what music was sung. John Jasper, a musician of considerable accomplishment, plays the accompaniment while Rosa Bud sings. But what does she sing? Something characteristic of the time, doubtless; perhaps "'Tis but a Little Faded Flower" would do very well, but we would greatly like to know for a certainty.

Dickens was not the only Victorian novelist to refuse to take this fence. In *The Warden* Trollope assures us that the Reverend Septimus Harding played the cello admirably, and was devoted to his instrument, but we are not told what music he plays.

A number of Dickens's novels have been turned into "musicals" in the twentieth century and one, *Oliver!*, has been a great success. But it must be considered on its own terms; it is not Dickensian in feeling. Its rowdy geniality throws harsh light into a dark book. Other works, of which *Great Expectations* and *Pickwick* have had some success, have been brought to the musical stage but the same criticism applies. It seems odd that so fragile a story as *The Cricket on the Hearth* was chosen for full operatic treatment by two composers, Carl Goldmark and Alexander Mackenzie. Neither work has held the stage. Dickens's music is very deeply inherent in his prose and resists attempts to drag it to the surface. For, after all, only Ulysses can draw the bow of Ulysses.

28

———— ∞ ————

FOLK-SONG: A LOST WORLD
OF ARCHETYPES

WHEN DAVIES WAS ASKED TO LECTURE to the Analytical
Psychology Society of Ontario, at the Ontario Institute for Studies
in Education in Toronto, he was able to talk about a favourite
subject – folk-song. He managed to amaze his audience by doing
some singing himself.

On May 5, 1986, he wrote about the Toronto event: *I lecture
on Archetypes and Folk-song at OISE to a full, rather over-full
house, and it goes admirably, especially when I sang. But O, how
badly these things are run! I thought I had hidden at the interval, for a rest, but was winkled out by a woman who was "very
much into rock and country" and wanted to gab about it. The
question period was three-quarters of an hour and like most question periods a waste of time; various people wanted to talk about
favourite rock stars, and although Stephen Clarkson and I
wrought manfully, we could not get them to see that such man-
ufactured goods had nothing to do with folk-song. There was
of course the advocate of "spirituals" and the Aggrieved Woman,*

who wanted to get me on some charge that was never made clear. Question periods never add anything to a lecture, and it is always a few wilful and often wrong-headed people who take over and ask all the questions. But it went very well, and though I was weary, I was pleased.

It was rather unusual for Davies to read a lecture twice. But on the same trip to New York in which he was awarded the Medal of Honor for Literature by the National Arts Club on February 24, 1987 (and delivered the speech "A Canadian Author" that appears in *The Merry Heart*), he was asked to speak to the C. G. Jung Foundation in that city on February 26. Dr. Philip Zabriskie was the Chairman of the Board and Dr. Mandelbaum was Executive Director. Davies recorded the following about the evening:

Dr. Mandelbaum calls for us with his girl friend, the opera singer Diana Rubin, a charmer. A full house for the speech; Zabriskie once again makes me blush by his introduction; he really knows my books. But can this remarkable fellow really be me? Can't quite believe it. Speech goes admirably, and they like being sung to, which of course they had not expected. Brenda says my singing is good, as explanation; *does not pretend to be art, but gives the spirit of the old tunes. Afterward we are taken to the Algonquin. A party of Mandelbaum and Rubin, Woitech the conductor and his jolly opera singer wife, Miss Haddas of the Jungian group, the girl who edits* Quadrant *and a man who lectures on analytical psychology at Harvard. Enjoy it greatly.*

------ ∽ ------

Let me begin with a question: How long is it since you sang a song? Another question: What was the song you sang?

Tonight I want to talk about the songs people used to sing, in the days when there was no recorded music, no radio or television, and entertainment, except in a few big places, was what people made for themselves. They sang at work and in pubs, they sang around the fireside and mothers sang to their children. And now all that world of song has utterly gone. Other people sing for us, and there is constant demand that the songs they sing should be new. Some of the singers, like the great rock-stars, have enormous and enthusiastic audiences, but do the audiences go away singing the songs they have heard? If they do, I never hear them. We have become a non-singing people, and something has gone out of our lives that was once very significant.

Please do not imagine that I am about to embark on one of those depressing whines about the Good Old Days, and the impoverishment of spirit with which we have paid for our great advances in technology and comfort. We who are students of Jung know that nothing completely disappears from human life; it may go underground, for a time, but it will appear again in a new place and perhaps in a new guise. The old songs have gone, and we never hear them except when a highly cultivated singer at a public performance sings some of them in greatly sophisticated versions. But that is not the same thing as the old songs in the old places. We must be grateful to the various folk-song societies for collecting and preserving the old songs, but they are now museum pieces, and what they gave to the lives of ordinary people must come, when it comes, from some other source.

It is about a century since people in country places sang songs easily and unselfconsciously, and almost everybody knew a few songs that they could be coaxed to sing when the time was right. There are other reasons for this change than simply the alteration in our lives made by constant, easily available music. The spread of education has made people self-conscious about simple things; they fear that they will be thought *simple*, in a derisive sense of the word, if they do what their forebears did. I remember what that feeling was like from my own childhood, when I spent some important years of my life in a town that was the centre of a large country district. Whenever there was an important occasion of any sort, it was usual for a street-dance to be organized; part of the main street was roped off and anybody who felt inclined could dance to the music of a small local orchestra. There were two kinds of dancing. During the early part of the evening the more sophisticated members of the population danced to the new music – which now sounds like old music. It was –

Smile the while, I kiss you sad adieu

and –

I'm forever blowing bubbles.

But as the evening wore on the orchestra began to play country dances – jigs and reels and square-dances, and then the young sophisticates of our small town withdrew to the sidelines and the young farmers and lumbermen from the country districts took their girls onto the dancing-floor and bobbed and jumped and whisked around very happily, at the direction of the "caller-off" who was a local wit of some renown. But the young sophisticates – like my brothers and their friends – smiled and even laughed at what they called "the hicks," who had not kept up with the times.

I can remember also local concerts, usually organized by churches, where another local wit always sang a song – usually to the tune of "It ain't goin' to rain no more, no more," in which he satirized in extemporary verse, various members of his audience. Very often he concluded by singing –

Now all you here
   Don't tell anybody
That I have sang a song;
   Because if you look outside the winda
You'll see that I sang wrong!
Oh – it ain't goin' to rain no more –

As a child I enjoyed all this greatly. The country-dances were so lively, even though they did not allow of the cheek-to-cheek intimacy that was thought so daring by the sophisticates. And the improvised song was – although I did not know it then – a peep into a past era when songs that made gentle fun of the audience were a feature of virtually every Celtic party. In Wales it was especially practised, and the rhyming of the satirical verses was of great complication, for it was an art that had descended through many centuries. I am glad to have had a part in this old-fashioned jollity.

When I grew older and became deeply interested in folk-song and folk-music I realized that I had seen with my own eyes the last shadows of a very long tradition.

For many years before my time that tradition was being rescued and preserved by people who recognized how fine the old songs and dances were. But those people were not merely sophisticated; they were super-sophisticated, and what they made of the old music was somewhat artificial, even when it was performed with love and deep seriousness.

The artificiality was inevitable, for the super-sophisticates could not bear to preserve the roughness and sometimes the obscenity of the old songs. So they corrected the grammar and rewrote the words of many songs, and what they so carefully edited and printed gives us an artificial notion of the past, unless we use our sixth sense and discern beneath their careful editing what the editors had originally heard. A dear friend of mine was an active member of the Welsh Folk-song Society, and she told me that when she was a girl of seventeen or eighteen, at the turn of the century, she spent every Saturday visiting the workhouses where old people who might know some old songs were then living. By careful coaxing, and bribes of tea and snuff and tobacco, she could persuade the old women to sing for her, and she said they still sang in voices of extraordinary sweetness, because they had never shouted their voices away in large concert-halls. But she said it was always a nervous experience, because some wicked old hag, having sung of love and the pain of love in songs of great beauty, would roll a laughing eye at her fellow-inmates of the workhouse ward, and launch into a song of such horrifying lewdness that my friend would have to pack up her notebook and her recording machine and withdraw with flaming cheeks, while the old women hooted with laughter.

We can guess what the collectors of folk-songs did, in their self-imposed job of cleaning up the past, and perhaps I may give you one, reasonably inoffensive, example. Do any of you know the old English song called "The Two Magicians"? It begins like this:

O she looked out at the window
    As white as any milk;
And he looked in at the window
    As black as any silk.
Hullo, hullo, hullo, hullo
    You coal-black smith;
You have done me no harm;
    And you never shall change my maiden name
That I have kept so long.
    For I'd rather die a maid
(Yes, but then she said)
    And be buried all in my grave;
Than have such a nasty musty fusty dusty coal-black smith,
    A maiden I will die.

Then follows a series of verses in which the smith chases the milk-white maiden. She becomes a duck, a duck all on the stream; and he becomes a water-dog and brings her back again. Then she becomes a hare, a hare all on the plain; and he becomes a greyhound dog and brings her back again. Then she becomes a fly; a fly all in the air; and he became a spider and fetched her to his lair. And with every change she declares that he shall not change her maiden name, that she has kept so long. But he persists.

We know what the original was. It was not her maiden name that the smith was seeking; it was her maidenhead, and in the end he got his wish; and the last verse of the song ended in the wildest shriek the singer could muster, and the delighted laughter of her hearers. The original version of the song – and there were probably many more verses, each one suggestive of the climax – tells us more about the world of our ancestors, who were not absurdly delicate in what they said and sang, than does the cleaned-up version.

We know this song in English, but there are versions of it in Spain, Italy, Roumania, Greece, Moravia and Poland, and it is said – though I have not checked it – that there is a story of this kind in the *Arabian Nights*. It is an archetypal theme, of a primal quest and its achievement, and people who are devoted to the cause of Women's Lib will take satisfaction in the hard time the maiden gives the coal-black smith before he gets what he wants, and which – in the depths of her unconscious – she certainly meant to give him from the beginning of the chase. No girl calls a man such hard names if she does not seek to attract his attention.

Inevitably love was one of the great themes of the old songs of the people – I somewhat dislike the word "folk" which seems to make them quaint, and sets them at an unnecessary distance from our sophisticated selves. Nowadays, when romantic love is in disrepute, novels and films about the past often suggest that our ancestors knew little of the gentler and more poetic aspects of love, and went in, rather, for rape and a grim subjection of women. I can't believe that that was so, although it must have been one side of the traffic between the sexes, just as it is today. But if there were no romance and no poetic feeling, how do you account for this opening verse of an old song –

She's like the swallow that flies so high;
She's like the river that never runs dry;
She's like the sunlight on the lee shore;
   I loved my love, but love is no more.

Did you ever hear so much archetypal imagery of the most exquisite poetic feeling in three lines? And where does that song come from? It was collected in Newfoundland a few decades ago.

Lost love, and unhappy love, is one of the great themes of these songs of the people. There are countless examples, but I shall speak of one that will be familiar to many of you; it is the fine song of "Barbara Allen." There are many versions, and two endings. Here is how it begins:

In Scarlet town, where I was born,
    There was a fair maid dwellin'
Made every youth cry Well-a-day!
    Her name was Barbara Allen.

All in the merry month of May
    When green buds they were swellin';
Young Jemmy Grove on his death-bed lay,
    For love of Barbara Allen.

The young man sends for Barbara to come to him:

So slowly, she put on her clothes,
    So slowly she came nigh him;
And when she came to his bedside
    She said, Young man, you're dying.

He pleads for a kiss before he dies:

Oh, don't you mind, young man, says she
    When the red wine ye were fillin'
That ye made the healths go round and round
    But ye slighted Barbara Allen?

He turn'd his face unto the wall
    And death was with him dealin'
Adieu, adieu my dear friends all
    And be kind to Barbara Allen.

As she was walking up the groves
    And met his corpse a-comin';
Stay, stay, she cried, and stop awhile
    That I may gaze upon him.

The more she gazed, the more she smiled
    Till she burst out a-laughin';

And her parents cried out: Fie, for shame,
  Hard-hearted Barbara Allen.

So, Barbara Allen has killed by her cruelty the young man who
slighted her, and it takes no great penetration to know that there was
strong feeling behind it, and that she was not simply a capricious flirt.
So – how does the story end? Here is one of the endings:

As she was walkin' o'er the fields
  She heard the death-bell knellin'
And every jow the death-bell gave
  Cried Woe to Barbara Allen!

Come, mother, come, make up my bed,
  Make it both long and narrow;
My true love died for me yesterday
  I'll die for him tomorrow.

And he was buried in Edmondstone
  And she was buried in Cold Harbour
And out of him sprang roses red
  And out of her sweet briar.

It grew and grew so very high
  Till it could grow no higher;
And around the top growed a true-lover's knot
  And around it twined sweet-briar.

It is a simple and somewhat terrible story, but it happens often
today as it happened in the past, and death may not be the worst of
it. Even so you are likely to find the story of *Othello* embedded
in the singularly unpoetic language of the police force, and what
newspapermen make of police reports, in your daily paper. The
themes of these old songs are deathless, because they are part of the
very fabric of life. One of the questions that bothers us is – who
wrote them?

Somebody must have done so, at one time. The notion that was once put forward that these songs rose, in some mystical way, from the soul of the folk, simply will not bear serious examination. There are at least twenty-seven versions of "Barbara Allen" in England and Scotland, and several in Ireland. The version I read to you was made up of verses from two of these versions. It is one of the most popular of all the old ballads, but who wrote the original? Was it someone who had really known Barbara and her unfortunate lover? Luckily we do not have to bother our heads too much about such matters, but we ought to take heed of the great popularity of the song. It embodies something which really happened, no doubt, but there must have been scores of Barbaras and Jemmys all over the British Isles, and those who had not known them in life, were ready enough to know them in song, because the song satisfied the desire for a particular aspect of love – the swain who treats his love lightly, feels the lash of her revenge, and the repentance of the girl too late. It is certainly an archetypal theme: is there any man here who has not said to himself, "She'd be sorry if I died," or a woman who has not said, "I could kill him for that"? The song speaks to something very close to the heart.

But surely it didn't happen precisely like that? We can be sure it did not. How do certain incidents become the subject of ballads, and in so doing take on an archetypal quality, and a clarity of narration, which may not have been evident in the happening itself?

A relevant passage comes to our assistance in Mircea Eliade's *The Myth of the Eternal Return*. This is how it goes:

> Sometimes, though very rarely, an investigator chances to come upon the actual transformation of an event into myth. Just before the last war [that would be in the 1930s] the Romanian folklorist Constantin Brailion had occasion to record an admirable ballad in the village of Maramures. [That is, in the foothills of the Transylvanian mountains.] Its subject was a tragedy of love: the young suitor had been bewitched by a mountain fairy, and a few days before he was to be married, the

fairy, driven by jealousy, had him flung from a cliff. The next day, shepherds found his body and, caught in a tree, his hat. They carried the body back to the village and his fiancée came out to meet them; upon seeing her love dead, she poured out a funeral lament full of mythological allusions, a liturgical text of rustic beauty. Such was the content of the ballad. In the course of recording the variants that he was able to collect, the folklorist tried to learn the period when the tragedy had occurred; he was told that it was a very old story, which had happened "long ago." Pursuing his enquiries, however, he learned that the event had taken place not quite forty years earlier. He finally discovered that the heroine was still alive. He went to see her and heard the story from her own lips. It was quite a commonplace tragedy: one evening her lover had slipped and fallen over a cliff; he had not died instantly; his cries had been heard by mountaineers; he had been carried to the village, where he died soon after. At the funeral, his fiancée, with other women of the village, had repeated the customary ritual lamentations, without the slightest allusion to the mountain fairy.

Thus, despite the presence of the principal witness, a few years had sufficed to strip the event of all historical authenticity, to transform it into a legendary tale: the jealous fairy, the murder of the young man, the discovery of the dead body, the lament, rich in mythological themes, chanted by the fiancée. Almost all the people of the village had been contemporaries of the authentic historical fact; *but this fact, as such, could not satisfy them: the tragic death of the young man on the eve of his marriage was something different from a simple death by accident; it had an occult meaning that could only be revealed by its identification with the category of myth.* The mythicization of the accident had not stopped at the creation of a ballad; people told the story of the jealous fairy even when they were talking freely, "prosaically," of the young man's death. When the folklorist drew the villagers' attention to the authentic version, they replied the old woman had forgotten, that her great grief had almost destroyed her mind. It was the myth that told the truth, the real story was already only a falsification. *Besides, was not myth truer by the fact that it made the real story yield a deeper and richer meaning, revealing a tragic destiny?*

That tells us a great deal about the origin of folk-song, and ballad. A ballad is by definition a song that tells a story, often a story rooted in historical fact. But we would look in vain in ballads for historical fact of the kind we get in well-written history books. Ballads were written by and for people who had no historical sense in the way in which we now use that expression. They were mostly illiterate, and those who could read had no newspapers, no radio and TV pumping the news of the day into their houses with tireless energy. If they heard of, for instance, the Battle of Waterloo, what they heard was coloured with national feeling, and legends about Napoleon and the Duke of Wellington, so that the sole indisputable fact in their possession was that the duke had beaten Boney, and it was up to the ballad-maker to fill in the details.

We need look no further than our own Canadian folk-song for an illustration. Do you know the ballad of "Brave Wolfe"? It tells of the victory on the Plains of Abraham, but it decorates the story with a romantic attachment between Wolfe and a young lady back in England, and it describes Wolfe and Montcalm walking together between the opposed French and English armies, discussing the conflict that lies before them. It is a very moving ballad, but it is not history. It is not a description of what really happened, but what the imagination of the people wished had happened. It is, in fact, myth, and in its evocation of a great historical crisis decided by a battle of heroes, it is archetypal.

Is this archaic thinking? I suppose it is. But as Jung reminds us, there are people all around us who think in archaic terms, at least part of the time, just as there are devoutly religious people whose mode of religious thinking is still medieval. We are getting into dangerous territory when we look down on such thinking, because there are dangers in being remorselessly contemporary, whatever that may mean. When, on January 26 last, the launching of the Challenger Rocket was aborted, and the seven astronauts on board were atomized in an instant, great numbers of people seemed to take refuge in archaic thinking. There were other accidents very near in time to that one – plane wrecks and train wrecks – in which greater numbers of people were killed, but the explosion of the Challenger Rocket touched the popular mind in a special way. On television we were shown pictures of schoolrooms full of children praying. Nobody said who they were praying to, and I wonder how many of them could have told us. Nobody said what they were praying for, and if they were praying for the souls of the departed there had certainly been an extraordinary regression in the thinking of the educational authorities of the U.S.A. Suddenly the much talked of division between Church and State seems to have been forgotten in a great wave of archaic thinking. "God has humbled us in a vital area; we must abase ourselves before God and try, somehow, to square him before the next launching." To the Jungian mind it was an astonishing resurgence of archaic thinking.

We have all encountered it, in one way or another; I still recall vividly my astonishment when, as a boy of eight, I met with such thinking in a schoolmate. He was an unfortunate boy, a poor boy, illegitimate, whose mother fought poverty as best she could by doing the hardest kind of daily housework. Walking with that boy one day at lunchtime I, aware that I was going home to something appetizing, asked him what he was going to have for lunch. He said: "I don't know till I get home. Every day at noon the Sun comes down and brings my mother and me something to eat." Every day? I asked. Yes, he said, that was the way he and his mother lived. When I reached home I told my mother about it. She looked very grave, and said she was afraid the boy and his mother might find the Sun a meagre provider. Was it a lie, then, I asked. She said she would not call it a lie, exactly, but a sad and brave answer to a question I should not have asked. The boy died not many months later, and I had some puzzling reflections about what the Sun might have meant by that. I have never forgotten that incident, because of the sense I had of a mythical world of which I knew nothing, but which was obviously intensely real to that unfortunate boy. If he had lived, I think ballads would have made more sense to him than the very dry Canadian history we were learning in school. He might even have become a ballad-maker himself, if his luck had changed.

Whenever something gets into the news which arouses strong feeling, we hear the voice of archaic thinking in the people who demand some terrible public vengeance for a rape, or a murder, or a bomb outrage. Not simply capital punishment, but the harshest kind of retributive justice of the sort the Ayatollah Khomeini has made familiar to us, is what they want, because the spiritual followers of the Ayatollah are by no means all confined to his own country.

Perhaps we should spare a few minutes to examine more carefully this question of the human pull toward myth, and the conversion of historical happenings that everybody knows about into a mythical form, which may become a song that spreads widely and achieves great popularity.

There is no lack of incidents in our own history that would make good ballads. Consider this one: in March of 1977 the wife of the Prime Minister of Canada deserted her husband and her children and ran off with a group of rock musicians called The Rolling Stones. She was young – much younger than her husband – and she was beautiful. Of course the press made a great deal of the incident, and there was an effective play, called *Maggie and Pierre*, that was popular for a while. But neither the press nor the stage could take the mythical line in dealing with the incident so that, forty years later, it would seem to have happened in some distant dream-time of romance.

But suppose a ballad had been made, what would it have been like? Fortunately a very similar incident is described in a ballad that goes like this:

There were three gypsies a–came to my door,
And downstairs ran this a–lady O!
One sang high and another sang low
   And the other sang bonny, bonny Biscay, O!

Then she pulled off her silk-finished gown
And put on hose of leather, O!
The ragged, ragged rags about our door;
   She's gone with the wraggle-taggle gypsies, O!

It was late last night when my lord came home,
Enquiring for his lady-o;
The servants said, on every hand,
   "She's gone with the wraggle-taggle gypsies O."

"Go saddle to me my milk-white steed,
Go and fetch me my pony-o,
That I may ride and seek my bride,
   Who is gone with the wraggle-taggle gypsies-O."

Then he rode high and he rode low
He rode through woods and copses too
Till at last he came to an open field
   And there he espied his lady-o.

"What makes you leave your house and land
What makes you leave your money-o,
What makes you leave your new-wedded lord,
   To go with the wraggle-taggle gypsies O?"

"O what care I for my house and land?
And what care I for my money-o?
What care I for my new-wedded lord?
   I'm off with the wraggle-taggle gypsies O."

"Last night you slept in a goose-feather bed
With the sheet turned down so bravely O;
Tonight you shall lie in a cold open field
   Along with the wraggle-taggle gypsies, O."

"O what care I for a goose-feather bed
With the sheet turned down so bravely, O?
For tonight I shall sleep in a cold, open field
    Along with the wraggle-taggle gypsies, O."

There, you see; that is archaic thinking and also archetypal thinking and I am sure you see its virtues, which lie in its simplicities.
There is something in the young woman that cannot be appeased
even by what most people would regard as great good fortune; she
demands a kind of freedom which is, like all freedom, expensive in
several kinds of coin. The old ballad makes no judgements; it sides
neither with the lord nor his rebellious lady. It simply gives us a
version of the story that allows us to think what we please, but which
– especially in the magnificent tune that goes with it – stirs our blood
and gives us a sense of the variety and wonder of life.

Not all archaic thinking is harsh. What characterizes it, at least in
part, is a directness which can find expression in fine poetry. Consider
the folk-song called "The Unquiet Grave"; it is a dialogue between
a young man and his dead love:

Cold blows the wind to my true love
    And gently drops the rain;
I never had but one sweetheart
    And in greenwood she lies slain.

I'll do as much for my sweetheart
    As any young man may;
I'll sit and mourn all on her grave
    For a twelvemonth and a day.

When the twelvemonth and one day was past
    The ghost began to speak;
Why sittest here all on my grave
    And will not let me sleep?

There's one thing that I want, sweetheart,
    There's one thing that I crave;
And that is a kiss from your lily-white lips
    Then I'll go from your grave.

My breast it is as cold as clay,
    My breath smells earthy strong,
And if you kiss my clay-cold lips
    Your days they won't be long.

Go fetch me water from the desert,
    And blood out of a stone,
Go fetch me milk from a fair maid's breast
    That a young man never has known.

O down in yonder grave, sweetheart
    Where you and I would walk,
The first flower that I ever saw
    Is withered to a stalk.

The stalk is withered dry, sweetheart,
    And the flower will never return,
And since I lost my own sweetheart
    What can I do but mourn?

When shall we meet again, sweetheart,
    When shall we meet again?
When oaken leaves that fall from the trees
    Are green and come up again.

There's a fine pagan poem of mourning and lost love for you! And we must remember that the people who sang this song by their firesides doubtless were regular attendants in the church of their parish, and heard the parson expounding the doctrine of Eternal Life. But what sort of Eternal Life is offered in the song? Decay and dissolution and unless the lover is able to perform certain mythological tasks – bringing water from the desert, blood from a stone, milk from the breast of a virgin – he must join his loved one in the grave which is still unquiet with unfulfilled love.

The Church used to teach – may still teach for anything I know to the contrary – that the soul of man is naturally Christian. We may not be so certain, but could we agree that the soul of man is naturally religious? The yearning for the numinous, for what provides not only comfort and reassurance but also awe and a sense of splendour beyond the daily task, is a powerful element in the spirit of man, which asserts itself in extraordinary and poetic and also sometimes laughable ways.

These old songs about which I have been talking were widely popular among simple people because they gave a dimension to their lives which they profoundly needed. Have we grown into a period of civilization where that need is no longer felt? The question is too absurd to require an answer. Where do we find our sense of the numinous today? There are still people who find it in religion, but it must be said that many of the churches have turned determinedly toward social gospels and what they call "relevance" – which so often seems to mean what is basely contemporary. Even the Catholic Church has abandoned much of its splendour, and has translated its superbly poetic Mass into an English which is not much above the level of a bank's yearly report. Where does modern man look for uplifting marvels?

It seems to me that the movies do as much for him as any readily accessible form. The lists of what's on in Toronto abound in pictures about space adventure, or ventures into what may be called the realm of the spooky. Much of the magic of the Challenger space shuttle lay in its promise of numinosity – what was impossibly distant and potentially magnificent was to be encountered and made our own; the sense of desolation that followed its failure was far more than can be accounted for by any scientific mishap. An outreaching toward unknown wonders had been abruptly snubbed. Mere train wrecks, whatever their cost in life, do not have that quality of numinosity. What is mystifying and wonderful is that the mourners for the

Challenger never suspect that an even greater exploration lies readily to hand: not the great journey without, but the greater journey within. No wonder the Gnostics asserted, with chilly calm, that salvation is not attainable by the spiritually lazy.

As for the movies, I wonder how many of you saw that popular and successful film *Cocoon*? In it, you recall, a number of people living in a colony for the old in Florida discovered the Fountain of Youth, and were at last carried away in a sort of flying saucer to a Greater Florida in the Sky, where they would forever, presumably, play golf, and bridge, and quarrel with one another, and never have to fear God, honour the King, or give a thought to anything beyond the intellectual gamut of the *Reader's Digest*. As one watches such a film one does not know whether to laugh in derision or weep for the spiritual abyss from which such frightened, vulgar garbage makes its way into the Hollywood mind – to use the word mind in a very general sense.

The point I offer for your consideration is this: the soul of mankind is naturally religious, and that means that the soul of mankind is also naturally poetic, and seeks refreshment and reassurance in the rich imagery of poetry. We Jungians, as we puzzle our brains over difficult and sometimes woefully badly-written books that explore Jung's thought, may sometimes forget that in poetry lies just about everything we are seeking, and frequently in more accessible and nobler form. The folk-song we have been discussing – necessarily in extremely abbreviated terms – embodies not only the lighter pleasures of human life but also its profundities. Jung says repeatedly that psychological wholeness is not solely to be found in the analyst's consulting-room; it may be found in a life lived fully, and thousands of quite simple people, said Jung, achieve this wholeness through the experience of a life deeply lived, in individual terms, in all sorts of occupations. The people who achieve such integration may never have heard of psychology.

Folk-song embodied much of this folk wisdom in simple and sometimes rough verse which carried, none the less, a great poetic strength in what it said and what it implied. This verse was supported

and given additional beauty and impressiveness by some of the loveli-
est melodies ever to emerge from the musical genius of mankind.
The songs without the tunes are only half themselves, and, of course,
I have not ventured to sing to you, though, as a man of Welsh descent
I value song as one of the great human expressions.

Because of that I want to conclude by speaking of two magnificent
folk-songs that come from Wales, but which you must encounter in
English. That is a pity, for the Welsh language is a pithy language, rich
in poetic overtone, but the English versions give you the sense of
what the songs say, and what is lacking you must fill in from your
own store of poetic insight.

These songs deal with themes which are not the commonest in
folk-song, but they touch on aspects of life that should be strongly
relevant to Jungian thought.

The first deals not with a story but with an emotion. It is called
"Hiraeth" and that is a Welsh word that is not easy to translate. The
best dictionary defines it as "longing" or "nostalgia" but that is not
the full meaning, because no single word in English quite encom-
passes all that "hiraeth" means. It includes also a sense of loss, of a
yearning for something irrecoverable, but not to be pinned down to
lost love, or a wish to return to childhood. It is a particular form of
melancholy to which Celtic people seem to be disposed, but the
Welsh have given it a special place in their emotional life. I can give
you the words, but not, unfortunately, the melody, which is simple
and of great evocative power. This is an English translation:

Tell me, all ye men of learning
    Who doth weave, with fatal yearning
Grievous longing past all bearing,
    Ceasing not through constant wearing?

Riches perish, so do pleasures,
    Velvet, silk, and costly treasures,
All the splendours that I cherish,
    Yet my longing ne'er will perish.

Cruel longing, ne'er forsaking,
  Longing brings my heart to breaking,
And when slumber gently takes me,
  Longing comes and rudely wakes me.

Although the Welsh have identified it and given it a name of its own, I do not think that emotion is particularly theirs. I have known people of many races who have suffered from it. It is not quite the melancholy of the romantic poets, who can tell us where their melancholy comes from, but a tormenting and indefinable feeling. It is the triumph of a folk-song to have defined it in so far as it can be defined, with an elegant simplicity. What do you, as Jungian thinkers, make of it?

The second is, in my opinion, even deeper in import. It is called "Yr Hen Wr Mwyn," which means "the kind old man." It is a funny song – funny in depth – and the joke lies to a great degree in the tune. It begins very mournfully, as some kind-hearted boys meet a nice old man on the road, and their hearts are filled with pity for his age and decrepitude. Obviously he is drawing toward the end of life. O, the pity of it! Slowly and softly the boys ask him where he has been wandering; they seem to think he is lost. But then the tune changes to one of great merriment; he has been fishing, he says, and ends with words – nonsense syllables, really – that suggest that he dances a little jig. The mournful boys ask what he caught? O, nothing very wonderful. How did he get so wet? Fell in the river, boys. Why does he shiver? Because he got a wetting. But what if you die, you kind old man? O, surely, you'll bury me, boys. Where would you like to be buried, you dear old man? Bury me under the hearth-stone, boys. But why under the hearthstone, you poor old soul? So I can hear the porridge bubbling, boys. And the old man ends with his little jig.

What have we here? The solemnity with which youth thinks of old age and death, wonderfully contrasted with the merriment, the downright irreverence, with which the old consider these same two facts of life. The sweetness and kindness of the boys does great credit

320   ROBERTSON DAVIES: HAPPY ALCHEMY

to the goodness of their hearts, but of course they don't know what they are talking about, because they have never experienced it. However, we would not want them to think otherwise; what they think must be in agreement with what they are – that is to say, very kind, nice boys who feel for someone at the other end of life. But the old man has the real Jungian spirit. Dr. Jung said that the way to meet old age was to live as if one expected to live forever. That is what the kind old man in the song has been doing; fishing, not catching much, getting into trouble because he falls in the river and gets wet, but still abundantly happy, still joking, still meeting destiny with resolution and some mockery. And at the end, we get the genuine feel of folk-song, which is never sanctimonious and very rarely religious in a purely Christian way. The old man wants to be buried under the hearthstone, in the midst of the world in which he has lived and gained his wisdom, and he will find his happiness when he hears the porridge boil.

It is a wonderful song, and of course without the music you have half – perhaps less than half – of what it implies. For the music speaks to pure feeling, unmixed with the complexities of words. It is the gift of music to be able to go behind the part of the mind that is dominated by language. Many of us take heart from the consolations of religion when we grow old. But there is another side of us – a pagan side which folk-song often evokes – that makes light of death and accepts it as inevitable and very possibly happy. Philosophers and professional "thinkers" in general can be very bad guides to the latter part of life. Consider Cicero's much admired – and to my way of thinking, over-praised – essay *De Senectute*. Stripped of its sonorous Latin, what a load of cliché, of gloomy codswallop it is. It is just the praiseworthy literary exercise of a good dull gentleman Roman lawyer, and as such we may mark it *beta +*. No: the Chinese knew better than that, and the Welsh folk-song speaks of the true Jungian spirit in our precious Celtic heritage. Not second childhood in the sense of senility, but the freedom from cant and hypocrisy of the child, revisited through the experience of a lifetime, is the truest gift of old age. We contrast this with the poetic evocation of death in "The Unquiet Grave," of which I spoke earlier. But "The Unquiet

Grave" is a song of youth and love, whereas "The Kind Old Man" is a song of age and life understood. Of course every stage of life finds its expression in folk-song. There is a wonderful Welsh folk-song called "The Mother-in-Law's Complaint," which is that her daughter-in-law washes her husband's clothes with this new-fangled, wasteful soap, instead of banging them on the rocks beside the stream, which has always been good enough for decent women. An archetypal situation, I'm sure every daughter-in-law among you will agree.

29

———— ∞ ————

HARPER OF THE STONES

THIS UNUSUAL PIECE IS A ghost story with music and was written in November 1986. Davies produced it at the request of Chamber Concerts and it was set to music by Louis Applebaum, one of Canada's most prodigious composers. The ghost story was staged at the Young People's Theatre in Toronto for the "Musical Mondays Series" and Davies narrated the tale at the first performances on May 11, 1987.

He recorded in his diary: *By 10:15 at the Children's Theatre. Rehearse with Lou and the orchestra until twelve; the orchestra are a very nice group and the violinist proved to be the concert master of the Hamilton orchestra . . . Jenny comes with Brenda to rehearsal and we eat a picnic in our car on the street, then I go back for the performance at 1:30. Full house of children from seven and eight to sixteen; attentive, and applaud generously but do not laugh or show any sign of involvement while the thing is going on. It was very well received, and I exerted myself to put a spell on them . . . Rest and a light dinner, then back for the performance at eight. House chiefly adults, and the piece goes much better and received with laughs, also with some dread. A little girl behind Brenda clung to her mother and whispered "I'm frightened." Good questions afterward. None of the "How much money do you make?" order . . . Enjoyed this departure from routine, though it cost me a good deal, as public performance always does, but I greatly enjoy working with Lou, a fine composer and a delightful man.*

———— ∽ ————

I live in the country because I need quiet for my work. Not that one gets complete quiet in the country; it is full of sound. For instance:

The natural sounds of birds. (MUSIC)

The sound of a farmer in a field far away cutting hay. (MUSIC)

The sound of a jet plane passing overhead. (MUSIC)

On Sunday night there is the wavering hum of traffic on the highway, as the city folk hurry back to be ready for work and school on Monday morning. How I pity them! (MUSIC)

And sometimes there are unhappy sounds. They come in the night when the animals we call brush wolves capture something. The brush wolves will not attack a man, but they are terrible to rabbits, raccoons, and even an animal as big as a deer. Then we hear the sound of Nature in her harsh mood, for Nature is not the dear old lady that foolish people think she is. (MUSIC)

What I do not hear in the country is music, and that is why, when I heard the harp last Hallowe'en, I went out at once to see what was happening. (MUSIC)

I live on the slope of a hill, and I have a fine view. There, looking at my view, and sitting on one of my stones, meditatively playing a large harp, was an old man.

"Good day," I said.

"Good day to you," said he, but not in a friendly tone. He was a very dirty old man, dressed in clothes so worn and stained I could not tell whether they were of cloth or leather. He wore a huge hat and had a dirty bandage over his right eye. An evil-looking old man, I thought. But I had the right of proprietorship.

"I must inform you that you are trespassing," I said.

"Must you inform me of that? Well, now!" he said. "And what if I asked you who you are?"

A hard case, I decided. "I am the owner of this property," said I. "I live here because I need quiet for my work."

"And what work would that be?" he said.

"I write stories," said I.

For the first time he showed something other than contempt for me.

"Do you so?" he said. "Then maybe there's some good in you after all. Maybe you and I have something to say to one another."

"What I have to say to you," said I, "is that you are trespassing on my land, and you must go. I can see that life has not used you generously, so I should be glad to give you something to help you on your way. But you cannot stay here."

"Can I not?" said he. "You'd better believe I can't go anywhere else."

Did I mention that it was a rather foggy day? That it was Hallowe'en? As I looked at him I understood that I was seeing a ghost. (MUSIC)

I know a good deal about ghosts. They are part of my profession. When you meet a ghost, there is one question you must always ask.

"What have you come for?" I said.

"Because it is what you call Hallowe'en, but it's rightly called Samhain [pronounced Sawen] in the Old Language. I come here every year on this day to play for the stones."

He touched his harp. Oh, it was easily seen that he was a fine harper! We have all heard harps, the graceful gold-plated concert harps that give so much beauty to every orchestra. But this harp was taller and thinner than those, and it was made of wood, and on the front of it was carved a woman's head. This was none of your French-made orchestral harps and I saw now that it was one of those harps

with three rows of strings, such as harps had before the inventio
pedals. The strings were made of gut, and some of them were ve
thick. And the sound that came from them! It was the sound of \
harp, but it was not − I don't know how to describe it − it was not
a concert-hall sound at all. Not what you would think of as a civilized sound. I can best describe it as a very ancient sound. (MUSIC)

"Tell me," I said, "why do you play to the stones?"

"I didn't say I played *to* them. I said I played *for* them," he said.

"What is the difference?"

"What a fool you are! But that's to be expected in a man of your
time," said he. "Maybe you're not as big a fool as you look."

I did not take offence. As I told you, I am a writer, and every time
I write something a few critics tell me what a fool I am. But even
though he was very cross in his speech, this old man did not seem
to be a critic. And what he said next proved it.

"Stay here by me, and you'll see why I play for the stones."

"I don't want to seem inquisitive, but after all I live here. Are you
telling me that this is a magic place?"

"All places are magic places, though fools everywhere pretend otherwise," said he. "But there are some places where the foolishness is
thinner than others, and this is one of them. Have you such a thing
as a drop of drink about you?"

He was becoming friendlier. I went into the house and got something to drink and hurried back to him.

"That's more like it," said he. "Gimme aholt of that bottle."

He snatched the bottle out of my hand and without troubling
about the glass I had brought he took a great swig out of it.

"Not bad," said he. "Not good, because it has a kind of a government taste about it, but I've drunk worse."

I managed to get the bottle away from him long enough to pour
a heartening drop for myself. It was the best straight malt whisky, and
I had been saving it for a special occasion. I knew that this was certainly a special occasion. The drink had made the old man talkative.

"Is this a magic place, you said. Well, boy, that's just what it is, and
I knew it the first time I set eyes on it."

"When was that?" I asked.

"Not long ago. About a hundred and seventy years ago, I suppose it was. I come here from the Old Land to make my fortune, and it was here I settled."

"And made your fortune?" said I.

"Not what the world calls a fortune. But what I knew was a fortune, because I knew at once that the Old People had been here, and were still here, for people like myself with the gift to see it," said he.

"I suppose you mean Indians," I said.

"There were Indians, sure enough, but they're not the Old People. Oh, there's been lots of people here, you know. Before me and my life there were some Frenchmen – just passing through. Great explorers, the French. (MUSIC)

"And before the French there were some fellas from just across the water. Norsemen, they called 'em. A very rough lot they were, but brave – Oh, they were very brave. (MUSIC)

"But before any of them, there were Indians, the people of the lightest step you ever knew. The French cut their way through the forest. The Norsemen just burst their way through the forest. But the Indians glided through the forest with never a sound to say where they were. (MUSIC)

"But before the Indians – long, long before them – were the quietest people of all. They were the fishes."

"Fishes?" I said in astonishment.

"Aw, sure the fishes," said the old man. "How ignorant you are! Did you not know that where we are now used to be under the water? That was when Lake Ontario, as they now call it, was a great inland sea, and this was the farthest shore of it. Have you never digged up any fossils, as they call 'em, in your garden? Those were the fish folk. And very quiet folk they would have seemed if there had been any men around to listen out for them. But they were not quiet to themselves, you see. They had a sound of their own. Have you never heard fish talking? (MUSIC)

"But even before the great sea was the ice, and the great sea came when the ice melted. Now the ice had a very queer sound, let me tell you. (MUSIC)

"When the ice went away, it left the stones behind. Because, you see, the ice had brought the stones with it down, down, down from the farthest north, from what you must call Ultima Thule. And these very great stones that you see all around this land that you say was yours, came from Ultima Thule."

I began to remember some things I had been told by my neighbours as local history. "Then you must be Old MacLir, who tried to make a farm in these stoney fields and broke his heart doing it," I said – and at once I knew I had made a mistake, for he looked scornfully at me and spat a ghostly gobbet on the grass.

"You've been listening to fool talk," he said. "I did not break my heart and I made a very good farm, around the stones. I was a popular man, let me tell you. A very popular character, I was. I was the only musician of note in this whole Irish settlement. Of course there were others – inconsiderable bosthoons who could do well enough at a wedding or a hooly – that's what we called a social evening, if you don't know the word. There was a fella played the tin whistle, and another one who could manage a fiddle. They were good enough for a hooly of the cheapest quality. (MUSIC)

"But for music – for real music – there was nobody to touch me. Ah, boy, you should have heard me at a wake! Solemn and lamenting to begin with, then wild and merry as the drink took hold. That was music for you! (MUSIC)

"But for the great music I came here where we are sitting now, and I played for the stones."

"I am afraid I don't understand," I said. "Why did you play for the stones? Did you imagine the stones could hear you?"

"I imagined nothing at all," said Old MacLir. "They heard me, right enough. To begin with I had to guess what music they would like. So I began very gently. (MUSIC)

"Nothing happened, but I knew they were listening, so I grew bolder, and played louder. (MUSIC)

"I knew they were pleased. You see, boy, fools never heed a stone. The farmers around here thought the stones were just nuisances. They put chains on them and dragged them to the boundaries of their fields, to make rough fences to keep their cows from straying.

The stones didn't like that, not at all. They knew they were hated, and treated with scorn. Never hate a stone, boy. The stone may decide to hate you. There were terrible accidents, when stones rolled on a man's leg, or knocked down a horse so there was nothing to do but shoot it. But I respected the stones, and never moved one of them, and the other farmers said I had a poor farm, no better than a stone-heap. They said I was lazy. But I knew what I was doing. Do you know what I was doing?"

I thought I knew, but it would have been tactless to say so, so I shook my head.

"No, of course you don't know. But I'll tell you. I was wooing the stones, boy. I was seeking their trust and their favour. And at last I had it. They taught me their music."

I thought the time had come to speak boldly. "Could you give me just a hint – just a few measures – so that I may know what their music was like?"

"Ah, you're like all the rest of the people nowadays," he said. "You want to know in a few minutes what it took me years to learn. You want all the gain, and none of the pain. It was slow – slow. For years I played to them, and nothing could be seen, but much could be felt. I felt I was getting nearer and nearer. Then one day I knew I had hit it, fair and square. I played my best, I can tell you, and then I knew I had learned their music."

"How did you know?"

"I knew it when the stones began to dance."

I knew he was mad. I looked all around us, and there were great stones – huge boulders of granite, some grey and some pink, scattered about the fields in front of us. A friend of mine, who is a great geophysicist, once told me that those stones were not less than a billion years old, belonging to a time long before man was on the earth – or in this part of the earth, at any rate.

I told you I know something about ghosts. I have met a few, but never before had I met a ghost who was mad. It was an astonishing experience. He heard my thought.

"You think I'm a madman," said Old MacLir.

I did not answer.

"I'll show you how mad I am," said he. And then he struck a great chord on his harp. (MUSIC)

He played, and I believe it was some sort of Irish jig, but enlarged and elevated beyond anything you might hear at a hooly. I looked around me at the stones. They did not budge. Of course the old man was mad, but his music was great. (MUSIC)

"I know what you're thinking," he said, and once again I knew he had heard my thought – because ghosts can do that, and you should keep it in mind when you meet one. "You're thinking I'm mad, and the stones aren't dancing at all.

"They're not dancing because they want to make me wait. They want to humiliate me, to put shame on me because of something I once did when I was young and foolish.

"I might as well tell you what it was. The first time I succeeded, the first time the stones danced, I was wild with joy and pride. 'O amn't I the marvellous fella!' I thought. 'O amn't I the greatest harper in the world.' And I began to dance myself and left my harp and pranced around like the proud goat I was, and bowed to the stones and grinned at them as if I was at a military ball. I thought how obliged to me they were. I even thought they were my servants, to do what I wanted. I went up to a big stone and I put out my hands as if it were a lady who would dance with me. And sure enough the stone took a lurch, and though I sprang back as sharp as I could, it fell on my leg, and crushed it, and though I lay there all the night through calling and calling it wasn't until the next morning that a boy heard me and fetched help and it took four strong men with crow-bars and chains and horses to get that stone off my leg, and then the doctor came and cut it down to a stump, and left me as you see."

True enough, I saw then that he had only one leg, and a wooden peg that was held in place by straps that went over his shoulder.

"That taught me not to try to dance with my betters," he said. "The stones are very proud and high, you see. What you call aristocratic, because they are so old and have been in the country so long. And now they always make me play a while before they begin to dance, to show me that they don't do it because of me, but because it is their wish. But now I think the fine lords and ladies are ready."

He grabbed the bottle from me and drained it to the dregs. A heroic swallow that would stagger any drinker who was not a ghost. Then he smashed the bottle, as if to give a signal. Again he struck the harp, and began the jig. But this time it was such music as never came from a harp. It was the wildest, strangest music you ever heard, full of the sound of birds and the cries of animals and the wind and the rain, and the thunder and the lightning, and the dashing of huge waves against the shores of a great cold ocean that was formed from ice that had made its way slowly down from Ultima Thule. It was the sound of a world before mankind. It was the sound of the great merriment God must have known during the long days of Creation. (MUSIC)

The stones were dancing now. O yes, they were dancing! But it was not hopping and skipping like jigs or reels, nor was it the dismal revolving of a ballroom.

Not a stone moved from its place, but they rocked and turned, slowly and with the greatest dignity, as if to say: "We are the lords of the earth and of the water. We shall stand when all has gone. We shall endure until better things come. But what can be better than we? So we shall endure forever." (MUSIC)

I watched for as long as I could bear it. How long that was I cannot tell, but night came, and the stars broke out of the sky, and the moon shone down on the strange dancing. It seemed to me as if the stones sang, in the strangest voices, in the language of Ultima Thule.

When at last dawn began to appear the music ceased, and the stones were immovable in their places.

And Old MacLir was gone. Gone, I suppose, until the next Samhain, when the stones would dance again. (MUSIC)

30

—— ❧ ——

JUNG AND THE WRITER

SEVERAL OF THE PIECES in this book have mentioned Carl
Gustav Jung, and his influence on his work was frequently
acknowledged by Davies. Here, however, is one of the clearest
tributes he was to make to Jung, and, since it was originally made
in Sweden, it has not been widely disseminated.

Although Davies always maintained that he disliked travel, he
managed to see a great deal of the world. For this 1989 lecture
he went to the Gothenburg Book Fair in Sweden, where his publishers were promoting his latest novel *The Lyre of Orpheus*. On
the way back to Canada he gave the same lecture in London to
The Society of Analytical Psychology on October 10, 1989,
whose members may have been struck by his confession of mis-
chief in the matter of defending his title *Fifth Business*.

On July 24, 1989, Davies wrote to a Swedish friend: *A very
important reason why I have been so busy is that I am to visit
Sweden in September to speak at the Gothenburg Book Fair (or
should it be spelled Göteborg? Nobody will tell me). I gather that*

*it is a very big fair and they have a great many speakers. My pub-
lishers are bringing me and Brenda from Canada for three days,
I believe it is, and I am to speak on Torsdag 7 September, the
program tells me, and my subject is "Jung and the Writer," which
sounds very solemn, though I shall try not to be too heavy. But
it is not exactly what could be called a humorous subject, and
the program I have received is full of funny pictures, so I hope the
audience is not expecting a funny speech. But there will only be
a few people present, I fear, because there are so many other
things to attract the crowd. The star of the Fair, I gather, is to be
a writer called Jackie Collins, of whom I have never heard. Do
you know anything about her? But my publishers seem anxious
to work me off my feet, and have sent me a long list of things I
am to do, besides the speech.*

In his travel diary, Davies described the day of the lecture in
Sweden, which was September 7, 1989: *Then at 4:00, my address
on "Jung and the Writer" to a full attentive house. Chairman,
Heidi von Born, a great enthusiast and a good speaker. She told
me that, as a child, she had actually seen a flea circus: fleas pulled
carts, duelled, etc. Says public health legislation put an end to
this sort of show. My speech is listened to with extraordinary
attention and seems to be a great success. All the Wahlström &
Widstrand people very pleased and Mrs. Danielsson listened as
the audience left and said the comment was remarkable. One
woman said, "No I won't go home by tram: I want to walk and
think about it." What could be better. Several children present
me with scraps of paper for autographs: obviously don't know
who I am and don't care. I sign "Jackie Collins" and they go away
quite content. They presented me with flowers and a heavy
wrought-iron candlestick: how do I get that home? – A rest and
then dinner at an excellent restaurant: aquavit, caviar and blinis;
sole, Chablis, an ice, cognac, all of the best.*

——— ❧ ———

Y̶ou have been told that I am
going to talk about "Jung and the Writer," and that is what I shall
certainly do. But let me assure you that I do not mean to talk about
C. G. Jung's psychology in detail and at length. Indeed, I am
unqualified to do so, for, although I have read extensively in Jung's
works, I have made no systematized study of them, and I am wholly
lacking in that scientific quality of mind that would enable me to
make them any clearer to you than would be the case if you read
them for yourself. Indeed, a beautiful clarity and regularity is not
characteristic of Jung's thought; he possessed an abundant, bountiful
mind and a compelling curiosity which led him in a number of directions which dismayed his scientific colleagues and disgusted his
master, Sigmund Freud, and was one of the reasons for the break
between those two great men.

When I was a young man, I read extensively in Freud, and was
captured and delighted by the elegance and apparent inevitability
with which he reached his conclusions. But when I approached
middle life I began to read Jung, and came under his spell, and have
remained there ever since.

To explain why this was so, I must be perfectly honest with you.
Indeed, I have resolved to be as honest as possible in everything I say
to you, even when I have to speak of some very personal matters.
The longer I studied Freud, the more I was repelled by his pessimism
and the powerfully reductive trend of his thinking. I simply could
not swallow the idea that sex was the dominating factor in human
survival and in the human mind. As I looked about me I saw all kinds
of people who appeared to live effective and even admirable lives
without any discernible sexual concern, but I never met anyone who
could go for a day without food without becoming deeply concerned
with getting something to eat. To me it was obvious that self-preser-
vation was the dominating force.

Perhaps this was a more personal reflection than I supposed. Critics
have observed that my books are full of descriptions of meals, and
people eating and drinking. But be that as it may, I thought Dr. Freud
was stretching things farther than was justifiable by life as I saw it.

Also I was struck by the fact that all the commentators on Freud, all his disciples, could not deny themselves the satisfaction of saying nasty things about Carl Gustav Jung, and I determined to find out why this was so.

It did not take me long to make my discovery. Jung, though not as good a writer as Freud, possessed a far-ranging and, I must say, a poetical mind, and I found this deeply congenial to me as a writer. A psychological approach to the human mind and the human spirit which was generous toward the creative faculty suited me admirably, and in a humble way I became a Jungian. I should say at once that I have never been analysed, either in the Jungian or the Freudian manner. I have not lost my high regard for Freud, whom I still think of as one of the greatest liberators of the human spirit in the history of our culture. But the cast of his mind – and every mind, great or modest in its scope, must have some broad determining attitude – was reductive, and when it came to the consideration of the creative faculty as it shows itself in art of all kinds, he simply said that he had to throw up his hands and declare himself vanquished. Not so Gustav Jung; he attacked the creative faculty and brought to bear upon it a mind that was primarily that of a scientist, but also that of a great humanist, and that was what I wanted.

I never thought that Jung was right and Freud was wrong, though I did think that Freud was most concerned with the sick mind, whereas Jung appeared to assume that the human mind, in its infinite variety, tended toward health and wholeness.

I must also tell you, because as I have said already I am anxious to be frank with you, that Jung appealed to me because he was, like me, brought up a Protestant – he a Lutheran and I a Calvinist – and Jung was a man who had in childhood lived in rural surroundings where there were all kinds of people and all kinds of animals; fields and trees and all the marvels of nature were everywhere about him, whereas Freud, despite his passion for mountain holidays, was a city man, and an overwhelming number of his patients seemed to be unhappy Viennese of the wealthy class. To a country-bred Calvinist of Celtic background, like myself, Jung's appeal was irresistible.

Nothing that has happened to me in the years since I was thirty-five or so, has shaken this loyalty. Indeed, since I began to approach the world as a writer, and to achieve some modest acceptance as a writer, everything has strengthened my fidelity to the Jungian approach.

This has been a source of strength to me, but it has also caused me a great deal of annoyance, because once it had become known that I was a student of Jung, large numbers of people have been quick to assume that I am nothing else. Studies of my writings have been published – a few of them even swollen to the length of books – that have demonstrated to the satisfaction of the authors that nothing I have written is not to be traced to that influence.

Many of the critics who think they know a great deal about me appear to know very little – certainly not enough – about Jung. Some of them have read extensively in Jung, but they have brought an unswervingly academic cast of mind to their reading. They are eager for certainties, and one of the things Jung makes very clear is that there are no certainties that are not personal certainties. These critics are looking for a system, and Jung is quick to insist that he is not a systematizer, but a man who in a large, general way, invites you to make up your own mind.

The learned critics have been by no means the worst of my trials. Education in North America has developed a deplorable tendency to invite very young and inexperienced school boys and girls to form opinions about aspects of life of which they have no personal experience. I have in my files – because I am one of those people who cannot bear to throw anything away – discussions of my books by children of sixteen and seventeen, in which they explain my books, and me, in terms of a Jungian system foisted on them by their teachers, who are not – I speak with the greatest moderation – people who know much about Jung. I receive, every year, a number of letters from schoolchildren who send me questions set down in lists – and ask me to answer them briefly and clearly. To what Jungian type do I think that I belong? By what means do I apply the teachings of Jung to my writing? Are my characters constructed according to his typology? Some characters in my books seem to be hostile toward their mothers – what was wrong between me and my mother, and why? But this sort of interrogation does not end with letters. I receive telephone calls from students of all sorts wanting answers to questions their teachers have asked of them. (I should explain that in Canada, at least, teachers often tell their pupils that they will award specially high marks to anyone who has made direct contact with me and, so to speak, put me on the spot.) The most dismaying call of this kind came one night at nine o'clock from a youth of sixteen who said: "I've got to have this essay ready to hand in tomorrow morning, and I'm stuck. Can you give me some help with these-here Jungian archeotypes?" It was impossible to explain to him that no telephone conversation could help him; indeed, in his agony, I do not know what would have helped him except sudden and merciful death.

I assure you that I am not hostile to these children, but I refuse to strip myself naked and dance while they make films of the performance to show in their classrooms. As for the adult critics, I am totally floored by them. They have such marvellous certainty! Many of them appear to regard an author as an *idiot savant* – a wretch gifted in one realm, but wholly incapable of understanding what he does. But I know that writers understand very well what they do.

To put it briefly, in Jungian terms, a writer has unusual access to his Unconscious, and he has encouraged and developed that ability because it is in that way his best work is done.

That is the simple statement, and of course it calls for development. First of all, what is the Unconscious?

As the name implies, it is that area of the mind which is perpetually alive, which never sleeps, but is not directly involved in logical thought. It is the well in which memory of every kind, be it of experiences, feelings, fleeting impressions, things heard and said and, of course, of things read, is stored, not according to any logical plan, but in an *olla podrída* in which things unknown and unrelated may come to the top, usually unexpectedly.

We all know what this is. It is the matter which floats across our consciousness when we are not thinking in a determined fashion about a particular subject. It can be embarrassingly trivial, or sentimental, or obscene; it can seize upon us unexpectedly, thrusting upward some idea, or criticism or ill-timed joke. It is the thing that makes us laugh when our outward circumstances say that we should weep. It is the source of desires, or disloyalties, or bursts of anger or tenderness of which we have not previously been aware. Most of us thrust such fleeting wisps of thought back down into the Unconscious, with impatience or shame, because they seem to have nothing to do with the matter at hand. But they do – O, indeed they do – if we seize upon them and track them down, and ask them to yield up their secret. Which is what writers do.

J. B. Priestley once wrote that he was always amazed, and surprised, when he read that some writers – Dickens, for example – developed their plots, or were visited by their finest inspirations, when they were walking. He confessed that when he was walking he never thought in any coherent way, at all. His mind was like a cinema screen across which all sorts of odds and ends of irrelevant, unconnected trivialities passed in a perpetual foolish picture-show. I know exactly what he meant. But I also know – and I think he knew as well – that some of a writer's best fishing in the Unconscious is done when that foolish picture-show seems to be in command of his mind.

Coherent thought is not the only kind of thought, and perhaps it is not the most productive thought. It was Bertrand Russell, who certainly ought to have known what he was talking about, who said, "Intellect, except at white heat, is apt to be trivial."

If we hope to know someone well, we must have some access to his mind that goes beyond his intellectual approach to life. The characters in fiction who are most real to us are those whose thoughts as they related to his Unconscious mind are imparted to us. Hamlet's soliloquies tell us more about him than his conversations with his friends and enemies. Indeed, Hamlet's father's Ghost tells us more about Hamlet than about the Ghost. And in his extraordinary novel *Ulysses* James Joyce takes us into the character of Leopold Bloom by admitting us to some – not all, for that would be unendurably boring – but some of what Bloom allows to rise from his Unconscious as he walks about Dublin. And when Joyce permits us to overhear, so to speak, the minds of that simple, foolish, unhappy girl Gertie MacDowell, in the Nausicaa chapter, we learn how greatly the colour and the quality of her mind differs from that of Mr. Bloom, and a sense of the variety and complexity of human experience is made manifest to us in a manner that is truly wonderful. But the greatest marvel of all is the insight we are granted into the life of Mrs. Bloom, the former Marion Tweedie, in the final books of *Ulysses*, the Penelope chapter, which has been called one of the most extraordinary revelations of feminine psychology in all literature.

Certainly no one could pretend that James Joyce's command of such material came from a study of Jung. He did not, I believe, ever read a word of Jung, and his only contact with Jung was when he asked Jung to examine his greatly troubled daughter Lucia; in a later talk with Joyce, Jung said that in his opinion Lucia's grave illness was associated with her father's neurotic dependence on her. Joyce was furious, and never afterward ceased to speak ill of Jung. Obviously, no influence there. No, Joyce's insight into the workings of the Unconscious was a part of his gift as a writer, and all through the history of literature we come upon examples of writers with insight of this kind, centuries before depth psychology as a scientific study came into being.

There are writers other than Joyce who were contemptuous of all depth psychology, either Freudian or Jungian. The names of Evelyn Waugh and Vladimir Nabokov come instantly to mind. Were they fearful that their artistic gift was being "explained" and therefore diminished? They need not have feared. Both Freud and Jung were deeply respectful of the writer, and declared that the secret of artistic creation was beyond their power to explain.

But this chaos of memories and feelings and impressions we call the Unconscious is not all; it is merely the personal element in this Unconscious realm where creative work has its beginning. There is another and far deeper Unconsciousness which is not personal in the sense that it belongs to any single man or woman, but is the foundation of our common humanity. Jung has given it the name of the Collective Unconscious, and in it lies the memory and the instinct and the emotional structure of mankind, which exists in forms he calls archetypes. The word "archetype" has been dreadfully abused by people who think that it means, simply, a pattern. They do not distinguish between an archetype and a stereotype. An archetype is a pattern, certainly, but not in any simple sense; it is part of the inherited psychological structure of man and it is linked with instinct; the thing about it which is most difficult to grasp is that it cannot be identified in any single form and is evident only through its manifestations. You cannot nail it down but you can see what it does.

Archetypes were not original with Jung and he never pretended that they were. Plato was aware of them and wrote most eloquently about them, and they are recognized by his followers as Platonic Ideas. They are by no means simply literary or artistic in their nature and manifestation; they lie at the root of all that makes us human beings, rather than animals, though archetypal ideas are present in animals, as well.

For instance, I am told that day-old chicks will run to their mother for protection if you pass a hawk-shaped piece of cardboard over their pen, and cast the shadow of a hawk upon them. But if you pass the same shadow over them, but backwards, they are not interested. The hawk-shadow constellates in these not very intelligent little creatures an Archetype of Danger, and they respond at once. The archetypes that affect human beings are, understandably, vastly more complex.

Albert Einstein, the great mathematical physicist, was very much aware of the archetypal elements in his own work, and he called them "universal elementary laws." But for our purpose today, we shall speak of archetypes as they apply to the creative life of the writer. Access to these archetypes, which must necessarily be interpreted personally, is to be found in all literary production of the highest kind, which we define as classical.

The writings of Homer, of Virgil, of Dante, are full of archetypal apprehensions of the Hero-Struggle, of the Heroic Journey, of the Divine Woman. We find them everywhere in the plays of Shakespeare. In *Romeo and Juliet* and *Antony and Cleopatra* we find the archetype of – no, not of Romantic Love, for that seems to be a fairly new idea in the human psyche – but of Obsession, of Thralldom to another human creature. Doubtless we could find examples of that archetype in this room, if we chose to do so. The archetype of Ambition lies at the heart of *Macbeth*, and the archetype of Pride is fundamental to *Coriolanus* and *King Lear*. It is needless to multiply examples in Shakespeare. His access to the archetypal world is without equal.

A writer whose access to the world of Archetypes seems also to have been extraordinary, and whose work may be more familiar to such an audience as this, was Goethe. Put aside his poetry and his novels for the moment and think only of *Faust*, for it offers a superb example of both the personal and the collective realms of the Unconscious. In the first part of *Faust*, written when Goethe was at the beginning of his long life, it is the Personal Unconscious that dominates, but in the second part, which was the product of his maturity, we meet with a wealth of archetypal material from the Collective Unconscious which leaves us stunned, and often baffled by whatever we can grasp of its significance.

If there are Goethe scholars among you, I ask your forgiveness for this blunt approach to one of the supremely great works of Western literature. I am not sufficiently skilled in German to do more than stumble though the play in its original, but I have, of course, read many translations and I assure you that their value is directly concerned with the degree of understanding the translators have of the archetypal roots of what the poet has to say. Translators must be poets themselves, and fine poets, to make head or tail of that astonishing work. It has often been said that the second part of *Faust* cannot be successfully presented on the stage. I can only say that I have seen it brilliantly and lovingly acted, and it was one of the two or three supreme theatre experiences of my life.

Of modern exemplars of such access to the Collective Unconscious of mankind I shall not attempt to speak, but the name of James Joyce has already turned up, as it must, in this discussion, and perhaps some of you may recall a passage in Thomas Mann's *Memoirs of an Unpolitical Man*, which expresses with admirable brevity the characteristic attitude of the literary artist.

> The look that one directs at things [says Mann] both outward and inward, as an artist, is not the same as that with which one would regard the same as a man, but at once colder and more

passionate. As a man, you might be well-disposed, patient, loving, positive, and have a wholly uncritical inclination to look upon everything as all right; but as an artist, your daemon constrains you to "observe"; to take note, of every detail that is characteristic, distinctive, significant, providing insights that are useful and relevant. You see these things as though you had no human relationship to the observed object whatever – coolly and deliberately – and in your work then, everything comes to light. . . .

I invite you to take special heed of that phrase "coolly and deliberately." It is this apparent want of ordinary human charity and forgiveness, allied to intensity of feeling, that has won for many writers a reputation for being somewhat remote people; they see too deeply to be at all times agreeable companions, sharing the feelings of those around them. Unless they can learn to keep their mouths shut, and to reserve what they see for what they write, instead of letting it spill out in conversation, they can be ugly customers indeed, and when they are in the company of other writers they may sometimes be quarrelsome. They are too sensitive to be ordinary social beings, and unless they learn to wear a mask – such a mask as Thomas Mann wore, and which earned him a reputation as an extremely formal and reserved man – they can be difficult friends and uncomfortable companions. They are sometimes the prey of bad habits, of which heavy drinking is one of the commonest. The wives of authors – poor souls – know all about this.

Perhaps you are wondering, is he never going to tell us anything we did not know? This is like an introductory lecture on Jungian psychology. Do not be uneasy; I am going to tell you a few things now which are drawn from my personal experience, and which may give you an insight into how at least one writer goes about his business and the way in which these Jungian ideas relate to him. I assure you that I do not really wish to do so, I dislike personal confession, and as I have already told you, it sometimes leads overconfident people to think that they know me better than they do. But I said I would be honest with you; so here goes.

I shall talk for a while about my own work, and the way in which the processes I have spoken about manifest themselves in my writing.

I am very often asked, where do your writings originate? School-children phrase it more directly. They say: where do you get your ideas? The answer, which is the most honest answer I can give, usually stops them in their tracks. I do not "get" my ideas – they "get" me. Let me offer an example.

In 1970 I published a novel called *Fifth Business*; it is still in print. People seem to like it very much, and some people study it in schools and universities. It had its beginning at least as early as 1960, and it did not appear as the germ of a novel or as a story of any sort. It came as a haunting image, which floated to the surface of my mind when I was idle, or sleepy, or bored, and it was always the same.

It was, as I say, an image or picture, and it was simple and clear. I saw a village street at night, in which two boys were fighting with snowballs; one boy threw a snowball which I knew had a stone concealed in it. He wanted to hurt his companion. He was devoured by spite and ill-will. The loaded snowball was thrown, but it did not hit the boy at whom it was aimed; it hit a woman, who was severely hurt and who fell to the ground.

I did not pay much attention to this unexplained and idle fancy, but it kept reappearing until, after perhaps two years, I thought that I had better take a closer look at this image, and discover what it meant, and why it was so insistent. And that is what I did. I called up the image and invited it to tell me what it had to say. In a very short time the early part of the novel had taken shape in my mind. But it was not the story which eventually was written; as I first saw it, the story was about the husband of the woman who was hit by the loaded snowball, and whose child was born prematurely because of it, and who lost her reason because of the shock. This man was a parson, of a not very highly regarded Protestant sect, who was driven by this misfortune to devote his life to revenge on the boy who had destroyed his happiness. Revenge did not destroy his enemy, the boy, it destroyed the man himself.

But when I began to plan the story, it did not want to go in that direction at all. The emphasis was different. It wanted to be about the two boys who were fighting; it wanted to be about the child who was born prematurely because of their quarrel. It wanted to be about one of the boys whose whole life was dominated by his Calvinist feeling of guilt; the snowball which was meant for him had struck another, innocent person, and changed her life, and the life of her husband, the life of her child, so drastically that no such consequence could have been foreseen. And at last it influenced the life of the boy who had thrown the loaded snowball so that all his worldly success suddenly seemed valueless, and he died, whether by suicide or murder, in a characteristically spectacular way. As for the premature child, it made him a very unusual and special person.

It was a story of vengeance, but it was not the simple vengeance that I had at first foreseen, where the wronged parson sought the death of his child's enemy, and eventually brought about his own death. No: this was the vengeance of Fate, of Destiny, and it took more than fifty years to complete its spiderweb of events.

Vengeance, however, does not occur without some agency to bring it about. Who was the agency? It was the first boy, at whom the snowball had been thrown. Without doing anything directly about the matter, it was nonetheless his undying remembrance of that wicked action, and his weight of guilt because he thought that he was directly responsible for the misery of the mother and her unfortunate child, that eventually brought about the death of the evil-doer. Or did it? He never knew, and nobody could ever say with certainty quite what had happened, but somehow vengeance was demanded and achieved for the spiteful act of a thoughtless child.

Thus it became obvious to me that the boy acted the role of Fifth Business in the drama of my story.

What is Fifth Business? To explain that, let me pause for a moment and tell you a story which will throw some light on the psychology of at least one author, and also on the psychology of publishers, who are a very special class of people, as everybody at the Gothenburg Book Fair knows very well.

To me *Fifth Business* was the only possible title for the book, but it troubled the publishers who thought nobody would understand it. It is a theatrical and operatic term, used to describe the role in a play or an opera which is not the leading role – not the hero or heroine, the villain or the villainess – but is that of the man who explains the plot, and helps the plot along but who is not himself a leading figure in the plot; such a person used to be called the *raisonneur* in the French theatre. My book was about a man who played the part of Fifth Business in the plot, and I wanted to show what a very interesting person Fifth Business might be, if you examined him closely. But the publishers shook their heads.

The English publisher was especially troubled. "If only you could provide some satisfactory definition, right at the beginning of the book," he said, "something that would help the reader. Indeed," he said, "I must insist that you do that or I really do not think I can agree to publish the book."

So there I was. I had to have an authoritative definition and, as it happened, I had to have it within twenty-four hours. Was I stumped? Did I fail? I did not. The next morning I handed him this definition, which has appeared in every subsequent edition and translation of the book:

> *Those roles which, being neither those of Hero, Heroine, Confidante, or Villain, but which were nonetheless essential to bring about the Recognition or denouement, were called the Fifth Business in drama and opera companies organized according to the old style; the player who acted these parts was often referred to as Fifth Business.*

The quotation was attributed to the Danish theatre historian Thomas Overskou, in his valuable work *Den Danske Skueplads*.

The publisher was overjoyed. He did not know that *Den Danske Skueplads* had never been translated into English, and that I knew no Danish. He did not know that in the succeeding twenty years a number of toilsome scholars would seek for that quotation in Overskou's many volumes, without ever being able to find it. He did not know that a considerable number of other scholars would accept the quotation as something Overskou might very well have written if he had thought of it. Nor did he, in spite of his great experience, appear to understand that writers are children of the god Mercurius or, as Thomas Mann has explained at length, that they have a strong element of the Trickster in them, and that if you ask them for a quotation they are very likely to provide you with one, and it will be just what you want. He did not understand that a novelist is a writer of fiction, and that not all the fiction may be confined to his books. The writer's mind is ambiguous in its deepest nature, and it is this quality of ambiguity which makes him a writer.

Ambiguitas is the adjective which Ovid applies to Proteus, whose gift it was to assume different shapes, in order to avoid being questioned. Never ask an author too many questions or you may get answers that you cannot wholly trust.

Why is that? Is it because the author is, to put it bluntly, a crook? No, I think it is because the author's access to his Unconscious makes him constantly aware of how deceptive even the world of seeming fact may be. If you doubt me, ask any honest judge how much of the evidence he hears in court is contradictory, even when the witnesses believe every word they are saying.

Now let us return to the writing of that novel *Fifth Business*, the origin of which I have explained. Did the story appear to me complete in form and detail? I have already explained that when I began to write the book the emphasis of the plot proved to be different from what I had expected when I wrote out a rough plan of the first few chapters. Nor did the plot come to me complete. It developed as I wrote, and I assure you that at the beginning I did not know how it would end. Of course I knew that by the end of the book the villain – if you want to call him that – would receive what is called in English, Poetic Justice – which means that he would have to pay for his evil act, though it had taken place fifty years earlier.

The foundation of the book, you see, is the belief I have long held, and which was impressed on me in my Calvinist childhood, that no good action is ever lost – and that no evil action is ever lost, either. Because I believe a work of fiction must be drama, the stone which so powerfully influenced so many lives when it was wrapped in that snowball, appeared at last to play a part in the death of the man who had thrown it. When I began the book I did not know how that would happen, but I trusted that I would find out. And so I did.

It is this sort of explanation, I know, which persuades some critics that an author is indeed an *idiot savant*, who does not know what he is doing. But that is a misunderstanding of the creative process. The author may not know consciously every detail of his story when he begins it, but his Unconscious knows, and it is from the Unconscious that he works. And if he is writing *Fifth Business* he must be aware that the Archetype of Retribution – of the Scales of Justice – is at work in the depths of his being. I say "being" rather than mind, because I believe that a writer's work is the product of the totality of his being, which invents far more effectively than the logical surface of his thought.

As I talk to you in this way, I fear that some of you may be saying to yourselves: "Ah, yes, it is just as we thought; these Jungians are mystics." I assure you that is not so. Gustav Jung was no mystic; indeed, he often spoke of himself as an empirical scientist, and if you read some of his case-histories you will understand why. I am certainly no mystic, but because I am a writer, and have given my best energies to that form of art, I have learned to trust some of my mental processes, to approach them with confidence. I assure you that I do not warm myself at fantastic fires and dance in the light of glow-worms. I do nothing that great numbers of people do not do, but I pay attention to what my Unconscious says to me. Let me give you another example.

When I was writing *Fifth Business* and was about halfway through the book, I became aware that I knew a great deal more about my characters than could be suitably included in the novel which was in progress. I realized that I was writing about three men – the one who was called Fifth Business and whose life had been utterly changed by the accident with the snowball, but also about the boy who threw the snowball, and who had lived what he considered an enviable and successful life, until he came to the end of the road; and there was also the third man, the child who had been born prematurely as a result of the unlucky snowball, and whose life took a course that nobody could have predicted, because he became world famous in an unusual profession. I must tell their stories, I decided, as those stories were already lying around in my mind, in bits and pieces, waiting to be put together.

But when I began the second book, I found myself in a difficulty. That rich successful man could never tell his own story, for he knew too little about himself to have any genuine insight; therefore I decided to tell about his life as it affected the life of his son, who was a victim of his unreflecting admiration for his father. But who was this son? He was a lawyer, and a brilliant one; a true gladiator of the courtroom. He was also a drunkard, and did not know why. What indeed was he?

The answer came to me in what, for want of a more accurate word, I must call a vision. Yet I dislike using the word vision, for it plays into the hands of those people who do not have visions, and think that those who do are not quite rational. But there it was – one summer's day, I was sitting looking out over the valley which lies below my house, when a strange creature appeared, quite close to me. It was an animal of some sort, for it had a lion's body and mane, but it had a long tail with a forked end like a scorpion, dragon's claws, and – the face of a man. The man, moreover, whom I knew at once to be the hero of my story. This was a manticore, a fabulous beast to which I had never given any particular thought. This extraordinary creature was being led on a golden chain by a beautiful woman, in classical dress. These are not precisely the visitors one expects in the middle of a Canadian landscape. They remained with me for perhaps two or three minutes, and when they vanished I had my story and my character complete. My hero was not wholly a man, for he was as fierce as a lion, as venomous as a scorpion, as incalculable as a dragon – and yet he had the face of a deeply unhappy man. The beautiful woman, I knew, was leading him to his salvation, where the animal and mythical elements in his nature would be integrated into a whole and true human being. And so it was. I wrote the book, and called it *The Manticore*. Once again the publishers were not sure what to do with such a strange title, but this time they did not ask me for a quotation to explain it; they could look up "manticore" in any good dictionary, and discover that it was a fabulous beast.

These creative adventures of mine are not, I assure you, improved upon or touched up to make a good story. I tell them to you exactly as they happened. Is this what happens to all writers? Certainly not in the same way, but I am certain that all writers worthy of the name have flashes and intuitions from the Unconscious which are basic to their work. We have all read books which are purely invented – by which I mean that the writer has determined to write a story and has made one up by logical processes. Sometimes they work beautifully, like a good watch; detective stories, at their best, belong to this sort of writing. But they do not grip the reader, and give him flashes of insight about his own life; they do not enlarge his imagination or his sense of the astonishments and splendours that rise from the Unconscious to meet those who welcome them. Jung called these logically constructed works of literature "psychological" and he distinguished them from what he called "visionary writing."

Jung had some extremely interesting things to say about visionary writing, and the unseen current that seems to sweep the writer along when he is working at his best. He spoke of the social significance of literature, constantly at work educating the spirit of the age, conjuring up forms in which the age is most lacking. And indeed this applies to all the arts; much of the mystery of modern painting rises from the determination of the painter to show the world something that the world is deeply reluctant to see. And Jung says, "art" – he was speaking of literature but it applies to all arts – "art represents a process of self-regulation in the life of nations and epochs."

This process, however, should not be pushed to absurd and simple-minded extremes. At present there is a great vogue for the sort of writer who is described as *engagé*, which too often means that he writes a kind of superior journalism about the troubles of his times. Certainly admirable books have been written from inside knowledge of a world situation, or from a burning indignation at some contemporary injustice. But when the world situation has changed or the injustice been dispelled, or given a different form, these books seem to dwindle in their effect. It was Jorge Luis Borges who said, very truly, that of all the obligations that an author can impose upon himself, the most common and doubtlessly most harmful is that of being "modern." To write in the very latest style, about the most impressive contemporary theme, sounds convincing indeed, but unless the writing rises from the only true fountain of inspiration – and the Unconscious has shown itself to be not timely, but timeless – it will not be first-rate.

Once again I quote James Joyce to you. He said, "The supreme question about a work of art is out of how deep a life does it spring?" He did not mean how philosophically trained a life, or how extensively educated a life, but a life that was deep in self-knowledge and heedful of what that painfully acquired self-knowledge had to tell the writer who had fought for it. You remember that Ibsen said that life was a struggle with trolls, but the trolls may be persuaded to yield deep secrets. They may, to some heroes of the inner struggle, yield what Jung spoke of as "primordial experiences" – secrets from the depths of human spirit.

I spoke earlier of the questions that schoolchildren ask me. I return to these questions often because they are innocent; they are not cloaked in layers of literary theory. They often ask me: Are you religious? When I talk to them, and try to get to the bottom of their question, I find that they meet with things in my books which they cannot account for except as being associated with religion. But when I ask them, "Are *you* religious?" they often deny it, because they have the modern notion that to be religious means that one believes a lot of things that are plainly untrue. I explain to them that I must certainly call myself religious, but that the things I believe are indeed true, and I have seen them at work during what I must now agree has been a long life.

What does the word "religious" really mean? It comes from a Latin word which means to take care, to pay heed, to give thought to something. That is the word *religere* which is the opposite of *neglegere*, from which our word "neglect" comes – to ignore, to close one's eyes to things, to live on the surface of life. Therefore I tell my enquirers that to be religious – at least as I interpret the word – is to be attentive, concerned, careful, and to look at life through eyes that are as clear as one can make them, and to bring conscientious scruple and a measure of intuition to whatever life presents to one's experience. Of course the word now means to give heed to godly matters, but I stick with the older meaning, and I am encouraged once again by Albert Einstein, who said that in our day the scientist is the truly religious man, because he has trained himself to neglect nothing, to set nothing aside as trivial, because the truth may lie hidden under a mass of triviality. But the artist, and as you know from what I have been saying, I consider the writer, if he takes his work seriously, to be very much an artist, is also religious in his attention to everything, and his willingness to see everything as a manifestation of the human spirit, which is itself a manifestation of God and God's will. This is tough chewing for very young people, to whom the very word God is irrelevant to what they think they know. They suppose that to be religious is to live under a yoke of codified beliefs which exclude or reject many things they think important. But the truth is very far from anything of that sort. The religious man is the man who tries, in so far as he can, to see everything as clearly as he can, even when what he is observing is shrouded in ambiguities. He understands that he cannot expect to understand everything, but he dare not ignore anything that lies within the scope of his vision, or that rises from the realm of the Unconscious.

When he has looked as clearly and as deeply as he dares, does he then slap down everything he has discerned on paper, and offer it to the world? No: indeed he does not. He must present his vision of life in terms of his art, with all the skill in language, all the tact, all the special quality that marks it as his own. He may choose to write in the tragic mode, if that is where his gift lies. Or he may write in the humorous mode, which will certainly expose him to misunderstanding and probably to accusations of triviality. But he must go in the direction to which his gift guides him.

You see, I have now come to the point where I must use the word "gift," which means no more in this context than that some people are born to be writers and some are not. We live in an age when many universities and schools offer instruction in what they call "Creative Writing." I cannot, however hard I try, convince myself that any teacher can show somebody else how to be creative, though of course he may uncover and encourage a creative gift if it already exists. Anybody who wishes to do so may enter into a friendly association with his Unconscious, but that will not make him a writer. Dredging up stuff from the Unconscious may put some ingredients on the kitchen table, but without a gifted cook it will never be turned into a meal that anybody wants to eat.

So, at the end, we find ourselves where Freud and Jung found themselves when they confessed that they had no explanation for the creative gift. We know a little more about it, perhaps, but we have not trapped its secret and we cannot give the secret to anybody else.

A modern writer who is much admired – though I confess that my own enthusiasm for him is well-controlled – used a Russian word to speak of the writer's gift. That was Vladimir Nabokov, and the word he used was *shamanstvo*. A Russian friend tells me that it means the quality of the enchanter, the magician, the worker of wonders. It does not mean the stage conjuror, who has a repertoire of clever tricks. It means the *shaman* who by gift and training is the source through which important things are imparted to his tribe.

The writer, if he is a serious writer, man or woman, tragedian or comedian, writer on epic themes like Tolstoy or on apparently slight themes, like Jane Austen, is one who brings great and important things for the consideration of his tribe. And he speaks to those of the tribe who are disposed to share his vision.

My theme, you remember, was "Jung and the Writer." Gustav Jung brought some very important things for the consideration of the whole world, but it does not lie in his power to make anyone a writer. But he may help you to a better understanding of your work, if you are a writer to begin with.

31

———— ⌀ ————

THE VALUE OF A COHERENT NOTION
OF CULTURE

THIS LECTURE WAS GIVEN as part of The Walter Gordon Series of Lectures in Public Policy at Hart House in the University of Toronto on Wednesday, September 23, 1992, chaired by the Master of Massey College, Ann Saddlemyer. It was the third of the series and the participants were Carlos Fuentes and Robertson Davies, with Fuentes speaking first. The title of the event was "An Emerging North American Culture," and Davies took the opportunity to voice the general Canadian weariness with the attempts of the unpopular government of Brian Mulroney to amend the Constitution through apparently endless negotiations conducted at places like Meech Lake and Charlottetown. The audience roared their approval as he laid into the politicians and their "tiny minds."

On August 24, 1992 Davies wrote to a friend: *Next month I have to join in a public discussion of North American Culture (what a pompous title) with Carlos Fuentes, the Mexican writer (and a very fine one). Both Canada and Mexico know what it is*

like to live side by side with the U.S.A., and to be taken for
granted by its government and its people. I expect we shall have
a lively time and I look forward greatly to meeting Fuentes.

———— ⌦ ————

Ever since I was told that the
subject of this discussion would be "An Emerging North American
Culture" I have puzzled over the implications of that title. It cannot
mean that there is no North American culture at present; any community has a culture of some kind. Does it mean that something lurks
in the womb of the existing culture, something markedly different,
which is going to leap upon us after the millennium which is now a
mere eight years away? What does it mean by "culture"?

I presume that it means the civilization, customs, artistic and
scientific achievements of a people, or group of people, in this case
Canada, the U.S.A., and Mexico; the word is often extended to
mean simply a way of life. After all, the life of an entire continent
is influenced by a similarity in culture; but in a certain degree also
national cultures are inescapable. The most determined hermit
would have trouble escaping completely from the culture that
encloses his solitude.

If that is so, North America unquestionably has a culture, and it
is rooted in the European culture which is the dominant aspect of
civilization among the principal countries of our time. We have
developed and altered some aspects of that European culture to suit
our own needs and tastes. Are we here tonight to discuss the possibility that something wholly new will appear on this continent in the
course of – let us say – the next five hundred years? Frankly, I think
that anything of that kind is most unlikely.

Very soon, however, in a mere two or three hundred years (which
is nothing in terms of the growth of a culture) we shall surely find
that the culture of North America will have taken on several attitudes and developments which come from the Orient. I cannot guess
how many of you are familiar with Oswald Spengler's remarkable

and prophetic work, *The Decline of the West*, in which he foresees the decline of the Western world and a corresponding rise of Asiatic and African powers. He puts forward a theory of cyclic progression, according to which great cultures and continents undergo a period of growth, followed by maturity and then decline. The theory is briefly expressed in Bishop Berkeley's "Westward the course of empire takes its way"; it is interesting to recall that the Bishop wrote those words in a poem called "On the Prospect of Planting Arts and Learning in America." But Spengler had less faith in arts and learning than in industrialism and technology. I cannot claim any authority in such matters as these, but we are all aware that it is common talk now that the United States is losing its industrial and technological supremacy to Japan, which is unquestionably establishing itself as a dominant force in industrial and technological affairs. If Japan takes the lead in industry and technology, this continent will certainly adopt, perforce, many Japanese characteristics.

Things which seem in themselves to be trivial may often be straws which show the way the wind is blowing. In the great days of Rome the mark of a truly influential citizen was the possession of a Greek secretary; since the end of the Second World War the mark of distinction in the U.S. is the possession of an English secretary; the modern Japanese produce admirable secretaries of their own, but they show dominance by the possession of a few pictures by Van Gogh and a cellar of the finest French wines. Draw what conclusions you will. When the cultivation and elegance of one nation become the coveted possessions of another, it seems that the clouds are beginning to gather over the skies of the nation which provides the greatly desired toys.

Please do not assume from what I am saying that I am wholly pessimistic about the Western world of which we are a part and whose industrial, technological, and artistic achievements we not only share, but to which we make an honourable contribution. Unfashionable as it is nowadays to say so, I firmly believe that there are attributes which belong to blood and race which cannot be copied with total success. Imitation, even on the highest level, is not creation.

I think of the world of music. Some of the finest executants on our concert stages and even on our operatic stages are now Orientals.

They come *very close to the best*, but if you will allow me to express a personal opinion – music has been a lifetime preoccupation of mine and I think that my opinion is not uninformed – they are not *quite* the best. Our own artists, in the performance of our Western music, have still that quality which makes the difference between the admirable and the transcendent; it is the quality which distinguishes the uttermost that can be achieved by intelligence from that which is the essence of spirit, and, if I may use an unpopular four-letter word, of soul.

This is to speak of musical performance only. What about the writing of music of a high order? This is an area in which the East has not excelled. It would be absurd to say that it may not yet do so, but it is mere fact to say that it has not done so yet.

So: does the course of empire really take its journey westward until it arrives at last in what we have been used to call the East? I am inclined to think that it is so, but I do not think the movement will be completed in our time or in our children's time or in our grandchildren's time. Our decline, if decline we must, will be slow, and for some of us the best may be yet to come.

Doubtless you have been wondering when I would get to Canada, because these lectures are expected to have a Canadian relevance. In what I am about to say I beg you to believe that I am not lambasting my country because I scorn it; I speak as I do because it has long been the privilege of a country's authors to speak of what they see with the special vision which is theirs. If I utter warnings, you must think of me as akin to the sacred geese who warned Rome that the enemy was attacking the Capitol; by their clamour and their scolding they saved Rome. Can our writers save Canada? We can try but we must not expect that Canada will like us for it. We all know the fate of the prophet in his own country.

In discussing this matter of a North American culture it is obvious that Senor Fuentes has been asked to join us because his country and ours may be said to enclose the United States, which is of course the dominant power on this continent. Mexico and Canada are in a sense parentheses around those words The United States of America. Parentheses are used for many purposes and sometimes they confer a hint of irony. The United States of America – it is a somewhat vaunting title, for those states do not yet include Mexico or Canada, but we overlook it. We pay it no mind, just as we do not worry that a small local baseball contest is vaingloriously named The World Series. The parentheses – Mexico and Canada – are used to our great neighbour talking always at the top of his voice. Do we parentheses have anything of importance to say? Senor Fuentes has spoken for Mexico; let me say something about Canada, though I shall certainly not forget Mexico.

We Canadians are all, I think, a little exhausted by the hullabaloo, the brouhaha, the pow-wow that has gone on in our country about our Constitution. We have wearied of the incessant pitter-patter of tiny minds trotting across our land to say, at one place or another, what they will or will not put up with as the structure of our country. But we may have missed, in our irritation, something of great importance that is not at once apparent. This constitutional wrangle is our version of a civil war. It is a psychological rather than a military conflict but nonetheless important because it is a war of ideas, fought somewhat ineptly with words. When we think of civil wars we think of the Roundheads confronting the Cavaliers, and making their point by beheading a King; we think of the Blue and the Grey involved in bloody struggle to maintain the Union. Our Mexican friends have known many civil insurrections, and, like ourselves in 1812, have fought the United States on land to preserve what is their own. Those wars are embalmed in the glory of military exploits and their story can be stripped down to make a chronicle understandable on a low level by children. But our present conflict is a Canadian version of a civil war, and dowdy and dispiriting though it may appear, it is none the less the struggle for the soul of a country and the identification of a national entity, and if what emerges is a pitiful lost soul and an entity in tatters, it will be nobody's fault but our own.

Why our own fault? Because we shall not have produced the people capable of dealing with great things in a great style. Because we have been content with a form of democracy which too readily slithers downhill into a conspiracy of mediocrity directed against a nation. Because our country, which could have boasted at one time of being one of the most politically sophisticated countries among the democratic lands, lost its way, lost its touch, ran out of gas. These things happen, and we may not pretend that they cannot happen to us. We shall have shown that those who laugh at us as a dull and spiritless people have been right.

Or is it as bad as that? I do not think so.

We are not a country populated by fools, but I fear that we are a lazy people, accepting our good fortune as though it came by divine right. The present constitutional dispute has shown, among other things, how indifferent we can be to things of the highest importance. We show no anxiety to distinguish ourselves in the world of the intellect, and in matters of business we are not, as a people, as aggressive as our southern neighbour. Except, of course, in the Province of Quebec whose leaders, armed with empurpled rhetoric which is so characteristically French, face, and face down, the tongue-tied anglophones, who sputter in terms of political correctness like damp firecrackers.

It has not always been so. In practical affairs and in the world of science we have made valuable contributions to the civilization of which I have spoken – the civilization that is known and shared by the most advanced nations on the globe. We have in our time produced statesmen of distinguished mind, great energy, noble eloquence, and devotion to our national cause, and these statesmen have come from both the dominant races of our country. Our contribution to the arts has been, until comparatively recently, confined to performers and interpreters, but there we have given the world artists whom the world has cherished. Of our contribution to the arts on the creative level I shall speak later, because it is of special significance to what I have to say this evening.

At the moment, however, it seems that we are in a trough, obviously bereft of political talent, which is the place from which we understandably expect the most potent leadership to come. I do not want you to think that I take any particular pleasure in scolding the people (men and women) who at present are in control of – no, not of our destiny, but of our immediate future – but I cannot forbear to say that they are a sorry lot. Out of the innumerable deliberations of our leaders on the present constitutional crisis have you read a solitary word that you can recall as being charged with piercing insight, or strong feeling, to say nothing of eloquence? It was reported a few weeks ago that one of our national leaders has in his entourage two speech-writers, one of whom is paid $100,000 a year and the other $70,000, but from this gentleman – he is not our prime minister, by the way – we have not heard a word that I, as a professional assessor of words, would value at one of our base metal dollars. Even these highly paid bards, it seems, are utterly bereft of song when their theme is Canada. Nobody has any eloquence, nobody has any passion, and it is because nobody has any intellectual vigour or strength of feeling. In our political world we face intellectual bankruptcy in all the major parties.

Who is to blame? We are. These are the people we have elected to think for us and to speak for us, and if they cannot do it it is our own fault. It is not a simple matter of political expediency or political choice. Of course our electoral system in Canada, as elsewhere in the world, has become, in essence, a vast popularity contest, in which a candidate's television quality is of greater importance than his intellectual endowment or his most cherished principles. But even when that is said, what is wrong is that our choice is so limited, and our power to choose so stupidly exercised.

Any attempt to answer that question would keep us here far longer than would be endurable, so I must talk about a single element in our national life which I think contributes heavily to the malaise of which I have spoken, that rheumatoid arthritis of the intellect and of the will which is the present Canadian disease. I want to talk about education.

We are met here in a university ambience and so education may fittingly come under survey. But it is by no means only at the university level that education in Canada must bear heavy blame for what is wrong with the country. To put the matter simply, we do not take education seriously enough. We still cling to the notion, which descends from our pioneer ancestors, that education above the simplest level is an affectation, and that a limited acquaintance with the primary skills of reading, writing, and arithmetic is good enough for anybody. Anyone who confesses openly to a cultivated taste in anything whatever is regarded as an oddity, desirous of raising himself above his fellows. Our Ideal Canadian is an oaf. Of course we do not say so openly, but we make the message clear enough in our legislatures, where the first move of a government faced with financial troubles is to cut down on what the lower level of our legislators do not hesitate to call "frills," by which they mean the arts, the sciences, and education. The majority of our legislators are wholly untouched by education. Oh yes, I am sure you can produce statements to show that the chairs in our parliaments are warmed by the rumps of a large number of B.A.s and possessors of professional degrees. But would you know it if you were not told? Does their manner of expressing themselves suggest any real acquaintance with the tongue that Milton spake? (Not to speak of the manner in which Milton thought.) The plain fact is that they do not believe in education or in culture and think these things the concern of lesser, impractical, inconsiderable folk, to be encouraged or set aside as expediency dictates.

The trouble begins at the bottom. The education in our schools simply is not good enough, because it is not rooted in any coherent notion of culture. If you were to enter a classroom in any elementary school in our ten provinces and say to the teacher: "Are you laying the groundwork here for the acquirement and extension of a national culture on the level of, say, France, or Sweden, or Finland?" I wonder what the response would be, or if you would receive a response? Yet that is what we need, and what we are paying for.

What is the trouble? I think it lies in our expectations, arising from what – to use a term very popular among educators – our "role-model" is. We are imitating the United States, and not on the highest American level.

In the United States there is more than one level of education. There is what the serious people among the rich can afford for their children, and below that schools of lesser quality degenerating into schools from which one averts one's eyes in dismay. The United States has a group of universities that are not dependent on governmental whim for their maintenance, and are thus free to give education above the level that politicians can understand. In Canada we have no such universities and the sad consequence is that our universities are at the mercy of uneducated people who have no idea of what education really is.

What is that? What *is* education? Let me tell you an illustrative anecdote. Some years ago, when I was Master of Massey College in this university, I knew a young man, a member of the college, who was a first-class student of history. He wrote an excellent thesis, and got his Doctorate of Philosophy in history. But then he needed a job, and the world of history offered none. So, to keep bread in his mouth, he took a minor post in a financial house dealing in stocks and bonds. He rose rapidly. When I met him about four years later, and asked him how things were going, he said, "I've learned one important thing, above all others; there's nothing in the financial world that a good grasp of history doesn't help."

There spoke a really educated man. He was not educated in finance, but I gather that in that world it is possible to learn by practical experience. To learn, if you already know what learning is. If you know what real mental application is. If you have something in your head that conditions your outlook on the world that is more extensive than the confines of the stock market. If you are, in fact, a truly educated person and not simply a trained peasant. But are politicians aware of this concept of the educated man? Have they any awareness of a mental capacity that extends beyond the boundaries of the job in hand, whatever it may be? Of low cunning, they have some awareness, because they employ that in their own lives. But of real education, what do they know?

A few weeks ago I was at the Stratford Festival, which has, for forty years, been one of the cultural glories of our country, and I was watching a performance of *Love's Labour's Lost*. There came that splendid moment when the curate, Sir Nathaniel, says of the stupid oaf Costard:

Sir, he hath never fed of the dainties that are bred in a book. He hath not eat paper, as it were; he hath not drunk ink; his intellect is not replenished; he is only an animal, only sensible in the duller parts.

At that moment I wanted to leap to my feet and cry: "Say it again! Say it again! Send a fax to every member of a provincial legislature and to every Member of Parliament and let him remember it when next he hears the word 'education.'"

You think that I am speaking in extreme terms, don't you? Remember those sacred geese that saved Rome; did they restrain themselves? My dear friends, how carefully do you read your daily newspaper? Do you not recall that earlier this year a Member of Parliament from North Vancouver told the legislators of our country that their poor assistance to the Canadian publishing industry was money wasted? Why? Because, he said, only 10 per cent of Canadians read books; he himself was a great reader (and at this point he gave the names of two writers of mingled crime and pornographic books as his favourites) but he read no Canadian stuff because it just wasn't good enough. There was nothing whatever to be gained, he said, by giving any assistance to literature in his country. The honourable member's name was Chuck Cook.

Is there anything to be said in support of Chuck Cook? I am afraid that there is. A recent survey under the auspices of the United Nations to discover how many people read books in forty-four literate countries revealed that Canada ranked forty-third. We were ahead of only one other country, and that was the United States. But we have still a claim to the lowest rung on the ladder because we tax books, and no other civilized country does so.

Where does the blame lie? With our systems of education, surely. And what is the remedy? Not to press on with the present prevailing attitude toward education, which seems to be that all subjects must be made diverting and easily mastered, and that what used to be called The Play Way in learning should dominate our educational ethos. Tell young people that something is easy, and they will certainly treat it easily and regard it as trivial. Reduce the tough chewing of history to vague generalities called Social Studies, lower the sights of literary instruction to exclude Shakespeare and the Bible as the foundations of English prose, teach mathematics as a collection of puzzles rather than as a mode of thought and reasoning, and you reduce the foundations of education to rubble. Education is hard work, not play, and its rewards are a seriously informed, wide-ranging attitude toward the whole of life, and the beginning of a great adventure, which, without it, can sink into an incoherent mess.

I imagine that there are among you university teachers who are familiar with the dispiriting work of teaching university students basic things that they should have learned before they appeared in your classes, to say nothing of teaching them what logical argument is, and the necessity to express considered opinions in concise and literate prose. But you are too often faced with young men and women who have no experience of intellectual rigour, and no conception of the root of all education, which is the thirst for knowledge which can only be slaked through self-education.

But to return to Chuck Cook, a man whose name fascinates me as a novelist, because only the highest inspiration could find so appropriate a name for a man who holds his opinions. Is he right in saying that there are no Canadian books worthy of intelligent attention? I confess that in such a matter I am a biased witness, and I am biased because the reception of my own writing by my fellow Canadians has been, on the whole, generous. But if I depended for my livelihood on my earnings within Canada, I should certainly live in a manner of humble restraint. However, like a number of other Canadian authors, my books appear in many countries and in twenty or more languages, and the reception they receive is warming and encouraging.

I do not say that boastfully but in refutation of what Chuck Cook implies when he says that Canadian books are not "good enough." They are good enough to carry the name of Canada and the ideas of Canada and a Canadian way of thinking and feeling to the rest of the world where they are received with respect and pleasure. They are good enough to make Canada appear as a country with something to say that the civilized world wants to hear about the condition of mankind and the way in which man's hopes and man's fears are encountered in the northern reaches of this immense continent. They have an individuality of viewpoint which is not that of the United States, but a soberer, darker, and, I venture to say, richer point of view than that which pertains to our south. I am not knocking the literature of the U.S.; that would be absurd. But I am asserting that our Canadian writing at its best has a flavour of its own and that the literate world enjoys that flavour and finds it reassuring as evidence of unity amid the diversity of civilized people the world over.

This is what a national literature does. This is what our guest, Senor Fuentes, has done so splendidly for Mexico, and it is what perhaps a dozen Canadian writers are at present doing for Canada. Canadian literature is a travelling ambassador of incalculable influence for what is best in this country. It is a message to the world that the intellect is not dead here, whatever the Chuck Cooks and the whole rabble of half-baked politicians, whose vision does not extend beyond the next election, may be signalling from their legislative buildings. The wine of political thought in Canada is a very watery tipple at the moment, but the brandy of Canadian literature is well over proof.

Limitations of time have compelled me to restrict my remarks about Canadian art to literature alone, but our sister arts can, and do, speak eloquently for themselves. I have been severe, but not, I think, too severe, about the Canadian people as a whole. Like our neighbours to the south we are self-declared seekers after happiness, but again like our neighbours to the south, we have no firm idea of where happiness is to be found.

Around the Great Hall of the neighbouring Massey College, these words are written, and I commend them to you: "Happiness is impossible, and even inconceivable, to a mind without scope and without pause, a mind driven by craving, pleasure, or fear. To be happy, you must be wise." Perhaps Senor Fuentes recognizes those words. They are by the Spanish American philosopher George Santayana; he is not much in favour at the moment, but he is nonetheless a perceptive and potent thinker.

Our neighbour to the south exhibits in its political world (using that phrase in the broadest sense) what happens when honest wisdom gives place to pleasure, craving, and fear. Can we learn the obvious lesson and abandon those delusive attitudes in so far as they have already seized upon our governors? Can we not demand of them that

they state their opinions more clearly on matters of the highest importance – and certainly our national culture is of the highest importance.
We should do so, because if we do not do so we shall go the way of
all stupid, greedy, covetous, frightened peoples.

And it will be nobody's fault but our own.

32

— ❧ —

HOW I WRITE A BOOK

MANY ADMIRERS OF DAVIES' WORK wrote and asked him how he imagined, developed, and wrote a novel. He had the opportunity to answer these questions in an article for the *Toronto Star* which was published on September 19, 1987. On a very hot August 18, he went to Massey College, which has no air conditioning, to begin his task. His daily diary entry provides a somewhat untypical picture of Robertson Davies at work:

Walk to the College in intense heat and arrive drenched, so I hang up my shirt and sit topless for the a.m. Outside the CNE [Canadian National Exhibition] procession is marshalling, so there is much noise from bad, out-of-tune bands and shouting from organizers. I set to work and write my Star *article.*

— ❧ —

Isuppose there must be as many ways of writing novels as there are authors, and in our time, when literacy is supposed to be in danger, there are hundreds of thousands of authors. Industry, though praiseworthy, will not produce a good book, and an author who drinks, drugs, womanizes and gambles, will not, for those reasons, produce a bad one. If you really mean to write a book you will find your own way of doing it.

Nevertheless countless people, many of whom wish to become authors, want to know how an author works. The *Star* has asked me to tell you how I work. I wish the answer were more interesting.

Very briefly, what I do is this: I yield to a theme, I ponder over it, I make a mass of notes, then I begin writing and write every morning from 9:30 until 12:30, Sunday included, until the book is done; I have it professionally typed, I revise the text rigorously, then I have it retyped and send it to my agent, who sends it to the publishers and takes care of all the business arrangements. All told it takes about three years.

Sounds simple and clear, doesn't it? But let us look a little more closely.

I said I "yielded" to a theme. Like all writers, I get great numbers of letters and many of them are from students who ask, bluntly, "Where do you get your ideas from?" The answer, which they are reluctant to believe, is that I do not "get" ideas; ideas get me. I do not invent plots; they arise in my mind, beginning usually with some mental picture that will not go away. It demands to be examined and thought about. And as I think about it something like a plot emerges. It is not always a plot that I particularly like, but it likes me and won't go away.

That is why I have written to countless aspiring writers that if they do not have any ideas that demand to be written about, perhaps they should consider seriously whether writing is the life for them. In the words of my old friend, Nicholas Goldschmidt, "In the world of art, if you haven't got it, you've had it."

Did I say I "pondered"? Yes, I did, and I know it sounds pretentious, as if "think about" would not be grand enough for what I do. But "pondered" is the right word, because I do not *think* coherently

about my theme. I let it present itself in a variety of shapes, and offer
me characters and situations I know I cannot use. Then, as the pondering becomes more and more insistent, I begin to make notes, and
that is often the longest part of the work of writing a novel. I try to
be tidy about the notes, numbering and indexing them in a special
book, and sometimes the notes fill 150 or 200 closely written pages.
As the notes swell in number I read them over, and wonder what I
can make of them. Because, somehow or other, a way must be found
of telling the story.

This presents real difficulties and sometimes several methods will
have to be explored before the right one declares itself. Shall it be
first-person narration, and if so, shall there be more than one narra-
tor? If this method is chosen, how do I deal with the problem that
there are things in the story that no single person can know?
Sometimes, as in *What's Bred in the Bone*, there are things no human
being can know, but which the reader must be told, and then I have
to call on spirits who have special knowledge. I have been sharply
criticized for this, but if the critics can do it any other way, they are
at liberty to try.

The method of narration is profoundly characteristic of the
author, and no two authors have precisely the same character. Henry
James is leisurely and profuse; Graham Greene is so compact as sometimes to be telegraphic. Who would wish either man to be other than
what he is? Dickens whoops and guffaws and weeps in print;
Thackeray is coolly ironic, and both are right. Tolstoy seems not to
know when to shut up; Stendahl measures out his narrative like an
apothecary. Flaubert agonizes over every word and Trollope writes
his daily stint without, apparently, crossing out a line. Both have their
immense virtues. Balzac intrudes his personality on every page, and
E. M. Forster hides himself behind a veil, but a single, unattributed
paragraph would enable us to identify either man. Only critics, those
great and good men, would wish any author to write in a way other
than his own. As the Welsh proverb has it, we must sing with the
voices God gave us.

My own way of writing has been called, in a very complimentary phrase, magic realism – a mingling of realism based on close

observation with elements which most people find quite out of this world, though not out of the world as it appears to me. I write of life as I perceive it to be, and luckily for me quite a large number of readers, in several languages, want to hear about it.

Then comes the actual writing. If I have suggested above that I am a pattern of industry, I only wish it were so. I try to write every day, but now and then I am tired, or written out, or even ill. I have never written a book in my life without having to pause for some wretched illness to take its course. This happens, I think, to everybody. Even Bernard Shaw, who presented himself to the world as a man without weaknesses and a monster of assiduity, reveals in his diaries (which we now have) that often he sat idle at his desk, utterly used up, eating boiled sweets, for which he had a child-like passion.

Then of course there is the Black Dog, the horrible, depleting depression to which Byron gave that name; when the Black Dog is on me, I look upon myself and curse my fate, and trouble deaf Heaven with my bootless cries. I have never known or heard of an author who was a stranger to the Black Dog.

Somehow, however, the book gets itself written, and now and then the passages written when the Black Dog was at his most malignant may be the best.

The book, once written, must cool off. That is while my secretary is at work. It takes quite a while for a typescript of five or six hundred pages to be transcribed in that neat, elegant, enviable professional form, in which every flaw is pitilessly revealed.

This is where the real fun begins. Revision! Cutting off some of the fat, but not all. Tightening and tidying. Making sure that the heroine does not have red hair on page 100 and raven locks on page 300. Catching shameful, pretentious mistakes, misquotations, and follies so stupid that the author blushes at them. Above all, shining up the vocabulary.

This does not mean substituting fancy words for common ones. More often it means substituting plain but strong words for flabby ones. It means giving every line of dialogue, so far as possible, the right flavour for whoever is speaking, and making the words spoken give the clue to how they are spoken, so that it is not necessary to fall back on nonsense like, " 'Do you love me?' she wailed, clench-ing her hands till the nails drew blood from the flesh."

I try to write, so far as I can, dialogue in Standard English. Slang may be outdated by the time the book is in print, and attempting to write dialogue that suggests the speech of an uneducated person very quickly becomes patronizing. A word or two should be sufficient to show the level of literacy to which a character belongs. If the reader is attentive, a too-elegant expression, or a snatch of professional jargon, tells all that need be told.

Revision could go on indefinitely, and the author must know when to call a halt. Too much revision can ruin a book, just as too much kneading may spoil a loaf of bread.

After that, the fate of the book rests with its readers, and the author reflects that, if he is lucky, some of those readers have not yet been born.

What might keep it alive? Not being a best-seller, certainly. Try reading a few best-sellers of days gone by and see for yourself. Read *The Rosary* by Florence Barclay, or *If Winter Comes* by A. S. M. Hutchinson; best-sellers once, but who reads them now? What keeps a book alive is what Nabokov calls "the more or less irrational *shamanstvo* of a book"; the Russian word means enchanter-quality. It is not essential in a best-seller, which is a commercial product, but a book must possess it if it is to live.

Writers, unless they have very bad habits, tend to live long lives, and go on writing so long as they can drag themselves to the – oh yes, the typewriter. I write on a machine, a simple affair; I don't want a word-processor. I process my own words. Helpful people assure me that a word-processor would save me a great deal of time. But I don't want to save time. I want to write the best book I can, and I have whatever time it takes to make that attempt.

I am old-fashioned enough to think that a book is a work of art. That is to say, the unique result of a unique temperament. Many are not, but that is what a real writer wishes to produce.

Art, as somebody – I think it was a Roman – has said, is long.

33

How to Be a Collector

LATE IN HIS LIFE ROBERTSON DAVIES was invited to become an Honorary Fellow of the Pierpont Morgan Library in New York, an honour he accepted with alacrity. He attended the Board Meeting of the Library on May 9, 1995, to accept the Fellowship and then made this speech before a dinner given at the Library. Wishing to respond to the great honour the Library had done him, he presented the Board with two handwritten, unpublished poems by Max Beerbohm which he had in his collection.

On April 23 Davies wrote: *Finish the Morgan piece and read it to Brenda; she thinks it first-rate and funny, which is odd as it was born of fatigue and despair . . .* On May 9 he writes: *Brenda goes shopping and I to Doubleday, but feel unwell and tottery and am displeased with myself therefore . . . We lunch at the Club and rest; I am plagued with nerves. The Pierces pick us up, and we go to the Library and to the reception . . . Then I give my speech which goes well but demands a great deal of effort from me as I am under par.*

The title of my speech is "How to Be a Collector Without Having the Wealth of a J. P. Morgan." I must make it plain at once that I did not choose this title; your Director did so and it was not until later that I realized how deeply embarrassing it was. The suggestion that my personal fortune falls short of that achieved by J. P. Morgan I find humiliating and hasten at once to assure you that I am a man of substantial means. I have never in my life gone without a meal or owned less than two pairs of shoes; I change my shirt according to a program which I have perfected over the years, which ensures that I always give the appearance of wearing a *clean* shirt but not always a truly *virginal* shirt. I frequently ride in taxis – not, I assure you, for pleasure, because nobody crawls into those dirty moving prisons for pleasure – but to show the world that I am a man of means. A man above the subway, indeed. Could Mr. Morgan, for all his vast wealth, say more? Could he sit in more than one chair at a time, eat more than one meal at a time, wear more than one suit of clothes at a time? There is a limit to the privilege that wealth brings. Mr. Morgan and I are more alike than we are unlike and if Fortune had decreed that we should meet I am sure we should have found much to say to one another.

Mr. Morgan was a collector, and I am a collector, and that establishes a bond between us and explains why I am now talking to you about my humble collection in the midst of Mr. Morgan's immense and splendid collection.

My collection is not like Mr. Morgan's. Our tastes were different. But did his collection give him any greater pleasure than mine gives me? It is possible that it did so; he was a bulkier man than I am and there was more of him to be pleased. But mine gives me all the pleasure I can contain.

Like Mr. Morgan, books are the things I collect, and to be perfectly honest with you, it was not until a few years ago that I realized that what I possessed was indeed a collection; up until that time I had simply thought of it as an accumulation. But if an accumulation is truly the mirror of a mind, it will end up being a collection. My collection is a mirror of my mind, or a large part of it, and sometimes I think what a sorry, frivolous mess it is. But then I remember that French priest who, early in this century, began saving the weekly supplement of the paper, *L'Illustration*, in which a play currently appearing in Paris was printed. Because he was a priest and lived far from Paris he could not attend the theatre, but through those printed texts he could indulge his love of it. And behold, after thirty years or so, he had on his shelves an enviable assemblage of all that had delighted the playgoers of the capital – a collection, in fact. My enthusiasm, the theme of my collection, is the theatre.

I did not begin in this frivolous vein. My ideas about collecting were from an impeccable source, nothing less than the *Philobiblon* of Richard de Bury, who was Bishop of Durham in the fourteenth century. He was a very great collector. He owned more books than all the other English bishops put together; his bedroom was full of books and he could not walk or stand without treading on them. How do I know about him? Because some of his books are in the library of Balliol College in Oxford, and that is my own college, and when I read his confession that "in books I find the dead as if they were alive" I knew that this was the man for me. And I loved him when I read that "no dearness of price ought to hinder a man from buying books . . . how shall the bargain be shown to be dear when an infinite good is being bought?" I sometimes had to speak eloquently to persuade my father of this truth, for he thought my book bills rather high. But fathers can be indulgent. Some years ago Arthur Houghton, who presented his very great library to Harvard, told me that when he was an undergraduate, his father visited him one January and found that he had no overcoat. Somewhat shamefaced, he confessed that he had sold his overcoat in order to buy a book he coveted. His father laughed and bought him another coat. We fathers are a very fine and greatly misunderstood class of society.

The Bishop of Durham and I saw eye to eye on many things. He hated people who were dirty or neglectful of books. He would have loathed Samuel Johnson, who would break a large book into several pieces in order to read it more comfortably. As a boy I sometimes made use of a library which was also used by uncommonly dirty people; many of the books were heavily thumbed, and others showed evidence of bread and butter – even peanut butter; I remember one volume in which a reader had used a dirty pipe-cleaner as a book-mark. Later in life, when I was the head of a college in a large university, and thereby the custodian of a very good library, I used to be driven to fury by students who cut whole articles out of expensive books of reference, with no thought for others who might need them. To be frank with you, I have never much liked public collections and of late years have avoided them totally. If I want a book, I buy it, and if it cannot be bought, I find a way of doing without. There is a joy known only to collectors in possessing the physical form of a book, quite apart from its contents. A library is a personal possession, not a brothel open to all comers. Of course we honour the names of the great collectors who have left their darlings to be enjoyed by others, but we collectors are also a jealous, miserly lot, and while we live, what is our own, remains our own. Collectors are rarely lenders. Remember what happened to David Garrick, who lent precious volumes to his friend Dr. Samuel Johnson – who promptly broke their backs and, in a word, strumpeted them, and was reluctant to return them.

I don't think that the great Bishop of Durham would have approved of the direction my love of books took very early in my life. But then, in his time the theatre was in a very primitive condition. I had always been in love with the theatre, as were my parents before me, and I could not resist books which fed and assuaged that passion. Many which I saw when I was a student I could not hope to buy.

How I remember them! My special study was Shakespeare, and I had to find out all I could about Shakespeare's theatre. It was always a good plan when you want to investigate some matter buried in the past to take a look at what its enemies said about it. One of the great enemies of the theatre, not precisely in Shakespeare's time but not long after – it was seventeen years after Shakespeare's death – was one William Prynne, a rancorous Puritan, who wrote a book called *Histriomastix, The Players Scourge or Actors Tragaedie*, in which he flails the stage through 1,006 pages of vituperative hate. I dutifully read that awful book as it was important to my subject, which was the circumstance that in Shakespeare's day all the female roles in his plays were acted by youths, often described as boys, but rather too old for that category. They were probably between fifteen and twenty years old and in that time more experienced than their counterparts today. I wished that I might have *Histriomastix* for myself, having read it in the Bodleian Library. I never thought to achieve my ambition, but at least twenty-five years later I was snooping through the antiquarian collection in Brentano's on Fifth Avenue in this very city, and there it was – an enviable copy. Faint with desire and dread, I looked for the price: obviously nobody at Brentano's knew anything about the book, which is of considerable rarity, or else they judged that *Histriomastix* would not move quickly off their shelves. I sought the price, and could not believe my eyes: Brentano's wanted – what? could it be? – they wanted ten dollars for that book! Trembling like a thief and gloating like a collector I laid down my money, expecting somebody to rush forward and demand a revision of the price. But no. I escaped into the street, bathed in that unholy glow that suffuses a collector who has, for once in a way, got the best of a bookseller. What was ten dollars to Brentano's was priceless to me.

In my student days I found bargains, too, but in the main the Oxford booksellers were well aware of the value of what they had. I knew what I wanted, and often viewed it covetously on Blackwell's shelves. *Bell's British Theatre* in thirty-two volumes, published in 1791; beyond my reach. And the great collections of Mrs. Elizabeth Inchbald, herself a dramatist and editor of the twenty-five volumes of her *British Theatre*, ten volumes of her *Modern Theatre* (modern in 1811, that is to say), and the seven volumes of her *British Farces*. I knew quite a lot about Mrs. Inchbald, who was celebrated for her beauty and her charm – though one critic records that she had no bosom, not a hint of any such thing; how he knew I shudder to think. But Mrs. Inchbald was out of my welkin. The prices asked in those days were trivial compared with what I have had to pay for those collections in later years, and I did not at that time have the wealth of a J. P. Morgan, nor did my father. But I have them now and am happy that my finances have at last pulled even with my desires.

Without being very strongly aware of it, I had established the confines of my collection; it would contain anything I could find that related to the theatre between 1660, when the Puritan ban on the playhouses was lifted by the restored King, Charles II, and the age in which I was living. I was especially attracted to the nineteenth century, which was the last great inclusive age of theatre. In our century, the movies and television have taken over a huge area of entertainment which used to be occupied by the live theatre; for us, the theatre has become almost a coterie art, aimed at highbrows. I do not speak of course of the giant musicals that dominate so much of our theatre; they are a phenomenon in themselves. But for us, the theatre has drifted toward being a socially conscious concern, attacking modern problems with a seriousness which appears to excuse a want of what would once have been thought of as theatrical art. We go to the theatre to be harassed about the agonies of abused children, or battered wives, or people with AIDS. Comedies are rare and sometimes it is hard to recognize them as comedies. But in the nineteenth century the theatre had to satisfy a huge audience eager for entertainment, and every theatre offered a night's pleasure that included a tragedy, and also a comedy, and after that a farce, to conclude an evening's entertainment that extended from half-past six until midnight. A big theatre, like Covent Garden or Drury Lane, might have a staff of performers that included not simply actors and actresses, but musicians, singers, dancers, and the large crew of stagehands and gasmen necessary to provide stage spectacles that were by no means simple — were, indeed, ingenious and beautiful on a scale that the modern theatre has not surpassed. And what did they offer?

It was not hard to find out, if one had patience, because all of those melodramas, farces, comedies, and whatnot had been printed, and the printed booklets, cheap and shabby, with orange paper covers and small, broken type within, could be found on the barrows outside the second-hand bookshops on Tottenham Court Road in London. I spent hours grubbing through those barrows, getting dirtier and dirtier and in my own terms richer and richer as I pieced out the repertoire of the nineteenth-century theatre in England. I early

decided that I could not cope with the American theatre, for that
would have extended my range far beyond what I could manage.
Those little playbooks cost, as a usual thing, sixpence, and that meant
that for a pound I could get forty of them, and a pound on each hunt
was about what I could afford. My mother used to wonder what I
wanted with so many grubby, tattered, often smelly, little books, but
I knew. I was studying the popular entertainment, and therefore the
taste, of a bygone age.

Because that is what the theatre is, you see. When Shakespeare said
that its purpose was to hold the mirror up to nature I am sure he
included popular taste in the category of nature. What does society
admire? What does society fear? What are people thinking about,
worrying about, laughing about? The theatre will tell you and tell
you honestly. The theatre has told me a great deal about the nineteenth century.

But did you do it a play at a time, you ask? Well, no. I did what I
could when I was young, but later in life I had a chance to secure a
very large collection of those nineteenth-century playbooks, and I
was able to snatch it from under the nose of a great library that took
too long making up its mind. So now I have rather more than a thousand of those little playbooks, and in addition about 2,500 which
various enthusiasts had, for one reason or another, caused to be bound
up, sometimes very handsomely.

Was it a determined search, attempting to complete some precise
catalogue of popular theatre? Not at all. It was whatever I could find,
it was always exciting, and sometimes it was hilarious. Because, you
see, it led to a study of fashion in humour. What did people think
was funny, three hundred, two hundred, one hundred years ago?
Frequently now people complain of the jokes in Shakespeare; they
don't seem like jokes at all. Did people ever laugh at such stuff? Of
course they did. And all through my four hundred years people have
laughed heartily at things which now don't seem funny at all. Those
of you whose memories extend back to the days of vaudeville can
remember jokes that would not do on the stage today, and when you
go to the modern theatre you hear jokes which would have caused
a theatre to be closed fifty years ago. In our solemn day we have

wrapped a cloak of seriousness about a great many subjects which our parents found irresistibly funny. Indeed, it sometimes seems to be a miracle that we have anything at all left to laugh at and are not smothered under a wet blanket of Political Correctness.

Do I laugh at the ancient jokes I find in my old plays? Yes, I do, but not as the original audience laughed. What makes me laugh is the change in ideas of humour. And it supports my long-held belief that very few people have any real sense of humour, any deep appreciation of the ludicrous, any acquaintance with that elusive essence that is called comedy. What they have is a carefully circumscribed idea of what it is fashionable to think funny, and that idea is changing all the time. If you doubt me, leaf through some of the first years of *The New Yorker* and compare it with the latest copy you have received. What has happened to all the jokes about Bella Gross and her family, who aspired to move to a district they called "The Concuss." What happened to that Hollywood agent Benny Greenspan, whose English was all his own – who searched "every nook and granny" and who called anybody who was stupid about money "an incomepoop." What has happened to that feature called "Letters from Coloured Maids"? What has happened to the world of Peter Arno, and those richly mustached elderly gentlemen who seemed always to be accompanied by pretty but cripplingly stupid chorus girls? Compare them now with the jokes about the sophisticated man and woman who converse, it appears, in incomprehensible monosyllables. Why are they funny and to whom?

What did people laugh at in the theatre of the past? Well – they laughed at sex, of course, and the way in which sex is dealt with, from age to age, is utterly fascinating. To begin in my period – that is to say, in 1660 when Charles Stuart had been returned to the throne as Charles II – sex was almost the only joke. That was a reaction against the Puritan rule which had been overthrown and which was savage in its condemnation of what Puritans called "the more than Solomitical uncleanness of the players." The great comedies of the Restoration are well known – the works of Congreve, Wycherley, and Vanbrugh – and they are funny about sex with an elegance that still makes us laugh. But read some of the plays by the lesser playwrights of the period – Thomas Shadwell, for instance – and it will wipe the smile off your face. A lot of the plays that Samuel Pepys, for instance, enjoyed, were simply dirty. We seem to be making a return to what is simply dirty, in our time. In London, recently, I was taken to a play called *Dead Funny*, which might have been written by Shadwell, except that Shadwell did have a certain sense of humour.

In the eighteenth century sentimentality became the fashionable mode, and the jokes about sex began to be less explicit. But it is in the nineteenth century that we find a theatre where sex was virtually excluded from the range of permissible subjects for comedy. Not entirely; it was still permitted to make harsh fun of old maids, and to attribute to them an unappeasable sexual appetite. But jokes about marriage, about courtship, and about anything that might involve an unmarried girl had to be managed with the greatest circumspection. As the nineteenth century retreated, a greater freedom in dealing with sexual matters was regarded as passable material for stage comedy, but it was still very mild by the standards of today. Such rib-ticklers as *Getting Gertie's Garter* and *Up in Mabel's Room* are not likely to raise any blushes now. What, indeed, does raise a blush now?

How did the nineteenth-century theatre manage without sex? By a very curious device; it concentrated on puns and word-play. It delighted in "insider" jokes, as for instance in one comedy; the scene was ancient Greece, and a picnic basket appeared on stage and on its side was printed the name of the most famous of London food shops, Fortnum and Mason. But the name was printed in Greek letters and so only those in the audience who knew Greek got the joke. Indeed, Greek jokes had quite a vogue. I recall one comedy about ancient Greece in which two ruffians were called Ragtagaides and Bobtailos. That made me laugh for I am quite enough of a snob to enjoy a joke that not everybody sees.

As for puns, nineteenth-century burlesque and burletta – as it was called – abounded with them. Nineteenth-century audiences must have had very quick ears and quick wits. I am tempted to give you a lot of examples, but I shall content myself with one exchange between a pair of girls discussing suitors. Once again the scene is ancient Greece:

ACTACA: There's young Cockeyes; choose him.

PARTHENIA: That I shan't
            He *squints!* – the man pretends to see *as can't.*

ACTACA: He's well off.

PARTHENIA: But if Fortune him forsook
            You'd find he didn't know *which way to look.*

Grim stuff, I think you will admit.

What do you say to a pantomime of *Little Red Riding Hood* in which Jack the Woodcutter rescues the heroine from the Wolf "quite by axey-dent," when the Wolf is paying his "devoirs" to the pretty girl. Red Riding Hood's mother, Dame Margery, is described as a "crusty *rôle*, and very ill-bread." The Fairy Felicia who is the good spirit of the pantomime is said to be "quite *au fay* in magic." As the puns pile up the mind grows dizzy and one is haunted by the fear that one has missed something – as puns always remind us is likely to happen. Many of these puns involve Greek, Latin, and French. What quick wits the children must have had who laughed at such stuff. Or perhaps the children were laughing because their parents laughed. Perhaps the parents laughed because they saw their betters laughing; humour is no stranger to snobbery. But not all the laughter can have been imitative. The Victorians were quick-witted in ways we are not.

Not plays alone engaged my rapt attention. I delighted in theatrical reminiscence, such as Tate Wilkinson's *Memoirs*. I have two copies of that not easily accessible book; for one I paid a pretty penny at Quaritch's in London, and the other I bought for ten dollars from a Canadian bookseller who didn't know what it was, but who thought as it was bound in leather it should bring an easy ten. The autobiographies of nineteenth-century actors are good fun, because they are so wondrously grandiloquent. When John Ryder, for instance, writes "I utter valediction to the author of my being,"

he means simply that he said goodbye to his mother. Reminiscences
of triumphs, though charming, are not such good fun as descriptions of performances that went wrong, actors who were drunk and
similar disasters. One of my favourites is from the diary of Rev.
R. H. Barham, who will be familiar to some of you as the author
of the *Ingoldsby Legends*. He was a jolly fellow – the nineteenth
century seems to have abounded with jolly clergymen – and he
writes of a dinner party he gave. It tells of what must surely have
been the strangest presentation of a very popular tragedy, called
Douglas. It was popular because it was gloomy and it was Scotch, and
both gloom and Scotland were very popular at the end of the eighteenth century and the beginning of the nineteenth. It was widely
quoted, especially such lines as –

    He seldom errs
Who thinks the worst he can of womankind.

That was accepted as great poetry and was extravagantly praised in
Scotland itself. Indeed, the story goes that when *Douglas* was first presented in Edinburgh, an excitable patriot bawled from the gallery –

Whaur's your Wullie Shakespeare now?

The hero of *Douglas* is a young shepherd called Norval, and of
course he isn't a shepherd but a great nobleman who has been
brought up by peasants, for reasons highly melodramatic. He first
appears, nobility outshining his simple shepherd's dress, and his introductory speech is this:

My name is Norval: on the Grampian hills
My father feeds his flocks; a frugal swain,
Whose constant cares were to increase his store
And to keep me, his only son, at home.

There's noble simplicity for you! Little boys were taught to spout
those lines in the nursery. But it was possible for things to go wrong

even in *Douglas*. Hear what Barham writes in his diary for March 13, 1828 –

Lord W. Lennox, Sir Andrew Barnard, Theodore Hood, Mr. Price, Captain E. Smart and Cannon dined here. The last [that was Cannon] told a story of a manager at a country theatre who, having given out the play of *Douglas*, found the whole entertainment nearly put to a stop by the arrest of Young Norval for debt as he was entering the theatre. In this dilemma, no other performer of the company being able to take the part, he dressed up a tall, gawky lad who snuffed the candles, in a plaid and a philabeg, and pushing him on the stage, advanced himself to the footlights with the book in his hand, and addressed the audience "Ladies and Gentlemen –

This young gentleman's name is Norval. On the Grampian hills
His father feeds his flock, a frugal swain
Whose constant care was to increase his store,
And keep his only son (this young gentleman) at home.
For this young gentleman had heard of battles, and he long'd
To follow to the field some warlike lord;
And Heaven soon granted what – this young gentleman's sire denied.
The moon which rose last night, round as this gentleman's shield
Had not yet filled her horns," etc.

And so on through the whole play, much to the delectation of the audience.

As every collector knows, one thing leads to another and it is often difficult to know where to stop. Not only the plays, and the reminiscences of the players, but the history of the drama became an absorbing concern of mine, and I greatly desired a rare book in ten volumes called *The History of the Drama and Stage in England from 1660 to 1830*. It was printed in Bath in 1832, and the title pages modestly give no name for the author. But it was a clergyman called the Reverend John Genest, who became an invalid – I believe his illness was tuberculosis – and retired to Bath where, to employ his time, he did the enormous research involved in the book I have mentioned. It is a marvel, because subsequent investigation by armies of scholars equipped with every sort of research assistance has revealed very few errors in it, and Genest corrects innumerable errors in books written before his time. He read and annotated every play, and his literary style is a constant delight, as he describes the plots of the plays of which he writes. He is just, and gentle; perhaps the most damning comment he makes upon a play is "This Tragedy may be considered more apt for perusal than for performance." I honour John Genest, and I used to hold him up to the graduate students whose theses it was my duty to supervise as a model of scholarship, for he did all the work himself, and as the *Dictionary of National Biography* says, "Few books of reference are equally trustworthy." Trustworthy, yes, and wonderfully good reading, a feast for the browser.

Did I say that one thing led to another? Yes, and I am afraid that in my enthusiasm I may dodge hither and thither in my collection until you are thoroughly weary of the subject and of me. Because there seems to be no end to it, and in my enthusiasm for books relating to the theatre, and in my pursuit of rarities, some of which I happened on by luck, and some of which I had to pay for in grievous sums, I found myself also involved in the pursuit of those little pictures of popular actors in their most successful roles, which were sold for a penny to theatre enthusiasts between roughly 1800 and 1830. The penny pictures were uncoloured; for tuppence you could get them beautifully adorned with the richest reds, greens, and purples. There is a story that William Blake, during a time when his fortunes were at a low ebb, earned a pittance by such colouring, and every time I buy one if the date is right I think that I may have acquired an original Blake.

That is one of the byways into which my collecting has led me. Another lies in the direction that I have never known to be taken by another collector, and this is children's drama, for in those days when the children of affluent parents had large nurseries and governesses who were eager to find amusement for them, quite a few plays were written for nursery performance before, one presumes, audiences of parents, friends, and nannies. In *Little Plays for Little Players, Dick Whittington and His Cat* and *Cinderella* and *Beauty and the Beast* are all given a thoroughly moral treatment, which was not always the case with plays written for adult amateurs. I have several collections of *those*, and although they made a pretence of innocence they provide plenty of opportunities for flirting, and one imagines that the rehearsals must have been very enjoyable. Some of these are what might be called "potted Shakespeare," in which the more demanding works of the Bard are adapted for the use of amateurs in the drawing room. It is noteworthy that in all of these the costumes of the ladies are described in detail. In one, for instance, the scene is that in which Romeo and Juliet part, after their marriage and which we are now accustomed to see in Juliet's bedroom, with both lovers as near naked as the most rigorous realist could desire. Not so the Victorian amateurs; "The stage represents a nicely furnished room, with a small table and chair on the left side, near the front, a large armchair on the right, and a small stand, with a vase of flowers upon it." Just the thing for the wedding night. It is suggested that the love duet from *Faust* might be played (offstage, presumably, by the governess). It is all very touching and determinedly chaste, and it must have been great fun to see and to do.

Amateurs also acted innumerable charades, for which books of directions exist and some of them seem to have demanded almost as much trouble as a full scale theatrical performance. How, for instance, would you act out the word "Surgeon"? Would it occur to you to set some of the action in the Middle Ages? Perhaps you do not amuse yourself with charades? But they must have been such fun that I am sure they will enjoy a revival at some future period.

Some of the most attractive things that have come my way are actual promptbooks of stage productions of an earlier day. Have you ever seen one of those? They are interleaved copies of the play, in which the prompter has carefully marked all the action and stage business of the actors, all the properties needed, details of the stage setting, and everything that related to a stage mounting. By chance I came upon one prepared for a production of *She Stoops to Conquer*, late in the eighteenth century; another is a prompt copy of Lord Byron's play *Werner* which was immensely popular in the repertoire of the great tragedian Macready after 1830; my copy was prepared by Macready's prompter. But such treasures are hard to find, and book-sellers are now alive to their value. Mine cost me a trifle because they looked like spoiled copies.

I am aware that one person's enthusiasm quickly becomes another person's boredom, and the time has come for me to hold my peace. I could go on until you were all fainting from hunger and ennui. I could tell you about my collection of failed plays written by great writers who proved to have no talent for the theatre; some very great names are in that group – Dickens, Browning, Henry James, and many more. One of the worst playwrights among great authors was Sir Walter Scott; I have all his stage works in first editions – there do not seem to have been any second editions – and I cherish also first editions of the plays of Matthew Gregory Lewis, who might be called the father of the vampire-and-monster dramas that now abound on the screen. I promised not to speak of these, and as you see, I have not done so.

But have I explained why I collect the books – not beautiful on the shelf, not delightful in the hand – that have absorbed so much of my leisure and my income – my income which is somewhat less than that of J. P. Morgan? Did I not at the beginning quote the great Bishop of Durham, Richard de Bury, who said "in books I find the dead as if they were alive"? In my collection, to me at least, the theatre of the past lives again and those long-dead playwrights and actors have in me an enthralled audience of one, and I applaud them across the centuries.